public administration

public administration

Policy-Making in Government Agencies

Ira Sharkansky
Hebrew University of Jerusalem
and University of Wisconsin at Madison

Fourth Edition

Rand McNally College Publishing Company/Chicago

For my mother
Beatrice Mines Sharkansky

78 79 80 10 9 8 7 6 5 4 3 2 1

Contents

Preface xiii

1 INTRODUCTION 1

The Nature of Administrators 3

Pervasive Administration 4

Our Approach to Public Administration 6
  Environment and Inputs 9
  Conversion Process 10
  Outputs 11
  Feedback 13

The Systems Framework 13

The Borders of Administrative Systems 16

The Organization of this Book 17

2 COMPARISON IN THE STUDY OF PUBLIC ADMINISTRATION 19

Comparative Analysis of Administrative Systems
in the United States 21
  Economic Interpretations of Policy 24

Comparative Analysis Across National Boundaries 28
  The Importance of "Development" 29

Administrative Systems in More-Developed Countries 31

Administrative Coherence in More-Developed Countries 33
  The Costs of Incoherence 36

Administrative Systems in Less-Developed Countries 38
  Traditional-Autocratic 43
  Bureaucratic Elite 43
  Polyarchal Competitive 43
  Dominant-Party Mobilization 44

Administrative Systems in Less-Developed (U.S.) States
and Less-Developed Countries 44
  Environmental Parallels 45
  Parallels in Public Policy 47
  *Relevance of Parallels Between Less-Developed States
    and Countries* 48

Lessons of Comparison: Policies of Financial Aid
and Technical Assistance   49
   International Aid to Poor Countries   49
   Domestic Aid to Poor States   52

Summary   53

Part One
The Conversion Process
of the Administrative System   54

3   DECISION-MAKING IN ADMINISTRATIVE AGENCIES   56

A Model of Rational Decision-Making and Its Shortcomings   57
   The Multitude of Problems, Goals, and Policy Commitments   59
   Limited Information   62
   Needs, Commitments, Inhibitions, and
      Inadequacies of Administrators   64
   Structural Difficulties Within Administrative Units and
      Involving Their Relations with Legislators and
      the Chief Executive   65
   The Deviant Behavior of Administrators   67

Problems of Rational Choice Amid Ambiguity and
Controversy: Growth vs. Conservation   69
   Some Problems that Complicate Rational Decisions About Growth   70

Decision-Making in Administrative Units: Compromises
with the Rational Model   73
   Satisficing with Respect to the Multitude of
      Problems, Goals, and Policies   74
   Satisficing with Respect to Limits on Information   75
   Satisficing with Respect to the Needs, Commitments,
      Inhibitions, and Inadequacies of Administrators   76
   Satisficing with Respect to Structural Problems   78

The Use of Decision Rules   79
   Reliance on Tensions   79
   Mutual Adjustment   80
   Routines   82
   Opportunities for Innovation in Administrators' Decisions:
      Deviations from Routines   88

Rationalist Efforts to Reform Decision-Making:
The Case of Budgeting   91
   Planning-Programming-Budgeting: Its Promise and Problems   92

Dispute in PPB: Competing Combinations of
    Assumptions, Calculations, and Findings   95
    The End of PPB in the National Government   97
    Summary   98

4 ADMINISTRATIVE ORGANIZATION AND ADMINISTRATIVE
   CONTROL UNITS: STRUCTURES AND THEIR
   INTELLECTUAL ROOTS   101
   Administrative Organization as Political Controversy   101
   Intellectual Roots of Administrative Organization   104
       Political Accountability   105
       Separation of Powers—Checks and Balances   107
       Professional Expertise   109
       Hierarchical Management   110

   Administrative Organization in the National Government   113
       Cabinet Departments and Independent Offices   115
       "Independent" Regulatory Commissions   120
       Government Corporations   122
       Federally Aided Corporations   123
       Government Contractors   124
       Administrative Hybrids   127

   Regional Character of National Administration   129

   Administrative Control Units in the National Government   130
       Executive Units for Administrative Control   132
       Congressional Mechanisms for Administrative Control   136
       Judicial Mechanisms for Administrative Control   138
       The Civil Service Commission   139

   Administrative Organizations of State Governments
   and Their Control Mechanisms   141

   Administrative Organizations of Local Governments
   and Their Control Mechanisms   145

   Growth of Administrative Units in the 20th Century   148

   Administrative Discretion and the Issues of Control   153

   Summary   155

5 THE PERSONNEL OF ADMINISTRATIVE AGENCIES   157
   Recruiting, Selecting, and Training Policy-Makers for
   Administrative Agencies   158

   "Nonpolitical" Personnel Procedures in the
   National Administration   160

   Collective Bargaining in the Public Service:
   Confrontations with Personnel Administration   163

Personnel Procedures for Political Appointees in
the National Administration   166

Significance of Administrators' Personal Traits in
Administrative Organizations   169

Who Are Public Administrators?   171

Career Routes and Success in Administrative Agencies   173

Government Employment of the Socially Disadvantaged   176
    Blacks in Government   177
    Women in Government   180

Values, Aspirations, and Personalities in
Administrative Agencies   181

Summary   184

6 THE MANAGEMENT OF GOVERNMENT AGENCIES   187

Administrative Units as Complex Systems   189
    Authority   189
    Communications   192
    Incentives   193
    Leadership   195

Three Modes of Organizational Control   197
    Scientific Management   197
    Human Relations   200
    New Synthesis in Management Techniques   201

Employee-Centered Organization:
The Minnowbrook Perspective   204

Consumerism and Accountability   206

Summary   208

Part Two
**The Inputs
of the Administrative System**   210

7 THE STATUS OF PUBLIC ADMINISTRATION   212

Assessments of Administrative Agencies in
Past Political Literature   213

Contemporary Views of Public Administration   217

The Public's View of Public Administration   220

Political Cultures and Administrative Organizations
in States and Regions   223

Summary   226

8 CITIZEN DEMANDS AND ADMINISTRATIVE AGENCIES   228

Individual Citizens as Providers of Inputs to
Administrative Agencies   228

Citizen Involvement in Policy-Making and Administration:
The Case of Neighborhood Democracy   231

The Mass Media as Intermediaries between
Citizens and Administrators   233

Public Opinion Polls as Intermediaries between
Citizens and Administrators   235

Elections as Intermediaries between
Citizens and Administrators   238

Interest Groups as Intermediaries between
Citizens and Administrators   240
   Administrators' Pursuit of Interest-Group Allies   242
   Government Interest Groups   244
   Limitations on the Influence of Interest Groups   247

Political Parties as Intermediaries between
Citizens and Administrators   248
   The Machine as the Archetype of Party Government   251

Administrative Agencies as Collectors of Information   253
The Ombudsman   255
Summary   256

9 EXECUTIVES, LEGISLATORS, AND ADMINISTRATORS   259

Legislative Weakness in Relations with
Administrative Agencies   261

Sources of Legislative Strength in Relations with
Administrative Agencies   262

Executive Weakness in Relations with Administrative Agencies   264

Sources of Executive Strength in Relations with
Administrative Agencies   267

Variations in Relations among the Executive and
Legislative Branches and Administrative Agencies   269
   Party Influence on Administrative-Legislative-Executive Relations 270
   Changes in the Status of Administrators   271
   Changes in the Leadership of Administrative Agencies   272
   A Cost-Benefit Analysis of Legislative "Oversight"   273
   Formal Powers of the Legislative and Executive Branches 273

Budget Relations among Legislators, Executives,
and Administrators   275
   Chronology of Budgeting   275
   Formulation in the Executive   276

Congressional Action 277
Budget Execution 281
Nature of Budget Decisions in the Executive and
    Legislative Branches 281
General Accounting Office: Administrative Nemesis
    with Little Public Renown 288

Tensions among Executives, Legislators, and Administrators 290

President Nixon vs. Congress and Administrators:
The Case of Impoundment 294

Summary 295

Part Three

The Outputs
of the Administrative System 298

10 INTERGOVERNMENTAL RELATIONS 301

The Meanings of Federalism for Administrators 302
Types of Intergovernmental Relations:
Federal to State and Local 305
    Financial Aid 306
    Revenue-Sharing 310
    Growth in Financial Aids 311
    Other Federal Aids to States and Localities 312

State Aids to Local Governments 315

Urban-Centered Outputs of National and State Agencies 318
    Explanations of Urban-Centered Intergovernmental Aid 320

Evaluation and Accountability in Vertical
Intergovernmental Relations 324

Interlocal and Interstate "Horizontal" Relations 325
    Stimuli of Horizontal Intergovernmental Relations 326
    Instruments of Horizontal Relations 327
    Regional Similarities in Public Policy 329

The Mixed Realities of Intergovernmental Relations 331
Summary 338

11 VARIETIES OF ADMINISTRATIVE OUTPUTS 340
Administrative Efforts and Public Services 341
Information as an Output 342

Opportunities for Changes in Output   345

Effects of Administrative Outputs   347
    Who Pays the Bills? Who Gets the Benefits?   347
    A Test of Community Action Programs   349
    The Success of Regulatory Agencies   352
    Administrative Efforts and Public Service   355
    The Payoffs from Spending   355

The General Assessment of Administrative Output:
Do We Like What Government is Doing?   357

Summary   358

Suggestions for Additional Reading   361

Index   373

It is common within the academic profession for writers to say how their approach to a subject differs from the approach of others. In this case, it is especially appropriate to make such a statement. This book *is* different from other texts in the field of public administration in that it emphasizes the political processes within and surrounding administrative agencies more than it stresses the management techniques that a budding administrator should master. It is written for the student who seeks to understand the operations of public administration in its political environment.

Public administration lends itself to contrasting approaches. At times, it is taught in the political science departments of liberal arts colleges. Presumably, those courses focus on the activities of administrative units in relation to other activities in the larger political process; the end product is more likely to be *understanding,* rather than *training* in the techniques of administration. Elsewhere, public administration is separated from political science and is offered to students as professional training. It is also subordinated to programs that offer instruction in the general field of "administration." Public administration has both "liberal arts" and "professional" clientele. Textbooks can be written for a liberal arts college or for the professional school of a large university.

It is not only the differing perspectives of a liberal arts department and a professional school which generate disputes about public administration. It is marked with disputes among faculty members within the same organization. In many political science departments that consider themselves to be solidly implanted in the liberal tradition, courses in public administration may be offered from the liberal or professional perspective. Students who aspire to a government career are urged to take the courses; the instructor may have some administrative experience; and the text materials often provide information useful to a public administrator. A popular introductory text includes chapters on leadership; decision-making; personnel recruiting, examining, evaluating, and promoting; employee relations; the impact of computer technology upon public administration; preparation, authorization, and execution of the budget; and judicial review of administrative decisions. After taking an introductory course in public administration, an undergraduate can take additional courses in "public financial administration," and "public personnel administration."

Among political scientists, public administration specialists are set apart not only by their interests in administrative training, but often because their scholarship is "traditional," "institutional," or "nonscientific." To the practicing administrator in government, however, the instructor in public administration is often viewed as too "academic," "theoretical," or "impractical."

Another conflict divides those who study *public* administration as a distinct entity and those who agree that the proper inquiry is *administration* per se. Those who take the larger view see administration as a generic process. It may be divided into "public," "private," "business," "educational," "military," or other forms of administration. However, each segment is said to have less distinctiveness than the general process of which they are all parts. From this perspective, the study of *public* administration represents a distraction. To understand or to practice administration of any kind, *administration* should be examined in several of its forms.

This book does not resolve the questions about the generic nature of administration or about the distinctiveness of *public* administration. Its principal roots are in political science; and it seeks to bring together that information about administration that is most relevant to an understanding of the larger political process. Of necessity, much of this information concerns *public* administration. It includes information about the public's regard for government bureaucracies; about the personal characteristics of public administrators; about interactions among public administrators and political parties, interest groups, and the executive and legislative branches of government; and about interactions between public administrators and government officials from different units in the federal system. At times we consider some information about the behavior of administrators in nongovernmental contexts. In dealing with decision-making within administrative organizations, for example, it appears that certain features of decision-making prevail in both public and private administrative organizations of a certain size. We also find some striking similarities in the social backgrounds of high-level administrators in both government agencies and large business firms. For the most part, however, the focus is on those attributes and activities of *public* administrators. The emphasis is on the contribution of public administration to public policy-making. While some features of administration appear common to both public and private arenas, any detailed inquiry into their commonness or distinctiveness is secondary to our task.

Much has happened to affect the field of public administration since the first edition of this book appeared. The size and scope of public agencies have grown, meaning that more of the population works in public administration, more of the student body aspires to an administrative career, and all of us have more contacts with administrators in which we receive the benefits of their services or feel the weight of their regulations. Skepticism toward administrators has grown with their importance. Ranking politicians—among them the governor of California and the president of the United States—have stressed in their campaigns that more money for the bureaucracy will not necessarily produce more or better services. Institutions like the ombudsman have spread throughout the United States and other countries to help citizens sort out their problems with insensitive or ignorant administrators.

The study of public administration has grown and changed along with its subject matter. Not only are there more students, more courses, and more formal programs to train administrators, but the increased number of faculty and other commentators drawn to the bureaucracy have produced a literature that is both larger and more rich. In order to remain useful, an introductory textbook must grow and change with its field.

This edition preserves the systems framework that its predecessors introduced to the study of public administration. The systems framework should clarify the policy roles of public administration and should highlight the significance of administration for other features of politics. This book deals with several features that seem capable of affecting policy-making in administrative units and—insofar as this is permitted by the available literature—describes the interactions among these features and the influence that each of them has upon the policy roles of the administrator. Among the questions that the book tries to answer are some of the classic inquiries of political science, as reformulated to make them relevant for a study of public administration:

- *Who gets what, when, and how from the decisions of administrative units?*
- *What share do administrators have in policy-making, as compared to elected legislators, chief executives, and members of the judiciary?*

- *How do administrators affect the benefits that citizens receive from governments?*
- *How do administrators affect the constraints on citizens' behavior that come from government agencies?*

Systems language has served well here as in other fields of political and social science. It retains a capacity to help a student comprehend relationships between the numerous parts of a complex field. Yet, it is best that systems language not lay too heavily on an introductory text. There is much in public administration that should be appreciated for its own sake, without a need to fit every last bit onto its proper spot of the system. The administrative system described here is a guide for understanding. It should clarify and suggest relationships between administrative agencies and the factors in their environment that impose influence upon them, or feel the influence of the agencies' activities.

The structure of this book highlights its use of the systems framework. After two introductory chapters that explain the systems concepts and describe the merits of comparison in the field of public administration, a group of four chapters deals with the *conversion process* of the administrative system. The conversion process converts the *inputs* of a system into its *outputs*. These chapters examine decision-making in administrative agencies; the structures of administrative agencies and their formal ties with other branches of government; the personnel who staff administrative agencies; and the management of agencies.

Then a group of three chapters deals with several sources of inputs to administrative units: the political culture and its predispositions toward public administration; citizen demands; and demands and resources that come from the executive and legislative branches of an administrator's own government. Finally, two chapters examine the *outputs* that administrative units provide to other governments and to other actors in their environment.

If there is a theme that emerges from the changes introduced in the fourth edition, it is a complex one—pointing more than earlier editions, on the one hand, to factors that add to the richness, complexity, and perhaps lack of coherence in administrative institutions, and, on the other hand, to the numerous ways used to monitor and control what administrators do. This edition deals with signs of public displeasure with —and alienation from—government; legislators' efforts to increase their capacity to control the bureaucracy, including the new budget procedures defined by the Congress and the creation of the Congressional Budget Office; the rise of consumerism and the ombudsman; citizen involvement in administration; technical and managerial efforts to control administrators; and the concern of administrators themselves to organize in defense of their own interests and to control their own activities. There is also discussion of interpretations that find positive signs in the seeming chaos of increasingly complex organizations.

This edition retains a commitment to the areas where public administration and political science come together. It has sought to infuse its presentations with more current and more lively discussions of the politics that pervades and surrounds administrative agencies and of the issues that complicate the lives of professional administrators as well as elected officials.

Just as a father gets much of his ego gratification from the successes of his children, an author derives great pleasure from the success of his books. *Public Administration* has done well. As I read the list of universities whose faculty members have adopted it for their class text, I found a geographic spread from the Universities of Alaska and Guam to the Universities of Maine and Miami. Although I wrote the book with the American undergraduate as my primary audience, I was flattered to learn that it was translated into Spanish, Portuguese, and other languages for students in foreign countries.

This is not to say that the book has received universal praise. An author needs a thick skin, even for those barbs that he expects. When some friendly—and some not-so-friendly—critics said the subject matter of this text is not "public administration," I had to remind myself that I did not intend the book to emphasize certain traditional approaches to the subject.

Numerous colleagues have taken the trouble to point out problems in the previous edition and to make suggestions for the fourth. I owe special thanks to George T. Menake, Sylvan H. Cohen, and Judith Merkle for their detailed reviews and recommendations. But because a text cannot appeal to all interests without losing its distinctiveness, I have not followed all of their recommendations. I, therefore, acknowledge responsibility for the results while expressing sincere appreciation for help in the process of revision.

1

Introduction

Many of the goods and bads that we receive from society come from public administrators. Administrators spend most of the $651 billion estimated for the budgets of national, state, and local governments in 1977.

Administrative spending accounts for some 36 percent of the gross national product, a commonly used measure of total national resources. About 15 million civilians work for public agencies, and more than 2 million others are members of the armed forces.

The administrative branches of national, state, and local governments include accountants, clerks, inspectors, lawyers, and other functionaries who fit the common image of "bureaucrats," plus physicians, social workers, college professors, and police. Indeed, the whole range of occupations finds representatives in government agencies. Public administrators arranged the involuntary sterilization of adolescent black females in Alabama, and others in military uniform massacred the civilian population of My Lai. Administrators also pursued the investigations of both these actions. Administrators provide us with public services and regulate our activities; they perform much of the supervision and control of those officers who come into direct contact with the public. As the range of public activities expands, the United States and other countries become more and more administrative states.

When President Gerald R. Ford came into office in 1974, he sought to reduce the size of the national government's workforce. He had his eye on a target of 40,000 fewer employees, which had been set earlier by President Richard M. Nixon. Yet, the actual figures show a growth of 31,000 in the full-time permanent staff in the 1974–76 period. While some agencies were able to trim their staffs, there was irrestible pressure from new programs in the fields of energy, law enforcement, bank examining, tax auditing, and veterans' medical care, plus a general pressure to increase personnel to meet the needs of a growing population. If the people and their elected officials want increased services, they—and even a nonelected president with a decidedly conservative frame of mind—will find it difficult to get by with fewer administrators.

For the student of public affairs, two questions increase in importance with the growing roles of administrators: *What are the activities of public administrators?* and *How are administrators controlled by the democratic mechanisms of government?*

The simple answer to the first question is *administrators do most of the work of government.* The simple answer to the second question is *administrators are controlled mostly by other administrators, but they are set in a complex system that includes supervision by elected executives and legislators, courts, and a variety of unattached politicians, political parties, interest groups, journalists, and interested private citizens.* For longer and more thorough answers to these questions, proceed through the remaining pages of this book.

These questions touch directly on some of the most profound issues of political thought. Since the ancient Greeks, writers have labored over the problems of directing government along paths that are consistent with moral virtue and public preference. As more and more of governments' actions become the direct responsibility of individuals who are not themselves chosen by the voters, these tasks of direction and control become more difficult.

There are profound technical and moral problems involved in administrative control. It is not a simple issue of "telling administrators what to do." The more we know about administration, the more we realize that "people don't always do what they're told." Moreover, we recognize that administrators have some rights to express their own preferences about public policy and—in some cases—to refuse compliance with instructions that go against their own norms. Indeed, we punish some administrators for obeying superiors, i.e., when their superiors' instructions violate the most basic of moral precepts. Yet, we require administrators to remain silent about information that is classified secret. We also expect administrators to avoid public criticism of their superiors and accuse some violators of insubordination. It is a matter of some dispute whether federal and state laws permit certain administrators to express political views or to run for elective office.

Many readers will have special problems with these issues. Taking a course in public administration already signals a greater-than-average interest in public affairs. In all probability, these students are already concerned with issues of controlling the government and keeping administrators responsive to public demands; many already are—or will become —public administrators. For these people, the issues are not only control of other people who are bureaucrats but control of their own activities and the likely surrender of certain liberties. When working in government, they may find themselves acting in ways they do not entirely approve, perhaps constrained by regulations or informal norms from publicly expressing their opposition to policy or acting contrary to their superiors' instructions.

THE NATURE OF ADMINISTRATORS

The activities of a "typical" public administrator cannot be described simply. Some administrators are concerned with routine tasks that have been detailed by actions of the legislature. In this category is the caseworker who decides what benefits should be paid to an applicant under the provisions of a government welfare program. Other administrators manage routine operations. The caseworker's superior allocates workloads, processes vacation schedules, sees to the maintenance of the local office, and deals with clients who are not satisfied with the routine decisions of the subordinates. Still other administrators involve themselves in the most innovative work of government. They help to push forward the frontiers of social progress by drafting proposals for new laws and by lobbying in behalf of these proposals among members of the federal or state legislatures. Administrators must also implement innovative programs. The way in which administrators use their discretion can mean success or failure for a project involving many citizens. A field representative of the U.S. Office of Education who negotiates with school systems about racial desegregation is vital to the program's success. Schools do not desegregate by themselves or simply in response to court orders. As well as having a personal commitment to the principles of equal opportunity, such administrators must have great sensitivity to the constraints operating on a local school board. It may be necessary for an administrator to balance sharply conflicting interests in order to help local officials make a concession to "the government in Washington" without losing their local political support.

The physical strength of the military is one kind of power resource which is available to public administrators. Other administrators wield power when they design programs for public schools and universities; allocate research funds to projects in medicine and the natural and social sciences; negotiate with landowners about the price to be paid for a highway's right-of-way; develop health and safety standards for foods, drugs, cosmetics, automobiles, and airplanes; and test individual products for their compliance with these standards. Our lives and fortunes are governed by the agencies that regulate the economy. Those of us working for government agencies have our salaries, fringe benefits, and work assignments subject to administrators' decisions.

Our society's dependence upon administrators does not mean we are enslaved. Certain administrative procedures protect the rights and interests of individual citizens. Some of the "redtape" that is a subject of derision is essential to monitor and control the decisions of administrators. In some ways, administrators are more "representative" of the diverse social and economic interests in the United States than are the elected members of the legislative and executive branches.[1]

The label "public administrator" is used in different ways. In some contexts, it means all the employees of governments, except those in the legislative and judicial branches and the elected chief executive. Such a designation includes the file clerks and sweepers, as well as persons in high- and middle-range positions in government departments. In other contexts, the term is reserved for high-level employees of government departments or agencies, i.e., the personnel who make the nonroutine decisions that set the standards to be carried out by their subordinates. For the most part, we concern ourselves with the more selective group of public administrators. Most of our discussions are about those officials who make important decisions within administrative units and who interact with officials in other branches of government. At times, however, we enlarge our focus and report about the larger group of administrative employees.

PERVASIVE ADMINISTRATION

The problems of describing public administrators reflect their presence throughout policy-making and implementation. Administrators are everywhere. They dominate the stages of formulating, executing, monitoring, and reformulating policy. In modern states where a large part of the labor force works directly or indirectly for government, important details of policy concern administrators' salaries, fringe benefits, duties, rights, and privileges.

---

1. Norton E. Long, "Bureaucracy and Constitutionalism," American Political Science Review 46 (September 1952): 808–18; and Samuel Kristov, Representative Bureaucracy (Englewood Cliffs, N.J.: Prentice-Hall, 1974).

What is the source of new policy? Frequently it is the administrators who work with existing policy and become familiar with its flaws. When administrators themselves do not originate proposals, they usually receive them from interest groups, legislators, or others who do conceive them. It is difficult to pass a bill through a legislature unless the relevant agencies have reviewed it and agree as to its administrative feasibility. Among the items considered by policy-makers is the availability of administrative resources. This means money and personnel. New programs require an adequate supply of personnel already trained, or trainable in the skills required, plus managers capable of integrating the new activities with related programs already in operation.

Once a program is on the books, it is up to administrators to recruit the staff, establish workspace, arrange the procedures, and serve the clients. Along the way, it is also necessary to fill in the chinks left in the basic definition of the program. Acts of Congress and executive orders set goals and deal with program features that seem important and solvable at the time. Designers may leave to administrators knotty problems that resist compromise in the legislature, as well as new issues that appear only when the program is in operation. Administrators themselves feel conflicting pressures as they proceed to resolve difficult issues. Just what level of polluted emissions will satisfy the standards of air-control legislation? What kind of safety devices will be approved for industrial machinery, automobiles, or household appliances? What evidence will satisfy requirements for testing new drugs?

Who is to control administrators? Mostly other administrators are the answer. Modern governments divide the tasks of control among numerous specialized agencies that review budget proposals; monitor the hiring, promotion, and discipline of personnel; check the compliance of government contractors; supervise the work of corporations owned wholly or partly by the government; review citizen complaints; and check on the legality and efficiency of spending. Organizationally, these bodies may be linked with the chief executive or the legislature, or they may have certain assurances of independence. Their chiefs may be professional civil servants or prominent appointees of major elected officials. In any case, it is inevitable that the working staffs of control bodies will be administrators. *Who controls the controllers* is itself a problem. The staffs of the president of the United States and Congress, appointed ostensibly to help them govern the bureaucracy, have themselves grown to unwieldy numbers. The Watergate scandal was partly a case of uncontrolled presidential staffers. Congressional staffs have also had their own problems, like Bobby Baker, a free-wheeling aide of Senate Majority Leader Lyndon B. Johnson.

The many controllers do not assure sanitized government. Both in the units that control and that are controlled a great deal rests on the judgments of individual officials. How the police officer, tax auditor, teacher, or social worker treats a client will, in most cases, never receive a systematic review. The administrator is alone with the agency's manual of rules, a course of training that urged flexibility in the case of unusual circumstances, a client wanting special treatment, a code of ethics with numerous abstract principles, plus complex personal feelings about certain types of cases or clients. How far to bend the rules? When to ask for the supervisor's advice? When to accuse a client—like a taxpayer—of a simple error or an attempt at criminal fraud? When to blow the whistle on a client's suggestion of goodies in exchange for a favorable ruling? All of these issues are likely to bother most administrators at one time or another.

Much policy not only passes through the hands of administrators, but it is about administrators. With a sizable percentage of the workforce in the public sector, there are continuous demands for better salaries and better work conditions. The one-time issue about the propriety of public employee strikes has bowed to a rash of lost workdays and legislation permitting collective bargaining for public employees. Civil service advocates demand expanded freedoms to campaign for public office and to speak publicly about controversial issues. What is the ultimate line that will keep the government's employees from becoming its masters? Whatever the answer, it is likely to be formulated and enforced by the administrative employees of one or another agency.

OUR APPROACH TO PUBLIC ADMINISTRATION

This book is for a student's first course in public administration. Its goals are both more ambitious and less ambitious than are those of many introductory texts. The primary goal is to make the study of public administration relevant and interesting for the student of political science. As a result, the book is concerned only minimally with several of the topics that are included in other books about public administration. It concentrates on those components that appear to be most relevant to the political process and that have received the most thorough attention by political scientists. One factor that links much of the material in public administration with other fields of political science is their common concern with *public policy*.

The meaning of the term "policy" is ambiguous. Policy can refer to a proposal, an ongoing program, the goals of a program, major decisions, or the refusal to make certain decisions. The uses of the term include such broad phrases as "the United States' foreign policy" and "the domestic policy of Jimmy Carter." In a more precise manner, it is used to denote limited aspects of complicated activities: "the policy toward oil depletion allowances advocated by the Treasury Department" or "the policies followed by a university in dealing with student demands." It would be misleading to specify one definition of policy at this point. Throughout the book, various of the above connotations will be implied; but the context in which the term is used should indicate the intended meaning in that instance.

The *policy process* includes the formulation, approval, and implementation of government programs. It joins public administrators to numerous other actors who have a stake in policy; these include officials in other branches of government, private citizens, interest groups, political parties, and sometimes the representatives of foreign governments. Also, within the policy process are the ideas, resources, stimuli, and constraints that influence the participants. The policy process is dynamic and is affected by intense controversies. Participants argue about the proper goals of government, about the programs that are suitable for obtaining each goal, about the probable impact of government programs on various segments of the population, and about the implications of certain programs for other government activities. Many of these arguments proceed with a surplus of emotion and a dearth of information. Policy-makers frequently make important decisions with nothing more than a "best guess" about the effects of these decisions on the problems they are designed to resolve.

In order to be successful in introducing a student to public administration and the policy process, a book should array its material in a framework that leads the reader to comprehend both the important features of the policy process and the relationships that make each feature important for the others. The framework of this book focuses on (1) an *environment* that both stimulates administrators and receives the products of their work; (2) the *inputs* that carry stimuli from the environment to administrators; (3) the *outputs* that carry the results of administrative action to the environment; (4) a *conversion process* that transforms (converts) inputs into outputs; and (5) *feedback* that transmits the outputs of one period—as they interact with features in the environment—back to the conversion process as the inputs of a later time. All of these features interact with one another. Together they form the *administrative system,* outlined in Figure 1–1.

This system will serve as a framework to guide the student through

FIGURE 1 1

The Administrative System

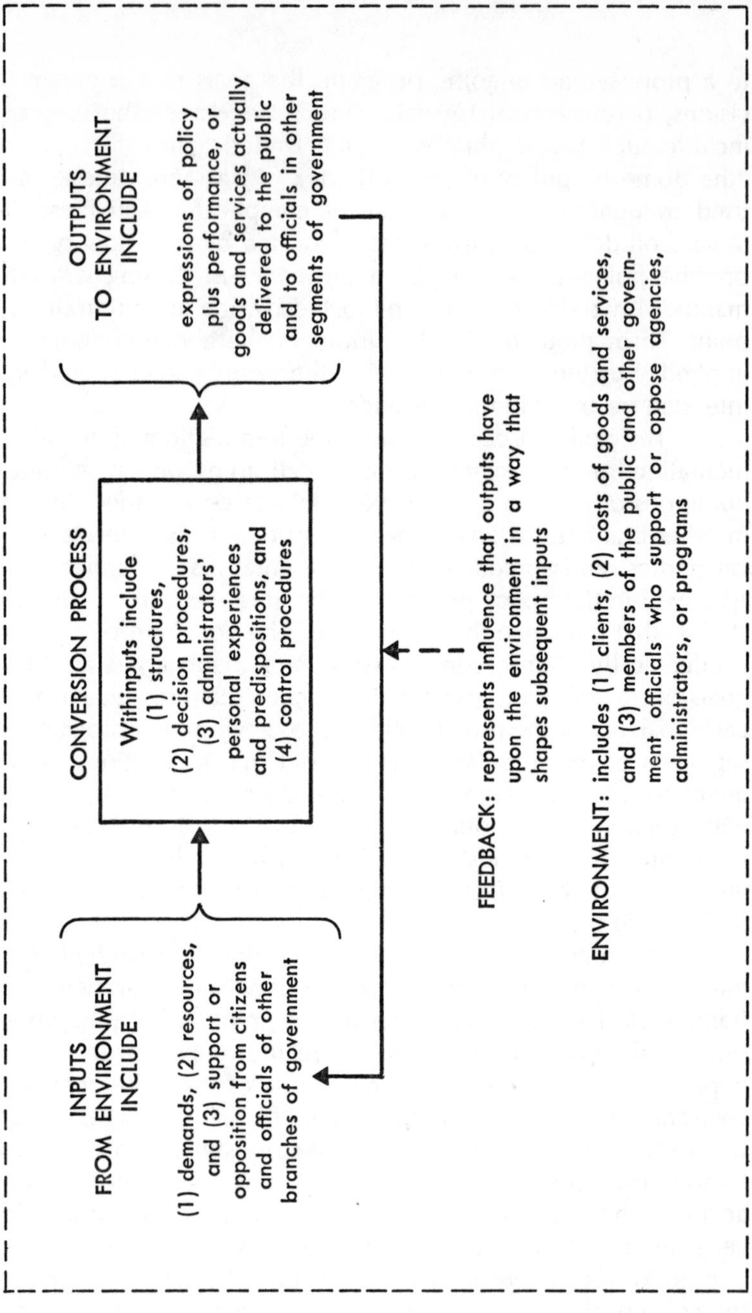

INPUTS
FROM ENVIRONMENT
INCLUDE

(1) demands, (2) resources, and (3) support or opposition from citizens and officials of other branches of government

CONVERSION PROCESS

Withinputs include
(1) structures,
(2) decision procedures,
(3) administrators' personal experiences and predispositions, and
(4) control procedures

OUTPUTS
TO ENVIRONMENT
INCLUDE

expressions of policy plus performance, or goods and services actually delivered to the public and to officials in other segments of government

FEEDBACK: represents influence that outputs have upon the environment in a way that shapes subsequent inputs

ENVIRONMENT: includes (1) clients, (2) costs of goods and services, and (3) members of the public and other government officials who support or oppose agencies, administrators, or programs

the numerous materials to be included in a book about public administration. The administrative system is a guide more than a theory. It does not explain how the various parts come together. Such information will come only as the reader takes information from this source and others to see what actually takes place within and between the pieces labeled inputs, outputs, conversion process, and feedback. The administrative system borrows concepts from other fields of social science to construct a framework for assembling various materials. Here we rest with a simple discussion of the system and its parts. Its complexities will become apparent as the student reads subsequent chapters. Readers themselves may elaborate on the categories presented here. Each part of the system is itself a complex world of individuals, groups, and institutions that interact in regular or irregular ways. It is possible to describe discrete subsystems that deal in budgeting, education, national defense, or other components of policy. The system outlined here is conceived in the most general terms. It is meant as the beginning, not as the end, of inquiry into public administration.

Environment and Inputs

The environment includes the host of social, economic, and political conditions that present problems to the policy-makers and that subsequently assist or confound their efforts to resolve these problems. Within the environment are the clients who are to benefit from a policy; a market that sets costs for the goods and services to be consumed by a policy; plus interest groups, members of the public and other units of government that express political support for—or opposition to—a policy. While some features of an environment facilitate policy-making and the solution of social problems, other features "harden" the problems and frustrate the policy-maker's efforts to cope with them.

Policy inputs are the transmissions sent from the environment to the conversion process of the administrative system. Inputs include demands for policy; resources; and support, opposition, or apathy toward the actions of administrators. People demand public goods and services for their own use, e.g., recreation facilities, education, transportation, and health services. They also demand the regulation of other people's behavior, e.g., by the police, commissions that limit the actions of business and labor, and the military. In addition, people demand the emotional satisfactions that derive from symbolic statements or gestures, e.g., from the celebration of patriotic, ethnic, or religious holidays. A "demand" is an analytic concept; it does not necessarily describe the nature of the citizen-administrator interaction. A demand may take the form of a routine request for service, such as filing an application with a welfare office or a state university; it may simply be a statement that an agency should introduce a new service; or it could be a public confrontation with all the hoopla of placards, civil disobedience, police, and tear gas. Resources include personnel, skills, materials, technology, and money. Support, opposition, or apathy shows itself in the degree of willingness of a population to pay taxes, to accept government employment, and to accept the government's regulation of behavior; it is also evidenced by their patience in the face of adversity and by their sentiments toward administrative personnel. Sentiment toward administrators can range from the enthusiasm of Support Your Local Police to the animosity of a campaign to oust a schoolteacher or principal. Between these extremes are the more typically passive attitudes toward government employees. The status of public administrators in the United States is below that of numerous other professional or technical groups. This has an implication for public policy: because many people consider government service to be an undesirable profession, government recruiters may not attract a sufficient number of applications from highly qualified college graduates.

The private sector is not the only source of inputs to the administrative system. The executive, legislative, and judicial branches of government send their administrators demands in the form of statutes, instructions, requests, or judgments. They also supply resources, support or opposition in the form of funds, and legal authority to perform services. Some of these governmental inputs are informal, and some are not even expressed. Administrators receive suggestions and recommendations from legislators during legislative hearings and throughout the year as the legislators clarify the intentions behind enacted statutes. Administrators continually anticipate demands they might receive from other branches of government by extrapolating from existing committee reports, court decisions, or public speeches. Administrators try to discern what the desires of another official will be or whether an official will be so irked by an administrative action that the official will invoke sanctions.

Conversion Process

It is not only inputs that influence the actions of administrators. Features of the conversion process itself affect their actions. These features are given a separate label in order to distinguish them from the inputs that come from the environment. Because they originate within the conversion process, they are called *withinputs*. Withinputs include chains of command and other formal structures found within administrative agencies; the procedures used by officials to make their decisions; the administrators' personal experiences and predispositions; and the ways that administrative superiors control their subordinates. Among the features that may be found in the conversion process are conflicts between the formal rules of the organization and the personal values of administrators; clashes among administrators that increase the problems in making agency outputs; decision-makers' use of routine procedures to simplify complex and numerous inputs; and tendencies toward rigid maintenance of the status quo in the face of innovative demands. An agency's leadership and staff may disagree about proper salaries, working conditions, and services to the agency's clients. Like other segments of government, administration is usually involved in some controversy.

Outputs

Outputs that administrators provide to their environment include services, tangible goods, and behavioral regulations, plus gestures, statements, and activities that give symbolic messages to those who are tuned in. To the private sector, administrators provide many of the material and symbolic needs of the citizenry. Administrators also provide direct benefits—information, technical advice, and concrete proposals necessary for policy formulation—to officials in other government units. Legislators and executives make their living by promising and delivering services to voters. Most of these services ultimately must come from administrative agencies. While the politician can supply the necessary resources to the administrator and can urge him to make the desired product for the public, it is the administrator who generally implements the statutory power enacted by the legislature and makes the actual delivery of public service. The administrator's failure to provide desired services may offend both the citizen and the elected members of the legislative branch. Such failures are "negative outputs." They carry short-term deprivations for persons in the administrator's environment; they threaten long-term deprivations for the administrators themselves.

It is helpful to think of outputs as including both *policies* and *performance*. *Policies* are the goals and actions of administrators undertaken in an effort to shape the quantity or quality of public services. Yet policies do not always produce their intended results. Conflicting policies, being pursued by the same or different agencies, may produce a net result of zero. The Federal Reserve Board's efforts to hold down inflation by requiring banks to increase reserve funds may have little success if other federal agencies increase spending or if the Treasury Department pursues tax reductions to increase employment. Social problems that are the targets of policies are often more substantial than first believed. Difficulties of lower-income families persist in the face of different policies for welfare payments, counseling, and job training. Certain children continue to do poorly in school no matter how much money is spent on their education. In other cases, conflicting demands from the environment lead officials to compromise their objectives so programs cannot perform as intended. This has happened with programs designed to control pollution, to regulate monopolistic business practices, and to eliminate racial inequities in jobs and housing.

Policy, then, represents efforts of administrators and other officials. *Performance* represents the work that is actually delivered. Policies can aim at services by defining expenditures, salary levels, employee workloads, and the rules that govern treatment of clients. *Performance* may reflect the influence of policies, but it also reflects the influence of various factors that complicate the delivery of policy. It is often difficult to judge administrators' *performance*, partly because a policy may have several goals spelled out in the legislation or the statements of administrators. Public education, for example, tries to impart basic skills of language and calculation; plus substantive knowledge across a wide range of academic fields; plus social amenities and patriotism. Welfare also has numerous goals, including material sustenance, employment skills and ambition, and sometimes the clients' acceptance of certain moral standards. For each policy, there may be different ways of measuring performance: by the frequency with which services are actually made available; by the evaluation of services by clients or professional experts; or by changes in the traits of clients as a result of a program. Insofar as the determination of "successful" or "unsuccessful" evaluation of performance is likely to influence a policy's future (and that of its administrators and clients), then the choice of an instrument to measure performance and the interpretation of its results is likely to be a matter of some controversy.

Who actually makes "policy" in an administrative system? Who is responsible for "performance"? There are no simple answers to these questions. Some policies are defined by administrators and other officials together: legislators and the chief executive authorize programs and define levels of spending, but they typically rely heavily on the advice of administrators who will implement these policies. On other occasions, administrators have more direct roles as when statutes or executive orders specify general goals but allow an administrative officer to define the specific features of each program and to pursue performance with the efforts of operating personnel. The heads of such bodies as the Food and Drug Administration and the Environmental Protection Agency have considerable discretion in defining the regulations to be imposed on business firms, as well as the responsibility to monitor business practices and to enforce agency policies.

Feedback

Feedback represents the influence of earlier outputs upon the demands, resources, support, or opposition (i.e., inputs) that an administrative system receives. Existing tax legislation influences the flow of economic resources into administrative agencies. Public services and regulatory policies affect citizens' satisfactions and thus shape the demands they make. Past efforts to promote economic development may affect social and economic conditions in ways that influence both the resources provided by existing taxes and the demands and supports coming from the population.

Feedback mechanisms are evident in the continuity of interactions among administrators and the many sources of their inputs and the recipients of their outputs. Citizens, legislators, and the chief executive are seldom satisfied once and for all times. Some always ask for more. They may demand improvement of existing services, expansion of the magnitude of services to provide for increased population, and expansion of the scope of a program to provide for certain needs left unmet by present activities. The annual budget cycle requires an agency staff to defend its activities of the current year and its proposals for the coming year in hearings before officials in both the executive and legislative branches. On these occasions, evidence of program accomplishments and of unmet demands come back to the administrators in the form of program instructions and budget ceilings for the coming year. Groups that receive an agency's services or feel the impact of its regulations join with allies in the legislature and try to alter the legal authority of an agency or its level of appropriations. In less formal ways, client groups and legislators are always making some effort to get administrators to change their policies or their decisions in particular cases.

THE SYSTEMS FRAMEWORK

The environment, inputs, conversion process, outputs, and feedback relate to and interact with one another in the manner shown in Figure 1–1. An entire set of these elements and their interactions is called an *admin-*

istrative system. A system is not simply the administrative unit contained in the conversion process. An administrative system is the combination of the administrative unit and all of the elements and processes that interact with the unit: that is, the (1) environment within which the administrative unit operates and which influences and is influenced by the unit, and the (2) inputs to the (3) outputs from the unit that are connected to each other by the (4) conversion process and by (5) feedback mechanisms. A system such as this is a useful framework for treating individual items; it focuses attention not merely on a simple description of discrete parts, but on the importance and relationship of these parts to one another.

As a conceptual framework, an administrative system helps us think about public administration. It is not a fixed set of actors and activities. It can be used to guide our ideas about universal happenings (i.e., generalizations about administrative activities in all governments) or about particular happenings (i.e., administrative activities in certain settings). We can devise an administrative system to include the actions of most public administrators in the United States; this system would include legislative and judicial officials of state, local, and national governments, as well as all the principal interest groups that involve themselves in prominent issues. For other purposes, we might devise an administrative system to explain the actions of one agency. A system focusing on the Federal Bureau of Investigation, for example, would include a limited collection of resources, government officials, interest groups, and citizens.

By thinking about public administration in a systems framework, we should discipline ourselves to ask about the relevance of the individual components: *What implications for outputs are to be found in the various features of the conversion process? How does the character of the conversion process respond to inputs from the environment? What kind of constraints over outputs are exercised by the amount of resources that come into the conversion process from the environment?* This kind of questioning establishes the relevance of public administration to politics, to economics, and to other features of its environment that interest us as political scientists and as citizens.[2] The administrative system is not

---

2. The theoretical work that is most frequently cited in connection with the systems approach to political science is David Easton, *A Systems Analysis of Political Life* (New York: Wiley, 1965). See also David Easton, *A Framework for Political Analysis* (Englewood Cliffs, N.J.: Prentice-Hall, 1965); Gabriel Almond and G. Bingham Powell, Jr., *Comparative Politics: A Developmental Approach* (Boston: Little, Brown, 1966); Thomas R. Dye, *Politics, Economics, and the Public: Policy Outcomes in the American States* (Chicago: Rand McNally, 1966); Richard F. Fenno, *The Power of the Purse: Appropriations*

a set of fixed patterns in which administrators engage in documented relations with their environment. The system is a *conceptual framework* whose purpose is to aid the study of public administration. Inputs and feedback suggest the kinds of stimuli likely to influence activities in the conversion process; outputs are merely a label for that category of phenomena that reflect the products of administrators' work. As a conceptual framework, the system guides the selection and organization of information about public administration. With the system as a guide, we shall collect information about items that seem to function as conversion components, inputs, outputs, and feedback mechanisms. We shall then see how these items actually do interact with one another.

The linkages among environment, inputs, conversion, outputs, and feedback may appear to be a closed system in which decision-makers respond continuously to the impact that their own previous decisions have had upon their environment. Figure 1–1 may suggest such "closure" to some readers. However, the diagram only shows which items in a system may interact with others; it does not portray the character of these relationships. There is much slippage among components of a system. In the real world, there are numerous features that can influence the decisions of the participants. Environments change in response to national and international politics, economic events, and natural disasters. New inputs continuously come from the demands of citizens and citizen organizations. Officials have many options in reviewing the feedback from their previous decisions: officials differ in the weight they assign to precedent, to the demands that come from citizens or from other officials, and to their own assessment about the success of current activities.

An administrative system may attain stability if its decision-makers succeed in satisfying demands and in living within the resources conveniently available. For the administrators who will be described in this book, however, stability is—at most—an elusive goal. For many participants, stability is neither apparent nor desired; they prefer major changes in their agency or in its surroundings. For some, the quest for stability is frustrated by an environment that provides not only shifting and ambiguous goals, but also resources and supports that change in response to numerous and complex determinants.

Politics in Congress (Boston: Little, Brown, 1966); John C. Wahlke et al., *The Legislative System* (New York: Wiley, 1962); and Karl W. Deutsch, *The Nerves of Government* (New York: Free Press of Glencoe, 1963).

A "systems approach" is not the only way to organize a book about public administration. For a discussion of the author's reasons for this choice, see the preface.

THE BORDERS OF
ADMINISTRATIVE SYSTEMS

In order to examine the systems that link administrative units with their environments, it is necessary to mark the borders that surround the conversion process and that separate it from inputs and outputs. The conversion process includes units that provide services, collect taxes, and impose regulations. Administrative units are variously termed "departments," "bureaus," "agencies," "commissions," "offices," "services," or whatever label the designers of a unit consider appropriate. In the national government, for example, we can find the *Department* of Justice, the *Office* of Education, the *Agency* for International Development, the Public Health *Service*, the *Bureau* of Indian Affairs, the Interstate Commerce *Commission* and the Tennessee Valley *Authority*. They comprise the "bureaucracy"—the offices and the personnel that staff them—that has long been the subject of serious analysis and some ridicule. Some writers call these "line" units of government. They are distinguished in this way from the "staff" units that serve the chief executive in supervising and controlling the administrative branch. We consider line units to be within the conversion process of administrative systems. Excluded from the conversion process and assigned to the "environment" of our conceptual framework are the chief executive, legislators, judges, and their immediate supporting staffs. On the federal level, such institutions as the Office of Management and Budget and the White House Office are considered to be part of the executive (or "presidency") and are, therefore, in the environment of the administrative system. Along with other legislative, judicial, and executive units, these provide inputs to administrative agencies. Note that we distinguish the *administrative branch* from the *executive*. The executive is described along with other political phenomena that provide direction to administrators and seek to control their activities.

Admittedly, these borders are diffuse. Some of the work of administrative units bears close resemblance to the work of executives, legislators, and judges. The heads of numerous departments in state and local governments are elected by the voters and act as the executives of their own departments, separate from the chief executive. Department heads and their assistants who are appointed by the chief executive may identify more with the executive branch than with administrators. Regulatory agencies are charged with the formal responsibilities of legislating —and then adjudicating—their own rules. Some organizations serve part-time as units of public administration and part-time as members of the private sector (e.g., government contractors). Administrators do not simply carry out decisions that are made in the legislative, judicial, and executive units of government. Administrators suggest policies to members of other branches and frequently write the bills that are enacted by the legislative branch. Administrators also exercise great discretion in carrying out assignments given to them. In describing the work of administrators, we shall be dealing with persons and institutions that make their own important contributions to the policies of government.

Despite the irregularity of the borders of the conversion process, it remains a valid subject for this book. Our focus is on the "fourth branch of government": those persons and organizations that are not usually included in the simple tripartite divisions of executive, legislative, and judicial.

Within the United States—which is the primary focus of this book—there are variations in the inputs received, in the nature of conversions, and in the outputs of administrative units at different levels of government. Within each level of government, moreover, important features of administrative systems may also vary from one agency to another. The use of a systems approach does not signify uniformities in behavior. It provides a framework that assists in the identification of general tendencies and deviant cases and in the understanding of those features that produce the deviations. On some occasions, we shall employ a system that has general application to administrative units. Elsewhere, we shall refer to a system that is relevant for only a limited number of administrative units.

THE ORGANIZATION OF THIS BOOK

Although these pages focus on the abstract categories of administrative systems, the book itself is not devoid of the dynamic, throbbing life of politics. Later chapters deal with the support given administrators by the political culture of the United States; with the social backgrounds of administrators and their own views about their jobs; with efforts they make to influence policy; with conflicts between administrative units that are ostensibly the subordinates of a common chief executive; and with methods that officials use to make decisions when their environment precludes a "rational" procedure. The systems framework shows itself most clearly in the book's overall structure. Four consecutive chapters examine aspects of the conversion process; three chapters examine inputs; and two concluding chapters deal with outputs and feedback.

Before these, however, a second introductory chapter explores the use of comparative research as an adjunct to the systems framework. It reports on comparisons of administrative systems within the United States and on comparisons of American administrative systems with some foreign examples.

As noted above, understanding of the administrative system is not complete. Also, despite the obvious necessity for organizing this book into specific chapters, there can be no simple compartmentalizing of *all* of the material into particular system categories. Some factors appear to straddle more than one category and thus require an arbitrary choice as to location in one or another chapter. On several occasions, we discuss a feature of the system in one section (e.g., as part of the conversion process), but we also note how it could be viewed in other contexts. The test of the systems framework for this book lies in the amount of clarity it brings to the subject, in the success with which it indicates important relationships among various components of the system, and—ultimately—in whatever research it provokes to clarify features of the system that presently are subjects of speculation.

2

Comparison in the Study of Public Administration

This book focuses on administrative systems within the United States. By concentrating on domestic materials, we can obtain depth of coverage. As a result, we must—albeit regrettably—sacrifice breadth in our treatment of the subject. Such a focus does not reflect any negative assessment of the rich and growing field of cross-cultural comparative public administration. The systems framework supports—and indeed requires—comparative analysis. Many studies compare administrative activities in various settings—both within the context of a single country and among different countries. By means of comparative studies, we see, for example, how administrators respond to different kinds of inputs and how outputs vary with the nature of administrative activities. This chapter illustrates some of the advantages that come to political scientists if they compare different administrative systems within the United States. It then examines some features of administrative systems throughout the world. It also examines parallels between the administrative systems of certain American states and those of developing countries. Certain features of environments may have similar influences on administrative units the world over. This chapter is placed early in the book to highlight the advantages of comparative study. Some readers may wish to postpone it until they have read the remaining chapters and have become familiar with the various elements of the administrative system in the American setting.

A focus on the administrative systems within the national, state, and local governments of the United States does not signify any parochial attachment to the boundaries of this country. The inputs to and outputs from American public administration are global in scope. This is most apparent in the fields of diplomacy, international aid, and military policy.

In other programs whose clientele are more uniformly domestic, there are also international inputs and outputs. In 1974, about 5 percent of the civilian employees of the federal government were stationed outside of the United States. The U.S. Public Health Service concerns itself with diseases wherever they occur. The U.S. Office of Education sponsors research into the educational programs of other countries—partly as an aid program for educators in those countries and partly to acquire information for the United States about teaching techniques that have been developed elsewhere. City planners and transportation experts study public housing and mass transit operations in cities throughout the world. They do this to broaden their knowledge of alternatives at home. It frequently happens that administrative actions have both international *and* domestic repercussions. This is certainly the case with research and development programs for weapons for the military. A new venture in this field gives signals to foreign governments about possible changes in our weapons strength and about likely offensive or defensive strategies; and such a venture simultaneously provides economic rewards to the American communities in which the weapons will be manufactured or based. One of the most controversial policy issues that connects administrative, political, and industrial sectors both within the United States and overseas concerns the "military-industrial complex." This is an alleged web of interconnected ambitions which is said to impel the United States toward high levels of military expenditure and dangerous international arms competition. Behind these expenditures, supposedly, are alliances of industrialists who want the profits to be made from building weapons, politicians who want military bases or industrial payrolls for their constituencies, party leaders who want the best "defense plank" for their candidates, and military officers who want power.

Comparison is essential to the use of the systems framework. By comparing different administrative systems, we can see how their parts correspond to one another. How regularly do certain environmental conditions occur with certain kinds of conversion processes? Or with certain kinds of output? This book makes a concerted effort to utilize the comparative method of analysis. As much as possible, it draws upon studies that are explicitly comparative in their examination of administrative processes in several agencies of the federal government or in several states, localities, or countries.

The comparative method indicates differences in form and process within varying contexts; identifies the range across which administrative phenomena vary; and demonstrates the patterns whereby certain features of administrative systems tend to occur together. As a result of comparative analysis, for example, we have learned a great deal about the influence of economic conditions—a feature of the environment—over the kinds of outputs that administrative agencies produce.

COMPARATIVE ANALYSIS OF ADMINISTRATIVE SYSTEMS IN THE UNITED STATES

The American states provide a natural laboratory for comparative analysis. If we examine the expenditures of each state, we can determine which states' administrative systems are given greater or lesser amounts of financial resources and which are likely to have greater or lesser impact on their environments. If we look at the salaries and other perquisites of officials in each state, we can judge which states have made greater or lesser efforts to professionalize their public service.[1] As a measure of the fiscal resources allocated to state administrators, we use total state government expenditures. Only a small fraction of this total amount is used to support the governor, the legislature, or the judiciary. Figures compiled by the U.S. Bureau of the Census for 1975 show that these three branches are allocated on average less than 1 percent of total state government expenditures.

In studying variations in states' expenditures, we must correct raw figures for state-to-state differences in population and eliminate state expenditures for liquor stores and insurance trust funds. The resulting figure—*general expenditures per capita*—is the measure that is used most frequently to judge the fiscal resources made available in each state to support its public services. Table 2–1 ranks the states according to this measure for 1975.

Alaska and Hawaii outspend each of the other states due, in part, to the high cost of goods and services in these newest states. The lowest per capita spender is Missouri, which may come as a surprise to those who automatically expect a southern state to hold this position. Other wealthy states scoring near the bottom of this list are Indiana and Ohio. Administrative agencies in these state governments have been lethargic in supporting programs that are popular elsewhere; they have also left massive spending responsibilities to local governments. When 1975 state

---

1. This section relies on Ira Sharkansky, "State Administrators in the Political Process," in Herbert Jacob and Kenneth N. Vines, eds., *Politics in the American States*, 2nd ed. (Boston: Little, Brown, 1971).

TABLE 2–1
State Government Total General Expenditures per Capita, by Rank, 1975

	Rank	General Expenditures per Capita
Alaska	1	$2,266.75
Hawaii	2	1,251.41
Delaware	3	889.43
Vermont	4	872.88
New York	5	866.70
Wyoming	6	803.86
Maryland	7	765.37
Washington	8	752.19
Massachusetts	9	748.25
New Mexico	10	747.68
Minnesota	11	744.30
Wisconsin	12	739.46
North Dakota	13	731.32
California	14	720.87
Michigan	15	709.80
Rhode Island	16	707.67
Maine	17	695.63
Nevada	18	695.22
West Virginia	19	682.60
Louisiana	20	681.91
Utah	21	671.09
Pennsylvania	22	670.81
South Carolina	23	658.25
Arizona	24	656.35
Oregon	25	655.37
Idaho	26	654.13
Illinois	27	638.78
Colorado	28	637.80
Montana	29	637.05
Connecticut	30	623.66
Iowa	31	616.94
Virginia	32	612.23
Mississippi	33	611.10
Kentucky	34	598.50
South Dakota	35	595.58
North Carolina	36	591.91
New Jersey	37	591.27
Alabama	38	567.18
Oklahoma	39	566.60
Georgia	40	561.20
Florida	41	541.87
Kansas	42	541.87

TABLE 2–1 (Cont.)
State Government Total General Expenditures per Capita, by Rank, 1975

	Rank	General Expenditures per Capita
Arkansas	43	$536.67
New Hampshire	44	530.51
Nebraska	45	529.62
Tennessee	46	522.39
Indiana	47	509.70
Ohio	48	506.50
Texas	49	470.26
Missouri	50	466.06

SOURCE: U.S. Bureau of the Census, *State Government Finances in 1975* (Washington, D.C.: U.S. Government Printing Office, 1976). General expenditures are for those functions pursued in common by almost all of the states. They exclude expenditures of state liquor stores and insurance trust funds.

and local spending is combined for each state, the lowest-ranking states become Arkansas, West Virginia, Alabama, and Mississippi.

State administrators compensate for weaknesses that exist elsewhere in their jurisdiction. State expenditures are often high where the administrative systems of local governments are relatively weak and where private resources (as measured by population and industrialization) are meager. Where citizens and local governments are poor, state authorities tend to collect sizable revenues and provide a disproportionate share of the services received by the population.

Several features help to explain the amount of resources available to the administrators of poor states. Low-income citizens cannot provide for themselves the levels of education, health, or recreation that are obtained through the market mechanisms in affluent settings. Moreover, many local governments in poor states (especially rural counties) are hard-pressed to meet service demands with their own resources. Part of the problem faced by local governments rests on their enforced reliance on a tax base that is dependent upon the local economy. State constitutions generally restrict localities to the tax on real property that is located within their borders. This imposes a severe burden on poor localities.

State administrators can make up for some needs of local authorities who must function in low-income conditions: the states have legal access to the economic resources within their larger jurisdiction; they benefit from a more generous selection of federal aids; and they have a more productive tax system with which to extract revenue from available sources. State income taxes and sales taxes have remained more productive in the face of depressed economic conditions than has the local property tax.

States also differ from one another in their efforts to professionalize their administrative systems. A "professional" cadre of administrators has several attributes: advanced training in their fields of specialization, an active concern to stay abreast of the latest developments, and a desire to implement the most advanced level of service that is available. Deil Wright reports an opinion survey of 933 state administrators from across the country that shows one dimension of their professionalism. The large majority of his respondents (76 percent) want an expansion of their own agency's services and expenditures. The administrators had a choice of expansion at levels of 0–5 percent, 5–10 percent, 10–15 percent, and over 15 percent. Almost one-third of the respondents chose the uppermost range of expansion. If Wright's specific alternatives had gone beyond 15 percent, we might have been able to gauge the upper limits of administrators' desires. As it is, many administrators seem to want a greater magnitude of expansion than Professor Wright expected.[2]

Employees' salaries show part of the states' efforts to professionalize their administrative systems. One group of states scores consistently high in the salaries paid to employees generally and to the heads of major units, e.g., the chief budget officer and the heads of departments for education, welfare, and health. The highest-ranking states in this group are New York, California, Ohio, Michigan, Pennsylvania, and Illinois. The states with low scores on administrative salaries are Montana, Louisiana, Delaware, Idaho, Mississippi, and Wyoming. As these lists suggest, salaries correspond with state economies. A high level of industrialization, in particular, may provide the resources necessary to support high levels of spending on the civil service, and it may provide models of salary levels in the private sector that are adopted by the state government.

Economic Interpretations of Policy

Thomas R. Dye provides substantial evidence that the level of economic development within a jurisdiction affects the nature of policy outputs from its administrative system.[3] He finds high levels of economic

2. Deil S. Wright, "Executive Leadership in State Administration," *Midwest Journal of Political Science* 11 (February 1967): 1–26.

3. Thomas R. Dye, *Politics, Economics, and the Public: Policy Outcomes in the American States* (Chicago: Rand McNally, 1966). See also Richard E. Dawson and James

development generally associated with high levels of expenditures in the fields of education, welfare, and health; state and local governments in the wealthiest, most urbanized states spend the most and offer the most attractive programs. In the fields of highways and natural resources, however, economic development is *inversely* associated with levels of spending and services; the poorest states offer the most attractive programs.

Professor Dye does not explain the economic-output linkages in a direct fashion. His comments suggest that the economy offers a set of material resources that either provides the wherewithal or imposes limits for administrators and other policy-makers:

> There is little doubt that the ability of states to raise revenues is a function of their level of economic development. Both tax revenues and total revenues per capita are closely related to wealth, as is the ability to carry larger per capita debt levels. Tax burdens, or the percentage of personal income devoted to taxes, is a function of industrialization. The greater the degree of industrialization, the lower the tax burden.[4]

This is a *resource* view of the economic-output linkage. In its simplest form, this view implies that citizen demands are similar from one state to another. Poor states offer the most generous policies that their resources permit. Wealthy states offer the most generous levels of policy on an absolute scale; at the same time, because of the great resources of these states, policies in wealthy states may be supported with relatively low tax burdens.

It is not only through a resource-output linkage that a state's level of economic development can affect administrators' programs. The economy may affect the needs felt by the population and perceived by policy-makers. This is called a *need* view of the economic-output linkage. In low-income states, in particular, this view deemphasizes the importance of available resources. Administrators in poor states may tax their citizens with unusual severity to provide the demanded level of services. Dye uses a *need* explanation for his findings that low-income rural states score high on their road programs:

> Quite clearly, rural politics are much more highway-oriented than urban politics. Part of this phenomenon may be a product of the historical problems

---

A. Robinson, "Inter-party Competition, Economic Variables, and Welfare Policies in the American States," *Journal of Politics* 25 (May 1963): 265–89; Richard I. Hofferbert, "The Relation between Public Policy and Some Structural and Environmental Variables in the American States," *American Political Science Review* 60 (March 1966): 73–82; and Ira Sharkansky, "Regionalism, Economic Status and the Public Policies of American States," *Social Science Quarterly* 49 (June 1968): 9–26.

4. Dye, *Politics, Economics, and the Public,* p. 290.

of rural isolation. "Let's Get Out of the Mud" was a familiar battlecry in rural politics a few years ago.[5]

There is nothing objectionable about using a *resource* view of the policy process to explain some statistical relationships between measures of the economy and policy and using a *need* view to explain other relationships. Each kind of linkage probably exists some of the time. When there is no awareness of their distinction, however, we may fail to perceive the full nature of the economic-output linkages that actually exist. It is true that welfare benefits in most states correspond with the level of wealth. In these cases, there is a resource-output process: both wealthy and poor states are paying a level of benefits commensurate with their resources. A fixation upon the resource view may hide the finding that welfare benefits of other states reflect a different kind of economic-output process. States like New Hampshire, North Dakota, and Vermont —with relatively low levels of economic development, but with high welfare benefits—reflect a need-policy linkage; their administrators spend an unusual portion of the state's economic resources to serve welfare clients.

The influence of the economy on policy can change with conditions. The economy varies in its influence at different levels of government, at different periods of time, and among different kinds of public services. Economic development has greater influence on the outputs of local governments than it does on the outputs of state governments.[6] As noted earlier, most local governments must draw upon a narrowly limited geographical area for resources; in addition, they are confined to only one major revenue source (the property tax), which generates a great deal of political controversy. State governments draw upon their larger jurisdiction and can transfer resources from "have" to "have-not" communities. State officials also have wider revenue options that include taxes on income and retail sales. The state income tax and sales tax appear to be less upsetting politically than is the local property tax; and the state taxes appear to be less vulnerable to an economic recession. As a result, state officials can escape many of the constraints on policy which seem to originate in the economic sector and to limit the policy discretion of local government officials. Officials of the national govern-

---

5. Dye, *Politics, Economics, and the Public,* p. 161.
6. Compare the findings reported in Harvey E. Brazer, *City Expenditures in the United States* (New York: National Bureau of Economic Research, 1959), with those in Ira Sharkansky, *Spending in the American States* (Chicago: Rand McNally, 1968), chapter 4.

ment appear to be hindered even less by economic constraints, partly because of their power to tax the resources of the wealthy areas of the country and partly because of their ability to borrow in the face of current deficits in the taxing-spending balance. The national government operates numerous programs to influence levels of employment, interest, and wages and at times may be as much the master as the subordinate of the economy.

The influence of economic conditions on state and local government policies appears to be diminishing.[7] Policy-makers now have more opportunities to spend at levels above the "norm" for their economic conditions. Some of this increased flexibility may reflect growth in magnitude of federal aids. By transferring resources from "have" to "have-not" jurisdictions, the federal government makes up for some of the differentials among the states. Also, state and local governments now have more flexible tax structures. With state taxes on personal incomes and/or retail sales now used by over 40 of the states (whereas no state used either tax at the beginning of the century) and with numerous local governments now also turning to these forms of taxation, policy-makers can tap an increasing proportion of the resources within their own jurisdictions. Even the poorest states (e.g., Mississippi, South Carolina, Arkansas, Vermont) have some pockets of wealth that can help support services in their poorest counties.

Economic conditions exercise less of a constraint on some kinds of policy than on others. The political saliency of a policy is one of the factors that can lessen the influence of economics. A program's popularity can provoke the use of substantially more resources than is normally associated with the jurisdiction's level of wealth. Officials "try harder" under the impetus of public demand. Under different conditions—when public sentiment runs counter to a program—there is less performance than would be expected on the basis of economic conditions.[8]

Economic resources vary in the ways they affect different features of public policy: the *total service output* of a jurisdiction and the *distribution of service benefits* among different income groups. The magnitude of resources in a jurisdiction seems to affect the total volume

7. Alan K. Campbell and Seymour Sachs, *Metropolitan America: Fiscal Patterns and Governmental Systems* (New York: Free Press of Glencoe, 1967), p. 57.

8. See Charles F. Cnudde and Donald J. McCrone, "Party Competition and Welfare Policies in the American States," *American Political Science Review* 63 (September 1969): 858–66; and Ira Sharkansky and Richard I. Hofferbert, "Dimensions of State Politics, Economics and Public Policy," *American Political Science Review* 63 (September 1969): 867–79.

of benefits produced, more than it affects the distribution of these benefits to residents of different income groups.[9] Policy-makers may be sensitive to the total resources available when facing such issues as the number of teachers to be hired, the number of schoolrooms to be built, the miles of highway to be constructed, the number of acres to be purchased for state parks, or the amount of money to be spent on public welfare. Policy-makers may be more sensitive to noneconomic political constraints when they consider questions of distribution: where to assign the teachers or to build the schoolrooms, which sites to select for the highways or the parks, or how much to pay different classes of welfare recipients.

Such findings about the influence of economic conditions upon the outputs of administrative systems may apply only to the United States, or they may also apply to analogous situations in other countries. The findings can be expressed in an interrogative fashion that would suggest international comparisons. Are the administrative units of national governments less constrained by economic conditions than are those of local or regional governments—owing to the greater jurisdiction of the national governments, to their opportunity to redistribute resources from "have" to "have-not" areas, and to their opportunity to exercise greater controls over their own economic development? Has the influence of economic conditions over policy declined in recent years—perhaps with increases in wealth and technological capacity? Does the politicization of an issue make policy decisions less dependent on economic resources? Does the total volume of economic resources in a country exercise more influence over the total outputs of its administrative systems than over the distribution of those outputs among high- and low-income groups? Questions of this detail have not been addressed in a sophisticated fashion in cross-national comparisons of administrative systems.

COMPARATIVE ANALYSIS ACROSS NATIONAL BOUNDARIES

This section employs the comparative method across national borders. These comparisons will not be as detailed as those among American units. In part, this limitation is included by design. We hope to maintain

---

9. Thomas R. Dye, "Income Inequality and American State Politics," *American Political Science Review* 63 (March 1969): 157–62; and Bryan Fry and Richard Winter, "The Politics of Redistribution," *American Political Science Review* 64 (June 1970): 508–22.

the focus and depth of a domestic analysis. In part, too, the limitation is required by the lack of cross-national information. Although the field of comparative administration has progressed far in recent years, it has not yet provided the thoroughness or breadth of coverage that is available from intranational comparisons.

This brief cross-national comparison provides some of the same benefits as are furnished by the more thorough domestic comparisons. It identifies the global range of differences in some administrative forms and processes. This exercise should convince the reader that there is nothing "natural" or "universal" about American public administration. It also suggests the utility of a systems framework for cross-national comparison. As in domestic analysis, the systems ordering of environment, inputs, outputs, conversion, and feedback can highlight the features of administrative systems that are related to one another. With this type of knowledge, we can gain some understanding of the processes that might bring about changes in administrative forms or procedures or in the outputs that administrative units provide to their clients.

The Importance of "Development"

At the present, comparative public administration has not progressed so far in its cross-national investigations as to define the numerous linkages that exist between administrative features and their environment. However, there is one environmental characteristic that often seems important to the nature of public administration: the level of "development."[10]

"Development" is a complicated concept. It is not a tangible commodity that a country either has or does not have. As the term is used in the literature, it refers to an aggregate of economic, social, and political variables, each of which exists on a continuum ranging from less- to more-developed. An individual country may simultaneously exhibit some traits that appear to be developed and others that appear to be less-developed. Some features of public administration may likewise appear developed, while others in the same country—indeed in the same capital city—may resemble the administrative features of a less-developed country. There are differences in public administration at each pole of

---

10. A number of labels have appeared for the "less-developed" countries. Some of the most common alternatives include "emergent," "transitional," "developing," and "expectant"; "underdeveloped" seems no longer popular, perhaps because it carries the onus of a connotation of permanence. Terms suggesting movement toward some more-developed stage seem to be the most acceptable.

the development continuum that do not reflect the stage of development as much as they reflect peculiar historical experiences or cultural traits. Great Britain, France, Germany, and the United States, for example, are currently at about the same stage of advanced development. However, each of these nations demonstrates peculiarities in public administration that reflect its own evolution.

Social scientists tend to disagree among themselves about the characteristics of development. To some, it is equated with the capacity to produce large amounts of tangible resources in relation to size of population—translated into industrial output, agricultural produce, raw materials, gross national product, and personal income. Others, who focus not so much on material production as on the forms of social and economic organization, argue that *development* exists in societies (1) that have *relatively equal distributions of benefits;* (2) that utilize *modern technology;* (3) that assign rewards according to *personal achievement* and not according to family, caste, or tribal background; (4) that use *specialists* in economic and governmental roles, instead of generalists who must provide leadership in a full range of activities; and (5) that have governmental units that *can adjust* to social or economic change and acquire "new capabilities" to meet new demands.[11]

Each trait of development is a distinct variable. However, many countries that score more-developed on one variable also score more-developed on other variables. Thus, the dimensions of development seem to reinforce one another. For example, the uses of sophisticated technologies seem to impel a society toward specialization and toward the distribution of rewards according to the criteria of personal achievement. Where there are complicated programs of medicine, agriculture, or industry, it is typical to allocate much of the educational resources to the training of technicians and professionals. In such a context, it is incongruous to give prestige and political power to religious and tribal leaders and not to those who have mastered both the sophisticated technologies and the large-scale organizations that seem to accompany these technologies.

Despite the tendency toward a clustering of the development characteristics, each of the most well-developed nations also shows some features of less-developed societies. Each has experienced some civil strife that reflects an inability to resolve the intense demands of certain social groups. Moreover, each has some "backward" regions that have been bypassed by some of the organizational traits and material wealth

---

11. The following pages rely on materials in Ferrel Heady, *Public Administration: A Comparative Perspective* (Englewood Cliffs, N.J.: Prentice-Hall, 1966).

of development. Indeed, regions in the United States offer economic and political traits sufficiently like those of Africa, Asia, and Latin America to question the United States' designation as a "developed" country.

ADMINISTRATIVE SYSTEMS IN MORE-DEVELOPED COUNTRIES

When writers describe well-developed nations, they generally focus on the most modern countries of Western Europe and those elsewhere that have followed European models. The list typically includes Great Britain, France, Germany, the United States, Scandinavia, "white" nations of the British Commonwealth (Canada, Australia, New Zealand), the Soviet Union, Japan, and Israel. The features that are generally shared by these countries include the following:

1. The organization of government is patterned after the organization of the private sector, in the sense that there is a high degree of task-specialization and that roles are assigned according to the personal achievements of individuals rather than according to family status or social class.

2. Political decisions and legal judgments are made according to secular standards of rationality; traditional (e.g., religious or tribal) elites have lost any real power to affect major governmental decisions.

3. Government activity extends over a wide range of public and personal affairs; and it tends toward further expansion into all major spheres.

4. Popular interest and involvement in public affairs is widespread.

5. Those persons who occupy positions of political or governmental leadership are widely viewed as legitimate holders of those positions, and transfers of leadership tend to occur according to prescribed, orderly procedures.

Some of these characteristics have counterparts in the nature of the public bureaucracies of more-developed nations:

1. The bureaucracy is large and has numerous, distinct subunits. Many of these units require highly specialized employees, and together they represent the full range of occupational specializations that are found in the society. This reflects both task-specialization and the wide range of government activities.

2. The bureaucracy tends to accept policy directions that come

from other branches of government. This reflects both task-specialization and the legitimacy of elected officials.

3. The bureaucracy is considered to be professional, both by its own members and by other participants in the policy process. Professionalization is a sign of specialization among bureaucrats.

Among the well-developed nations, there are considerable differences in bureaucratic forms and procedures which reflect peculiar historical experiences. One writer has likened public administration in France and Germany and has contrasted it with that in Great Britain and the United States.[12] Officials in the upper levels of French and German administration have achieved a distinct status, separate from other occupational groups in their societies. They undergo a long period of training in elite institutions of higher education. This training helps to maintain both the historic upper-class backgrounds of public officials and the antidemocratic bias in their norms. The separateness of public administration is enforced even further by elaborate procedures for administrative self-government. The recruiting of new officials is controlled by the administrators themselves. Upper-echelon administrators are selected by promotion from within the career service. Each of these countries has a system of administrative courts that is distinct from the civil-court system. Administrative courts hear charges brought against administrative actions by private citizens and charges brought by administrators themselves concerning their rank, salary, or pension.

In Great Britain and the United States, the tradition is to avoid any clear separation between public administrators and other occupational groups. In contrast to the continental model of distinctive training for high-level administrative positions, the British and American services recruit from persons with a generalized training. In some details of their selection procedures, however, the British and Americans diverge from one another. The British are more inclined to select recruits from among the graduates of elite universities than from curricula specifically designed for professional administrators. British graduates in literature or the classics have traditionally been favored by essay examinations in general knowledge.

Americans have a Jacksonian tradition that any citizen is fit to perform the chores of a public employee. Related to this is the practice—still observed in numerous state and local governments and for some

---

12. Heady, *Public Administration*, pp. 44ff.

federal positions—of filling government jobs on the basis of political appointments without regard to the details of a candidate's training. Both Britain and the United States have moved toward selection procedures that emphasize specialized competence in the administrative tasks to be performed. Yet neither has approached the French and German models of elite training schools for professional administrators, and neither emphasizes the distinctiveness of a government career to the extent emphasized by the French and Germans. In Britain or the United States, there is no pervasive concern among public officials to distinguish their rank and status from those of the citizen, and there are no separate administrative courts. On the matter of "distance" from the population, however, there are some important differences between the United States and Britain. By tradition, British civil servants have more typically come from the upper social class, while in America some effort has been made to ensure that civil servants are "representative" of the population. The British generally appoint high-level administrators from within the ranks of the civil service. At both federal and state levels in the United States, however, many high-level administrative positions are filled with "outsiders." American executives in government and in the private sector believe that the "transient" business-government administrator can infuse the government bureaucracy with an innovative stimulus from outside.

ADMINISTRATIVE COHERENCE IN MORE-DEVELOPED COUNTRIES

A problem that appears widely in more-developed countries is a lack of coherence in relations between numerous service and regulatory agencies. The problem is often pronounced at local levels, where authorities design and implement their own programs, as well as implement programs designed and funded in part by national authorities. *Who controls what?* is a topic of some concern when many units share policy design, funding, and implementation. A typical result is control by bureaucratic elites who operate within their specialized domains. There is occasional dominance by politicians who take an interest in a particular matter, but there is also a lack of general integration of programs by elected officials.

Americans who wish to comprehend their government must take account of 78,000 local authorities, plus uncounted thousands of administrative entities within these authorities as well as government corporations and contractors that operate on the fringes of government. Some 22 percent of the resources allocated to domestic activities are transferred among authorities, which adds a dimension approaching international relations to activities with shared financing, program design, and implementation.[13] Elected officials generally feel left out of decisions that are dominated by bureaucrats who speak for their different governments at the points where they come together.[14] Much of the resources transfer in programs that are defined with a vagueness that defies control by elected officials or their immediate agents.[15] The thickest segments of the intergovernmental maze occur in metropolitan areas, where central city and suburban municipalities share territory with districts providing school and other services, as well as regional consultative bodies—like councils of governments—that try to systematize certain intergovernmental relations. In all of this, there is a fair amount of distrust and alienation directed against certain local officials.[16]

The fragmented nature of British government in urban areas appears no more coherent. There are counties, boroughs, urban and rural districts, parish councils and meetings, metropolitan counties and districts, plus a variety of administrative bodies having responsibility for particular services, sometimes with their territories scattered in patchwork fashion. Within a single jurisdiction, the civil servants of different departments may follow their own procedures for recruitment, promotion, salary, and control. There is no unifying national civil service as in several European countries and no strong local chief executive along the lines of an American mayor or city manager who might work to integrate the activities of different agencies or authorities.[17]

Sweden's localities also show a lack of integration. With elected councils as the political basis of control, actual administration is given over to executive boards. The boards deal with representatives of the national government and public corporations that also have a stake in a common venture. Protracted negotiation appears to be a dominant fea-

13. Ira Sharkansky, "Intergovernmental Relations," in Paul C. Nystrom and William H. Starbuck, eds., *Handbook of Organizational Design* (Amsterdam: Elsevier, 1978).

14. See Michael D. Reagan, *The New Federalism* (New York: Oxford, 1972); and Deil S. Wright, *Federal Grants-In-Aid: Perspectives and Alternatives* (Washington, D.C.: American Enterprise Institute, 1968).

15. Elmer B. Staats, "New Problems of Accountability for Federal Programs," in Bruce L. R. Smith, ed., *The New Political Economy: The Public Use of the Private Sector* (London: Macmillan & Co., 1975).

16. M. Kent Jennings and Harmon Zeigler, "The Salience of American State Politics," *American Political Science Review* 64 (June 1970): 523–35; and Joel D. Aberbach and Jack L. Walker, *Race in the City: Political Trust and Public Policy in the New Urban System* (Boston: Little, Brown, 1973).

17. Lord Redcliffe-Maud and Bruce Wood, *English Local Government Reformed* (London: Oxford, 1974).

ture of their relationships, with no single actor having clear authority to coordinate the bodies that must deal with each other.[18]

The incoherence of local authorities is no stranger to the socialist bloc. One Polish expert summarizes local decision-making in his country in words that fit many settings farther west:

Everyone who has examined local power in Poland knows the difficulties encountered in obtaining information, or sometimes even the impossibility of getting answers to questions concerning roles in the decision process. In my opinion, the context...in which the majority of local decisions are made creates the situation in which the process seems unclear, even to the actors.[19]

Israel's cities depict a standoff between equally aggressive national ministers or senior civil servants, on the one hand, and local officials, on the other. Israel's public sector has its own maze of state and local authorities: universities, hospitals, and other public institutions; corporations associated with the state, local authorities, or the labor federation that deal in the urban-relevant areas of housing, industry, mass transit, and banking; plus other corporations that are subsidiaries of these corporations or joint ventures between them. Each unit may have its own source of funds in Israel, as well as a well-cultivated group of friends in the international Jewish community.

A certain degree of local incoherence may be inevitable in a state that provides many different services to the population. Incoherence may be especially strong in a democratic context, but the Polish material suggests that democracy is not a requirement. Different aspects of social services develop at different times with aggressive politicians and civil servants more concerned about their own activities than with principles of administrative integration. Local authorities provide the setting for the implementation of many activities designed and funded in part or wholly by national ministries. There are incentives for local and national actors to continue the lack of organizational coherence. Occasionally, there may surface a strong demand for reorganization to simplify the structure for reasons of popular control, but such demands must compete with the incentives of senior bureaucrats and politicians to meet their funding needs through existing arrangements.

---

18. Hans Calmfors, Francine F. Rabinowitz, and Daniel J. Alesch, *Urban Government for Greater Stockholm* (New York: Praeger, 1968).

19. Jacek Tarkowski, "Decision-Making in the Polish Local Political System," in F. C. Bruhs, F. Cazzola, and J. Wiatr, eds., *Local Politics, Development and Participation: A Cross-National Study of Interrelationships* (Pittsburgh: University Center for International Studies, 1974).

The Costs of Incoherence

The incoherence that marks local organization has its costs in matters of equity, service delivery, and control. The issue of *equity* has several parts: The equality of taxes that is demanded from the residents in different urban areas; the equality of resources available to locally provided public services; and the equality of services actually provided to urban residents. At times, the inequalities come together in the most pernicious fashion, as some residents pay disproportionately high taxes, yet encounter services of disproportionately low quantity or quality.

These issues may be clearest in the United States, where there is the most overt independence of local authorities. With a minimum of control by superior levels of governments, local authorities that neighbor one another may impose widely different rates of taxation on their residents and provide different levels of service. The residents of low-income residential communities may pay high taxes in relation to the value of their property, but the sums collected may allow only minimum services.

In a more centralized system, like Israel, national standards may be applied in local taxation and services. Part of every local authority's programs depends on the mayor's skill in arranging special deals with government ministers, with foreign patrons, or with the public corporatious located in the community. Much that determines *who gets what* operates informally. Because it is extralegal (although perhaps not illegal), its practice and its understanding depends upon covert information and political insight. There are frequent allegations of special deals and no little admiration for the political figures thought capable of arranging them.

The multiplicity of actors involved in major urban policies has a negative effect on policy-making and implementation. In matters big and small, the incoherence of institutions leads to program delay and dilution. Such problems may reinforce equalities. Groups that are wealthier, better educated, or more involved in politics are more likely to understand the mechanics. They are also more able to bring the weight of their resources to bear on the machinery and receive a richer dose or a more rapid delivery of services in response to their demands. In short, the complexity of government seems likely to induce informal ways of cutting through the maze and to benefit those with the resources to play such games.

A by-product of organizational complexity is the figure who rises to power via a demonstrated ability to comprehend the system and to get things done. One variant is the political boss on the model of Chicago's late Mayor Richard Daley. Daley used his leverage over certain institutions (the Chicago municipality and the Cook County Democratic party) to extract special consideration from other institutions (the legislative and executive branches of Illinois and the national government). Another variant is the technocrat who develops a career outside of electoral politics, but on a similar basis is able to cut across a maze of institutions like banks, foundations, and numerous public bodies. Robert Moses was such a figure in New York. He was able to bring together important individuals in public and private organizations who had various powers over the development of New York's ports, bridges, and highways.

Who is responsible for what? is a continuing issue in complex urban settings. It disturbs actors who must arrange multiple approvals in order to initiate a new project, as well as actors who must discern the regulatory process in order to keep someone from trampling on established norms. The development of the *ombudsman* is one sign of the responsibility issue. The ombudsman's function is to help individuals receive just service or protection from the complex institutions of a welfare state.[20] Characteristically the ombudsman is limited to clarifying a citizen's case and bringing the pressure of its advice against an errant bureaucracy. However, the citizen may face confusion in the multiplicity of ombudsmen and like institutions. Israel offers a national ombudsman located in the office of the state comptroller, plus specialized ombudsmen in certain ministries and some municipalities as well as a variety of complaint bureaus and an infinite number of friends and neighbors who will tender advice on how to work the system. The citizen who wishes redress from the bureaucracy needs a certain amount of knowledge and determination to work through the agencies established to offer protection from other bureaucrats.

Another aspect of responsibility lies outside the ombudsman's concern for the individual complaint. The issue of political control over the principles of policy flounders in the incoherence of local institutions. Elected officials need a great deal of help to work their way through the national and local authorities that deal with various matters.[21] Organizational decisions run along programmatic and geographical lines, with many *ad hoc* divisions of responsibility. The simple lines of control from voters, to their representatives, to the bureaucracy must detour through

---

20. Larry B. Hill, "Institutionalization, the Ombudsman, and Bureaucracy," *American Political Science Review* 68 (September 1974): 1075–85.
21. See Douglas M. Fox, ed., *The New Urban Politics: Cities and the Federal Government* (Pacific Palisades, Calif.: Goodyear, 1972), especially pp. 90–92.

key figures like Richard Daley and Robert Moses, or through professional staff institutions. The description and justification of all this requires sophisticated conceptions of democratic control.

ADMINISTRATIVE SYSTEMS IN LESS-DEVELOPED COUNTRIES

As might be expected, more differences in administrative systems are observed among the many less-developed nations than among the relatively few societies that qualify as more-developed. In part, this is merely a result of differences in numbers. It is also a result of the diverse cultures in which these two groups are found. Almost all of the more-developed societies are in Western European countries or in countries that are tied closely to the nations of Western Europe. They shared historical experiences with one another or were settled by immigrants who brought the governmental institutions of Western Europe with them. In contrast, the developing countries reflect a global range of political cultures. Some are in Western Europe (e.g., Portugal and Spain); but others are in Latin America, Africa, and Asia. Most of these countries experienced a period of control by the colonial powers of Western Europe; but this period was too brief or too superficial to overcome the centuries of "traditional" (i.e., pre-European) cultural evolution.

Despite the peculiarities in structures and processes in individual countries, the following traits have been observed throughout less-developed countries:

1. Among political elites, there is a widely shared commitment to "development." This commitment often takes on ideological trappings. The package of changes that is sought may vary from one country to another, but common goals are increase in agricultural or industrial production; increase in personal living standards; improved programs for public health, education, and individual pensions; changes in the traditional roles of women or of the lower castes; and the change of one's loyalties from a tribe to the newly conceived "nation."

2. There is a high reliance on the public sector for leadership. Many developing countries have evolved structures that have a socialist or Marxist orientation. However, it is frequently a local variety of socialism, reflecting evolution of "Marxist" doctrines outside of the European working-class context. Agriculture, rather than industry, is the economic base; and the people who feel oppressed have ethnic ties rather than affinity for an industrial working class. The proposals for specific reforms

differ from one country to another. However, they typically seek rapid economic development and identify government bodies as the indigenous actors most capable of generating this development and guiding it along paths that are socially desirable. As will be seen later, not all sectors of government are equally well developed in these countries, and the incidence of trained manpower in even the most well-developed sectors is less than the country needs. The typical results include a heavy reliance on the bureaucracy and a high incidence of frustrated goals and civil unrest.

3. The society suffers from incipient or actual political instability. This instability may be a carry-over of patterns that were developed within the native movements against a colonial power. In several countries, there was not only conflict between the colonial and native forces, but also internal strife among the native leaders. In many cases, the "country" was an artificial creation of the colonial power who simply combined into one administrative unit the lands of distinct tribal or ethnic groups. During the campaign for independence, or perhaps soon after independence was achieved, conflicts between these traditional groups erupted into violent confrontations. Also contributing to violence are the frustrations associated with unmet goals for development. Many campaigns for independence are coupled with rash promises made by the new elites. However, their limited economic resources and scarce supply of skilled manpower make these promises unfulfillable. Popular disappointments provide support for still newer leaders who challenge those who steered the course from colonialism. When economic frustrations are coupled with feelings of discrimination among members of diverse tribal, linguistic, or ethnic groups, the stimuli for violence are present. One study of 84 developing countries found successful coups or serious attempts to overthrow the government in 40 of them.[22]

4. A gap exists between the modernizing and the traditional elites. This may actually be a series of differences—in social background, in orientation toward change, and in linkages to the mass of the population. The modernizing elites tend to be urban, Western-oriented, young, well educated, and committed to economic, social, and political change. The traditional elites tend to be rural, oriented to local customs and to the indigenous religion, and opposed to change as a threat to these values. The new elites may control the technological skills that are vital to the nation's development; but the older elites may retain the intense loyalties of people in the countryside and the urban slums. The contrasting styles

22. Fred R. von der Mehden, *Politics of the Developing Nations* (Englewood Cliffs, N.J.: Prentice-Hall, 1964), pp. 1–2.

and orientations of the two elites may generate severe conflict between them and their followers.

5. There is an imbalance in the development of various political features. Former colonies tend to replicate the legislative, executive, and administrative forms of the former mother country. When these forms are imposed upon the institutions of the colonial and precolonial periods, however, they produce a wide gulf between formal procedures and actual practices. Legislative and executive branches often lack the ability to control the civil or military bureaucracies. The new bureaucracies usually show the most rapid development, often because the departing colonial power had already begun to staff its bureaucracy with natives. The administrative organization generally receives the most well-educated members of the new elite and thereby becomes the one institution with the expertise necessary to direct a program of social and economic development. The military sector may be even more well developed (at least in its office corps) than the civilian administration. The combination of a weak legislature and an inefficacious chief executive, plus a professional military, often results in government takeovers that are either engineered behind the scenes by the military or are led openly by military personnel. Less-developed nations throughout the world may share no one trait as much as they share the experience of having a uniformed and bemedalled chief executive who either took over the government in an overt *putsch* or used an election format (perhaps without tolerating real opposition) to obtain office.

Several traits of administrative forms and procedures in less-developed countries reflect the attributes of their environment. A number of them are clearly indicated in the previous discussion: lack of sufficient skills in the bureaucracy that are required by the regime's program of development; conflict between the decision processes expected by Westerners and the traditional relationships that are expected by some members of the indigenous elite and by many citizens; and the tendency of former colonial territories to carry over the formal administrative structures that were acquired from the departed Europeans. Two other features of less-developed public bureaucracies are typically described as "problems": pervasive corruption and a marked discrepancy between the forms and realities of administrative procedures.

The corruption that exists in the bureaucracies of less-developed countries affects both small and large decisions and involves proportionately minor and major resources. It includes the small bribe that officials expect in exchange for "expediting" a decision on behalf of an individual; the willingness of officials to evade formal personnel procedures to hire their own relatives or fellow tribesmen; and the massive bribes from foreign investors that assure a favorable decision about mining rights, a utility monopoly, or a commercial concession. In some cases, this corruption is so taken for granted that it is defended as "part of the system"—without which officials could not justify their decisions. Nepotism or tribal favoritism is a carry-over from traditional values and may disappear only when the norms that support them are no longer viable. The truly massive corruption may, in contrast, be a product of colonial times when outside investors bought concessions from traditional elites.

A discrepancy between form and reality is frequently the product of a combination of insufficient administrative resources and excessive aspirations. Governments establish procedures to resemble those observed in the capital city of the former colonial power or those prescribed by visiting American advisors. This trait has been labeled "formalism."[23] It has obvious implications for the citizens and elites of less-developed countries; it means that announced procedures may provide no reliable guidelines about the service to be rendered. Formalism rewards those who learn the informal procedures of administration and frustrates those who rest personal aspirations on the public promises of the government. Formalism also has important implications for students of comparative administration. It means that they cannot accept as similar (or "comparable") institutions those which carry similar labels in different countries. An interior ministry may not only be—as in more-developed countries—the superstructure of the police service, but it may also represent the single most powerful unit in the bureaucracy (perhaps excepting the army) and may even stand as the selector of the chief executive. The leading political party may not simply be the organization that currently has control of major government offices, but it may also be the only real vehicle that integrates the programs of leading figures in the army, the civilian bureaucracy, and other branches of the government. Elaborate programs for education, health benefits, or old-age pensions may be empty shells without operating administrators or budgets sufficient to meet the announced goals. The forms of federalism or local autonomy may belie the realities of strict central control via an authoritarian political party, a strong chief executive, and a centralized bureaucracy.

---

23. Fred W. Riggs, *Administration in Developing Countries: The Theory of Prismatic Society* (Boston: Houghton Mifflin, 1964), p. 12.

Since it can be misleading to compare administrative—and other governmental—institutions among less-developed countries merely on the basis of their labels, it is necessary to make comparisons according to the "functions" that various organs perform in the political system. Gabriel Almond has suggested a series of functions that might serve as the framework of comparative analysis. His principal functions are political socialization and recruitment; interest articulation; interest aggregation; political communication; rule-making; rule application; and rule adjudication.[24] To some, this list depends too much on the American pattern of competitive political parties, election campaigns, and interest groups, plus legislative, executive, and judicial branches; to others, it is so general as to be of little help in clarifying issues for comparison among the less-developed countries. Fred W. Riggs suggests more detailed kinds of functions that might be examined comparatively within less-developed nations: the creation of agricultural markets; price-setting; and the establishing of quality standards for agricultural produce. According to Riggs, comparative-administrative specialists should define features that coexist with various functional behaviors with the intent of understanding why various administrative units come to perform the kinds—and qualities—of functions that they do.[25]

The problem of formalism may also limit the extent to which the systems framework developed in this book lends itself to cross-national comparisons. Recall from Chapter 1 that the boundaries of our conversion process include administrative units found within the executive branch of national, state, and local governments in the United States. In order to compare the American conversion processes with those found elsewhere, it would be necessary to identify comparable units of public administration. This should be possible in most of the more-developed countries where there is a correspondence between the form and procedures within government structures. Even in the case of parliamentary governments, where the executive and legislative branches are merged to some extent, it should be possible to separate the "line" units of the administration and compare them and their environments with counterparts in the United States. In the case of many less-developed countries, however, the functions of "administration" as we know it here may not actually be performed in those units that are labeled as the line departments of government.

It would be misleading to end this discussion without asserting

---

24. Gabriel Almond and G. Bingham Powell, *Comparative Politics: A Developmental Approach* (Boston: Little, Brown, 1966), chapter 2.
25. Riggs, *Administration in Developing Countries*, pp. 31ff.

that a wide variety of administrative forms and procedures—both formal and informal—can be found among less-developed countries. As in the case of the more-developed countries, there is not a perfect correspondence between development and administrative forms and processes. Many factors peculiar to each country's history can shape its bureaucracy. Ferrel Heady suggests several categories of administrative types within the less-developed countries. The labels that he uses for some of these categories suggest the differences to be found within them: Traditional-Autocratic; Bureaucratic Elite; Polyarchal Competitive; and Dominant-Party Mobilization.[26]

Traditional-Autocratic

This type is traditional in its style of rule, with dominant political elites drawn from families with monarchic or aristocratic status. The political elite rely on military and civil bureaucracy to provide those changes in policy which are considered desirable and to inhibit those demands which are considered undesirable. With the exception of those countries blessed with huge oil deposits, little economic progress and little commitment toward such development are expressed by the political elite. Countries in this category include Saudi Arabia, Morocco, Iran, and Paraguay.

Bureaucratic Elite

In this type of system, traditional elites have been displaced from effective power, although they may retain some presence (perhaps as a figurehead monarch). Popular political participation is severely limited. Modernizing goals are proclaimed by leadership groups, but they are not embraced by the general public. Political power is largely in the hands of the civil and military bureaucracy. Military officials are usually more prominent and are in positions of highest power, often as a result of having led a coup against the prior regime. However, the military depends on civil bureaucracy to carry out nonmilitary developmental projects. Countries in this category include Brazil, Guatemala, Indonesia, Iraq, Nicaragua, Pakistan, Paraguay, Peru, South Korea, Sudan, Syria, and Thailand.

Polyarchal Competitive

This form of system has political structures that resemble the models of Western Europe and the United States with respect to popular

---

26. Heady, *Public Administration,* chapter 6.

participation, free elections, interest-oriented parties, and policy-making authority granted to representative government institutions. However, there are occasional interruptions by military interventions or other lapses in representative government. Typically, these interruptions are claimed to be only temporary. The *poly*archal label denotes the existence of several political elites whose base of power may be spread among urban merchants, landlords, military officers, labor leaders, and professionals. There is greater social mobility than in the more traditional societies. Due to competing parties' search for "consensus," government programs emphasize "pragmatic" policies that are easy to understand and offer short-range benefits in such fields as education, welfare, and health. Countries included in this category are the Philippines, Malaysia, Jamaica, Costa Rica, Greece, and Turkey.

Dominant-Party Mobilization

Within this type, there is little permissiveness in politics. The dominant party may be the only legal party, and it may assure its position with coercive techniques. There is usually a doctrinaire ideology and mass demonstrations of loyalty to the government. The elite group tends to be young, urban, well educated, and secular. Often a charismatic leader dominates the entire movement in which the programs stress nationalism and development. A well-trained civil. service is essential for the developmental goals of the regime; but there is frequent tension between the technical and professional people in the bureaucracy and the politicians who insist on the primacy of nationalism and loyalty to the current regime. Countries in this category include Algeria, Bolivia, Egypt, Guinea, Mali, Kenya, Tanzania, and Tunisia.

It remains to be tested how closely the administrative structures, procedures, and outputs of the countries in each of these categories resemble other political, social, or economic features. Admittedly, the designations are loosely conceived. The categories may be more useful as illustrations of variety among less-developed administrative systems than as tools for rigorous comparative analysis.

ADMINISTRATIVE SYSTEMS IN LESS-DEVELOPED (U.S.) STATES AND LESS-DEVELOPED COUNTRIES

Administrative systems in certain American states and the developing countries have several parallels that challenge any clear divisions between comparative analysis within the United States and cross-national comparisons, or between more- and less-developed countries.[27]

On some measures of economic development, the United States is at or near the top of the world scale. Gross domestic product per capita (GDP/c) is the single measure of economic development most widely used in international comparisons; it sums the market value of the total goods and services in any economy. For 1970, the GDP/c of the United States was $4,734; the average for a group of 13 black African countries was $172; for 16 lesser-developed Asian countries, $253; and for 19 Latin American countries, $473. Despite these marked differences and all they mean in terms of economic security and living standards, we find contrasts between the most- and least-affluent regions of the United States. The differences between the most comfortable sections of New York and California and the depressed regions of Mississippi, West Virginia, and New York City emphasize American problems of economic development. Rural backwaters, urban slums, and depressed social classes resemble counterparts in the Third World. We can learn about American administrative systems by looking at them from a developmental perspective. Several policy-relevant parallels appear to link the less-developed states of the United States with less-developed countries of Africa, Asia, and Latin America. The following traits tend to occur in the southern states, as well as in such other low-income states as Vermont, New Mexico, North Dakota, and Utah.

Environmental Parallels

Developing states and countries receive significant inputs of financial grants, soft loans, and technical assistance from other governments and from outside private sources. The chief governments that supply aid to the developing countries are the former colonial powers, with other assistance coming from the United States, the Soviet Union, Canada, Sweden, and West Germany. In the United States, the federal government provides more in per capita aid to the developing states than to wealthier states.

Citizens in both the developing states and countries feel they pay a price in the control of their economic resources by outsiders. Just as Chileans and Cubans have rallied against Yankee control of copper and sugar, so West Virginians, Kentuckians, and Georgians have declaimed Yankee control over their coalfields or railroads. A difference, of course,

---

27. This section relies on Ira Sharkansky, *The United States: A Study of a Developing Country* (New York: McKay, 1975).

lies in the options open to governments in the lesser-developed economies. A developing country may try to expropriate the resources of foreigners at the risk of substantial changes in its international relations. In the developing states of the United States, the governments have some leverage through the weight of their own representatives in the national legislature.

In both least-developed countries and states, there is a greater role for cultural traditions in the political process. Political campaigns are less concerned with the hard details of policy alternatives than with the efforts of candidates to identify themselves with folk symbols. In Kenya, for example, President Jomo Kenyatta features traditional dancing at many of his public appearances and often joins the dancers of different tribes to sway and kick through several routines. Likewise, an aspiring politician in the American South will mix with the folks and provide traditional food and music to attract them to his rallies. Of course, the importance of traditional symbols is not in the food or festivities of political rallies, but in their use in cementing alliances and shaping the predisposition of policy-makers. Developing countries and states provide examples where traditional loyalties slow the modernization that is feasible. In places where traditional politics features racial symbols in the United States (or tribalism in the Third World), they are likely to distribute outputs unequally between the citizens in different groups.

Two policy-relevant political traits that appear in the less-developed states and countries are "centralization" and "concentration." The centralization of government refers to the dominant role taken by the central, as opposed to the local, jurisdictions. In the lesser-developed American states, the "central government" is the state government. Centralization shows in the state government's collection of revenue, its distribution of financial aid to local units, its establishment of program standards to be followed by local governments, and its direct provision of services throughout the jurisdiction by means of central government officers. For the less-developed American states, centralization appears most clearly in the ratios of state to local activities in revenue collection and spending.

"Concentration" pertains to the aggregation of political options in relatively few hands; it determines the political opportunities available to the mass of citizens. A hallmark of concentration is limited competition between political parties. The dominance of single parties lessens the opportunities for citizens to make decisions on the basis of alternatives to present officeholders or public politics. In some developing countries, the major party has a monopoly that is written into the national laws and/or endorsed by the official police or the party thugs.

Concentration differs from "centralization," which pertains to the aggregation of powers to officials in the capital city. Yet "concentration" and
"centralization" complement one another; both permit a narrow base
of effective participation, with many citizens and officials left out of
real decision-making.

Strong executive leadership frequently accompanies the traits of
centralization and concentration. Huey Long is the archetype of a strong
executive in the context of a lesser-developed American state, with
George Wallace, Gene Talmadge, and Orval Faubus providing other examples. Virtually all of the developing countries offer their own parallels,
with some of the most striking cases being those nationalist leaders who
led their countries out of the colonial experience and became their first
presidents or heads of government: Kwame Nkrumah in Ghana, Jomo
Kenyatta in Kenya, Julius Nyere in Tanzania, Hastings Banda in Malawi,
and Sukarno in Indonesia. In most of the least-developed countries, the
bureaucracy—and often the military sector of the bureaucracy—joins the
chief executive in commanding the greatest leverage over public policy.
The bureaucracy attracts members of the best families and the best
graduates of the national universities; it commands a virtual monopoly
over technical expertise; and its police and military segments may use
their powers to control other branches of government.

Parallels in Public Policy

*Developing states and countries resemble one another in certain
efforts to induce economic growth.* Both pursue industrialization with
similar kinds of tax reductions for new industries, and both have problems with the marginal industries that are attracted by such schemes;
i.e., firms that teeter on the brink of bankruptcy, require extensive nurs-
ing by the government offices charged with economic development, offer
little in the way of transferable skills to their employees, or fail to pay
back the jurisdiction's investment in the form of substantial taxes or
resources added to the economy.

Regressive tax and spending policies also appear in both developing states and countries. A regressive tax or expenditure is one that takes
disproportionately from the lower-income population or provides its
benefits disproportionately to upper-income classes. In the developing
countries, the typical regressive taxes are the excise taxes on fuel, cloth,
processed food, beer, or manufactured goods, and the customs duty on
goods that permeate the society (e.g., imported radios and printed cloth,
or imported components that are assembled by local industries). In the
United States, the most prominent regressive taxes are those on retail

sales and real property. State individual and corporate income taxes, in contrast, are progressive. During 1971, the ten states with the least-developed economies drew only 10.3 percent of their revenues from income taxes, while the ten states with the most-developed economies took 20.6 percent of their revenues from such taxes.

The tendency to avoid progressive taxes has a further parallel in the tendency to give little support to those programs that have a progressive impact on the distribution of resources. Elementary and secondary education, welfare, and public health programs go disproportionately to citizens in the lower-income ranges; in the United States, these programs tend to receive smaller per capita allocations in the low-income states. Highway and natural resource programs, in contrast, represent investments in economic infrastructure and promise "growth"; they tend to receive greater per capita allocations in the states with lesser-developed industrial sectors. Similar allocations appear in the development plans of many lower-income countries and serve to complement their avoidance of progressive taxes. On the expenditure side, these plans feature transportation, electric power, and communications facilities plus investments in industry and commercial-scale agriculture.

Relevance of Parallels Between Less-Developed States and Countries

Elements of governmental centralization, political concentration, traditionalism in politics, and such policies as industrial promotion, plus tax and spending regressivity fit together in a syndrome that both reflects conditions of relative deprivation and may affect the processes of further economic development. Traditional politics lessens the opportunity for new perspectives to permeate policy-making. Centralization and concentration both serve to limit the claimants on public resources. With centralization, there is a minimum opportunity for regional and local groups to bolster their demands on public resources with the aid of any formal instruments built into the policy-making process. Political concentration lessens the power of citizens in regional or class groupings who would claim resources for their own welfare purposes. Centralization and concentration also permit the small number of trained and experienced administrators to keep the management of scarce resources in their own hands.

There is a view that prospects for economic development benefit from traditionalism, centralization, concentration, and regressive policies. This view is problematical and relies on one important assumption: that elites who benefit will use their economic and political leverage for public benefit rather than private gains. Traditional symbols may distract unsophisticated voters from their leaders' policies. Programs of industrialization, transportation, communications, improved agricultural techniques, as well as public health and education, and general improvements in the standard of living can result from a publicly minded elite investing rationally to stimulate economic development. On the other hand, some elites use their leverage to reinforce their own position, keep taxes low for their own social class, control the government for personal profit, and either bank the proceeds overseas or consume them in opulence at home. The developing states and countries provide examples both of asceticism and excess on the part of their elites.

LESSONS OF COMPARISON: POLICIES OF FINANCIAL AID AND TECHNICAL ASSISTANCE

The economic and political traits of rich and poor areas are important not only for their impact on administration or domestic policies for economic growth. These environmental traits also leave their mark on the financial aid and technical assistance that flow from richer to poorer areas. Although international aid has declined in recent years, it is still considerable. U.S. aid to other nations was about $5 billion in 1977. Domestically, funds flow from wealthy to poorer states through the mechanisms of the national government's taxes and aids. In 1975, the ten poorest states received some $5.3 billion from Washington, amounting to $235 per capita. Indeed, some American observers feel that the poorer states of the South have received more than their share of federal benefits and are growing economically at the expense of the older industrial region of the Northeast.

International Aid to Poor Countries

The diversity of poor regions is one of the factors that leaves its mark on the aid policies of outsiders. *What aid to offer?* is an issue that varies with the economic situation of the potential recipient as well as with the demands coming from the political elites of the recipient. These economic and political realities combine with cultural traditions and traits of geography, climate, soil, and water to affect the workability of various proposals. The recipient's traits complicate an outsider's efforts to bring about changes in economic, social, or administrative patterns. Presumably the problems of program design would be easier for the aid given within a country than for international aid between countries that have sharp differences in cultures and politics. Yet, one observer of Washington's aids to American states and localities has written—hopefully with tongue in cheek—that 40 percent of the time and funds are spent in designing aid projects and another 40 percent on evaluation.[28]

Not all of the problems associated with project choice and design reflect the complexities of recipients. Political inclinations and commitments change in the donor governments. Such changes affect not only the size of aid budgets, but also the targets likely to have appeal. Among the targets that have been stylish at various times include economic growth with primary concern for infrastructure items like roads, ports, power, irrigation, and key industries; a more balanced distribution of economic opportunities via programs of education or job opportunities in rural areas; a concern for political development toward greater participation and assurances of democratic liberties; or a more narrow concern with administrative reforms that may enhance a recipient's capacity to extract and manage the resources of its own economy.[29] The numerous motives for financial and technical assistance include the donor government's calculations of what will meet the current political demands coming out of its own society, as well as what efforts may win some support in international politics, plus some undefined measure of altruism. U.S. aid policies have changed considerably from the early 1960s, when the Alliance for Progress was pursuing political and economic reforms throughout Latin America. The Nixon-Ford administrations were more inclined to military and economic aid for the purposes of strengthening selected allies or extracting concessions in international negotiations. The early statements of the Carter administration in behalf of human rights suggest a shift back toward reformist goals.

Current definitions of "development administration" encompass diverse goals, with the participants in major projects having to face the conflicts that rage among the proponents of each. According to Professor Milton J. Esman, development administration "refers to those activities of government that foster economic growth, strengthen human and organizational capabilities, and promote equality in the distribution of opportunities, income, and power."[30]

The problems of recipient governments often frustrate the goals

---

28. David T. Stanley, "How Safe the Streets, How Good the Grant?" *Public Administration Review* 34 (July/August 1974): 380–89.

29. See Kenneth J. Rothwell, ed., *Administrative Issues in Developing Economies* (Lexington, Mass.: Heath, 1972).

30. Milton J. Esman, "Administrative Doctrine and Developmental Needs," in E. Philip Morgan, ed., *The Administration of Change in Africa* (New York: Dunellen, 1974), p. 3.

of aid projects. The entrenched conservatism of traditional peasants hinders the reform of agriculture, while entrenched bureaucrats thwart campaigns against corruption. Shortages of trained personnel and the unwillingness of university graduates to live outside the capital city hinder projects that require effective administration in regional centers. A great number of bureaucratic procedures—typically inherited from colonial rulers concerned with controlling the work of suspect natives— hamper development programs that require personnel to move quickly in response to local problems or opportunities.[31] The elites of recipient governments may look to technical advisors only for the backing of projects already chosen. The elites may demand obeisance to local pride more than the candid use of the advisor's expertise.[32] The details of these problems vary from one country to another, and within a country, from region to region or project to project. Behind many of the problems lie the poverty of resources, personnel, and administrative capabilities that are both the targets and the frustrations of programs for development.

The United States Internal Revenue Service has cooperated with the United States Agency for International Development in sending high-ranking experts in tax administration to poor countries on missions of technical assistance. Their "end of project" reports offer numerous examples of tax reforms that succeed in increasing government revenues. However, they also contain insights—sometimes veiled to protect the sensitivities of the recipient countries—into the problems faced by tax advisors: officials of the recipient government who seem to accept an advisor's recommendation, but who then do not deliver the resources or reforms which they seem to have promised; personnel resources that are too thin to make more than a symbolic effort to staff field offices outside of the capital city; efforts at tax enforcement which run afoul of outright corruption or political influence which protect errant tax-payers from an intensive audit or from prosecution; lack of elementary recordkeeping which results in many eligible citizens being missing from the tax roles, or which hinder the revenue department from keeping track of tax returns and correspondence; and political instability which hampers the implementation over time of any but the simplest of administrative reforms.[33]

31. See Gunnar Myrdal, *An Approach to the Asian Drama* (New York: Vintage, 1970); and Richard P. Taub, *Bureaucrats Under Stress: Administrators and Administration in an Indian State* (Berkeley: University of California Press, 1969).

32. G. E. Caiden, "International Consultants and Development Administration," *International Review of Administrative Sciences* 42 (1976): 1–7.

33. An important study of tax administration in poor countries is Alex Radian, "Resource Mobilization in Poor Countries: Implementing Tax Policies" (Ph.D. diss., University of California, Berkeley, 1977).

Domestic Aid to Poor States

The United States has its own share of difficulties in the design and implementation of domestic strategies for development. The regional development programs of the 1960s showed an undisciplined dissemination of resources over a wide variety of regions and for a diverse set of goals.[34] The early intention of the Kennedy administration was the development of the Appalachian region, modeled after Tennessee Valley Authority of Roosevelt days. Under the pressure of representatives, senators, and governors from states on the periphery of the original target area, the concept of Appalachia moved outward from the coal-mining counties of West Virginia and eastern Kentucky to include parts of 13 states from New York to Mississippi. Later the leaders of other poor regions demanded a share of the action. Eventually, there were regional development schemes in most sections of the country:

- The Ozarks Regional Commission included parts of Arkansas, Oklahoma, Kansas, and Missouri;
- The Four Corners Regional Commission included parts of Arizona, New Mexico, Colorado, and Utah;
- The Coastal Plains Regional Commission included parts of Georgia, North Carolina, and South Carolina (other sections of these states were attached to the Appalachian Region);
- The Upper Great Lakes Regional Commission included parts of Michigan, Wisconsin, and Minnesota;
- The New England Regional Commission included all of Connecticut, Maine, Massachusetts, New Hampshire, Rhode Island, and Vermont.

A further diffusion of resources for regional development occurred in the choices of programmatic goals. There were debates over the provision of aid to places or directly to individuals; over the focus on the most needy areas, on the areas most likely to develop, or the dispersal of aid to many sites; and over the kinds of programs to be offered as humanitarian aids or as inducements for economic growth. Just as the political process took the regional idea and applied it to many parts of the country at the same time, so there were tendencies to

---

34. See John H. Cumberland, *Regional Development Experiences and Prospects in the United States of America* (Paris: Mouton, 1971); and Monroe Newman, *The Political Economy of Appalachia: A Cast Study in Regional Integration* (Lexington, Mass.: Heath, 1972).

answer these issues in a multiplicity of ways and to divide resources among numerous kinds of projects. After the programs had been in operation for some time and faced the need for a legislative extension, the Nixon administration argued that the diffusion of goals and resources had blurred the disciplined pursuit of economic development. It sought to end the funding of regional commissions and to transfer their resources to such departments as transportation, commerce, and health, education and welfare. Yet the coalition of so many legislators (three-fifths of United States senators had a stake) found the president's arguments unpersuasive.

SUMMARY

In most of this book, a concentration on public administration within the United States will facilitate an in-depth coverage of material. This choice should neither disparage the exciting and rapidly growing field of comparative administration nor should it suggest that the American model is any more "natural" or worthy of emulation than are those in other countries. The systems approach to the subject encourages comparisons. Indeed, comparison of different administrative situations is necessary in order to find patterns in the occurrence of different kinds of agencies, controls, and policies or to test hypotheses about the influence of environmental traits—like a well-developed economy—on administration.

In other chapters, we employ the results of comparative research carried out within the United States. This permits us to identify some differences in structures and procedures among agencies of the federal, state, and local governments. In some cases, we can identify certain influences from the social, economic, or political environments that shape the administrative structures or procedures, or certain influences perhaps can be identified that administrative structures or procedures exert on other features of politics or the economy.

Characteristics of economic development seem important for aspects of administrative systems, both within the United States and around the world. There are complex disputes—that this chapter has not attempted to settle—about the nature of "development" and about the place of individual countries on several measures of development. This chapter has attempted to illustrate the range of variations in public administration throughout the world and to suggest the importance of development and of programs of assistance for development among the central issues of policy-making and administration.

Part One

THE CONVERSION PROCESS OF THE ADMINISTRATIVE SYSTEM

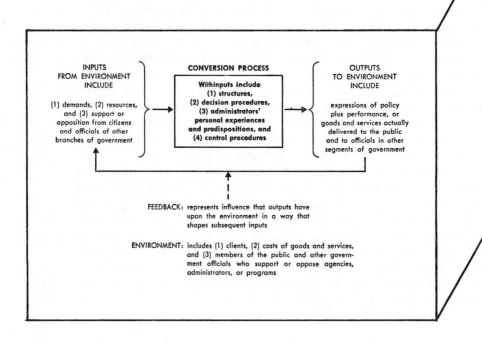

INPUTS
FROM ENVIRONMENT
INCLUDE

(1) demands, (2) resources, and (3) support or opposition from citizens and officials of other branches of government

CONVERSION PROCESS

**Withinputs include
(1) structures,
(2) decision procedures,
(3) administrators'
personal experiences
and predispositions, and
(4) control procedures**

OUTPUTS
TO ENVIRONMENT
INCLUDE

expressions of policy plus performance, or goods and services actually delivered to the public and to officials in other segments of government

FEEDBACK: represents influence that outputs have upon the environment in a way that shapes subsequent inputs

ENVIRONMENT: includes (1) clients, (2) costs of goods and services, and (3) members of the public and other government officials who support or oppose agencies, administrators, or programs

the reader that we are dealing with actions *within* the conversion process of the administrative system and not with the interface where those decisions encounter the environment.

Administrators are not free to make whatever decisions suit their fancy. To understand their decisions is not simply to understand the personal predilections that lead an agency official to make a certain choice. Administrators are subject to numerous demands and severe constraints. These include:

1. The regard for public administrators in the political culture and the specific attitudes that citizens hold about public programs and government employees;
2. Demands, resources, and political support from individual citizens, political parties, and interest groups;
3. Demands, resources, and political support from the legislative, executive, and judicial branches of government;
4. Demands, resources, and political support from individuals and institutions in other governments, through "vertical" or "horizontal" intergovernmental relations;
5. The social backgrounds, skills, and values of the administrators themselves; and
6. The structures, procedures, and precedents of administrative units.

The sheer number and variety of inputs and withinputs complicate the task of agency decision-makers. No simple procedure for making decisions can accommodate the factors that might be taken into consideration. In an effort to detail this complexity, we first describe a purely "rational" model of decision-making that urges administrators to "take everything into consideration." Then we identify several features that frustrate this kind of rationalism. Finally, we report some decision procedures that have evolved in various administrative units. These do not meet the sandards of the purely rational model. Indeed, they are attractive to administrators partly because they permit administrators to ignore certain factors and thus to simplify choices.

A MODEL OF RATIONAL DECISION-MAKING AND ITS SHORTCOMINGS

Rationality is a value that has wide respect in our culture. As might be expected, public administrators like to be as rational as the rest of us.

Certainly they are not going to admit that they make decisions "irrationally" or without taking into consideration all important issues. However, the demands of a completely rational decision are severe. It is costly to be perfectly rational, and few administrators seem to have sufficient resources to meet the price. It is unfair, however, to accuse administrators of making irrational decisions. This term implies that they make their choices in an undisciplined fashion, without paying heed to many of the considerations that most observers would consider to be important. As we unfold our description of administrative decision-making, we see that it is neither completely rational nor irrational. Complete rationality is an unattainable goal for administrative decision-makers in all but the most simple kinds of problems.[1] Yet most of their decisions appear to be disciplined and to be made after an assessment of several important issues.

We cannot extend this discussion further without a clear understanding of a rational model for decision-making. As noted above, this is a demanding model, against which the decisions of most administrative units score less than pure. According to one common formulation, a rational decision-maker would:

1. Identify his problem;
2. Clarify his goals, and then rank them as to their importance;
3. List all possible means or policies—for achieving each of his goals;
4. Assess all the costs and the benefits that would seem to accrue from each of the alternative policies; and
5. Select the package of goals and associated policies that would bring the greatest relative benefits and the least relative disadvantages.[2]

Decision-makers who follow these procedures should inform themselves about all possible opportunities and all possible consequences of each opportunity. This is an enormous assignment. It assumes that an administrative agency has vast resources that can be used to gather intelligence about the environment and about the capabilities of the agency itself. It also assumes that personnel are sufficiently uncommitted to—or against—any one set of goals or policies and, thus, can make their decisions on the basis of information that is systematically collected. This rational decision-making model seems inappropriate for most public agencies which are under pressure to produce policies quickly and

---

1. Herbert Simon, *Administrative Behavior* (New York: Macmillan, 1961), p. 70.
2. Charles E. Lindblom, *The Policy-Making Process* (Englewood Cliffs, N.J.: Prentice-Hall, 1968), p. 13.

which operate in environments that impose commitments upon them. Political demands require that certain goals and policies be favored in agency deliberations and that other goals and policies be avoided. The five major features of public administrative systems that block the fulfillment of rational decision-making by personnel in administrative units include:

1. The multitude of problems, goals, and policy commitments that are imposed on—or kept from—decision-makers by actors in the environment of an administrative unit;
2. Barriers to collecting adequate information about the variety of "acceptable" goals and policies;
3. The personal needs, commitments, inhibitions, and inadequacies of decision-makers which interfere in their assessment of goals and policies that are acceptable from their agency's point of view;
4. Structural difficulties within administrative units and involving their relations with legislative and executive branches of government; and
5. The deviant behavior of individual administrators.

These five items are not entirely separable. Each includes some features that are also apparent in others. However, each has been the subject of separate inquiries and has been shown to impose its own set of limitations on decision-makers who might—in an ideal world—desire to make rational choices. Aspects of Item 1 and Item 4 are inputs that affect decision-making in administrative units. The remainder are withinputs that operate largely within the borders of an administrative unit.

The Multitude of Problems, Goals, and Policy Commitments

This barrier to rational decision-making is actually a combination of two factors: the variety of problems and goals that can probably be selected as the target of administrative activity; and the commitments in the environment of an administrative agency that preclude a thorough assessment of each possible goal. Frequently, the full range of possibilities open to an agency is so great that even the task of defining one's problem (Step 1 in the sequence of rational decision-making) is obscured by the variety. A problem will, presumably, be signaled by difficulties perceived in the agency's environment. However, the difficulties perceived may not translate themselves directly into defined problems. One stumbling block may occur when officials try to distill a conception of "problems" from the "symptoms" they see. What are the problems that lie beneath unemployment or survey results showing increased levels of alienation? Are each of these symptoms to be treated by the selection of specific goals and policies that will solve the problems? Are they indeed symptoms of underlying difficulties that are themselves the problems to be treated? If there are underlying problems, what are they? Is there a common problem that generates each of these symptoms? If there is a common problem, the way in which it is defined has important implications for which agencies will deal with the problem and how they will define goals and policies with respect to the problem. There can be problems in the banking system; in international trade; in the prices of certain raw materials; in elementary, secondary, and higher education that is not adequately designed to meet the needs of certain clients; or a loss in the basic sense of community that once may have united the country. Each of these diagnoses has been made by observers of the contemporary scene. Without agreement as to the problem(s) that lies beneath perceived difficulties, it is not feasible to move through the goal- and policy-selection steps of a rational decision-making sequence. Problem definition is, at best, a difficult and ambiguous process. Problems not already defined must be defined through a process of observing, assessing, and abstracting from reality. This is done while under the influence of an agency's prior experiences and commitments. Thus, the process is somewhat less than "rational."

A problem may exist for a long time in a dormant state, without becoming an issue of public policy. Environmental pollution is objectively worse in some locales where it has failed to be an issue, while it has become more important to policy-makers elsewhere. Professor Cynthia H. Enloe describes some of the elements that are needed to make the environment—or other "facts of life"—into problems that policy-makers must face. These include officeholders who are both sensitive to the issue and who possess the legal authority and the political clout to make their views count; mass media, business groups, labor unions or other extragovernmental actors capable of developing interest in the topic; and economic and social settings that make it feasible to pursue this problem at a certain time. Environmental pollution is not likely to appear as a problem, for example, where the prevailing sentiment sees factory smoke as a welcome sign of economic progress.[3]

---

3. Cynthia H. Enloe, *The Politics of Pollution in a Comparative Perspective: Ecology and Power in Four Nations* (New York: McKay, 1975), especially chapters 1 and 2.

Once a problem is recognized and defined as such, there are additional difficulties involved in the definition of goals and policies. These do not flow naturally from one's sense of the problem. The definition of goals involves judgments that are as ambiguous as the definition of problems. Should a problem that is perceived as inadequate higher education, for example, be met with packages of goals and policies that er.vision changes in teaching techniques, the development of new curricula (e.g., courses about environmental quality), more financial aid for students, greater student-freedom from university controls, the "return" of universities to a preoccupation with liberal education, or the further refinement of specialization among institutions of higher education? The definition of goals involves a specification of what an agency will do in order to alleviate a problem. When a goal is defined, the agency personnel and actors in its environment (e.g., legislators, the chief executive, and interest groups) will receive signals about the future course of agency activity. With the variety of persons surrounding an agency who have something at stake in its activities, the choice of goals is not likely to produce a uniform reception. Disagreements will arise between members of the agency and those outsiders who feel affected by the agency. Even before the agency undertakes a course of action (i.e., before it chooses its policy), it may be set upon by actors who object to its goals.[4]

The persons chosen by a chief executive to be personal advisors or the heads of administrative departments can heighten or ameliorate the difficulties of making rational decisions. Critics of the Nixon administration focused on members of the White House staff who elevated loyalty to their chief above the wide-ranging consideration of policy alternatives.[5] Earlier, President Kennedy floundered in the Bay of Pigs incident partly because he relied on those advisors who were committed to the project and screened out warning signals from other segments of the bureaucracy. Among President Johnson's many problems with Vietnam were the personnel whose commitments to established programs led them to mislead one another—and the public—in their reports from the field.[6]

---

4. Richard M. Cyert and James G. March, *A Behavioral Theory of the Firm* (Englewood Cliffs, N.J.: Prentice-Hall, 1963), chapter 3.

5. For a relatively friendly critic, see William Safire, *Before the Fall: An Inside View of the Pre-Watergate White House* (New York: Belmont Tower, 1975).

6. See Alan C. Elms, *Personality in Politics* (New York: Harcourt Brace Jovanovich, 1976), especially chapter 5; and David Wise, *The Politics of Lying: Government Deception, Secrecy, and Power* (New York: Vintage, 1973).

Limited Information

The variety of perceivable problems in one's environment and the variety of specific solutions for these problems are elemental facts of an administrator's life that complicate the tasks of rational decision-making. A feature that makes such decision-making prohibitive is limited information. Some limitations are intentional, as when agencies limit their discussion of certain information. Participants mask their disagreements (e.g., on matters of basic philosophies or goals) by not discussing them, particularly if they agree on a particular course of action, each for their own unstated reasons. A second limitation is the sheer working time that can be devoted to analyzing an agency's environment and assessing the advantages and disadvantages that may be associated with each set of goals and policies. A third limitation is the ineradicable ignorance that may remain even after an organization has invested a great deal of its members' time and has risked offending individuals within the organization or its environment by looking into areas that are politically sensitive. The ignorance results from inadequate technologies for gathering or evaluating information. Consequently, administrators must extrapolate from certain kinds of information in order to make inferences about the future. These inferences are called "predictions" or "anticipations." They require a leap beyond the edge of one's information. Some inferences are based on the assumption that past trends will continue into the near future; these are not too risky if the trend being considered is a simple one that has shown past consistency in repeating itself from one period of time to the next. On other occasions, however, extrapolations are complicated by the nature of the assumptions that must be made. Some of the most complicated statements about the future are those that depend on assessing both the intentions of individuals or organizations and the likelihood of changes in these intentions.[7]

Anthony Downs lists three conditions that generally restrict organizations from acquiring the type of information required by the rational decision model:

1. Information is costly because it takes time, effort, and sometimes money to obtain data and comprehend their meaning;
2. Decision-makers have only limited capabilities regarding the amount of time they can spend making decisions, the number of issues they

---

7. Simon, *Administrative Behavior,* chapter V.

can consider simultaneously, and the amount of data they can absorb regarding any one problem; and

3. Although some uncertainty can be eliminated by acquiring information, an important degree of ineradicable uncertainty is usually involved in making decisions.[8]

Not all potential goals and policies can be examined for each of their implications. It is necessary for an organization to take some shortcuts. The important questions are *When does an administrator stop gathering information? When does he stop assessing that which has been gathered?*

The answer to both of these questions may be "Never!" Some administrative units never stop gathering and assessing information, but they do not delay action indefinitely in the hope of obtaining complete information or a finished assessment. They proceed with some activity, but they try to hold open the possibility of altering their actions if they acquire new information. Information-gathering and assessment may go into abeyance when a program actually reaches the operational stage. At this point, an agency makes its commitments to action. The commitments may become increasingly strong as persons inside and outside the organization get used to the established practice. Although new information can alter procedures, established procedures may acquire a life force of their own as they become ingrained in the expectations of officials and clients. Of course, different agencies cut off their active search procedures at different times. Some have greater staff resources that can be devoted to information-gathering; some may have greater tolerance for ambiguous or unresolved questions of policy; and some may experience greater conflicts (either internally or with external actors) requiring a prolonged search for policies that appear bland to all protagonists.[9]

The multiplicity of information-gatherers within administrative units may present problems to the decision-makers. Gatherers of information may have their own views of the problems facing the organization (and themselves) and of the goals that are appropriate for each perceived problem; these problems and goals help to govern the collected information. Because it is not a single mind collecting information, no single mind can make the unique rational assessment of that information; this, too, limits a rational approach to the organization's problems and goals.

----

8. Anthony Downs, *Inside Bureaucracy* (Boston: Little, Brown, 1967), p, 3.

9. Ashley L. Schiff, "Innovation and Administrative Decision-Making: A Study of the Conservation of Land Resources," *Administrative Science Quarterly* 11 (June 1966): 1–32.

Needs, Commitments, Inhibitions, and
Inadequacies of Administrators

The administrative organization is more than the simple sum of its parts, insofar that a well-ordered group can accomplish more than if each of its members pursued his or her own efforts alone. When it comes to the selection of goals and the development of policies, however, the organization must face the individuality of its members. Each has different values and attitudes; these tend to shape perceptions of the organization and its environment and to create preferences about the organization's goals and policies.[10] These perceptions and preferences are among the withinputs of an administrative unit that shape the decisions of the unit. Moreover, the perceptions and preferences of individuals may gather strength through informal alliances among like-minded administrators.

The goals of individual administrators—and their alliances—may reflect professional training or personal predilections. Professional training provides norms as well as skills; these norms affect both the professional's view of problems seen in the environment and the goals adopted to confront those problems. Federal, state, and local administrators represent a wide range of professions, e.g., law, medicine, engineering, and various social and natural sciences. Not each member of a profession has a common "professional" view of the world. There are different schools of thought within each profession. These may generate disputes among the members of one profession within an agency at the same time that other disputes occur between the members of different professions. Some disputes are nothing more than personality conflicts. Antagonisms developed in one context may carry over to other encounters between certain administrators and may generate severe arguments about the agency's definition of its problems or about its choice of goals or policies.

Because of diverse personal and professional interests within administrative organizations, the process of goal- and policy-formulation involves a continuing process of learning and bargaining. There is no once-and-for-all decision that reflects a "rational" assessment of problems, goals, policies, and the benefits and costs associated with each possible option. As changes occur in the organization's environment, it is necessary for participants to learn about the implications of these

---

10. This discussion relies on Cyert and March, *Behavioral Theory of the Firm,* chapter 3.

changes for the current set of goals or policies and perhaps to renegotiate. Coalitions in an agency form around members of similar professional orientation or personal predilection. Yet the coalitions are not always homogeneous or continuous. Certain coalitions may be viable only for a segment of the agency's activities. Inputs of demands and resources may come from the environment to change conditions inside an agency. Also, the personnel of the agency change due to retirements, resignations, and new recruitment. Certain coalitions may grow; others may disintegrate and contribute their members to a new set of coalitions.

The bargaining among coalitions that often marks decision-making within administrative agencies puts a premium on some skills not considered in the rational model. These include individual capacity to express oneself clearly and the ability to resist the blandishments of antagonists. As arguments do not always carry their own weight, they may require a combination of tact, assertiveness, and humor, as well as wisdom, in difficult bargaining sessions.

Structural Difficulties Within Administrative Units and Involving Their Relations with Legislators and the Chief Executive

Several structural difficulties hinder rational decision-making in administrative agencies. These include (1) the administrators' need to interact with legislators and with the chief executive; (2) the different messages received from the legislative and executive branches, whose competition with each other reflect the separation of powers and checks and balances; (3) limits on public administrators' control over subordinates; (4) standard operating procedures and redtape within administrative units that hinder innovation; and (5) conflicts between administrators in operating positions and administrators in positions of authority.

One incentive for administrators to avoid clear-cut decisions about goals is the fear of alienating powerful legislators and the chief executive. The lack of announcement about goals and the difficulties in predicting the outcomes of policy can rebound to the administrators' benefit. Elected officials can support an administrator's policy, even though they would reject certain results the policy *might* produce. If the anticipated results remain ambiguous, a policy may receive support from representatives and from a chief executive whose own long-run goals are likely to be achieved, as well as from those who can only hope that their own goals will be achieved.

Procedures that protect the jobs of individual administrators also complicate the tasks of agency heads. Sometimes subordinates choose to follow their own policy inclinations. The heads of many public agencies cannot readily discipline a subordinate who does not accept the instructions necessitated by a rational choice among alternatives. Civil service sanction procedures are lengthy and threaten to disrupt morale within an agency when they are invoked against an employee. Many administrators feel that it costs more in heartache to attempt dismissal proceedings than it would be worth in greater efficiency. Independent-minded administrators can shop around for a legislator to support their positions or can seek public support from the mass media or an interest group. A legislator may support an errant administrator with the intention of embarrassing an agency head or a chief executive who is a member of the opposite party. Because of the publicity involved as well as the difficult procedures necessary to dismiss employees who have civil service protections, a superior may not be able to fire obstreperous subordinates or even to transfer them to "harmless" assignments.[11]

Within administrative units, some procedures have a life force of their own and can resist changes in policy that might otherwise be dictated by an assessment of problems, goals, and policies. These are standard operating procedures which may be established in legislation, or they may only be the habitual practices of administrators. They are frequently designed to inhibit hasty decisions or to keep individual officials from making off with public resources in their own pockets. Such procedures are generally considered to be essential; but they often limit the flexibility with which an agency can cope with its environment. In the latter case, they lose the connotations of "safeguards" and acquire those of "redtape."

Another structural problem in some administrative units is the conflict that occurs between specialists who are loyal to certain norms of their own professions and persons who exercise managerial authority.[12] There may be a lack of communication, cooperation, and coordination among individuals with different training and career experiences and different responsibilities in the organization. The specialist is encouraged by training and experience to look out for the interests of one program; the specialist usually seeks the resources that are sufficient to operate this program and autonomy in making decisions. Specialists may resist the pressures of an agency head who wants activities to conform with the

---

11. Louis C. Gawthrop, *Bureaucratic Behavior in the Executive Branch: An Analysis of Organizational Change* (New York: Free Press of Glencoe, 1969).

12. Victor A. Thompson, *Modern Organization: A General Theory* (New York: Knopf, 1964), especially chapter 5.

needs of the larger organization. Such problems may be particularly acute during periods of scarce resources when the agency head must persuade several specialists to defer to the organization's needs. Because many agency heads themselves come from the ranks of specialists, conflicts between the specialist and the central authority may have a personal as well as an organizational dimension. The agency head may experience role conflict due to a promotion from a position of specialist to a position of central authority. The former specialist must make adjustments for the demands of a specific program against the demands on the total organization.

The Deviant Behavior of Administrators

Another factor which hinders rational decision-making in administrative agencies is the behavior of certain individuals who preclude the kind of communication that is required by rational decisions. In each of the preceding sections, we documented a number of behavioral patterns that are nonrational according to our model. In this section, however, the focus is on behavior which is not simply nonrational according to the severe standards of that model. Here the concern is with individuals whose behavior is "unreasonable" in that it precludes cooperative communications among members of an organization. In effect, this kind of behavior prevents organizations from making appropriate adjustments and from making decisions that approach some, if not all, of the standards of the rational model.

Like other factors that affect decision-making, the deviant behavior mentioned here is not found equally in all administrative units. Undoubtedly some units are free of all deviant behavior, while others have more than their fair share. If some of these deviant actions occur in high places within an organization, then some individuals may be more likely than others to show such traits. The actions themselves may reflect stress within administrative organizations; and the stress generated by some deviancy may produce even more stress. The stresses include the personal insecurity of organizational members; their inability to accept (either as superiors or subordinates) the status and power which adhere to hierarchical positions; and the gap between the authority incumbent in a formal position and the knowledge which the holders of that position may have about their responsibilities. Some deviant behavior actually derives from normal organizational behavior, but this behavior is an extreme manifestation of the normal activities. Such deviant behavior is called "bureaupathic," to signify its relation—but pushed to *pathological* proportions—to behavior that is "normal" in a bureaucracy.[13] Bureaupathic behavior includes excessive efforts on the part of persons in leadership positions to maintain aloofness from their subordinates; ritualistic attachments to formal procedures; petty insistence on the rights of one's status within the organization; insensitivity to the needs of subordinates or clients; resistance to conflict within an organization; and resistance to change. Some measure of each kind of behavior may be commensurate with the normal requirements of administrative organizations: the need to have persons in positions of authority; the use of standard procedures for making certain kinds of decisions and a stability of these procedures; and the need to make some decisions about subordinates or clients that run counter to the feelings produced by personal relations. However, the pathological variants of these activities hinder communications within the organization. These pathologies create distrust among members of the organization and between the organization and its clients. They threaten the kind of rapport necessary for a reasonable discussion of goals and for a consideration of alternate policies; thereby, they hinder the explicit definition of goals and the assessment of each possible policy that are demanded by the rational model.

It is not only in the bureaucracy where deviant behaviors affect the rational consideration of policy. Public dismay over numerous cases of government deception in relation to the war in Southeast Asia and Watergate has heightened awareness of the distortions disseminated by officials, both high and low in status. The problem of official lying is not a product of recent years. It has been found by historians in the earliest of American administrations. It also is not restricted to matters of great import, as in the case of Lyndon Johnson's false claim of a great-great-grandfather who died at the Alamo. Yet, officials' deception of one another and the public has appeared in matters of the greatest importance, as when distorted reports of North Vietnamese attacks provided the impetus for the Tonkin Gulf resolution that served as the major congressional authorization for the pursuit of war after 1964. Later, one of several efforts to encourage peace via halts in American bombing stumbled over the practice of General John D. Lavelle, whose men bombed without authorization and protected themselves—at the general's encouragement—with false reports of having been fired upon by the enemy. President Richard Nixon left office when his claims of innocence to the public and his congressional supporters were proved false by the contents of his own tape recordings.

---

13. Thompson, *Modern Organization*, chapter 8. See also Robert Prosthus, *Organizational Society* (New York: Knopf, 1962), chapter 9.

Such deceptions not only disturb officials' capacity to assess alternatives and make decisions according to rational procedures, but they weaken the foundation of public trust. Public opinion surveys showed sharp drops in public confidence in government's information over the 1964–72 period. After the lavishly publicized moon landing of 1970, a newspaper opinion poll in some cities found close to 20 percent of the people who did not believe the landing was real. Some felt it was staged somewhere on earth to fool the Russians and Chinese, and a few thought it was staged to make the Americans forget their troubles.[14]

PROBLEMS OF RATIONAL CHOICE AMID AMBIGUITY AND CONTROVERSY: GROWTH VS. CONSERVATION

Administrators who prefer to be rational are comparable to other policy-makers and citizens who face complex problems, coupled with conflicting or ambiguous information. The issues of economic growth, conservation, and equity offer prominent examples. By examining some of the conflicts inherent in these issues, the reader may sympathize with administrators who would prefer to decide issues "rationally," but who end up by evading the rational model.

The issues involve demands for continued economic growth. These demands are accompanied by claims that the United States is already an "overdeveloped" society and should concentrate on efforts to conserve resources and clean up pollution.

There are several points of view to be faced. From one perspective, we find serious problems of regional and social groups that do not share in the mainstream of economic benefits. As noted in Chapter 2, the least-developed states resemble the least-developed countries of Africa, Asia, and Latin America on politics, governmental structure, and public policy (see pp. 44–49). Blacks and other ethnic minorities show economic and social deprivations and express strident demands for change. The calls from low-income regions and classes within the United States are in chorus with the statements of officials in the less-developed states seeking continued economic growth.

The contrast to this view emphasizes the problems inherent in continued growth. Alvin Toffler's *Future Shock* focuses on the psychic problems. He argues that a triumverate of transcience, novelty, and di-

---

14. Wise, *Politics of Lying.*

versity are traits of today and tomorrow that will produce the symptoms of social pathology. He calls our society "super-industrial":

Millions sense the pathology that pervades the air, but fail to understand its roots. These roots . . . are traceable . . . to the uncontrolled, non-selective nature of our lunge into the future. They lie in our failure to direct, consciously and imaginatively, the advance toward super-industrialism. . . .[15]

Another argument points to physical threats of further economic growth. In this view, there are too many people, too much industrial production, and too much consumption of nonrenewable resources; impending pollution that will stifle the environment is the predicted result. In 1969, Paul Ehrlich, an articulate professor of biology, looked ahead only ten years and saw an "eco-catastrophe," with "the end of the ocean [coming] late in 1979."[16]

In a more temperate and persuasive piece, a group of researchers from the Massachusetts Institute of Technology projected growth rates for population, industrial and food production, resource consumption, and pollution. Their book, The Limits to Growth, reports computer printouts showing "the basic behavior mode of the world system is exponential growth of population and capital, followed by collapse."[17] The publisher's blurbs on the paperback edition's back cover indicate its basic message and reception:

The earth's interlocking resources—the global system of nature in which we all live—probably cannot support present rates of economic and population growth much beyond the year 2100, if that long, even with advanced technology.

And in the words of one prestigious reader:

If this book doesn't blow everybody's mind who can read without moving his lips, then the earth is kaput.

Some Problems that Complicate Rational Decisions About Growth

The view that growth produces doom makes serious demands on our attention. It is impossible to recommend continued economic growth

---

15. Alvin Toffler, Future Shock (New York: Bantam Books, 1971), p. 366. This discussion relies on Ira Sharkansky, The United States: A Study of a Developing Country (New York: McKay, 1975).

16. Paul Ehrlich, "Eco-Catastrophe," Ramparts (September 1969), as reprinted in Franklin Tugwell, Search for Alternatives: Public Policy and the Study of the Future (Cambridge, Mass.: Winthrop, 1973), especially p. 186.

17. Donella H. Meadows et al., The Limits to Growth (New York: Universe Books, 1972), p. 142.

without regard for avoidable consequences to the environment. Yet, the simple assertion that growth produces doom is no more satisfactory.

There have been serious efforts at challenging the growth-pro-duces-doom perspective with fresh information and reanalyses of the data used in *The Limits to Growth*. Here is a case of information limits being pushed back by reanalysis. To some eyes, however, the result is ambiguity, not clarity. In the reanalysis there are three arguments: (1) growth is not as rapid or universal as the doomsters predict and does not clearly threaten resource depletion or stifling pollution; (2) projections of unlimited growth have not reckoned with the continued technological growth that could blunt the adverse consequences; and (3) the issue of growth vs. no-growth is a sterile debate and distracts attention from the more important concerns of "what kind of growth?" and "how should its output be distributed?"

One group of demographers has challenged any projections that see population as continuously going upward. Their argument has two basic points. First, population forecasting should *not* be accepted without strong reservations:

No demographer has ever succeeded in forecasting the future of any population. However, demographers today are much better informed about the reasons for their failure, and their product is much more likely to be regarded with justifiable doubt. We call that progress.[18]

Second, existing figures about recent trends severely question any expectation of continued population growth. Indeed, the long trend among countries with advanced levels of economic development is population *decline*. This is true of the United States, with the magnitude and duration of the post-World War II "baby boom" the untypical occurrence, and thus the aberrant phenomenon to be explained. This phenomenon passed at about the mid-1960s, with the mean birth ratio declining by some 20–24 percent between 1961–65 and 1966–70. Declines have come partly with changes in technology (more widespread use of better contraception) and values (later marriages and fewer children wanted). The implication is that economic growth brings a modernization of attitudes and lifestyles and fewer children. There are occasional upward spurts in population, but there seems little in recent history to support any notions of continued exponential growth.

Another group of researchers from Sussex University in England

---

18. Norman B. Ryder, "The Future Growth of the American Population," in Charles F. Westoff et al., *Toward the End of Growth: Population in America* (Englewood Cliffs, N.J.: Prentice-Hall, 1973), pp. 85–86.

takes direct aim at the M.I.T. group. Their volume titled *Models of Doom: A Critique of the Limits to Growth*,[19] offers a systematic attack on the assumptions, methods, conclusions, and recommendations offered by their New England colleagues in *The Limits to Growth*. This may not be the place to referee the international match and award a cup to the winning university, but we can ally the Sussex response to the growth-produces-doom perspective. The Sussex group finds the M.I.T. people to be unreconstructed Malthusians. Thomas Malthus was a preacher of the early 19th century who forecast that population would grow so much faster than agriculture that mass starvation was inevitable. The Sussex group calls its colleagues on a failure to build technology changes into their projections of growth, resource depletion, and pollution. They remind us that Malthus was proved wrong on the basis of higher agricultural yields, as well as on the uneven nature of population growth, and that technological innovation has been a continuing feature of recent history. Just as any forecasting of energy supplies done in the mid-19th century could not have taken the (as yet undeveloped) use of petroleum into consideration, so any energy projections to the year 2100 must concede some unexpected progress toward new discoveries and innovation. The Sussex group also indicts M.I.T. for working with a whole-world model, thereby masking the numerous opportunities for continued resource exploitation, industrialization, and population growth in as yet undeveloped regions. The Sussex group concedes there are theoretical limits to growth, but the group is more impressed with the political than the physical constraints. The 1973–74 oil embargo on the United States lends some weight to this Sussex argument. By admitting some degree of technological change into their models, Sussex pushes the point of resource depletion beyond the time span of their models. For them, the issue is not growth vs. no-growth, but the *nature* of growth, its *location*, and the *use* of its outputs. These issues lend themselves to political analysis, which must focus on the most variable of elements that do not lend themselves to computer projection.

The Sussex group also questions the social goals of the M.I.T. researchers and introduces value questions that may complicate any effort to resolve these issues without a great deal of political controversy. The British find the New Englanders loyal to the intellectual and leisure values of their class and doubt they can acquire more tangible values without economic growth. They find in the M.I.T. perspective "an aris-

---

19. H. S. D. Cole et al., *Models of Doom: A Critique of the Limits to Growth* (New York: Universe Books, 1973).

tocratic concern for enjoying amenity and environment without distur-
bance by others" that also appeared in antigrowth writings of the 19th
century.[20] True to this indictment, the M.I.T. group would exclude from
its no-growth prescription the further development of those virtues "that
many people would list as the most desirable and satisfying activities of
man—education, art, music, religion, basic scientific research, athletics,
and social interactions."[21] To the Sussex critics, this may be the ideal list
named by "many people," but such judges would likely enunciate their
preferences with the accents of the well-educated upper class.

DECISION-MAKING IN ADMINISTRATIVE UNITS: COMPROMISES WITH THE RATIONAL MODEL

The failure of decision-makers to follow the rigorous prescriptions of
the rational model does not mean that their decisions are frenetic, un-
patterned, or made without benefit of human reason. The rational model
demands a central decision-maker who can—with the cooperation of
subordinates—define problems, establish goals, and survey all possible
policies before selecting those that will maximize benefits and minimize
costs. Some factors that hinder this kind of decision-making are features
of the democratic process, i.e., a large number of actors having a stake
in administrative decisions, many of whom have the political resources
to block decisions that threaten undesirable consequences. Politics can
—and does—enter into such big questions as Do we emphasize growth
or conservation? as well as such smaller questions as Do we build a new
road? and Where do we build it? Other factors that hinder strict rationality are limits on information-gathering technologies and the high cost
of information; a variety of goals relevant to an organization; personal
needs and commitments among members of the organization; and the
deviant behavior of individuals who show pathological responses to the
pressures of organizational life.

   This section describes several features that are observed in administrative decision-making. None can claim to be the one way in which
most decisions are made, but each represents a mode of decision-making
widely found in administrative systems. While none of these can claim
to be rational according to the standards of the purely rational model of
decision-making, they do represent *reasonable* ways for administrators to

   20. Cole et al., *Models of Doom*, p. 148.
   21. Cole et al., *Models of Doom*, p. 175.

cope with the numerous demands that come from their environment or from within their own organizations. One set of terms for labeling these different kinds of decisions is useful because it blunts the sharp contrast in connotations between rational and nonrational. The rational decision has been labeled an *optimal* procedure, i.e., one that would be desirable in the most ideal kinds of surroundings. In light of the problems described earlier, however, it is conceded that administrators make do with *satisfactory* decisions. These may not be ideal to all observers, but they are said to meet the needs of participants in a decision-making situation, after taking into account the information about goals, resources, and alternative courses of action that it is feasible for them to assemble.[22] There are "satisficing" techniques appropriate for each of the features that hinder rational or optimal decision-making.

Satisficing with Respect to the Multitude of Problems, Goals, and Policies

One of the practices used by administrators who must be content with satisfactory decisions is to define problems, goals, and policies that permit the use of existing agency resources and that are consistent with existing expectations of legislators, the chief executive, and interest groups. Administrators do not define problems, goals, and policies that reveal a marked departure from existing activities. Thus they avoid challenges from those—inside or outside the organization—who might object to any explicit goals they had not already learned to tolerate.

Many administrators are skilled bargainers. They often settle disputes over goals and policies by accommodating diverse interests. Bargains are made between persons with different interests within administrative agencies, between agencies and officials in other branches of government, and between agencies and interest groups or even prominent citizens. The test of a good bargain is its acceptance by individuals and groups that have control over resources important to an agency. Such a test is not featured in the model of rational decision-making, but it is prominent in democratic political theory.

Another practice is to avoid making any explicit definition of problems or goals. This may avoid one source of severe conflict for the leaders of an organization and still not preclude their mobilization of resources in behalf of certain policies. People who disagree over a definition of problems and goals might agree—each with his own conception

---

22. James March and Herbert Simon, *Organizations* (New York: Wiley, 1959), pp. 140–41.

of problems and goals—to work in behalf of specific policies. The announcement of an agency head's view of problems and goals may cost more in the antagonisms it creates than is warranted by the benefits it provides. Not only may it be possible, but it also may be necessary for an organization to proceed without having a clear or agreed-upon understanding of its major goals and of the social or economic problems these goals are designed to alleviate. Such a procedure departs from the norms of rational decision-making, but it is consistent with the variety of problems, goals, and policy commitments that exists within and around many administrative agencies. This satisficing technique may alleviate problems for a decision-maker that originate as conflicts within the agency, as well as those that reflect conflicts between agency members and legislators, the chief executive, or other political actors in the environment. Each of several participants may support a concrete policy without arguing with others about the long-range goals the policy might —or might not—realize. Work on a policy can go forth in spite of potential dissent that may lie dormant throughout the life of the policy. Administrators with different perspectives on the great problems of continued growth vs. conservation, for example, might avoid their basic disagreements and still cooperate on certifying nuclear power plants. They could face each plant's certification on a case-by-case basis and let the local needs for electric power, the particular circumstances with respect to pollutants, and the political weight of interested parties shape their decisions without an intra-agency clash about the propriety of economic growth, per se.

Satisficing with Respect to Limits on Information

Administrators often cut off their search for information about problems, goals, or policies when they discover a mode of operation that will involve the least profound change in their established programs.[23] They do not search out all possible alternatives until they find "the one best" way. Instead, they search until they find something that "will work," i.e., provides satisfactory relief from the perceived difficulties without threatening undesirable unrest within the agency and among the legislators, executives, and interest groups who involve themselves in its affairs.

The reluctance of an agency to fully search out results partly from the variety of goals held by agency personnel and by powerful outsiders,

---

23. Downs, *Inside Bureaucracy*, p. 173.

and partly from the sheer impossibility of finding one best solution that squares with all of these goals. Most large agencies delegate information-gathering for different projects to different individuals or units within the organization. Program specialization may govern the choice of information-gatherers. The specialists in each of the agency's numerous activities search for and assess information relevant to their program. The use of numerous information-gatherers and assessors may permit some goal satisfactions for a wide variety of members.[24] However, the result may also be a lack of coordination. This lack of coordination may cause fewer problems in some contexts than in others. When an organization recognizes it is in danger, it may coordinate information-gathering to gain an early warning of serious problems. But it may be difficult to discern a harmful situation and to govern the flow of information so that the coordinator is not smothered in a mass of undigested data.

Fragmentalization of perception inevitably produces an enormous amount of "noise" in the organization's communications networks. The officials at the bottom must be instructed to report all potentially dangerous situations immediately so the organization can have as much advanced warning as possible. Their preoccupation with their specialties and their desire to insure against the worst possible outcomes, plus other biases, all cause them to transmit signals with a degree of urgency that in most cases proves exaggerated after the fact. These overly urgent signals make it extremely difficult to tell in advance which alarms will prove warranted and which will not.

There are no easy solutions to this problem. With so many "Chicken Littles" running around claiming the sky is about to fall, the men at the top normally cannot do much until "Henney Penney" and "Foxy Loxy" have also started screaming for help, or there is a convergence of alarm signals from a number of unrelated sources within the organization.[25]

Satisficing with Respect to the Needs, Commitments, Inhibitions, and Inadequacies of Administrators

The presence of personal conflict among personnel does not mean an agency will be rent apart or even that individuals will be miserable on account of the fray. Several mechanisms can protect both the organization and its individuals from the conflict costs. These are *not* the mechanisms portrayed in the model of rational decision-making. They are, in contrast, mechanisms that permit the organization to make

---

24. Cyert and March, *Behavioral Theory of the Firm*, pp. 36–38.
25. Downs, *Inside Bureaucracy*, p. 190.

some decisions about goals or policy and to carry on its activity despite conflicts that prohibit agency leaders from making integrated, rational decisions for the entire organization.

The mechanisms that protect administrative organizations from the worst consequences of internal conflict include the selection of highly ambiguous or nonoperational goals; the use of slack resources to "buy-off" members who might be unhappy with the goals or policies selected; and the acceptance of precedent (i.e., goal- or policy-selections made in the past) to narrow conflicts to be faced in the present.

The selection of ambiguous or nonoperational goals defers conflict by obtaining agreement on a diffuse statement that does not commit participants in favor of—or against—any activity that threatens their own goals. Conflict may come when subgoals—or actual policies—are selected. At that time, however, the choice may not involve the entire organization. Decisions might be confined to subgroups. These might reach agreement about their own activities if they can deliberate without being the focus of widespread attention by a total membership who expects major goals to be chosen.

Organizational slack consists of resources that are not yet allocated, but that can be used to provide some rewards to administrators who are dissatisfied with goal- or policy-selections. The resources include money, status and other symbolic rewards, and policy commitments. When they are used to placate individuals who are miffed by major goal selections, they can be thought of as "side payments" that the organization makes to buy the acceptance of its decisions by unhappy personnel. Side payments can be an increase in salary or rank; a larger or more comfortable office or other amenities that make work easier or more pleasant; or a commitment to undertake a program tangential to the main effort of the agency. Such a program can be experimental or can be the continuation on a small scale of a project that had been larger. A side payment of an experimental program might be given to an officer who failed to have the organization adopt a massive effort in this new direction. A diminished continuation of a previously large activity may be granted to an individual who fought unsuccessfully to retain the program at its previous size.[26]

Many agencies use precedent to simplify the decisions they make about goals and policies. Previously made decisions tend to stand until they are overturned or replaced. Precedents narrow the range of goal-

---

26. Cyert and March, *Behavioral Theory of the Firm*, pp. 36–38.

and policy-questions that an organization must face. If a new problem can be defined to make an existing goal relevant, then such a definition will spare the organization from the turmoil of a new goal conflict. We shall see in a later discussion of decision-rules that precedent has several manifestations in administrative agencies. For example, decisions can become "routinized," so that there is no longer any conflict as the agency makes similar decisions in the future.

The mechanisms that protect the organization from the worst consequences of internal conflict also benefit individual members. When an agency selects ambiguous goals, it masks the threat to an individual of having been on the losing side in a confrontation. Reliance on precedent also permits many potential conflicts to pass unexamined. And the pool of slack resources provides some payoffs when an individual is faced with having lost a dispute over major goals. Individuals also have another protection from internal conflict: the tendency of specialists to focus their energies on a small fraction of the organization's problems. This permits individuals to identify problems and formulate goals that are only subproblems and subgoals for the larger organization. Other specialists may be pursuing subgoals that *might* come into conflict with one's own. However, as long as a confrontation does not occur, each group of specialists may pursue its own goals without regard for— perhaps without even knowing about—activities in other units of the organization.

Satisficing with Respect to Structural Problems

As in the case of other difficulties raised as barriers to rational decision-making, a common response to structural problems within administrative agencies, or between the agencies, legislators, or executives is a failure to make overt decisions about goals. Policies can proceed without the centralized deliberation and clear choices prescribed by the rational model. Organizations often "factor out" goal-setting and policy-formulation to specialized units. Matters requiring new programs are typically assigned to program specialists. The central authority is satisfied with an opportunity to review their proposals. The difficulties of coordinating different specialized units can be met by keeping coordination to a minimum. The news that specialized administrative units pursue duplicate, or even contradictory, programs reflects this lack of coordination. Certain decisions about goals or policies may be made at the insistence of individuals within an organization or at the insistence of legislators and executives on the outside. Even when this occurs, however, decision-makers may not meet the demands of the rational model. An order to "make a decision" may not be acceptable where specialists within an organization could not live with the implications for their own activities. Such a decision forced on an agency may be so vague or nonoperational as to avoid imposing any threat on the specialists involved. Thus it may require the devolution of subgoal- and policy-definition to specialists who will administer the eventual program.

THE USE OF DECISION RULES

Common to each of the satisficing techniques is the use of several kinds of decision rules. Three of these rules are prominent enough to merit separate attention. They are (1) administrators' reliance on *tensions* between established patterns and unmet needs to signal the need for a change in policy; (2) the tendency to make *adjustments* to demands, rather than initiate decision processes that seek a clear definition of goals or policy; and (3) the use of *routine procedures* to simplify the complex considerations potentially relevant to a decision-maker. Common to each of these features is the reluctance of administrators to make great departures from customary activities. This is not simply laziness, but it represents their appreciation of the numerous demands presented by members of their own organizations, by legislators and the chief executive of their own government, by officials of other governments with whom they have contact, and by their clients and other interest groups. Seldom is everyone satisfied with the current state of affairs. To change markedly from the current state, however, might arouse more unrest among the constituents than would be warranted from the benefits promised.

Reliance on Tensions

Administrative agencies do not look for trouble, as a reasonable person does not continually search the environment looking for unmet needs. Instead, they wait for tensions to signal dissatisfaction with current activities. Some dissatisfaction is always present, insofar as the agency lacks resources to adequately serve all demands. Several factors prevent an agency from making an active search for unmet needs and then seeking to alleviate these needs. These factors include a scarcity of personnel for these search processes; the desire to avoid provoking new conflicts within agencies or between agencies and other branches of government that might upset delicate agreements reached on other matters; and a scarcity of resources needed to support new programs of service. By relying on tensions, administrators wait for problems to present themselves. When problems become sufficiently severe to cause a tension, administrators make some effort to respond. Tensions can be thought of as a screening device between an administrative unit and its environment; unit members use it to determine when unmet demands are so severe as to require a response. The quality of the tension may indicate the source of the stress, the actors involved, and the intensity of their dissatisfaction.

The tension network appears to have both independence and substance, as if, instead of a network of logical relationships, it were a large computer receiving dozens of demands for service and matching them with hundreds of alternative service capabilities. In this process it manipulates the composite of all demands against the total available capacity to meet them. Since demands for service typically exceed capacities, rough priorities are established by a set of values and agreements, evolved over the years. These priorities do not go into process . . . as a logical list of things to be pursued, against which an incoming request is matched and then either accepted or rejected, but rather as a series of thresholds guaranteeing that the demand has a minimal amount of support. Thus, instead of a *rational structure of program values,* there is a series of barriers operating as thresholds; they screen the values that have meaning, relevance, and support from those that lack one of the requisites.[27]

Mutual Adjustment

An administrative unit that responds to tensions does not initiate policy-change according to any rationally defined set of priorities; it waits until a change is demanded. A set of procedures for accommodating demands has been labeled "mutual adjustment." Like the reliance on tensions, the concept of mutual adjustment refers not to a rational assessment of priorities; mutual adjustment is a pattern of response and negotiation. One of the terms used to identify decision-making by mutual adjustment is "muddling through."[28] This term suggests a lethargic organism that would detour around a problem rather than meet it head-on.

The techniques of adjustment include discussions with representatives for various interests; a reluctance to view any part of one's own

---

27. William J. Gore, *Administrative Decision-Making: A Heuristic Model* (New York: Wiley, 1964), p. 43 (italics added).
28. Charles Lindblom, "The Science of 'Muddling Through,'" *Public Administration Review* 19 (Spring 1959): 79–88.

position as inflexible; a willingness to bargain with a protagonist; the expectation that protagonists will negotiate in good faith and relinquish part of their demands in exchange for one's own concessions; and the view that goal-formation and policy-making is a continuing process, so that desires that are not satisfied in one period may be realized some time in the future.[29]

The pursuit of agreement among representatives of diverse interests stands as a major departure from the centralized choices that are assumed by the rational decision model. Officials create special task forces to represent the interests concerned with an issue or intra-agency committees that include representatives from different units. While these bodies may have only advisory functions, they often obtain agreement among their contending members and present their parent agency with a proposal that is accepted in whole or part.

Flexibility in the face of others' demands is a primary feature of mutual adjustment. It represents an admission that decision-makers lack incontrovertible evidence that any one set of goals or policies is "the one best way" to resolve their problems. Intellectual search and discovery is less to the point of mutual adjustment than is the acceptance of certain demands. The number of individuals who support a demand, their intensity, their alliances with key officials, and the possibility of modifying their position so that it appeals to an even wider population are useful criteria for mutual adjustment. *Adjustment* is not simply a process of rewarding overt power; it is a system of recognizing that power and demands are held by numerous interests and that each can modify its position somewhat to make demands more acceptable to one another.

Another component of mutual adjustment is flexibility over time. Decisions are not made once and for all, but in a sequence of continuing interactions; later decisions modify the impact of earlier ones. Demands that are not met in one phase of the sequence return again, often in different formulations and with different supporters. With some changes in content or style and with some additional changes in the context that might expand its appeal to other interests, a once-rejected demand can find wide acceptance and a generous provision of resources.

---

29. This discussion relies on the works of Charles E. Lindblom, especially *Policy-Making Process* and "Science of 'Muddling Through,'" and also "Decision-making in Taxation and Expenditure," in National Bureau of Economic Research, *Public Finances: Needs, Sources and Utilization* (Princeton, N.J.: Princeton University Press, 1961), pp. 295–336.

Routines are used by decision-makers in administrative systems to avoid the time-consuming, expensive, and impossible demands of the rational model. Routines are decision rules that specify which of the numerous inputs that might be relevant are actually considered in making decisions. Some routines are more elaborate than others and indicate the weight to be given each input; some even specify the response to be made under certain conditions. Routines help decision-makers select from among potentially relevant conditions by simplifying the inputs and, thereby, making the decision easier.

There are different types of routines in administrative systems. At the extreme of simplicity, an electronic computer uses a routine when it decides if the arithmetic is accurate on a citizen's tax return. At another stage, the computer uses a slightly more elaborate routine to determine if the citizen claims more for charitable contributions than is commensurate with total income. If the citizen does claim more, the computer identifies the tax return for human scrutiny. When the auditor examines the tax return and other documents the taxpayer is asked to bring in, the auditor employs additional routines. These are more flexible than those programmed into the computer; but they likewise provide a screening process for the inputs. They identify the kinds of evidence that are acceptable—and unacceptable—for showing the citizen's contributions. Other routines help the tax agency determine from the circumstances whether the citizen will simply pay back-taxes with interest, pay a fine in addition to the taxes and interest, or be prosecuted for tax evasion.

Many of the routines used by subordinates in administrative agencies reflect the working-out of procedures explicitly designed by their superiors. However, some of the most interesting routines are used in making policy decisions. They affect enormous financial, material, and personal resources. Often they are not pursued in a conscious manner. Decision-makers accept them because of their appeal as the simplifiers of complex situations. Like the routines mentioned above, those used by policy-makers select a few inputs from the many that face a decision-maker; sometimes they assign a weight to each of these inputs or even prescribe the decision-maker's response to a certain kind of input. At the same time that routines simplify the tasks of policy-makers, they also help to stabilize the political system. They do this by screening out certain kinds of inputs, especially those that would produce marked departures from prevailing activities. Three policy-making routines will be illustrated here: incremental budgeting; the tendency of state and local administrators to copy regional neighbors in formulating their own policies; and the tendency of policy-makers to seek an increase in spending when they perceive a need to improve their programs.

Incremental Budgeting

Incrementalism is a routine found in many types of government decision-making, but most clearly in the budgetary process. Budget-makers who follow an incremental approach fail to consider all of the alternatives that face them; they do not make their decisions on the basis of all relevant information. Incrementalists do not debate grand social goals. Their most salient concerns are immediate appropriations for specific agencies, rather than long-run benefits for society. They generally accept the legitimacy of established programs and agree to continue the previous level of expenditure. They limit their task by considering only the *increments of change* proposed for the new budget and by considering the narrow range of goals embodied in the departures from established activities. Their expectations tend to be short-range and pragmatic.

More clearly than other decision rules, incremental budgeting reveals its function as a conservative force in administrative agencies. Budget-makers consider no single criterion as important as their own decisions of the recent past. They accept established levels of spending and focus their inquiries (and their budget-cutting) on the increments of change that are requested.

There is some evidence that incremental budgeting is most confining in state and local governments. At the federal level, incrementalists seem willing to examine the changes in expenditure *and* service outputs that are requested for each agency.[30] In the state and local governments that have been studied closely, however, there is a more narrow concentration on the increments of dollars requested. In his study of budgeting in Illinois, Thomas J. Anton finds decision-makers relying on a simplistic set of rules that examines—and cuts—budget totals with little concern for the impact on programs.[31] Administrators often must expand services by shifting funds within budgets that reveal minimal overall change.

---

30. Aaron Wildavsky, *The Politics of the Budgetary Process* (Boston: Little, Brown, 1974), chapter 3. This discussion of routines relies heavily on Ira Sharkansky, *The Routines of Politics* (New York: Van Nostrand-Reinhold, 1970).

31. Thomas J. Anton, *The Politics of State Expenditure in Illinois* (Urbana: University of Illinois Press, 1966).

John P. Crecine's findings about budgeting in Detroit, Cleveland, and Pittsburgh document how incremental budget-makers can parcel out annual increases in revenues without concern for program values.[32] When budget-makers expect a revenue surplus, they distribute it among most agencies on the basis of routine priorities that are not rationally derived in regard to the situation at hand. Salaries are given first preference; equipment gets the second rewards; and maintenance gets the remainder. A contrary priority is used when the forecast indicates a need to reduce budgets below present levels. Cuts are made first in maintenance, then in equipment, and only then in salaries. Those items that promise the greatest political appeal—regardless of program—receive the best treatment. (A more-detailed description of incremental budgeting and of its influences on the expenditures of administrative agencies appears in Chapter 9, pp. 281–88).

Regional Consultation

Incremental budgeting is a routine that guides officials to take their decision-cues from within their own jurisdiction. The routine of regional consultation guides the administrators of state and local governments when they look outside their own arenas for decision-cues. When administrators look elsewhere for a model policy to copy for their own jurisdiction, they do not survey all the possible models throughout the country—as the rational model suggests. Instead, they look within their geographic region or, more typically, to a jurisdiction that borders directly on their own.

Many administrators believe that neighboring jurisdictions have problems similar to their own.[33] Because neighboring governments serve similar populations, it is likely that the people have common needs for public services and present similar demands to government agencies. The economies of the neighboring governments are generally alike, and they present to government agencies a comparable set of resources and needs. The political environment is also likely to be similar in neighboring jurisdictions. Politicians will probably support comparable levels of service, and there may be similar relationships among administrators, the executive, and the legislature. Southern states are said to be the arche-

---

32. John P. Crecine, "A Computer Simulation Model of Municipal Resource Allocation," a paper delivered at the Meeting of the Midwest Conference of Political Science, April 1966.
33. Ira Sharkansky, *Regionalism in American Politics* (Indianapolis: Bobbs-Merrill, 1970).

type of American regions. They share certain geographical features that have affected their politics through the intermediary of the cotton-plantation–slave syndrome. They also shared historical experiences of racial heterogeneity, Civil War, Reconstruction, continuing poverty, and limited political participation and competition. Many government services in the South are distinctive; but the South is not the only distinctive region. States in the Great Lakes and Rocky Mountain areas, in particular, share traits that seem to reflect common features of population, geography, history, economics, and politics.

It is not only policy-makers in administrative agencies who feel that regional neighbors are likely subjects of emulation. Politicians, journalists, and members of the public who take an interest in certain programs are accustomed to comparing efforts in their own state to those that are in their own circle of experience; and this circle typically is limited to the region. Thus, the inputs that come to an administrative agency often carry demands developed in a distinct regional context. State bureaus of research usually publish comparisons of their own state's demographic, economic, and public-service characteristics with those of regional partners. For example, the *Georgia Statistical Abstract* (published by the University of Georgia's Bureau of Business and Economic Research) compares data for the state as a whole with a figure for the entire United States and with separate figures for Alabama, Florida, North Carolina, South Carolina, and Tennessee. When a study committee of the University of Wisconsin analyzed tax burdens in that state, the comparisons were drawn with Illinois, Indiana, Iowa, Michigan, Minnesota, and Ohio.

The professional activities of administrators also lead them to regional neighbors for policy cues. Policy-makers and professional employees of state and local governments belong to formal organizations according to their subject-matter specialties. They include the National Association of State Budget Officers, the National Association of State Conservation Officers, and the National Association of Housing and Redevelopment Officials. They have both national and regional meetings that provide the opportunity for trading information about current problems and reinforcing friendships formed at earlier meetings. State and local officials indicate that they are more likely to attend the regional than the national meetings of these groups and that they acquire many of their professional contacts at these meetings.

Because administrators have consulted in the past with their counterparts in nearby governments, they have learned who can be trusted for credible information, candor, and good judgment. Unless officials are committed to an extensive program of research before making their own policy decisions, they will make only a few calls to individuals with whom they have dealt amicably in the past.

Several elements favor the development of nationwide similarities in the public policies of state and local governments. They include federal aid, improvements in transportation and communication, and the mobility of professional and technical personnel from schools or previous government jobs in one state to new jobs in other states. Yet regional patterns in policy have not succumbed to these influences. Distinct regional patterns remain in spending and service levels for the fields of education, highways, and welfare; in the nature of state and local revenue systems; and in the use of federal and state aids. The presence of these regional similarities in policy remains as a prominent indication of the routine of regional consultation.

The Spending-Service Cliché

The spending-service cliché is a routine that leads policy-makers to equate levels of expenditure with levels of service-output. Like other routines, the spending-service cliché gets its support from the need of decision-makers for a device that will simplify reality. In the field of program development, there are five principal elements that add to the appeal of the spending-service cliché: (1) the large number of factors—and complex interrelationships among these factors—that actually has an influence on the character of services an agency provides; (2) the lack of information among decision-makers about these service-factors; (3) the belief that some factors that influence the level of outputs are not conveniently subject to manipulation by public officials; (4) the commonality of money as an element that may influence many potential service-factors; and (5) the widespread belief among analysts and observers *outside* the decision-making arena that money is crucial among the factors that influence the level of service-outputs.

Among the factors that can influence the nature of public services are the nature of staff and leadership, physical facilities, the clientele who are to be served, the organizational structure of the service agencies, the economy of the jurisdiction receiving the service, and the political environment in which policy decisions are made. There is much folklore about the elements that will help to improve services, but there is little hard information about the results to be expected from certain combinations of ingredients under certain conditions. In a number of federal, state, and local agencies that have access to sophisticated staff assistance and electronic data-processing equipment, efforts are being made to identify salient features that have a bearing on the level of services produced. However, much of this work is still in the exploratory stage. It is not sufficiently widespread among government agencies, and its techniques are not sufficiently well accepted for it to have broad application.

Among the elements that seem likely to influence service levels, a number of them appears unamenable to direct manipulation by government officials. Because of this, decision-makers may be dissuaded from a thorough analysis of service-determinants and may be led to rely on the simple routine that assumes a spending-service relationship. The preparation of clients, their motivation for making the efforts that are part of the services to be rendered, market costs, the level of economic development in a community, and the attractiveness of a community as a residence for professional and technical personnel can have a bearing on the services that an agency can render. Although each of these elements may be altered by long-range campaigns directed specifically at them, it is unlikely that these changes can be made the responsibility of service agencies who have other, more immediate goals.

In the face of the complexities that face the decision-maker who would undertake a thorough analysis of the elements that influence an agency's level of services, the routine of the spending-service cliché offers both simplicity and credibility. Although money, per se, does not affect levels of service, it seems reasonable to believe that money will purchase many of the commodities that do affect services. Money is also subject to manipulation by government officials. If the present level of service is not satisfactory, it is always possible—assuming sufficient resources or sufficient willingness to increase taxes—to spend more money. With additional dollars, officials can seek to recruit and/or train leaders and scientific-technical-professional personnel for their agencies; they can pay existing personnel enough money to make it difficult for them to accept employment elsewhere; they can offer financial inducements so that personnel will accept changes in organizational structure or changes in agency norms; and they can buy the material and talents necessary to construct and maintain attractive physical facilities. Unfortunately, the willingness to spend more money may not solve the service problem. Not only is it true that some service-determinants are not subject to alteration by current spending, but it is also unclear as to which of the purchasable commodities—and how much of each—will do the desired job.

One of the factors that helps to make the spending-service cliché attractive to administrators is its popularity among those who observe and analyze public policy. Journalists frequently rank state or local governments on some readily available financial scale. Total spending, expenditures per client, and average salaries are favorite subjects for comparison. Several academic social scientists with solid reputations as scholars, consultants, and government executives also give high marks to the spending-service cliché. In much of the literature that examines government expenditures in the United States, we can find the assumption that spending provides the primary stimulant for public services.[34] Most writers who assume the expenditure-service correspondence fail to test their belief. On some occasions, they even overlook contrary data from their own tables.[35]

Opportunities for Innovation in Administrators' Decisions: Deviations from Routines

The use of set rules in making routine decisions does not fix the decisions that administrators can make. As noted earlier, routines are only one of several devices they use in making decisions. Others, like mutual adjustment, are more hospitable to innovative stimuli. Moreover, some officials recognize the biases in decision-makers' routines, and they devise strategies that play on the weaknesses of routines. Certain environmental conditions help to weaken routines and to permit innovative proposals to affect policy. Some officials are sufficiently won over to new ideas that they disregard their normal routines and make a new kind of decision.

Despite its widespread appeal, the spending-service cliché is not invincible. Successful politicians—like Governor Brown of California and President Carter—have appealed to the widespread skepticism about big spending that produces little tangible improvements in social problems. However, it is premature to conclude that they will be able to rationalize spending or make it pay off substantially more than at present. The massive size of the policy machinery, as well as all the inputs its masters would prefer to consider, will challenge new perspectives introduced at the top. Decision rules that simplify the policy-maker's con-

---

34. See, for example, Robert C. Wood, *1400 Governments* (Garden City, N.Y.: Anchor Books, 1961), p. 35; Jesse Burkhead, *Public School Finance* (Syracuse, N.Y.: Syracuse University Press, 1965), p. 50; and Philip C. Burch, *Highway Revenue and Expenditure Policy in the United States* (New Brunswick, N.J.: Rutgers University Press, 1962), p. 34.

35. In Burkhead's book, for example, the author is not troubled by the lack of significant statistical relationships between four measures of educational expenditure and such likely indicators of service as the salary of beginning teachers, the insurable value of school property, and the number of full-time employees in such auxiliary services as student health and counselling. For a test of the spending-service cliché, see Ira Sharkansky, "Government Expenditures and Public Services in the American States," *American Political Science Review* 61 (December 1967): 1066–78.

siderations, like the spending-service cliché, may resist even the most highly placed skeptics.

Aaron Wildavsky identifies a number of strategies that are used within the confines of incremental budgeting. The following set of strategies, for example, defends the "base" (an agency's current budget) against attack from legislative committees.[36]

Cut the popular program. By anticipating legislative insistence on a pruned budget, administrators can cut their requests for programs that they know are popular. When this happens, it is more than likely that the legislature will restore the cut and, hopefully, not make up for the restoration with a cut taken elsewhere.

Claim that any cut in a program will require its sacrifice. Any cut will be too great to allow the program to be continued. The risk with this kind of claim is that the legislature might view such a program as existing on too tenuous a foundation and scrap the whole works.

Separate programs in the budget presentation. This makes it difficult for legislators to cut "across the board" in a way that takes funds from anonymous programs. By forcing the legislature to cut out specific activities, an administrator can mobilize the supporters of those activities in opposition to the cut.

Wildavsky also identifies some strategies that administrators use to increase their budgets within the constraints of incrementalism. He calls them "increasing the base—inching ahead with existing programs."

Old stuff. Funds for new programs are difficult to obtain. Therefore, administrators say that their "new" money is for existing programs. "Our programs have grown a lot, but we have never begun anything we described as fundamentally new in the twenty years I have been [with the agency]."[37]

The transfer. Administrators maintain budget requests at constant levels, even though some older programs are phased out and have been replaced with others. This is one way of moving ahead in program development, while appearing to stand still.

The numbers game. Administrators claim that the *number* of programs has remained constant. This may be true. But while they try to focus attention on the number of their activities, the activities and the cost of each one can move ahead.

The wedge or camel's nose. This is a device that begins a new program with a sum that appears insignificant. Once this has been accepted, the administrator claims in the next budget period that the pro-

---

36. Wildavsky, *Politics of the Budgetary Process,* pp. 102ff.
37. Wildavsky, *Politics of the Budgetary Process,* pp. 109ff.

gram has become part of its base and that it must increase expenditures in order to go ahead and finish the task it has started.

If this, then that. This is implied in the claim that a new activity is integrally related to an existing program. Thus, the implied obligation to go on with the old passes on to the new.

The backlog. This is the claim that existing activities have not accomplished the assigned tasks. Therefore, additional expenditures are necessary to clean up the backlog of unfinished business.

The crisis. A proposed new program is identified with an event or set of circumstances that is widely viewed as a crisis: war, drought, depression, plant disease, social unrest. This strategy is related to the next device.

The defense motif. National defense has had wide appeal. It often enjoyed bipartisan support and a willingness to spend money that might otherwise be denied. It is not only the military that has received the benefit of the defense motif; other activities have tied themselves to this symbol with lucrative payoffs. The largest single highway program—and the costliest—in the nation's history is the "Interstate and Defense Highway System." One of the most generous and wide-ranging federal aids for education enacted during the 1950s is the "National Defense Education Act." Such labels vary in their appeal. In the years of the second Nixon administration with a hostile Congress that was especially tired of the war effort, the defense label was of questionable value in the budget game.

Historically, national crises have affected the use of such routines as incremental budgeting and the spending-service cliché. In particular, the Great Depression, wars, and postwar reconversions made untenable some of the factors that normally led officials to practice these routines. Intergovernmental aids can also upset the routines of recipient governments. And certain individuals, when elected to high public office, may be able to alter, at least temporarily, the routines of their governments while they implement policy.[38]

The Depression had it most severe impact on the routines of local governments. In many communities, the bottom dropped out of the real estate market at the same time that there were unprecedented unemployment and industrial shutdowns. The combination of these factors resulted in a great loss in local-government revenues from the property tax; in some places, it led to the actual bankruptcy of the municipality. Under these conditions, incremental budgeting was a luxury, and many localities cut deeply into the expenditure base of existing pro-

---

38. The discussion draws on Sharkansky, *Routines of Politics,* chapter X.

grams. World War II and, to a lesser extent, the Korean conflict also forced local, state, and *domestic* federal agencies to fall behind their previous year's expenditures. Both manpower and raw materials became less available for domestic purposes. The number of state and local government employees declined during World War II, and the magnitude of federal aids also declined.

The high levels of military expenditure reached during World War II seemed to lessen the willingness to continue with incrementalism and the spending-service cliché. In the executive branch, the reform movement that evolved to PPB (planning-programming-budgeting) got its beginning in 1946 when the Navy Department reorganized its budget to emphasize the program components that its expenditures would purchase. In 1949 the Hoover Commission urged the adoption of "performance budgeting" within federal agencies. This style of budgeting—like the earlier innovation in the Navy Department—would call the attention of budget reviewers to the levels of program output that were promised by each agency's request. Service levels, and not simply spending, would be examined by budget analysts. This reform was initiated in the Budget and Accounting Act of 1950, and a number of federal agencies took steps to clarify the outputs that funds would provide.

Grants-in-aid have some influence on the routines of state and local administrators. The sheer magnitude of grants coming into a state can distract state and local administrators from the routines of incremental budgeting. This has been true in the fields of highways and natural resources, reflecting the substantial amounts of the federal grants for these programs.[39] Federal funds represent "outside" money that is free from the constraints placed on additions to the base of state expenditures. Of course, the federal grant usually requires an outlay of "matching" state resources; but this can be justified by the amount of federal money that it "brings in."

RATIONALIST EFFORTS TO REFORM DECISION-MAKING: THE CASE OF BUDGETING

The procedures that administrators use to make "satisfactory" decisions have evolved in the face of constraints that inhibit "optimal" or "rational" decisions. Such satisficing procedures appeal to those observers

---

39. Ira Sharkansky, *Spending in the American States* (Chicago: Rand McNally, 1968), chapters IV and VIII.

who see insurmountable difficulties that block rational decisions. However, other observers are dissatisfied with existing procedures. They may not expect to mold decisions to the demands of the purely rational model, but they do want decision-makers to take more of a rational route to their decisions than has been the practice. Over the years, they have urged structural reforms for administrative systems—both on the agencies themselves and on legislative and executive institutions in their environment. The reforms are designed to encourage decision-makers to take more factors into consideration when choosing goals and when choosing policies that will realize their goals. If successful, these reforms would open policy decisions to a wider range of economic, social, and political inputs. Yet, failures of many proposals and sharp modifications of others when put into practice suggest the power of the features that hinder rational decision-making. Many of the reforms have focused on the budgetary process. They have resulted in the development of the Office of Management and Budget (see pp. 132–36), the Executive Office of the President (see pp. 133–34), and the PPB.

The creation of congressional budget committees and the Congressional Budget Office in 1974 represents the most recent efforts of the legislative branch to adapt analytic techniques for its own policy competitions with the executive branch. A more complete discussion of these reforms appears in Chapter 9, as part of executive-legislative relations. Here we concentrate on PPB, which stands as the most serious effort in recent years to rationalize decision-making, and whose analytic techniques were important in the later design of the congressional reforms.

Planning-Programming-Budgeting: Its Promise and Problems

PPB is actually an interrelated series of several devices whose description is clouded by the failure of advocates to agree on a common set of terms. Systems analysis, cost-benefits analysis, cost-effectiveness, and program budgeting have been used variously to describe individual components or the entirety of PPB. In budgeting, PPB seeks greater rationality by clarifying the choice of means used to attain agency goals. Its decision stages include the following:

1. Define the major programs in each area of public service;
2. Define the principal "outputs" (goals) of each program;
3. Identify the "inputs" that generate "outputs" (inputs include various combinations of personnel, facilities, and techniques of rendering service);

4. Compute the costs of alternative combinations of inputs and the value of the outputs likely to be produced by each combination; and
5. Calculate the cost-benefit ratio associated with each combination of inputs and outputs.

Presumably, PPB guides those who would employ public resources in the most efficient manner. If its practitioners are thorough, they should be able to clarify alternatives among goals and policies and to identify the set of inputs that produces the lowest cost-benefit ratio of inputs to outputs.

When the proponents of PPB speak about "systems analysis," they refer to the relationships among components 1–5 and the hope to take "everything into consideration" in making budget recommendations. By combining PPB's five decision stages, they hope to obtain a "systems-wide" view of a policy problem. In practice, however, some aspects of PPB are developed more fully than others. Analyses that claim to reflect a systems-wide view of a policy problem may actually produce only a microscopic examination into one part of a complex picture. Some shortcomings of PPB point to the continuing problems that have also shown through other attempts to make decisions rationally: an inability to assess the full range of political and economic issues associated with each major policy; and the failure of participants to subordinate their own loyalties to the recommendations that evolve from a new system.

A major criticism of PPB focuses on its inability to provide budgeteers with an evaluation of the political costs and benefits associated with their support of certain programs. Aaron Wildavsky was an early critic of PPB who cited it for failing to provide information about three types of political costs:

1. *Exchange costs*—the costs of calling in favors owed and the costs of making threats in order to get others to support a policy;
2. *Reputational costs*—the loss of popularity with the electorate, the loss of esteem and effectiveness with other officials, and the subsequent loss of one's ability to secure programs other than those currently under consideration; and
3. *The costs of undesirable redistributions of power*—those disadvantages that accrue from the increase in the power of individuals, organizations, or social groups who may become antagonistic to oneself.[40]

---

40. Aaron Wildavsky, "The Political Economy of Efficiency: Cost-Benefit Analysis, Systems Analysis, and Program Budgeting," *Public Administration Review* 26 (December 1966): 292–310.

An advantage to incremental budget-making is that it sharply limits the political costs that have to be calculated. When incrementalists accept the base of previous expenditures as legitimate, they excuse themselves from reviewing the whole range of tradition, habits, and prior commitments that are subsumed within existing programs. PPB threatens to perpetuate controversy (and discomfort for budget-makers) with its rationalist analysis of alternative approaches to each major program.

Another accusation directed at PPB is that it focuses on the ingredients of program inputs and outputs that are easy to investigate. Many systems analyses that have been published introduce their subject matter with an impressive list of potential service-determinants and likely products of the service. But the analysis itself typically deals with a few of the inputs and outputs, seemingly selected on no more substantial basis than the analyst's convenience. The inputs and outputs that are measured and subject to analysis may not be representative of other—unmeasured—components of the program. Budget allocations can be led astray by information that appears sophisticated but that deals with only a small portion of the relevant picture. Thus, practitioners of PPB may base their recommendations on a routine that is *no more comprehensive in its rationality* than is incremental budgeting.

PPB made its start in the military, where the major goals are clear and widely accepted among the officials who make budget decisions: deterrence of war, defense of country, and victory in war. Elsewhere, the goals of programs are subject to intense controversy. In many cases, different legislators and interest groups agree to support specific activities, even though bitter conflict would result if they had to agree about the long-range goals of the programs. Even in the case of agencies with relatively noncontroversial goals, the value of PPB is limited by the extent to which goals can be defined with precision and the costs and benefits of programs can be measured. Definitions of the "victory" being pursued in a military encounter may—as in Korea and Vietnam—be so ambiguous and controversial as to defy any precise statement. The life of an unlettered peasant in a foreign country, the value of an American soldier's life, or the payoffs of a research and development project must be considered in many phases of military planning; but they hardly lend themselves to simple or indisputable pricing. Some factors are worth more than their market price indicates.

Another problem is that PPB encourages centralized decision-making (i.e., by officials who assess information relevant to goals, resources, and prospective performance). Yet a prominent characteristic of American government is decentralized decision-making, with representa-

sive fashion, with wealthy families paying disproportionately for the education of students from poor families.[44]

The particular allegations about the merits and faults of the Hansen-Weisbrod argument are less important—for our purposes—than is the demonstration of controversy about the details of a cost-benefit analysis. The assumptions and research strategies of Hansen and Weisbrod—and their critics—have great impact on their findings about costs and benefits and on their budget recommendations.

With these kinds of discrepancies between competing PPB exercises, no policy-maker can accept any of the calculations without question. By seeing the conflict right at the heart of PPB, we should appreciate that it is not yet ready to claim status as the incarnation of rational decision-making. PPB may offer valuable tools for the policy-maker to test certain programs. However, when it enters the political arena, PPB may lend itself to controversy. Each side in a dispute may produce its own assessments of goals, inputs, and outputs and may be forced to argue the merits of each other's assumptions and calculations.

The End of PPB in the National Government

The death of PPB in the national government came with an Office of Management and Budget memorandum of June 21, 1971. No longer were agencies "required to submit with their budget submissions the multiyear program and financing plans, program memoranda and special analytical studies. . . ."

According to one political scientist who followed its life from the beginning: "PPB failed because it did not penetrate the vital routines of putting together and justifying a budget."[45] And yet, features of sophisticated analysis do remain in certain federal units, where voluntary responsibility for their operation was left by the Office of Management and Budget. Moreover, administrators in a number of states and localities, and other countries which took up the reform as it was developed and propagated by the national government, remain convinced of its usefulness.[46] Any summary judgment of PPB is made difficult by the diversity of its evolution in various settings and by the differences in what people mean by "PPB." PPB as a head-on effort to rationalize the budgetary

---

44. Pechman, "Distributional Effects," pp. 361–70.
45. Allen Schick, "A Death in the Bureaucracy: The Demise of Federal PPB," *Public Administration Review* 33 (March/April 1973): 146–56.
46. Allen Schick, *Budget Innovation in the States* (Washington, D.C.: Brookings Institution, 1971).

process has not mastered the full range of difficulties described earlier. Yet, there remain sophisticated procedures for costing certain inputs to programs and of weighing the values of competing goals.

The Congressional Budget Office has adapted sophisticated economic and programmatic analysis to the needs of the legislative branch, in conjunction with an ambitious reform of budget review in both the executive and legislative branches. The Office of Management and Budget has developed "management by objectives" (MBO) which requires cabinet departments and independent agencies to define priority objectives for their programs and to measure progress toward the objectives at various points through the fiscal year. While MBO lacks the elaborate procedures of PPB, it retains the concern of rationalist reforms to improve the calibre of policy-making. As the Ford administration was coming to an end and the Carter administration was assembling its parts, both the executive and legislative branches were inclined to improve their control over the policy issues associated with the budget. As we suggest here and in Chapter 9, however, the executive-legislative competition over policy control is one of the elements that limits the rationality that either can achieve.

SUMMARY

The variety of features both within administrative agencies and coming from their environment, along with the changes that continually occur in these features, complicate the administrator's task. For one thing, this variety makes the prescriptions of rational decision-making impractical.

If an administrator were to follow the standards of the rational model, the administrator would list and assess all goals that appear relevant to the agency's problems and would then do likewise for each of the policies that appeared capable of achieving each of the potential goals. On the basis of all relevant information about the probable advantages and disadvantages associated with each package of goals and policies, the administrator would then select the one best goal-and-policy combination to become the agency's program.

The rational model is widely respected by individuals and groups who comment about government activities. It presents a standard of "right thinking," which asks that officials take every issue into consideration and make clear decisions that can then guide the actions of subordinates. The result promises to be integrated policies that complement rather than conflict with one another. However, administrators who would accept the prescriptions of the rational model find their way blocked by a number of constraints. These constraints are integral to American politics. They reflect the heterogeneity and conflict that are considered—by many writers—components of the democratic process. The finding that they hinder rational policy-making is frustrating, however, and may account for part of the alienation that sets certain citizens —and even some administrators—against the procedures of administrative agencies.

The factors that stand in the way of rational policy-making include the variety of possible problems that can be perceived in an agency's environment; the numerous goals and policies that are potentially feasible; the high cost of information; the personal, ideological, and professional interests of policy-makers; structural disharmonies that generate conflict among administrators or between them and other participants in the policy process; and deviant (bureaupathic) behaviors that occur in administrative units.

In the face of these problems, policy-makers tend to avoid centralized decisions that are announced in an unambiguous fashion. They seek decisions that will be satisfactory rather than optimal. They avoid as many difficult choices as possible. Problems are avoided unless they appear with enough severity to generate tensions in an organization or its environment. Once tensions occur, an administrative unit may use the procedures of mutual adjustment. These include a combination of negotiation among interested parties, flexibility on the part of each protagonist in the face of others' demands, and an expectation that problem-solving will be a continuing process. Mutual adjusters do not seek final solutions to social or economic problems, but they recognize that the perception of problems as well as goals and policies are matters of dispute among reasonable individuals. They provide opportunities for dissatisfied interests to express their demands. It frequently happens that a demand raised and rejected in one context appears later under other conditions and receives some resources from decision-makers.

Another device that comprises some of the requirements of the rational model is a routine—a decision rule that identifies which of numerous inputs officials should take into account and that sometimes specifies how they should respond to specific inputs. Routines appeal to decision-makers because they simplify their choices. By limiting the kind of inputs likely to have an impact on policies, routines also help to stabilize policy and complicate the task of those who demand major innovations. The routines considered in this chapter are incremental budgeting, regional consultations, and the spending-service cliché.

Although routines bring some stability to policy-making, they do not choke off all innovation. As is evident in the strategies used in federal budgeting, participants can innovate within the constraints of a routine. Stimuli associated with national crises (e.g., wars, postwar reconversions, and depressions) have occasioned major departures from routine policy-making. Intergovernmental aids can also generate innovations in the policies of recipient agencies. And occasionally a powerful individual may upset—at least temporarily—the routines of entrenched officials. Moreover, reformers have not resisted the temptation to enhance the components of rationality in existing procedures. Their most recent effort—PPB—recently disappeared from manuals of the national government. Yet, aspects of this reform survive. If "rationality," in the strict sense, does not prevail in policy-making, there is some hope of improving the information employed.

4

Administrative Organization and Administrative Control Units: Structures and Their Intellectual Roots

ADMINISTRATIVE ORGANIZATION AS POLITICAL CONTROVERSY

As we have defined the conversion process of the administrative system, it is outlined by formal structures. It includes those agencies of government that are in neither the executive, legislative, nor judiciary, but that produce the goods and services government provides its citizens. The description of administrative organization is not a simple matter that can be accomplished in the manner of a tourist's guide. Agencies—and their relations with other branches of government—are designed partly by reference to theories that claim to have general application and partly by the politics surrounding the individual programs and the interests that either support or oppose them. Issues of administrative organization erupt prominently over the creation of new government agencies, over the elevation of existing federal units to "cabinet rank," over the transfer of a program from the auspices of one agency to another, over the design of powers that will strengthen or weaken the ability of the chief executive or legislature to control agencies, over a change in procedures that link "line" and "staff" agencies, or over the alteration of budgeting or other devices used to govern administrative units.

The model used most often to describe administrative organizations in the United States is the *hierarchy*. The typical organization chart shows several department heads who are directly responsible to the chief executive and whose own departments fan out beneath them to include several layers of leadership and, ultimately, the personnel who actually provide the services or impose the regulations that are the department's major tasks. The pinnacle of the hierarchy is the chief executive who reputedly exercises control over the department heads and through them reaches the activities of all administrative personnel. However, this simplified hierarchy is so often violated in practice that it hardly qualifies as a model of public administration.

The hierarchy is compromised by several features that weaken the chief executive's control over the department heads and that make the heads (and their own "subordinates") responsible to numerous actors besides the chief executive. Each of these features represents a desire to broaden control of administrative units beyond the interests that would be represented by the chief executive and his appointees. Those wanting a say in the policy-making of administrative units—and willing to violate hierarchical principles—include legislators; the clients of agencies and the interest groups who represent them; employees of the administrative units; and citizen groups who feel strongly about the use of special procedures (e.g., the "merit" selection of employees) for the control of administrative units.

One of the features that violates the model of the hierarchy is the direct popular election of department heads. This device, employed by all of the state governments for at least some of their department heads, is used by most states for the positions of attorney general, secretary of state, auditor, treasurer, and superintendent of public education. These administrators become politicians in their own right and may be independent of the governor in both party membership and policy orientation. At the federal level, the president is not bothered by subordinates who are elected independently; but there are other mechanisms to be coped with that are designed to impede the president's control of administrative departments. One of these is senatorial confirmation of appointees (e.g., cabinet officers and the heads of major agencies). Another is the Civil Service Commission, whose members are appointed by the president, but whose fixed terms of six years signify the concern of the Commission's founders to keep federal hiring outside of the president's control. State and federal legislators also destroy the symmetry of a simple administrative hierarchy by their control over the legal authority and the budgets of administrative agencies, and by their desire to influence specific decisions in certain programs. Legislatures are not content to write general policies and let the chief executive and his subordinates administer their departments accordingly. The history of legislative-executive-administrative interaction has seen countless devices employed by the legislature to retain detailed control over those aspects of program administration that interest them. These devices include specific recommendations in committee *reports* that administrators are expected to follow; detailed questioning during annual budget hearings on the minutiae of program administration; special investigations into the operation of agency field-installations; and statutory amendments designed to prohibit certain practices that legislators have found distasteful. At the federal level, Congress has established under its own auspices the General Accounting Office in order to supervise the expenditures of administrative agencies. This institution—large enough to employ over 5,000 persons and to spend $150 million in 1977—is a staff-arm of the legislature and has the power to question and to disallow individual items of agency expenditure.

Another factor that compromises the model of the hierarchy in administrative organizations is the disinclination of some chief executives to operate in a hierarchical manner. President Franklin Roosevelt often ignored the niceties of hierarchical etiquette. He dealt directly with bureau chiefs without going through their department heads, and he purposely generated conflict within the administration so that the noise of battle would inform him about the issues his subordinates debated. He guaranteed conflict by appointing likely antagonists to positions in which they had to deal intimately with one another. He also divided what appeared to be single jobs into multiple positions so that different officials would contend with one another in their operations. Another device that Roosevelt used to infiltrate the hierarchy was the freewheeling personal assistant. Harry Hopkins was in and out of several formal positions in the Roosevelt administration, but his most important assignments were ad hoc assignments that permitted Roosevelt more direct contact with significant decisions than he would have had if he relied upon the traditional hierarchy.[1] A more recent counterpart of Harry Hopkins was Robert F. Kennedy. In formal position, he was the attorney general in his brother's administration. But he served beyond the boundaries of the Justice Department and was an analyst and advisor in fields of defense, international relations, and domestic politics.

The plurality of governments that join together in order to formulate and implement policies also confound hierarchical principles. "Government" in the United States is actually some 78,000 separate entities—the nation, states, and numerous categories of local authorities—plus countless business firms, not-for-profit organizations and private individuals that work for governments on a contract basis. A later section of this chapter, as well as Chapter 10 on intergovernmental relations, focuses on important dealings among these various entities. At this point,

---

1. See Robert E. Sherwood, *Roosevelt and Hopkins* (New York: Grosset & Dunlap, 1948).

it is important to recognize that there is a great number of governmental and quasi-governmental jurisdictions in the United States and that each has some measure of independence from the others. When national, state, and local officials meet together to produce services in such fields as education, highways, or welfare, no one is clearly the superior or subordinate of another. Relationships among them do not work like a smooth chain of command. There is a great deal of haggling and compromise among officials who feel that they have a right to stand up for the distinct interests of their constituents.[2]

If the hierarchy is not the perfect model for public administrative organizations, there is no single model that serves better. The official charts portray hierarchical lines of authority within and between units at each level of government. Thus, the hierarchy is a useful departure for teaching purposes, even if we begin with the knowledge that it distorts reality. The varieties of administrative organization are numerous and reflect the peculiar turns that have been taken by controversies surrounding individual agencies and programs. We can better understand the varieties of existing organization after we have examined the four intellectual roots of administrative organization. One of the four roots lends its support to hierarchical forms of organization. These roots have not operated in isolation, but they are frequently compromised for reasons of political expediency. Their influence is evident, however, in the administrative units of national, state, and local governments.

INTELLECTUAL ROOTS OF ADMINISTRATIVE ORGANIZATION

Four intellectual roots are prominent in the structures of administrative organizations in the United States. Each is built on the assumption of certain political goals that are inconsistent with goals assumed by other roots. If nothing else existed to insert controversy into the construction of administrative institutions, the attempts to obtain some of the benefits from each of these goals would guarantee that conflict. The four roots are (1) the desire to maintain political accountability in public administration; (2) the desire to maintain the traditional equilibrium among the three constitutional branches of government by preserving the separation of powers and checks and balances; (3) the desire to insure that

2. Vincent Ostrom, *The Intellectual Crisis in American Public Administration* (University, Alabama: University of Alabama Press, 1974).

professional and technical skills are brought to bear on relevant matters of policy formulation and implementation; and (4) the desire to maximize the efficiency of resources by using a hierarchical form of organization.

Political Accountability

The political accountability of public administration is a general principle that includes several tenets and has been pursued in radically different ways. Indeed, there are such sharp controversies between the proponents of different forms of "accountability" that they could be termed distinctly antagonistic approaches to administrative organization. One approach—which can be termed "traditional" by virtue of its historical lineage—maintains that elected officials should have the final say over the activities of administrative agencies. This means that agency programs are defined by laws subject to the approval of the legislature and the chief executive. Moreover, annual or (in the case of many state governments) biennial budget requests are subject to similar law-making procedures and require the approval of the legislature and the chief executive. An element that sometimes accompanies this form of political accountability is executive and legislative control over agency personnel. At the extreme, this has meant both control over individual appointments by the political branches and the insistence that all administrators be contributing members of the party in power. The excesses of "Jacksonian" patronage are no longer evident at the federal level and are decreasingly apparent in state and local governments. Yet for many years, public bureaucracies experienced mass turnover with a change in party control of the executive. Although Jacksonianism is often equated with patronage for the sake of maintaining party strength, it was first presented to the country as an integral component of democratic political theory. President Andrew Jackson felt that the administration had become the possession of an elite class, and he sought to bring it within reach of the common man. He said:

Office is considered as a species of property and government rather as a means of promoting individual interests than as an instrument created solely for the service of the people. Corruption in some and in others a perversion of correct feelings and principles divert government from its legitimate ends and make it an engine for the support of the few at the expense of the many.

The duties of all public officers are, or at least admit of being made, so plain and simple that men of intelligence may readily qualify themselves for their performance; and I cannot but believe that more is lost by the long continuance of men in office than is generally to be gained by their experience.

In a country where offices are created solely for the benefit of the people, no one man has any more intrinsic right to official station than another. Offices were not established to give support to particular men at the public expense. No individual wrong is, therefore, done by removal, since neither appointment to nor continuance in office is a matter of right.... The proposed limitation would destroy the idea of property now so generally connected with official station, and although individual distress may be sometimes produced, it would, by promoting that rotation which constitutes a leading principle in the republican creed, give healthful action to the system.[3]

By now, a series of administrative reforms has all but eliminated the spoils system in the federal civil service and has curtailed it sharply in most state and local governments. Yet several features still testify to the remaining strength of this element in administrative organizations. Senior positions in many public agencies are filled by the chief executive's appointment of "outsiders" brought in from private life, rather than by people who have devoted their careers to the agency.[4] In this way, administration is thought to remain responsive to the wishes of the "people"—either because the elected chief executive makes the top appointment or because the appointees are citizens rather than professional bureaucrats.

A different approach to political accountability is direct client participation in agency decisions. This feature has recently attracted considerable public attention as it has been implemented through community action programs of the U.S. Office of Economic Opportunity. As these efforts began, there was direct clash between the two principal forms of political accountability. Elected officials—especially state governors and local mayors—felt their own control over administrative activities would be undercut by citizen selection of policy-making councils and citizen control over the selection of agency personnel. This was a clear instance of intense political conflict over the design of administrative structures. Elected officials charged that the "extreme" device of citizen participation would not only threaten their own capacity to supervise and control government activities, but it would also put untrained

---

3. Paul Van Riper, *History of the United States Civil Service* (Evanston, Ill.: Row, Peterson, 1958), pp. 36–37.

4. Prominent exceptions are the military and the police, but even in these cases top policy-makers are "civilians" (i.e., nonprofessionals) appointed by a popularly elected chief executive or by a commission that is itself appointed by the chief executive.

and irresponsible persons in control of public resources. They predicted that huge sums would be siphoned off for the support of new "political organizations"; that untrained supervisors would waste resources in poorly conceived and poorly managed programs; and that cadres of new revolutionaries would gain control of these programs and use them to challenge established norms. From the other side, the representatives for citizen participation alleged that existing programs for welfare, health, and education were poorly conceived to assist those people who were most in need and that recipients were the best qualified to formulate policies for their own benefit.

The recent political uproar over citizen participation in administrative systems suggests that this is indeed a revolutionary form of structure; but this is not the case. Several old and respectable government programs include provisions for client control. State programs to license and regulate the professions and trades, for example, usually include members of the regulated group on the policy-making boards. A board of physicians typically oversees the regulation of the medical profession, for example; and boards of barbers, plumbers, or electricians supervise the regulation of their trades. Several of the federal agricultural programs established in the 1930s include boards of farmers that make the crucial decisions about local operations. County committees for agricultural stabilization and conservation, for example, pass on farmers' applications for acreage allotments in the different crops of the region and for federally assisted conservation activities.[5]

Separation of Powers—Checks and Balances

The second intellectual root of administrative structure maintains a separation of powers, or checks and balances. Framers of the U.S. Constitution implemented this mode of organization and established it as a tradition to be followed by the builders of state and local governments. In the federal government, the separation of powers takes the form of a bicameral legislature, a separately elected chief executive, an independent judiciary, and a further division of powers between federal and state governments. Along with these divisions, each branch was given some tools to protect itself against the others: the chief executive was given a veto; the legislature was given the opportunity to override the veto with an extraordinary majority and the opportunity—in the Senate

---

5. Douglas, H. St. Angelo, "Formal and Routine Local Control of National Programs." *Southwestern Social Science Quarterly* 47 (March 1966): 416–27.

—to review major presidential appointments; the judiciary was given a vague grant of authority that it interpreted (in *Marbury* v. *Madison*) as the right to review the actions of other branches for their constitutionality. Finally, the personnel of each branch faced the threat of impeachment if they violated certain prohibitions on their own behavior.

Each of the state governments adopted the separation of powers, or checks and balances, although with slight variations in the nature of individual branches. Indeed, if any general statement can be made about the structures of state governments, it is that they are even *more divided and beset with internal checks* than the national government. In contrast to the opportunities of the president to appoint all the major officers in the administration, each of the governors must work with high-ranking department heads who are separately elected or are appointed by quasi-independent boards or commissions. In contrast to the freedom with which the U.S. Congress can determine its own prerogatives on matters of legislation, most of the state legislatures are limited to short sessions, are prohibited from borrowing sizable funds in a convenient manner, and have numerous other constraints against the types of legislation they may approve (see pp. 261–63).

The pervasive attachment of American constitution-makers to the separation of powers, or checks and balances, has several implications for administrative organizations. *First,* control of administrative units is not given entirely to any one of the constitutional branches. *Second,* this concern to divide the leadership of administration precludes the use of a simple administrative hierarchy in which control of the hierarchy is given to the chief executive. The chief executive must share prerogatives over administration with the legislature and the judiciary. The judiciary hears cases that aggrieved citizens bring against administrators and may void or restrict certain powers that the administrator had exercised. The legislature has many opportunities to affect the structure, procedures, and programs of administration. They include review of new program proposals; periodic review of agency budgets; the approval of key personnel appointments; special legislative investigations into the operation of certain programs; the legislature's ability to initiate (and to pass over the executive's veto of) new programs or to make changes in existing programs[6] and informal arrangements in which administrators seek the approval of key legislators for certain kinds of decisions. *Third,* each administrative unit may be subject to demands from competing superiors. A committee in the upper or lower house of the legislature and the chief

---

6. The Taft-Hartley Act is a prominent example.

executive may send conflicting directives to the administrator. While at times this may benefit the administrator—providing the excuse of conflicting instructions to explain a lack of compliance with any one of them —the conflict between superiors also presents problems for administrators. Each potential superior may have an advocate within an agency; the unit may be affected by internal conflict over the choice of superiors. Multiple loyalties within a department can upset the department head's control over an agency at the same time that they inhibit clear control by either the chief executive or the legislature.

Professional Expertise

Another root of administrative structure seeks to elevate professional and technical competence to secure positions in each agency. This root has had diverse manifestations, some of which have generated severe conflicts with the advocates of contrasting forms of organization. One prominent manifestation is the civil service movement. Several reform organizations have sought to protect federal, state, and local employees from patronage, the spoils system, or political control. Its most prominent success was the Pendleton Act, passed by Congress in 1883 and amended numerous times since then. Over 90 percent of the positions in the federal administration are now covered by merit provisions, as are an increasing number of positions in state and local governments. This has not been an easy process, however, as each major extension has removed patronage appointments from the control of the legislative and executive branches.

Employment on the basis of merit is only part of the more inclusive concern with technical competence. The merit programs merely remove the criteria of partisanship from personnel decisions; they have not—except in quite recent developments—been concerned with the development of recruitment, selection, and training procedures to increase the level of technical competence in administrative agencies. These later movements reflect the increased preoccupation of administrative agencies with programs that require highly trained specialists in the natural or social sciences, or other professions. Yet, this concern with professionalism has its political opponents. The motivation for citizen participation in welfare and education administration comes partly from those who feel that established professions are insensitive to needs of certain clients. Another kind of conflict sees the advocates of hierarchical organization doing battle with those who want professionals in charge of their own administrative structures. When this happens in a university, it is called "faculty" versus "administration." It happens when professionals make individual judgments, based on their training, on what a client needs and this clashes with the principles of hierarchical management that lead a superior to assert agency policies upon the decisions of subordinates. Where the manager and the professional employees do not share similar professional training and norms of service—or where the manager has acquired managerial values since leaving day-to-day work as a practicing professional—the intra-agency clash may find professional workers on one side and management on the other.

Hierarchical Management

Although the administrative hierarchy is often violated due to other "principles" or to the exigencies of special demands, it does have its own intellectual justification. It enjoys the support of a management theory that corresponds closely with some "principles" of managing large private firms. Its proponents describe their work as leading to "the one best way" to organize administrative personnel for the purpose of maintaining control over subordinates and maximizing the efficiency of their performance. This body of theory, responsible for the hierarchical outline evident in the organizational charts of most governments and private business firms in the United States, includes the following principles:

1. Activities should be grouped by purpose, process, clientele, place, or time and made the responsibilities of small units under the direct control of a supervisor.
2. Work units should be organized hierarchically, so that several units are grouped under the control of a single supervising unit (or supervisor) that is subsequently grouped with other supervisors under the control of a yet-higher supervisor.
3. There should be a narrow "span of control," with a limited number of subordinates under each supervisor. In this way, supervisory personnel can give sufficient attention to each subordinate unit or person.
4. There should be a clear "chain of command" and "communications through channels," so that superiors will have full information about the activities of subordinates and be assured that their directives will control their subordinates.
5. Executives should have sufficient authority to appoint and remove their subordinates.
6. Personnel appointments and promotions should be made on the basis of competence with no interference from "politicians" seeking to reward fellow partisans.
7. Executives should control the expenditures of administrative units.

8. There should be sufficient staff services that provide the executive with the information necessary to understand and control the activities of subordinates.[7]

These management principles have enjoyed strong support in the reports of prestigious commissions charged with proposing administrative reforms including the following: President Taft's Commission on Economy and Efficiency; President Franklin Roosevelt's Committee on Administrative Management; and the two Hoover Commissions set up by Presidents Truman and Eisenhower.[8] However, recent investigations have challenged several of their basic assumptions.

We have noted above that certain assumptions of the hierarchy are violated by persons in the executive and legislative branches who wish to exercise special controls over administrators. An increasing body of literature also finds that hierarchical structures face difficulties in private industry, even where there are no outside intruders with the status or power of an elected executive or legislature. The hierarchy is no longer in vogue among organizational theorists who concern themselves with the private sector. Among the major shortcomings of a hierarchy in both a private and a public organization are its failure to account for complex motivations of employees; conflict within administrative units; and the executive's inability to master all the information necessary to control subordinates. For a hierarchy to operate according to design, subordinates must accept their superior's definition of organizational goals. However, employees come to their task with a variety of personal and professional interests.[9] It is no easy task to win their loyalties for any common goal. Indeed, it is often difficult to define the common goal because department heads themselves may not agree with their own superiors on the proper tasks of their organizations. Conflict within a hierarchy may reflect the imperfect knowledge the chief executive had about the department head; the department head's need to compromise

---

7. Albert Lepawsky, *Administration: The Art and Science of Organization and Management* (New York: Knopf, 1949), chapter 8. For the theoretical foundation of hierarchy in bureaucratic organizations, see H. H. Gerth and C. Wright Mills, eds., *From Max Weber* (New York: Oxford, 1946).
8. See Frederick Cleveland and A. E. Buck, *The Budget and Responsible Government* (New York: Macmillan, 1920); Arthur Smithies, *The Budgetary Process in the United States* (New York: McGraw-Hill, 1955); and Barry Karl, *Executive Reorganization and Reform in the New Deal* (Cambridge, Mass.: Harvard University Press, 1963).
9. James March and Herbert Simon, *Organizations* (New York: Wiley, 1958), chapter 2.

Departments

FIGURE 4–1

Executive Branch of the Government

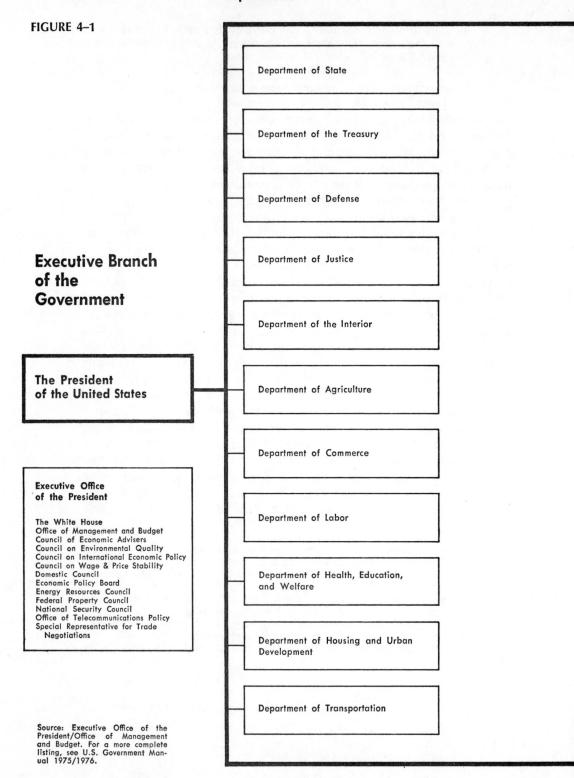

The President of the United States

Department of State

Department of the Treasury

Department of Defense

Department of Justice

Department of the Interior

Department of Agriculture

Department of Commerce

Department of Labor

Department of Health, Education, and Welfare

Department of Housing and Urban Development

Department of Transportation

Executive Office of the President

The White House
Office of Management and Budget
Council of Economic Advisers
Council on Environmental Quality
Council on International Economic Policy
Council on Wage & Price Stability
Domestic Council
Economic Policy Board
Energy Resources Council
Federal Property Council
National Security Council
Office of Telecommunications Policy
Special Representative for Trade
  Negotiations

Source: Executive Office of the President/Office of Management and Budget. For a more complete listing, see U.S. Government Manual 1975/1976.

Selected Agencies, Boards and Commissions

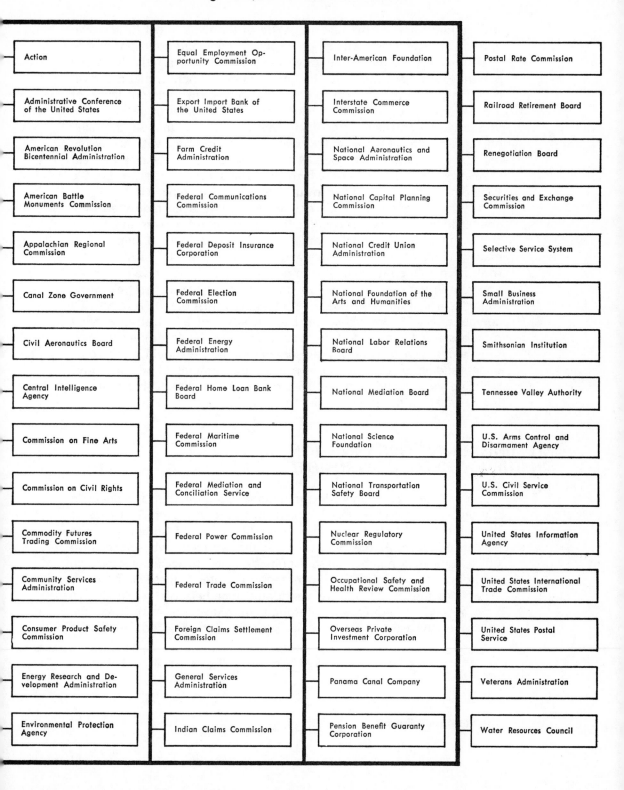

Action	Equal Employment Opportunity Commission	Inter-American Foundation	Postal Rate Commission
Administrative Conference of the United States	Export Import Bank of the United States	Interstate Commerce Commission	Railroad Retirement Board
American Revolution Bicentennial Administration	Farm Credit Administration	National Aeronautics and Space Administration	Renegotiation Board
American Battle Monuments Commission	Federal Communications Commission	National Capital Planning Commission	Securities and Exchange Commission
Appalachian Regional Commission	Federal Deposit Insurance Corporation	National Credit Union Administration	Selective Service System
Canal Zone Government	Federal Election Commission	National Foundation of the Arts and Humanities	Small Business Administration
Civil Aeronautics Board	Federal Energy Administration	National Labor Relations Board	Smithsonian Institution
Central Intelligence Agency	Federal Home Loan Bank Board	National Mediation Board	Tennessee Valley Authority
Commission on Fine Arts	Federal Maritime Commission	National Science Foundation	U.S. Arms Control and Disarmament Agency
Commission on Civil Rights	Federal Mediation and Conciliation Service	National Transportation Safety Board	U.S. Civil Service Commission
Commodity Futures Trading Commission	Federal Power Commission	Nuclear Regulatory Commission	United States Information Agency
Community Services Administration	Federal Trade Commission	Occupational Safety and Health Review Commission	United States International Trade Commission
Consumer Product Safety Commission	Foreign Claims Settlement Commission	Overseas Private Investment Corporation	United States Postal Service
Energy Research and Development Administration	General Services Administration	Panama Canal Company	Veterans Administration
Environmental Protection Agency	Indian Claims Commission	Pension Benefit Guaranty Corporation	Water Resources Council

with subordinates; or the diverse nature of the department head's own interests and the head's willingness to accept some, but not all, of others' goals for the department. Although the theory of managerial hierarchy prescribes strict adherence to the decisions of a superior, that is a difficult standard to obtain. The result of different goals, different levels of motivation, and different loyalties is often the inability of an organization to clearly articulate its goals. It may be easier to "muddle through" on the strength of agreements about specific programs without raising the spectre of long-range goals. A result, of course, is the lack of clear normative standards against which executives can screen prospective subordinates or can test their loyalty once they are employed.[10]

The designers of public organizations have been motivated by a combination of political accountability, separation of powers and checks and balances, professional competence, and principles of hierarchical management. At different times and in different minds, each of these roots have seemed more or less important. There is no *prevailing mode* apparent in the organizational schemes of administrative systems in the United States. If the basic outline is a hierarchy, that outline is frequently compromised. By describing the basic features of administrative organizations at national, state, and local levels, plus the governmental institutions designed to control these organizations, we should reach some understanding of what can happen when four notions of administrative structure coexist and some understanding of the stimuli that motivate the designers of particular administrative units.

ADMINISTRATIVE ORGANIZATION IN THE NATIONAL GOVERNMENT

The hierarchical component in the national administration is evident in the organizational chart that is shown in Figure 4–1. Note that cabinet departments are connected by a heavy black line of authority to the executive branch. At the head of this is the president, whose executive office contains a number of staff units designed to facilitate executive control of the administration. As noted in Chapter 1, these staff units—as well as the president—are considered members of the "executive branch" and therefore external to administrative units. We examine several of the executive staff units later in another section when we

---

10. Charles Lindblom, *The Policy-Making Process* (Englewood Cliffs, N.J.: Prentice-Hall, 1968).

Kennedy, and Johnson, however, spent relatively little time in formal cabinet meetings. They relied heavily on advice received privately from individual members of the cabinet, from officials holding noncabinet posts in the government, and from trusted private citizens. At first, President Nixon appeared to consult his cabinet more frequently than his two immediate predecessors did, but not as regularly as President Eisenhower. Indeed, as part of the general commotion surrounding President Nixon's second term, it became apparent that several members of his cabinet found it impossible to arrange appointments with him.

In their number of personnel and the size of their budgets, the cabinet departments are generally larger than independent offices. However, this difference is not uniform. In 1977, several independent offices —the National Aeronautics and Space Administration, the General Services Administration, the Postal Service, the Veterans Administration, the Environmental Protection Agency, and the Energy Research and Development Administration—had larger expenditures than four of the eleven cabinet departments. The expenditures of the Veterans Administration were surpassed only by those of the Defense, Treasury, Health, Education, and Welfare and Labor Departments. In number of employees, the Veterans Administration is topped only by the Defense Department. In fact, if we were to look at the organizational chart of the Veterans Administration, we would see the indication that its functions are every bit as broad in scope as those of most cabinet departments. Its units deal with services in the fields of education, health, real estate, insurance, and pensions. The agency's principal clientele are veterans of the armed services, plus their dependents, widows, and orphans who qualify for special services. If periodic wars continue, the Veterans Administration will probably remain in business as an important segment of the national government, even if it never attains cabinet rank.

With the exception of those few units that were already established at the time of the Constitutional Convention in 1787 (the Departments of State, War, and Treasury),[11] all of the cabinet departments began their organizational lives as independent offices or as components of other cabinet departments. When they became cabinet departments in their own right, it signified a victory for themselves, for clientele groups, and for other supporters who sought the increase in prestige. It is felt that the increased visibility of a cabinet department gains more support from the White House, from Congress, and from citizens' groups and

---

11. The Department of War was reorganized and merged with the Department of the Navy in 1947 to form the Department of Defense.

helps the agency in getting more legal authority, personnel, and funds. The elevation of some units to cabinet status has been opposed by some members of Congress or interest groups who were apprehensive about the growth of certain programs. Conservatives opposed the elevation of the Federal Security Agency to the Department of Health, Education, and Welfare and the elevation of the Housing and Home Finance Administration to the Department of Housing and Urban Development. The Housing and Home Finance Administration faced an additional hurdle when President Kennedy proposed it for cabinet rank: its administrator, Robert Weaver, semed likely to become the first black in the cabinet.

There has been a spurt in major cabinet alterations since World War II. Table 4–1 records the amalgamation of separate War and Navy departments into the Department of Defense; and the creation of the Departments of Health, Education, and Welfare, Housing and Urban Development, Transportation and Energy. In 1970 Congress approved President Nixon's proposal for the transformation of the Post Office Department into the Postal Service; this marks the first instance of a department's departure from the cabinet. In his 1971 State-of-the-Union Message, President Nixon recommended even more sweeping reform: he proposed to keep the Departments of Defense, State, and Treasury in their

TABLE 4–1
Chronology of Major Alterations in the President's Cabinet

1789:	Departments of State, Treasury, and War created
1798:	Department of Navy created
1814:	Office of Attorney General given cabinet rank
1829:	Postmaster General acquired cabinet rank, although Post Office remained in the Treasury Department
1849:	Department of the Interior created
1870:	Department of Justice created
1872:	Post Office Department separated from Treasury Department
1889:	Department of Agriculture acquired cabinet rank
1903:	Department of Commerce and Labor created
1913:	Departments of Commerce and Labor each given separate cabinet rank
1947:	Department of Defense emerged from an amalgam of War and Navy Departments
1953:	Department of Health, Education, and Welfare created
1965:	Department of Housing and Urban Development created
1967:	Department of Transportation created
1970:	Postal Service created; Post Office Department lost cabinet rank
1977:	Department of Energy created

SOURCE: Adapted from *Congressional Quarterly Weekly Report* 28, No. 25 (June 19, 1970): 1969.

present form, but he wanted to consolidate the remaining seven departments into four: Human Resources, Community Development, Natural Resources, and Economic Development. This proposal raised widespread concern about the "upsmanship" to be given programs and their supporters. Opposition to the change came from interest groups and members of Congress fearful of losing their existing lines of control to program administrators. The formal changes did not occur, but President Nixon sought to achieve some results by naming certain cabinet secretaries to simultaneous positions as White House advisors, with responsibility for matters beyond the boundaries of their own departments. A prominent example was George P. Schultz, whose role as secretary of the treasury and chief economic advisor came to resemble the president's conception of a secretary for economic development. In a related move, Dr. Henry Kissinger served simultaneously as secretary of state, chief of the National Security Council staff, and chief foreign policy advisor to the president.

Within both cabinet departments and independent offices, there have been additional controversies over the placement of units in one agency or another, or over their status in the hierarchy of a certain agency. Some conservation-minded friends of the Forest Service managed to have that agency transferred from the Interior Department to the Department of Agriculture. They argued that the Interior Department was less interested in conservation than in providing resources to commercial foresters and livestock ranchers. Friends of the Children's Bureau sought to have that unit elevated in the hierarchy of its parent agency. They wanted it shifted from a component unit of the Social Security Administration—which was one level below the top leadership in the Federal Security Agency—into a position of its own directly below the top leadership. They wanted it in a position of greater prominence, where it would be more visible, more likely to attract congressional and presidential support, and more able to develop its programs without having them limited by administrative superiors.[12] An early proposal of the Carter administration was to create a new Department of Energy, in order to consolidate and strengthen energy-related programs scattered in several departments and agencies.

While the status of a cabinet member has the appearance of great personal influence, that is not always the feeling inside a secretary's

12. See "The Transfer of the Children's Bureau," in Harold Stein, ed., *Public Administration and Policy Development: A Case Book* (New York: Harcourt, Brace, 1951), pp. 15–30.

office. Secretaries and those close to them describe the frustrations of trying to operate sprawling, complex organizations with a minimum of independent authority. The size and technological sophistication of most departments present some barriers to effective control by someone appointed from outside the organization. Other problems come from the intergovernmental nature of many programs and the secretary's reluctance to become involved with the operating details of state or local agencies. These details may determine the success or failure of a federal program. Other problems for cabinet secretaries come from their relationships with the White House. From the lofty pinnacle of the Oval Office a cabinet department may be lower in priority than other domestic or international issues. Presidential aides in the White House office may exercise detailed control over departmental affairs while the president attends to other matters. Aides—claiming to act in the president's name—may select the undersecretary and assistant secretaries of a department without consulting the secretary who is the nominal superior officer. White House aides also regulate the secretary's opportunity to meet with the president. For a person chosen as secretary on the basis of a prominent background as a governor, corporation president, or prestigious lawyer, it is something of a shock to encounter White House staff members standing in the way of dealing directly with the president, especially when the White House staff takes the shape of brash youngsters in their 20s and 30s.[13]

Aside from the cabinet departments and independent offices, there are several other kinds of organizations that enjoy peculiar relationships with the president, with Congress, and with other actors in the political system. These units exist near the "borders" of the conversion process in the administrative system. They include independent regulatory commissions, government corporations, federally aided corporations, government contractors, plus several additional "hybrids" that defy even a general label. We describe some of these units in order to illustrate the full range of organizational forms that exist in and near the federal administration.

"Independent" Regulatory Commissions

The independent regulatory commissions include units in charge of setting rules and regulating activities in several fields of commerce,

13. Joseph W. Bartlett and Douglas N. Jones, "Managing a Cabinet Agency: Problems of Performance at Commerce," *Public Administration Review* 34 (January/February 1974): 62–70.

transportation, finance, communications, and labor relations.[14] They differ from "normal" departments and offices in several ways, but it is tempting to exaggerate their uniqueness. Each of them is headed by boards of several members instead of by one secretary. Furthermore, fixed terms of commissioners, bipartisanship, and vague guarantees of job protection promise some "independence" from the presidency. Commissioners are appointed for terms ranging up to 14 years; their terms overlap in a way that makes it unlikely that any one president can staff an entire commission with appointees; and the members of each commission must include a "balance" of members with different party affiliations. Members of several commissions cannot be removed by the president except for certain "causes," which include inefficiency, neglect of duty, or malfeasance. These protections do not protect commissions from being made the subject of public instructions by the president, of investigations by Congress, or of budgetary controls by both the president and Congress. Moreover, the fixed terms of commissioners are not foolproof protections against "stacking" a commission by the president. Many commissioners resign before their terms expire and thereby make their posts available to the next appointee of the incumbent president.

The peculiar structure of the commissions seems to fit their often-delicate assignments. They make rules within the broad grants of discretion provided by the statutes, apply their own rules to specific cases, and adjudicate cases where parties appeal the commission's first decision. Because they seem to be more independent of the chief executive than are other agencies, the regulatory commissions take on some of the reputation of judicial bodies. This may win the acceptance of business firms that must endure adverse decisions. The commissions' independence of the president may also lessen the president's concern with their budgets and program development; thus they may become more subject to legislative control. This increases the appeal of regulatory commissions to members of Congress who might otherwise object to government regulation of private industry.

It is possible to exaggerate the uniqueness of the independent regulatory commissions. Other units within cabinet departments or independent offices likewise make rules, apply their own rules to specific cases of business regulation, and hear first appeals from dissatisfied firms. The unit that looks most like an independent regulatory commission—

14. The commissions include Interstate Commerce Commission, Federal Power Commission, Federal Trade Commission, U.S. Maritime Board, U.S. Tariff Commission, Securities and Exchange Commission, Federal Communications Commission, Civil Aeronautics Board, Federal Reserve Board, National Labor Relations Board, and Nuclear Regulatory Commission.

without the peculiar structure of a commission—is the Food and Drug Administration. It is headed by a single administrator who is appointed (and subject to removal) by the president. The FDA regulates the manufacture, advertising, and distribution of food, drugs, and cosmetics, and it determines which commodities or practices should be removed from the market. There is no clear explanation for the trappings of the independent commissions being given to some regulatory units, while others —like the Food and Drug Administration—are indistinguishable from companion agencies within cabinet departments. Perhaps some political contexts lend themselves to the development of elaborate safeguards against presidential dominance of a control mechanism—along the lines of the independent regulatory commission—while others permit regulation by a standard type of agency. (See Chapter 11 for a discussion of Ralph Nader's investigations of independent regulatory commissions and the FDA.)

Government Corporations

Several corporations are wholly owned by the federal government. They are subject to budget and basic policy controls of the president and Congress, but they also enjoy some of the freedoms of private firms. Their activities include banking, insurance, scientific research, electric power generation, land development, and the delivery of mail.[15] Their boards of directors are appointed by the president with approval of the Senate, and they are subject to the formal budget controls of the president and Congress. However, much of their funds comes from the sale of products or services in the private sector. The corporate format is said to permit them to use economic as opposed to political criteria in making their policies about pricing and the nature of products and services.

The businesslike status of government corporations does not protect them from political controversy. The Tennessee Valley Authority began in the 1930s as a major departure for the federal government. It undertook comprehensive programs for conservation, flood control, navigation, and electric power generation throughout the seven-state area that is drained by the Tennessee River and its many tributaries. During

---

15. They include Commodity Credit Corporation, Export-Import Bank of Washington, Federal Crop Insurance Corporation, Federal Deposit Insurance Corporation, Federal National Mortgage Association, Federal Prison Industries, Federal Savings and Loan Insurance Corporation, Panama Canal Corporation, Postal Service, Smithsonian Institution, and Tennessee Valley Authority.

its formative years, the TVA was engaged in controversies with individual landowners whose land would—or would not—be taken for a TVA project; with producers of electricity and fertilizer who felt the TVA would move into their market with an unfair price advantage; and with local governments who felt their tax base was "eroded" by tax-free TVA facilities or by the flooding caused by the TVA dams. One report indicates that the TVA remained controversial long after its establishment. Some of the charges reflect a change in status from a new and revolutionary agency to one which had made enemies by its programs; other charges were almost identical to those of 30 years earlier.

Conservationists in Tennessee and North Carolina accuse TVA dams of spreading pollution and of eliminating wild rivers and trout streams.

TVA developments are charged with providing an unjust advantage to private land speculators. It is alleged that the Authority makes excessive purchases of the land surrounding its reservoirs and sells this land to private developers.

TVA's insistence on cheap coal to run its generating plants is seen as a major incentive for strip-mining operations. It is alleged that TVA does not provide complementary incentives to have the coal industry clean up after a strip operation, replace the terrain to an attractive condition, or control stream pollution.

Local governments in the TVA region continue to charge that its payments in lieu of taxes for inundated lands are inadequate.

Other units of the federal government with overlapping responsibilities have engaged in conflicts with TVA over their mutual jurisdictions. The U.S. Army Corps of Engineers, the Fish and Wildlife Service, and the National Park Service overlap with the TVA on such matters as the development of wilderness areas and streams for navigation, flood control, wildlife, and recreation.[16]

Federally Aided Corporations

Even more ambiguous in their relations with the president and Congress are several institutions labeled "federally aided corporations." Several of these are housed for organizational purposes in the Department of Health, Education, and Welfare. They include the American Printing House for the Blind, Gallaudet College, and Howard University. Ostensibly these are private institutions whose boards of directors, executive officials, and personnel are free from the customary selection by the president and approval by the Senate. However, each institution re-

---

16. See John Egerton, "TVA: The Halo Slips," *The Nation* (July 3, 1967): 11–15.

ceives funds from the federal treasury and submits to annual reviews by the Office of Management and Budget plus appropriations committees. Each defends its peculiar relationship with the federal government by virtue of the socially desirable functions that it performs. Yet these are not the only institutions in the society performing desirable functions; their continued support rests on tenuous agreements with persons having budget responsibilities in the White House, in the Department of Health, Education, and Welfare, and in Congress.[17]

Government Contractors

For the most part members of the "private sector," government contractors serve important supplementary functions for government agencies. They build weapons for the military, construct post offices and other buildings for lease to the government, provide janitorial and protection services for government installations, and conduct research in numerous fields of social and natural science. What some agencies do for themselves, others (or the same agencies under other conditions) hire out to a contractor. Some decisions to contract are motivated by the agency's desire not to tie its funds up in capital construction. It takes less of an outlay for the Postal Service to lease a building than to build one itself. At times, the temporary nature of a program will lead an agency to contract for services rather than to enlarge its own staff. Contractors have some freedoms from federal standards that offer them flexibility in certain aspects of personnel, budgeting, and pricing. In the case of scientific or technical jobs, contractors can pay higher wages and more easily attract talent because of their freedom from the salary scales of the U.S. Civil Service Commission. On other features, however, they are subject to official procedures. Contractors must accept equal-opportunity provisions in hiring and may not segregate their employees on the basis of race. They are also subject to audits by the General Accounting Office and may have details of their expenditures and profits made public by that unit.

Contractors have long existed on the fringes of government and have often aroused controversy. Scandals of profiteering, selling inferior merchandise, and favoritism in the awarding of contracts have been part of American military activities since the Revolutionary War. Now the

---

17. Ira Sharkansky, "Four Agencies and an Appropriations Subcommittee: A Comparative Study of Budget Strategies," *Midwest Journal of Political Science* 9 (August 1965): 254–81.

contract has become a central feature of government, extending to all fields of service and blurring the lines between the public and private sectors. Professor Vincent Ostrom sees the growth of services under contract as a source of diversity and flexibility in the services offered to various publics.[18] Professor Bruce L. R. Smith is no less appreciative of the benefits that may come via contracts, but he is also concerned about the maintenance of control over service-providing units that are not clearly part of the government apparatus.[19]

The mechanism of the contract is infinitely flexible. It invites a great variety of arrangements and numerous justifications for establishing certain activities under contract rather than as an integral part of government. Contracts go to universities, nonprofit institutions, clinics, social welfare agencies, and industrial firms. A contractor's services may be offered directly to a government purchaser, as in the case of research and development ordered by the military; or they may be offered to citizen clients, as in the case of a clinic's medical diagnosis and treatments. The skills purchased by a contract may exist already in government departments, but not in sufficient quantity, in just the right place, or of just the quality for the need at hand. The use of a contract allows the government to avoid dealing with such support activities as the recruitment of personnel, the provision of pension rights, and the maintenance of quality controls over services rendered. In the case of a contract, there is no commitment to the continuation of a project or its personnel beyond the time specified. For some services, like medicine, there is an assumption that quality control and financial accountability can be left in the hands of peer review by established professional bodies. However, exposures of shoddy treatment and inflated bills indicate that contracting authorities must reinforce their usual reliance on peer review with some independent scrutiny of the professionals' activity.

The contract mechanism also serves to link governments for the sharing of specified services. Neighboring municipalities contract with one another for the sale or sharing of police, fire, and library services. Such arrangements allow for larger-scale economies than would be available to any one municipality working alone, as well as providing the opportunity for a community to negotiate for the package of services and costs most attractive to its residents. As in the case of other contracts,

---

18. Ostrom, *Intellectual Crisis.*
19. Bruce L. R. Smith, "The Public Use of the Private Sector," in Bruce L. R. Smith, ed., *The New Political Economy: The Public Use of the Private Sector* (London: Macmillan & Co., 1975).

the lack of permanence offers greater flexibility. Yet, the problems of control are also apparent, as additional organizational boundaries intervene between the citizen and the purveyor of services.

The government contract lends itself to both explicit and implicit uses. Many contracts serve purposes besides those for which they are obviously intended. Federal contracts with university professors for scientific research also funnel money into other features of higher education: (1) to support the graduate students who receive part of their training while apprenticed to the principal investigators and (2) to support the general programs of the university by providing "overhead" money to the universities as part of the research contract. Federal contracts for the construction of public works or military hardware also serve an economic function. On occasion, these contracts are made with a weather eye to levels of unemployment, and specific projects or firms are selected for their likely contribution to economic conditions. Certain firms acquire a vital status as purveyors of critical goods or services—like the Lockheed Corporation, the Penn-Central Railroad, and certain private universities—and governments come to their rescue when they reach the brink of bankruptcy. In these cases, the line between public and private becomes even more vague than in the case of other contractors. The peculiarities of the arrangements both delight those who applaud *flexibile pragmatism* or *muddling through* as principles of government and add to the anxiety of those concerned with the implications of precedent or the maintenance of accountability.

The issue of vital institutions that operate with some assurance of governmental maintenance raises the issue of multinational corporations. The giants among these bodies, for example, General Motors, Standard Oil, Shell, and ITT have greater economic resources than most countries of the world.[20] They are heavily engaged in the private and public sectors of the United States and other countries and have an importance that helps them defy some regulatory efforts of rich and poor countries. At times, it is difficult to know which is the bestower or recipient of contracts, as in the case of Lockheed payments that reached into the royal family of the Netherlands and the Prime Minister's office of Japan, and ITT payments that reached the White House of Richard Nixon. Often the multinationals seem to be the agents of their home countries, and this makes them targets of other populations who fear exploitation. However, the subsidies and payoffs of Lockheed and ITT

---

20. Lester R. Brown, *World Without Borders* (New York: Vintage, 1972), especially pp. 214–15.

suggest that the multinationals are primarily agents for themselves and should be viewed by any government with the same concern for accountability that contracting parties show toward each other in the private sector.

Problems of accountability do not rest only on the shoulders of the government party to a contract. Several kinds of controversy may affect a university, private research laboratory, or business firm that accepts a government contract. Even though the contractor is only partially a member of an administrative unit, some observers will identify the contractor as a part of the policy-making team. Students and faculty members who have objected to the activities of the Defense Department, the State Department, or the Central Intelligence Agency have been militant in their insistence that universities sever their contracts with these units. For similar reasons, industrial firms that make armaments have been picketed by citizens who object to the use of those arms by the military. The status of "government contractor" does not protect an institution from the political disputes that center on the agencies with which it does business. The boundaries of administrative organization are somewhat wider than the departments, offices, and agencies that are officially a part of the administration. Any attempt to assess the impact of government hiring practices, for example, must take account of the equal-opportunity practice standards which apply to federal contractors. And any assessment of the goods and services produced under the auspices of the federal government must include the numerous business firms, research organizations, and universities that do part of their work under government contracts.

Administrative Hybrids

One variety of administrative hybrids was illustrated by the Office of Economic Opportunity. The Office of Economic Opportunity acted very much like other "line" agencies of the federal government in providing services directly to the public and administering grants-in-aid to state and local agencies and to nongovernmental organizations. Initially its major programs were Job Corps, VISTA, and community action programs. What was curious about OEO was its initial placement in the Executive Office of the President. This is generally reserved for staff units that facilitate the president's control over operating agencies. OEO's location in the Executive Office made it a hybrid of administrative and executive features and testified to the fuzziness in the classic administrative concepts of "line" and "staff." As they are customarily used, these refer to administrative units with substantive, service-producing functions (line) or to units with planning, budgeting, or other functions designed to facilitate the executive's control of the administration (staff). The inclusion of the OEO in the Executive Office showed how an organizational innovator can flaunt the hierarchical model and place a unit where it "shouldn't be" in order to facilitate policy-making. There were several reasons for putting an innovative agency, like OEO, in the Executive Office of the President. Its location signaled President Johnson's concern for its programs and provided the agency with some protection from opponents in Congress or among the state and local authorities who were affected by its programs. Its prominent site also made OEO more susceptible to control by presidential aides and, thus, may have provided its opponents with some feeling of assurance that its "radical" programs would be kept under control.

Another kind of administrative hybrid is the presidential commission named to investigate a particular crisis.[21] Examples include the "Warren Commission," named to investigate the assassination of President John F. Kennedy and the "Kerner Commission," named to investigate urban riots in the summer of 1967. These are hybrids in the sense that they contain representatives of numerous sectors of government and private affairs. The Warren Commission was headed by Chief Justice Warren of the United States Supreme Court, and the Kerner Commission by Governor Kerner of Illinois. Presidential commissions typically include members of the federal Congress and administration, prominent officials of state or local governments, and distinguished private citizens. Each also has a staff that carries the burden of interviewing witnesses, taking testimony, and compiling the interim and final reports. At least for the short time of its existence, a commission may represent a considerable investment of human resources. Insofar as the crisis that provoked the commission has sufficient meaning for large numbers of people, commission reports are "important." In the case of the Warren Commission, its importance lay in the publicity given to the alternative explanations for President Kennedy's assassination and in the effort to legitimize the "Oswald-as-single-assassin" explanation. In the case of the Kerner Commission, an important product was the creation in several states and localities of "little Kerner Commissions," which were assigned the task

---

21. Some observers would quarrel with the definition of advisory commissions as "administrative hybrids" and would claim that they are more properly considered in the environment of the administrative system. See the essays in Thomas E. Cronin and Sanford D. Greenberg, eds., *The Presidential Advisory System* (New York: Harper & Row, 1969). See also pp. 253–55.

of discerning local relevance from the major report, making a local investigation, and producing some recommendations. These commissions perform several of the information-gathering and proposal-gathering functions of other units in the administrative organization. They lack any permanence or responsibility for program implementation, but they may have prestige and national prominence. These attributes may warrant the creation of special units partially outside the borders of established agencies.

Each of the units described above exists among—or on the borders of—the administrative organization of the national government. In systems terms, they are components of the conversion process in the administrative system of the national government. Some hold only a tenuous membership as administrative units; this is especially true of the federally aided corporations, the government contractors, and the administrative hybrids. The common link between each of these, however, is the resemblance between their tasks and those of cabinet departments and independent offices; they perform important supplementary tasks or, in some cases, identical tasks as the departments, but under peculiar organizational arrangements.

REGIONAL CHARACTER OF NATIONAL ADMINISTRATION

Although Washington, D.C. is the nation's capital, it does not contain the entire national administration. Only 12 percent of the government's civilian employees work in the Washington metropolitan area; about 83 percent are in various regional and local offices throughout the country; the remaining 5 percent are outside the United States.

The distribution of administrators reflects the decentralized character of the national administrative system. The actual delivery of most services occurs in the field, and much of the discretionary negotiations with state and local governments, private contractors, and individual clients occurs there as well. One justification of decentralization is its convenience to clients. Another is the greater capacity of national programs to adjust themselves to conditions in various parts of the country. And a third lies in the economic appeal of a regional federal office for the city chosen as its site. The offices provide steady payrolls, plus a stream of visitors who patronize local hotels and restaurants. Initially Congress spread these benefits to a large number of cities, with cabinet departments and other administrative units having different boundaries for their regions and different regional capitals. Many units had their southern office in Atlanta, but others used Jacksonville, Charlotte (N.C.), Charlottesville (Va.) Knoxville, Richmond, Birmingham, or New Orleans. A northeastern office may have appeared in Boston, New York, or Philadelphia. Chicago, St. Louis, Kansas City, and the "twin cities" competed for midwestern regional offices, and a western office could be anywhere between Dallas and Seattle.

The dispersion of regional capitals created problems in coordination. While they were conceived initially to save clients a trip to Washington, the regional capitals required state or local officers to make a series of visits to consult with the regional offices of different departments working with related programs in their state or city. At one time, the state of Kentucky was served by the regional offices of Housing and Urban Development in Atlanta; by Health, Education, and Welfare in Charlottesville, Virginia; by the Bureau of Employment Security in Cleveland; by the Bureau of Work Programs and OEO in Washington; and by the Economic Development Administration in Huntington, West Virginia.[22]

In order to combat this dispersion and facilitate coordination, President Nixon directed various units to adopt a uniform system of ten regions with common boundaries and headquarters cities. The favored cities and the regional borders appear in Figure 4–3. However, the president's order initially covered only five units (Labor, HEW, HUD, OEO, and the Small Business Administration), and it is not yet clear how thoroughly these and other regional offices have relocated themselves and their employees from old to new capitals.

ADMINISTRATIVE CONTROL UNITS IN THE NATIONAL GOVERNMENT

At this point in our discussion of the conversion process, it is advantageous to compromise the structure of the "administrative system" by describing several institutions that exist in the environment of the system and serve as control units of the administrative agencies. This description is placed in this chapter—and not in Part Two, along with other inputs to the conversion process—because much of the discussion inherent in

---

22. James L. Sundquist, *Making Federation Work* (Washington, D.C.: Brookings Institution, 1969) p. 276.

FIGURE 4-3

Map of the United States and Outlying Areas, Showing Federal Administrative Regions

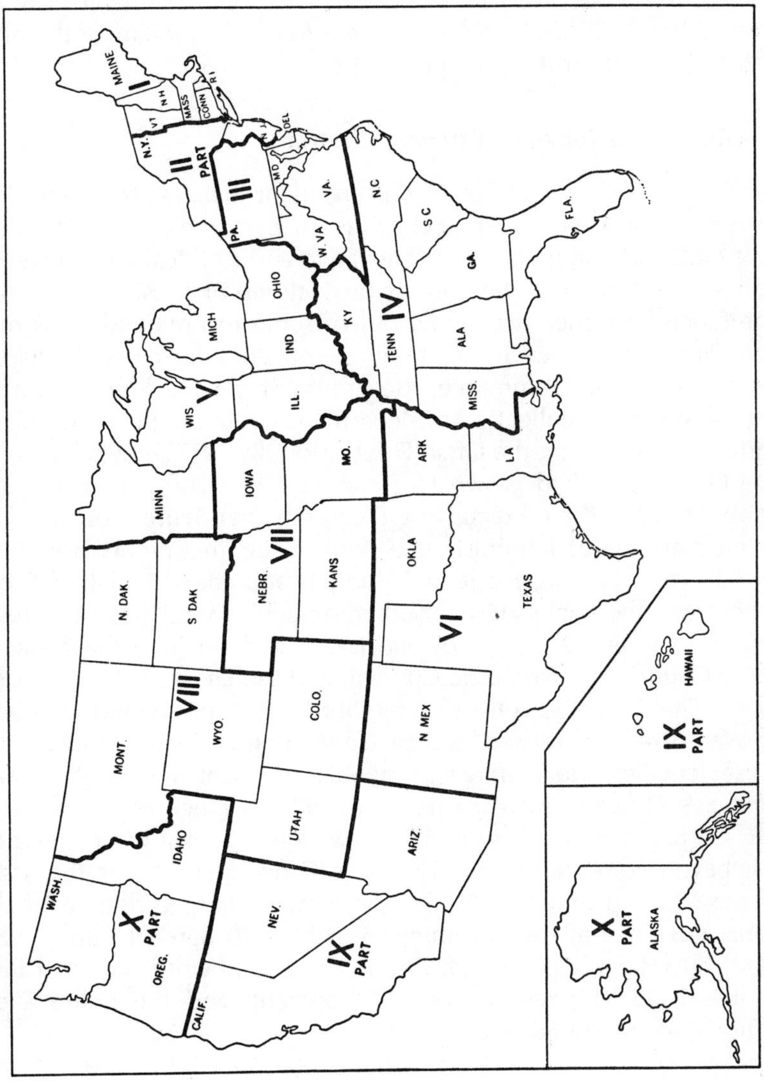

SOURCE: U.S. Bureau of the Census.

the four roots of administrative organization (pp. 104–13) concerns the structure of administrative relations with other branches of government. Institutions that control administrative units at the national level are included in all three constitutional branches of the federal government. One additional institution that does not fit neatly into any of the branches also helps to control the administration.

Executive Units for Administrative Control

The Executive Office of the President includes the control mechanisms of the executive branch, plus an occasional administrative unit (like OEO) whose traits as an innovative and politically sensitive institution seem to require the special protections of presidential proximity. The Executive Office developed out of some recommendations of President Franklin Roosevelt's Committee on Administrative Management. According to that committee, the president needed help in administering the sprawling collection of departments and independent offices that had grown up during the Great Depression. By 1977, however, the Executive Office itself had grown to some 13 units with a total expenditure of about $73 million. Executive Office units that figure most prominently as mechanisms of administrative control are the White House Office, the Office of Management and Budget, and the Council of Economic Advisors. Other units have information-advisory-coordinating responsibilities for a limited range of activities. These include the National Security Council, the Domestic Council, and the Energy Resources Council.

The Executive Office came into great prominence as a result of Watergate and related events. Depending on one's interpretation of those activities, the Watergate scandals represent the zenith or nadir of Executive Office growth, perhaps beyond the range of the chief executive's capacity to control (or to know) what transpired in this domain. It is beyond dispute that the Executive Office grew during the first years of the Nixon presidency. While the total civilian workforce of the national government was declining by almost 10 percent during 1969–73, the White House Office (that unit in the Executive Office most involved in the scandals) grew by some 70 percent, and the entire Executive Office grew by 9 percent.

White House Office

This office includes the most intimate of the presidential aides: the press and appointment secretaries for the president and the first lady;

the president's physician; and other members of his personal staff. More important from a policy-making point of view, the White House Office includes several key individuals, whose formal titles are unrevealing (e.g., special assistant, legislative counsel, special consultant, special counsel, or administrative assistant), but whose duties involve them in bill-drafting, in speechwriting, or in negotiations with legislators, administrative agencies, business firms, or foreign governments. The responsibilities of these assistants are not prescribed in any formal document. The White House Office is a flexible mechanism that permits the president to assign trusted individuals to major tasks of intelligence-gathering, policy-formulation, or negotiation. Before the White House Office was established, presidents were forced to do without some of these services or to employ private citizens (often without compensation) as their informal representatives. Private citizens (or government employees hired in other capacities) still advise the president and perform other services for him. However, the opportunities provided by the White House Office may have lessened the president's need for auxiliary helpers.

Office of Management and Budget

The Office of Management and Budget (OMB) was a creation of President Nixon. As presented to Congress, it was an expanded version of the Bureau of the Budget—long a major element in the Executive Office. The powers inherited by the OMB (as developed by the Bureau of the Budget) are primarily financial, but they also include controls over the substance of departmental programs that reinforce its financial roles. During the annual budget cycle, the OMB screens administrative requests before they are transmitted to Congress. Indeed, it is the OMB recommendations that the Congress considers. The rules of procedure prohibit any administrator from making a financial request of Congress that has not been cleared through the OMB. There is no prohibition against Congress granting more funds for a unit than had been requested by the OMB, so it sometimes happens that an administrator's budget will be larger after the congressional phase. In this event, the OMB has another weapon: it controls the allocation of funds from the Treasury to the agencies. Under certain conditions the OMB can prevent an agency from spending funds in excess of its earlier recommendation. The OMB can use this same control over allocations to hold spending below the level that it had recommended. The OMB has used this authority when economic conditions have signaled a decrease in expenditures or when a change in demand or policy has made certain programs appear less urgent. We return to the controversy generated by these "impoundments" of appropriated funds in Chapter 9.

Outside the financial area, the Office of Management and Budget has certain controls over the statutory authority of each department. Before any agency can formally initiate a request for new legislation, or even reply formally to a member of Congress' inquiry about new legislation, the communication must be cleared through the OMB. One of its units circulates the proposed communication to other agencies whose programs might be affected by the proposal. It then cumulates opinions and defines the implications of the proposal for the "president's program." Without a favorable evaluation from the OMB, a government agency cannot formally support a measure being considered in Congress. The Office of Management and Budget cannot stop Congress from granting powers to departments the OMB had not initially approved. However, the OMB has an opportunity to act again after Congress has acted. While a measure is awaiting presidential action, the OMB circulates it to relevant agencies, gathers their opinions, and then prepares a recommendation for the president's veto or approval.

During its earlier history from 1921 to 1970, the Bureau of the Budget earned a reputation for inviolability from members of Congress and interest groups. Members of Congress respected the Bureau's efforts as a reviewer and distiller of agency budget requests, and they hesitated to impose their own desires on the Bureau in order to avoid setting a precedent that others might follow. Interest groups failed to receive a sympathetic hearing from the Bureau and the rules of their game assigned it an "off limits" label. One manifestation of the political isolation of the Budget Bureau is the obscure nature of its decision processes. The Bureau did not welcome outsiders to study its processes. Despite its obvious importance in the policy-making process, political scientists have learned very little about its activities.[23]

Council of Economic Advisers

The Council of Economic Advisers (CEA) consists of three professional economists, plus a staff of assistants. The three professionals are appointed by the president with the consent of the Senate. The CEA traces its origin to the Employment Act of 1946 and is one of the instru-

---

23. For significant exceptions, see James W. Davis, Jr., and Randall B. Ripley, "The Bureau of the Budget and Executive Branch Agencies: Notes on their Interaction," *Journal of Politics* 29 (November 1967): 749–69; plus other literature cited in that article.

ments established by that Act to give the federal government responsibility for supervising—and hopefully controlling—the nation's economy.[24] The most prominent activity of the CEA is the annual *Economic Report of the President,* which is submitted to Congress early each January. In this and other reports, the CEA assesses the current state of economic growth and stability, balance of payments, and other international matters; appraises likely impacts on the economy from certain policy proposals; and recommends corrective measures for economic distress. The CEA has no direct role in the implementation of policy. However, its advice on the economic implications of current (or proposed) activities affects decisions of the president and the Office of Management and Budget and through them affects activities within administrative agencies.

Domestic Council

The Domestic Council appeared in the Nixon administration. Its design and operations show both the needs and the tactics of bringing together the sprawling resources of the Executive Office to focus on important issues that hitherto had suffered from inadequate attention. The Domestic Council was Nixon's way to get some greater energies focused on priority issues in the domestic sphere. He indicated that the Council was to be a counterpart of the prestigious National Security Council, and he employed symbols of bureaucratic prestige to indicate his intentions. Nixon named one of his most prominent aides—John D. Ehrlichman—as director of its staff and provided some 35 professional and 35 support positions; he located its offices in high-prestige areas—the west wing of the White House and on the White House side of the first floor in the adjacent Old Executive Office Building. In order to make room for the Domestic Council staff, personnel of other Executive Office units were moved to a more distant (and less prestigious) New Executive Office Building.

The formal "members" of the Domestic Council were ranking persons of the administration with roles in domestic affairs. It was chaired by the president and included the vice president, secretaries of agriculture, commerce, health, education and welfare, housing and urban development, interior, labor, treasury, and transportation; the attorney general; the directors of the Office of Management and Budget and

---

24. See Walter W. Heller, *New Dimensions of Political Economy* (New York: Norton, 1967).

ACTION, (American Council to Improve our Neighborhoods); Chairmen of the Council of Economic Advisors and the Council on Environmental Quality; and the administrators of the Environmental Protection Agency and the Veterans Administration. However, the key to the Council was its staff. Its members helped to draft legislation and shape congressional strategy. They also drafted executive orders for the president and directives for agency heads. Given the problems that the Nixon and Ford administrations faced with a heavily Democratic Congress, these kinds of administrative orders were the preferred route for policy changes. There was also public relations work for Domestic Council staff members—drafting policy components for speeches of the president and the other formal members of the Council and supplying materials on policies directly to newspaper and television reporters.[25]

Congressional Mechanisms for Administrative Control

The major control mechanisms in the legislative branch are the committees of the House and Senate, plus a unit that has all the earmarks of an administrative agency but is located in the legislature's jurisdiction —the General Accounting Office. The tools the committees use to control administrative units include statutory provisions, budget limits, formal recommendations in committee reports, and informal suggestions that are made by committee members.

The three types of committees which perform control functions with respect to the administration include legislative committees, appropriations committees, and special committees. In the first category are those committees that consider the substance of program legislation; they govern the scope and detail of departmental activities and typically review departmental operations as they consider proposals for adding to or amending the statutes that authorize the operations. Some programs are authorized for a limited period of time, so legislative committees must reexamine the administrators on a regular basis. The labels of most legislative committees suggest their responsibilities, e.g., Agriculture, Armed Services, Banking and Currency, Education and Labor. However, committee labels do not always specify the activities in the committee's jurisdiction. The Committee on Banking and Currency, for example, considers legislation that is concerned with public housing and

---

25. Raymond J. Waldmann, "The Domestic Council: Innovation in Presidential Government," *Public Administration Review* 36 (May/June 1976): 260–68.

urban renewal.[26] The label of the House Ways and Means Committee bears little resemblance to its major responsibilities—tax legislation and the social security program (i.e., old age, survivors, disability, and health insurance).[27]

The Appropriations Committees have the most regular opportunities for examining administrative activities. Once each year the heads of administrative units present their requests for the coming year and defend these requests (plus their performance during the past year) before subcommittees of the House and Senate Appropriations Committees. It is the subcommittees that make the detailed decisions on matters of appropriation. The subcommittee's budget recommendations are typically passed on unchanged to the full House or Senate by their parent Appropriations Committees.[28]

The subcommittees of the Appropriations Committees are divided according to those departments whose budgets they review; some subcommittees review the budgets of more than one department. The Appropriations Committees grant seniority privileges to the members of their subcommittees, so that the individual members can remain on their subcommittee from one year to the next and accumulate information about agency programs. Subcommittee labels indicate their responsibilities:

- Department of Agriculture and Related Agencies
- Department of Defense
- District of Columbia
- Foreign Operations
- Independent Offices
- Department of Interior and Related Agencies
- Departments of Labor and Health, Education, and Welfare and Related Agencies
- Legislative
- Military Construction
- Public Works

---

26. A link between the committee's label and the substance of housing–urban-renewal lies in the ingredients found within much of this legislation for financing provisions, the role of lending institutions, and the guarantees on loans that are provided by the federal government.

27. The link between tax and social security legislation lies in the provisions for financing the social security program—a special payroll tax.

28. See Richard F. Fenno, *The Power of the Purse: Appropriations Politics in Congress* (Boston: Little, Brown, 1966).

- Departments of State, Justice, and Commerce, the Judiciary, and Related Agencies
- Departments of Treasury and Post Office and the Executive Office

The committee structure of Congress is not static. It changes as members perceive new developments that require their attention. At times, Congress establishes special committees for the purpose of investigating certain institutions or events. A classic example was the committee that investigated the Japanese attack on Pearl Harbor. The committee's voluminous reports and conclusions are cited as justification for "preparedness" policies followed by the military in the later periods; and the reports had a direct effect on the careers of individual officers. In Chapter 9, we describe the activities of the Congressional Budget Committee and its staff arm, the Congressional Budget Office. These were created in 1974 to strengthen congressional control over the budget.

The General Accounting Office (GAO) is the principal auditing unit of the federal government. Although the chief officer of the GAO (the comptroller general) is appointed by the president, the term of office (fifteen years) guarantees considerable independence from the executive branch. The reports of the GAO are made to the presiding officers of the House and Senate, and it is formally responsible to these institutions.

Because of the role that spending plays in administration, the GAO is in a crucial position to enhance the legislature's control over the administrative activities. The GAO has auditing responsibility both for all expenditures of the federal government and for the spending of federal funds by state and local agencies that receive grants or loans. This is an enormous task; the GAO has simplified it by letting the operating agencies audit their own expenditures under approved procedures. The GAO reserves the right to disallow Treasury payment for any expenditures that are not within the provisions of appropriations acts. Moreover, the GAO makes extensive studies—either on its own initiative or at the request of Congress—of administrative procedures. Where it finds these practices to be ineffective, inefficient, or uneconomical (but not necessarily illegal), it makes a report to Congress and proposes reforms (see pp. 288–94).

Judicial Mechanisms for Administrative Control

The control mechanisms of the judiciary differ from those of the executive and legislative branches in their relative passivity. The federal judiciary does not seek out those instances of administrative behavior that it wishes to stimulate or curtail. This is not to say that the courts are weak partners or that they exercise no choice over their involvement in administrative control. It is the nature of the federal judiciary that it waits upon a case being brought to court by a party who considers himself wronged by an administrative decision. Then, depending on circumstances, the court's decision may be a narrow opinion that is relevant for only one instance, or it may be a sweeping judgment that governs administrative actions in many similar instances.

The basic units in the federal court system are the federal district courts. Their jurisdiction covers most of the problems raised by administrators' decisions. There is at least one district court in each state, and another in the District of Columbia. Citizens bring cases to the federal district court if they feel a federal administrative action is not consistent with the statutes, if they feel the statutes that underlie an administrator's actions are inconsistent with the Constitution, or if they feel the actions of a state or local administrator are inconsistent with the federal statutes or Constitution. There are also special courts that address themselves to limited concerns. These include the Court of Claims, which is concerned with compensation for the taking of property, with construction and supply contracts, and with the salaries or perquisites of government employees; the customs court, which is concerned with actions arising under tariff laws, reciprocal trade agreements, and other matters dealing with imported goods; the Court of Customs and Patent Appeals, which reviews certain decisions of the Customs and Patent Courts; and the Court of Military Appeals, which is the final appellate court for military court martials. The Tax Court operates as an independent agency in the executive branch, but it functions in much the same way as a judicial unit. It tries and judges controversies arising between taxpayers and the commissioner of internal revenue. The decisions of the Tax Court, like those of other specialized courts and the federal district courts, are subject to review by higher units in the federal judiciary, i.e., by the courts of appeals and/or the Supreme Court.

The Civil Service Commission

The Civil Service Commission consists of three commissioners and an extensive staff whose functions are to formulate personnel policies for administrative departments, to supervise the implementation of these policies by the departments, and to perform some personnel services for the departments. In many state and local governments (and in national governments of other countries), the personnel function is assigned to the chief executive. In the U.S. government, however, the Civil

Service Commission grew out of a 19th-century reaction to the excesses of the spoils system. The reformers of that time established the principle that control over federal personnel policies should be isolated from the chief executive. The Commission is not affiliated with either the executive, legislative, or judicial branches of government. The president appoints the commissioners, but no more than two of the three commissioners may be members of the same political party; moreover, their terms of six years each are staggered so that no president can fill more than two of the seats in one term (barring the premature retirement or death of a commissioner). We shall leave a further discussion of personnel procedures until Chapter 5. At this point, however, it is appropriate to list the principal activities of the Civil Service Commission and, thereby, to show the scope of controls that it exercises over administrative units.

1. Recruiting and examining candidates for positions in the departments;
2. Developing standards to be used by the departments for the selection, classification, training, promotion, and dismissal of employees;
3. Developing standards for employee safety procedures, health and life insurance, vacation provisions, and retirement plans;
4. Developing employee incentive programs to be used by the departments;
5. Supervising the departments' use of the standards and procedures that have been approved by the Commission;
6. Enforcing provisions of the Hatch Acts that limit the political activities of government employees;
7. Adjudicating the appeals of individuals and agencies that involve rights and interests of federal employees arising under laws, rules, or regulations administered by the Commission; and
8. Examining and making recommendations about the departments' efficient use of their personnel.

In dealing with these various external controllers of administrative units, we should not assume that they are the sole—or even the primary—instruments of control. The size and scope of administrative activities in the government of the United States and in the larger states and municipalities, plus the ranks of contractors operating on the fringes of the administrative units, exceed the capacities of courts, legislatures, and chief executives. Much of what passes for administrative control remains in the hands of administrators themselves. We look at this topic again in Chapter 6 and deal with administrative management and self-control.

ADMINISTRATIVE ORGANIZATIONS OF STATE GOVERNMENTS AND THEIR CONTROL MECHANISMS

In their gross outlines, the administrative organizations of state governments and their executive and legislative controls resemble those of the national government. Each has a number of departments that administer the major programs of the state. The structures of most resemble a hierarchy that culminates in the governor's office. Also, as in the case of the federal government, there are numerous compromises with hierarchical principles. As with the federal hierarchy, these compromises reflect the intellectual roots of political accountability, the separation of powers and checks and balances, and professional competence, as well as particular concerns relevant to each program. What distinguishes the administrative structures of state from federal governments is the extent of these compromises. The architects of state governments have been hypersensitive to the notion of political accountability and to the principle of separation of powers, or checks and balances. The results show themselves in the top levels of administrative departments and in governors and legislators whose controls over administrative units are weaker than their counterparts in the federal government.

The separation of powers, or checks and balances, and political accountability are highlighted in most state governments by severe limitations on the authority of the chief executives to govern their administrations. This takes the form of direct elections for the heads of major departments, the selection of other department heads by boards or commisions over which the governor has only partial control, the governor's obligation to share budget-controls with individuals who are not directly responsible to him or her, and more severe restrictions on the governor's tenure than those faced by the president.

In over half of the states, separately elected persons hold the following positions: attorney general, treasurer, secretary of state, auditor, and superintendent of education.[29] Other major appointments are made by boards or commissions (over whom the governor has limited power of participation or appointment). Because governors have little direct

---

29. This section on state administrative units and their control mechanisms relies on Joseph A. Schlesinger, "The Politics of the Executive," and Thomas R. Dye, "State Legislative Politics," both in Herbert Jacob and Kenneth N. Vines, eds., *Politics in the American States* (Boston: Little, Brown, 1971); tabular materials presented in Council of State Governments, *The Book of States, 1964–65* (Chicago: Council of State Governments, 1964); and John G. Grumm and Calvin W. Clark, *Compensation for Legislators in the Fifty States* (Kansas City, Mo.: Citizens Conference on State Legislators, 1966).

control over several important department heads, there is a high probability of internal tension and discord in the formulation of state policy. At times, the tensions break out in dramatic relief. During a period of party division between Republicans and Democrats in Wisconsin's legislative and executive branches, the Republican treasurer refused to honor the salary voucher of a man appointed to a state commission by the Democratic governor. Because the Republican attorney general also opposed the governor on this appointment, the "chief executive" had to obtain private legal counsel in order to press his case within the administration.

The budget powers of most governors are woefully inferior to those of the national chief executive. Whereas the president formulates the administration's budget with the assistance of an expert Office of Management and Budget headed by his own appointee, several governors must share budget formulation with persons who are politically independent. In Florida and West Virginia, the governor chairs a budgeting board that includes the separately elected secretary of state, comptroller, treasurer, attorney general, superintendent of public instruction, and commissioner of agriculture. In Mississippi, North Dakota, and South Carolina, the governor is chairman of a group containing separately elected administrative heads, plus the chairmen of the legislature's finance committees and members of the legislature named by the presiding officers. The governor of Indiana has only indirect access to the formulation of the budget as the governor's appointee sits on a board with legislators appointed by the presiding officers of the House and Senate. In 13 other states, the governor works with a chief budget officer who is either separately elected or chosen by the legislature or Civil Service Commission.

In about half of the states, the governor's tenure is restricted: governors cannot succeed themselves in 13 states, and another 12 states limit the governor to one reelection. This tenure barrier may limit the expertise the governor develops and restricts bargaining power with the legislature. When it is clear that the governor's term will soon end, individual legislators may be less inclined to accept gubernatorial persuasion. A study of state budgeting in Illinois summed up the financial powers of the governor with a crisp analogy:

The budget document may be compared to a huge mountain, which is constantly being pushed higher and higher by underground geologic convulsions. On top of the mountain is a single man, blindfolded, seeking to reduce the height of the mountain by dislodging pebbles with a teaspoon. That man is the Governor.[30]

The institutions that restrict the governor's control over the state administration are mirrored in further restrictions on the legislature's controls. State legislatures lack several of the features that enable the federal Congress to supervise and regulate administrative provisions: these include strong committees bolstered with seniority provisions and staff units that can work full-time on the tasks of administrative oversight.

In the legislatures of some states, committees are weakened by procedures that allow relatively new and inexperienced members to occupy chairmanships. The lack of a seniority system means that committee assignments and chairmanships are up for grabs at the beginning of each session. At one time, 76 percent of the committee chairmen in the senate of Alabama, 50 percent in the senates of Maryland and Kentucky, and 43 percent in Georgia had only one previous term of experience. In the lower houses of state legislatures, there was even less of a tendency for chairmen to be senior members; 50 percent of the chairmen in Vermont, 44 percent in New Hampshire, 100 percent in Alabama, 83 percent in Kentucky, and 43 percent in Montana, Tennessee, and Nevada had no more than one previous term in the lower house.[31] Without seniority provisions, state legislatures are unlikely to develop any expertise among their members. Where committees do not provide tenure and an opportunity for members to learn their jobs, they are likely to depend heavily upon the recommendations of administrative agencies.

The lack of viable seniority provisions in state legislatures reflects the unattractive nature of state legislatures and the high turnover of their members, as well as the lack of effort to build strong legislative institutions. The prestige, salary, and perquisites of state legislators are markedly inferior to those of members of Congress; and a turnover rate of 40 percent (much of it voluntary) is not unusual. Only 12 states paid their legislators $10,000 per year as of late 1973. The expense allowances and the clerical and professional staffs of legislators are similarly inadequate. In several states, the legislators have no office or secretary of their own. Few of the states provide their legislators anything like the expertise available to U.S. congressmen in the form of committee staffs or the General Accounting Office.

---

30. Thomas J. Anton, *The Politics of State Expenditure in Illinois* (Urbana: University of Illinois Press, 1966), p. 146.

31. G. Theodore Mitau, *State and Local Government: Politics and Processes* (New York: Scribner, 1960), p. 29.

State legislatures are restricted further by the length of time they are permitted to sit and by the nature of decisions they are allowed to make. Only 9 of the 50 state legislatures can stay in session for as much as four months every year without going through procedures to call a special session. In contrast, Congress faces no limitation on the length of its sessions other than its members' own endurance. Except for election years, the recent sessions of Congress have been almost year-long. In their dealing with budget policy, many state legislatures face difficult requirements that do not present themselves to Congress. While Congress can decide about expenditures separately from revenues (with the federal government's borrowing power making up for the deficit), the constitutions of several states require that expenditures not exceed projected revenues. In some states, additional restrictions also prevail. The legislatures of Maryland and West Virginia may reduce the funds that the governor recommends for any agency, but they may increase only those recommended for the legislature or (only in West Virginia) the judiciary. In Nebraska, a simple majority may reduce the governor's recommendations, but a three-fifths vote is necessary to increase them. In Rhode Island, any increases voted over the governor's recommendations must be covered by revenue estimates or existing surpluses or by additional financing enacted along with the budget.

The large number of administrative systems in state governments permits the use of comparative analysis to determine what effects different components of the administrative system may have upon each other. The literature is still limited, and the available findings pertain to few aspects of administrative systems. There are some findings, however, about control mechanisms that the governor can exercise over administrative agencies and about the power that these give the governor vis-à-vis policies.

One study of state budgeting found the governor's control over the appointment of agency heads, the potential for tenure, and the veto power have some bearing on gubernatorial influence over appropriations. Where the governor has substantial powers of appointment, the governor's own budget recommendations are more honored by the legislature than where there are many agencies headed by separately elected executives. The governor's appointment authority seems to give some measure of control over the demands of the agency and its tactics in the legislature. When the agency is headed by the governor's appointee, it lacks a separate base of political power, and it seems less able to pursue funds beyond those provided in the governor's budget. The governor's potential for tenure also provides strength with the agencies and in the legislature. When the governor is unhindered by the state constitution or by statutes from another term in office, the governor may remain for some time as a dispenser of patronage and a formulator of policy. Under these conditions, the governor's budget is more likely to pass the legislature without substantial deletions or additions. The governor's veto power seems to help in dealing directly with agency requests. Where the veto power is strong (i.e., where the governor can veto individual items in a budget and where it takes a large majority in the legislature to override the veto), the governor is better able to hold down agency requests for budget expansion.[32] The simple existence of strong veto powers may warn assertive agencies that resistance to the governor's wishes will not save them from eventual control.

During the same period of growth in the size and powers of the Executive Office of the President (1968–72), numerous changes in state governments also enhanced the governor's position. The 1972–73 edition of *The Book of the States*[33] records that more than 30 states had studied reorganization recently, and that some had completed substantial reorganizations in the preceding five years. The dominant pattern gave more power to the chief executive by consolidating departments; by permitting the governor to appoint more administrative heads; by allowing the governor through an executive order to further reorganize the administration, by extending the term of the governor, by removing limitations against successive terms in office, by providing a transition staff for a governor-elect, and by centralizing various revenue, budgetary, and expenditure controls under the governor's authority. With the advent of Watergate, however, these changes seemed to stop. An executive-oriented reorganization in Wisconsin bogged down in the legislature, barely one year after the same governor won the integration of higher education sought unsuccessfully by several of his predecessors. The only change in circumstances was the awareness of the national scandal and the problems that may occur when a chief executive becomes too powerful.

ADMINISTRATIVE ORGANIZATIONS OF LOCAL GOVERNMENTS AND THEIR CONTROL MECHANISMS

Local governments present even more diversity in their administrative systems than do state governments. In part, this reflects the great number

---

32. Ira Sharkansky, "Agency Requests, Gubernatorial Support, and Budget Success in State Legislatures," *American Political Science Review* 62 (December 1968): 1220–31.
33. Council of State Governments, *The Book of the States, 1972–73* (Chicago: Council of State Governments, 1972).

of local governments, the diversity of their economic and social characteristics, and the diversity of their legal responsibilities. There are approximately 78,000 "local governments" in the United States, with almost 3,200 municipalities having populations in excess of 5,000.[34] The diversity in local administrative systems also reflects the influence of the several intellectual roots of administrative structure we described earlier. Advocates for each of these roots express their desires with respect to local administrative organizations. Conflicts in local politics also play their part, as do the requirements of state laws and constitutions. In Chapter 10, we discuss several varieties of administrative units that provide services within metropolitan areas. Here we limit our attention to some prominent categories of executive and legislative forms in municipal governments. They are relevant for the kinds of controls they exercise over local administrators.

The form of municipal government that bears the closest resemblance to national and state governments includes a single elected executive and an elected legislature. Among these "mayor-council" cities, there is great variety in the powers assigned to the executive and to the legislature. However, executive and legislative bodies generally share control over the local administration. Department heads are typically appointed by the mayor or by commissions appointed by the mayor. The mayor generally compiles the budget requests of the departments and submits recommendations to the council.

Two forms of local government are most interesting for their departure from the models set by the national and state governments: the council-manager government, with an appointed professional executive, and the commission form of government, where a small group of elected officials serve both executive and legislative functions. The council-manager type represents greater attachment to professional expertise than other administrative forms of national, state, or local governments. It is found in about 40 percent of the cities of over 5,000 population and most often in cities of 25,000–250,000 population; over half of the cities in this class have appointed city managers. In the class of the largest cities, however (over 500,000 population), less than 20 percent have managers. The complexity of social and economic problems and the intensity of political demands in very large and heterogeneous cities

---

34. "Municipal" governments provide general government services to a city, town, or village; they are distinguished from "special-district" local governments which provide only a limited range of services, generally defined by their title (e.g., school or sewage districts). Counties are the other principal type of local government.

may require a government that permits politicized demands to filter through the executive as well as the legislature.[35]

In most manager cities, the appointed executive is responsible for the selection of department heads, the preparation of the budget for submission to the council, and the general management of the administration. One appeal of the manager form of government is the opportunity for a city to hire a professionally trained executive who is familiar with the technical problems of municipal services. At one time, the manager was considered isolated from matters of policy. Now, it is recognized that acts of budget preparation and personnel selection are intimately involved with matters of policy. A manager enters policy matters both in making recommendations to the council and when exercising the discretion assigned by the council. Successful managers must deal skillfully with the politicians in the city council and with the citizens' groups that urge policy changes on the city.

Some research finds tendencies for manager-governed cities to differ from mayor-governed cities in the kinds of policies they enact. Large population groups seem to exercise less influence over policy decisions where there is a city manager. This kind of structure is, by design, somewhat isolated from the special demands of political parties or distinct population groups. In contrast, government based upon the direct election of the chief executive is designed to bestow power on those groups who can muster support at the polls.

There is also lower "expenditure effort" (expenditure as a percentage of personal income) in communities governed by a city manager than in communities governed by an elected mayor.[36] This has been interpreted to mean that manager-governed structures occur in business-minded, conservative communities and that such structures work against high taxes and expenditures. Yet, a study of school-board expenditures finds the highest spending in communities governed by city-managers.[37] It is tempting to see some connection between city-manager governments and a policy emphasis on education. However, differences in research techniques limit any direct comparisons between the studies.

A city-commission form of government consists of from three to

35. Robert L. Lineberry and Edmund P. Fowler, "Reformism and Public Policies in American Cities," *American Political Science Review* 61 (September 1967): 701–16. See also Robert L. Lineberry and Ira Sharkansky, *Urban Politics and Public Policy* (New York: Harper & Row, 1974), especially chapter 4.

36. Lineberry and Fowler, "Reformism," pp. 701–16.

37. Thomas R. Dye, "Governmental Structure, Urban Environment, and Educational Policy," *Midwest Journal of Political Science* 11 (August 1967): 353–80.

seven commissioners, each of whom is popularly elected. One commissioner receives the title of mayor, but the mayor's duties are seldom more than ceremonial. The entire commission sits as the local legislature; and individual members serve also as the heads of major departments. This form of government is not widely used and seems to be declining in popularity. Less than 8 percent of cities of over 5,000 population have commission governments, and only one of the 27 cities over 500,000 population has a commission government.

GROWTH OF ADMINISTRATIVE UNITS IN THE 20TH CENTURY

We have seen that administrative structures are neither uniform nor static. They reflect the influences of four different intellectual roots and of demands for "special considerations" made in behalf of particular programs. Now we shall examine dramatic changes in the overall nature of administrative activities, as reflected by changes in their economic resources. Agencies have grown in magnitude, and new agencies have been created in response to increases in population, to new demands for public services, and to certain traumas that have generated widespread dependence on government services.

Before we can assess the growth of administrative units, we must agree on some rules of measurement. Several events have influenced the meaning of resources used by agencies and, thus, confound the inferences we can make. We measure the resources of administrative units by reference to government expenditures.[38] We cannot overlook the obvious facts that expenditures in raw dollars increase partly to provide fixed activities to an increasing population and partly because inflation diminishes the purchasing power of each dollar spent. By correcting expenditures for population increases and inflation, we avoid a gross exaggeration of growth in government bureaucracies. Between 1932 and 1975, uncorrected spending figures for the total of federal, state, and local governments increased by 4,386 percent: from $12.4 billion to $556.3 billion. During the same period, however, spending in *constant dollars* (at the 1954 level) *per capita* increased only 422 percent: from

---

38. A relatively small proportion of government expenditures support the legislative, judicial, and executive branches of government. The 1977 federal budget showed $1.4 *billion* in outlays for the legislative and judicial branches and for the Executive Office of the President. The bulk of the remaining outlays—$392.8 *billion*—were to be made by the administrative units.

$252.73 to $1,319.93.[39] We can also distort the appearance of growth at the federal level by failing to take account of the tremendous increase in the nature of responsibilities peculiar to the federal government. If our goal is to understand the factors that affect the resources given to federal, state, or local administrative agencies to operate the services they provide in common, we must exclude federal expenditures for defense, international affairs, space exploration, the postal service, and interest on the national debt. During the 1932–75 period, for example, spending for these five functions increased from 30 percent to 42 percent of the federal budget.

The figures shown in Tables 4–2 and 4–3 permit several kinds of analysis. In order to identify changes in the proportion of resources assigned to administrative units at federal, state, or local levels of government, we can use the percentage of spending for *common functions* made by federal, state, and local governments. To identify changes in the total resources made available to administrative units, we can use per capita expenditures in constant (1954) dollars.

Several patterns are evident in the records of administrative resources. First, total levels of expenditures have increased over the period from 1932 to 1975. The increase is much less, however, if we remove the activities of the federal government that are concerned largely with international and military activities. Second, the events of depression, war, and postwar reconversions seem to have triggered sharp spurts or lags in certain kinds of activities. Third, each of these major events had a different effect on the administrative systems of federal, state, and local government.

Total spending shows its greatest increases during the Depression, World War II, and the Korean and Vietnam conflicts.[40] The spending increases of the Depression were greatest during the 1934–36 period. Natural resources and public welfare accounted for much of this increase. During those years, federally aided programs were begun or enlarged for surplus commodity distribution, wildlife restoration, soil conservation, support for grazing lands, price parity, old age assistance, aid to families with dependent children, aid to the blind, and child welfare.

---

39. This section relies on Ira Sharkansky, *The Politics of Taxing and Spending* (Indianapolis: Bobbs-Merrill, 1969), Chapter V.

40. The years used to mark the beginning and end of the Depression, World War II, and the Korean and Vietnam conflicts are governed to some extent by the availability of data. The years of the Depression are considered to be 1932–40; World War II (including the prewar mobilization) is 1940–44; the Korean conflict is 1950–53; and the Vietnam war 1965–72.

TABLE 4–2

Expenditures of All American Governments, 1902–75

| | Total | | Common-Function | |
	Expenditures per Capita in Constant Dollars	As Percentage of GNP	Domestic Expenditures per Capita in Constant Dollars	As Percentage of GNP
1975	$1,319.93	37.1%	$761.11	21.4%
1972	1,218.48	34.5	621.43	17.6
1967	727.02	32.6	388.39	14.6
1965	631.91	30.0	343.36	13.6
1955	648.30	25.6	256.48	11.0
1953	701.49	30.1	235.21	10.1
1950	536.00	24.7	250.55	11.6
1944	1,253.02	52.0	211.47	8.8
1940	341.94	20.3	239.91	14.2
1936	297.09	20.3	233.52	15.9
1932	252.73	21.3	177.18	14.9
1927		11.7		8.2
1922		12.6		8.1
1913		8.0		5.7
1902		6.9		4.6

SOURCE: U.S. Bureau of the Census, *Historical Statistics on Governmental Finances nd Employment, U.S. Census of Governments, 1967* (Washington, D.C.: U.S. Government Printing Office, 1969) vol. 6(5); and U.S. Bureau of the Census, *Governmental Finances in 1974–75* (Washington, D.C.: U.S. Government Printing Office, 1976).

During World War II and the Korean conflict, there were sharp increases in total spending, but there was a decline in resources for domestic activities, especially in state and local governments. The decrease reflected scarcities brought about by the military mobilization. Manpower, capital equipment, and materials became less available for civilian purposes and precluded many opportunities for government agencies to pursue their activities at previous levels. There were sharp wartime declines in the percentages spent for public welfare and education. These reflected reduced demands for services. Reductions in welfare payments occurred with increases in employment and wage levels. Reductions in education reflected wartime drains on teaching staffs and college enrollments and, perhaps, the feeling that investments in education must wait until hostilities end.

After the wars, the availability of manpower, capital equipment, and materials, plus the backlog of needs for repairs and new facilities, spurted increases in government spending and employment. States and localities increased tax rates in order to meet their needs, and the federal government responded with increased financial aid. Significant new federal programs begun during the postwar years included aid for federally impacted school districts, national defense education, and interstate highways. Education and highways benefited most during the years immediately following World War II; both fields almost doubled their share of total spending during 1944–50. By the 1960s, the baby crops of the 1940s and 1950s were putting pressure on a wide range of government services. They—and now their children—have required vastly increased activities in the fields of elementary, secondary, and higher education, hospitals, correctional institutions, recreational facilities, and highways.

A different pattern emerged during the years of the Vietnam conflict. In contrast to the earlier wartime periods, domestic spending continued to grow. There was a "war on poverty," as well as a war in Southeast Asia. Public higher education, in particular, felt the onslaught of a population boom generated by earlier wars. Administrative systems of national, state, and local governments acquired new programs and funds. The increases in both domestic and military spending may have reflected the greater size of the economy or the lesser relative cost of the Vietnam conflict compared to World War II and Korea. No matter what the explanation, the United States bought lots of guns *and* butter during the 1965–72 period.

The Depression, wars, and postwar reconversions had different effects on the administrative systems of federal, state, and local governments. Table 4–3 shows the division of resources (spending for common domestic functions) among the three levels of government at selected years during the 1902–75 period. The resources of the federal government increased most dramatically during the Depression and during World War II. From 1932 to 1944, federal spending increased from 14 to 58 percent of the total expenditures. This change reflects a number of factors, including the relative isolation of the federal government from economic catastrophe, its capacity to obtain tight resources during periods of wartime scarcity, and its responsibility during wartime for many domestic programs that had a direct effect on the war effort. During the Depression, the federal government did not suffer—as did states and localities—from the dramatic diminution of the real property tax base. Moreover, the federal government had flexible borrowing powers that are denied the officials of most state and local governments by their own state constitutions. And compared to most state and local officials, federal officers

TABLE 4–3

All Governments' Common-Function Expenditures by Percentage Spent by Federal Government, States, and Localities, 1902–75

	1975	1972	1969	1965	1953	1950	1944	1940	1932	1922	1913	1902
Federal	36.7%	35.6%	31.4%	30.8%	32.1%	38.0%	58.0%	41.8%	13.6%	15.2%	10.9%	9.9%
State	48.2	48.8	47.8	43.9	39.8	37.3	24.3	30.6	31.7	22.3	16.9	16.7
Local	50.3	52.0	52.1	60.3	50.5	44.9	33.4	45.4	66.5	69.6	76.8	78.7

SOURCE: U.S. Bureau of the Census, *Historical Statistics on Governmental Finances and Employment, U.S. Census of Governments, 1967* (Washington, D.C.: U.S. Government Printing Office, 1969), 6 (5); and U.S. Bureau of the Census, *Governmental Finances in 1968–69 and 1974–75* (Washington, D.C.: U.S. Government Printing Office, 1970 and 1976).

NOTE: Percentages sum to more than 100 because intergovernmental expenditures are counted twice: once for the granting level and once for the level of final expenditure. This double-counting is justified by the assumption that both the grantor and the recipient governments employ the funds to shape services offered.

may have been better prepared philosophically to fight the Depression with new programs and increased spending. During World War II, the federal government invested in a number of domestic programs that made a contribution to the war effort. One of these was the improvement of ports and canals. Between 1940 and 1944, federal expenditures for these facilities increased from $321 million to $4.5 billion annually. Since World War II, there has been a resurgence of state and local activities in the domestic sector. Between 1944 and 1975, the federal share of common-function spending declined from 58 to 30 percent, and then increased to 38 percent. During this same period the shares of both state and local governments increased.

During the Depression and World War II, the state governments showed greater stability than the local governments in maintaining their share of total domestic resources. This stability reflects the more flexible financial position of state governments. Both state and local governments entered the Depression as heavy reliers on the property tax. When the value of real property suffered greatly and curtailed its use as a generous producer of government revenue, many state governments shifted to other forms of taxation. Beginning with Mississippi, 23 states adopted the retail sales tax during the 1930s. Local governments, however, were limited by their state constitutions to the declining tax base of real property. Also, state governments enjoyed a wider taxing jurisdiction than did localities and could redistribute resources from "have" to "have-not" areas.

The Vietnam conflict joined the Depression, World War II, and the Korean conflict in altering the distributions of resources to administrative agencies. During the 1965–72 period, the national and state governments showed the greatest increases in financial activity and the states showed the greatest increase in administrative personnel. In these years, the states assumed an increasing role in aiding local governments. The taxpayers of all governments voiced their complaints. However, it appears that payers of the property tax levied by local governments have mounted the greatest resistance and have helped to lower the financial contribution of local governments to the total.

ADMINISTRATIVE DISCRETION AND THE ISSUE OF CONTROL

In dealing with the topic of administrative organization and the various ways of controlling administrators, it is appropriate to ask *how much control actually occurs?* With the growth of administrative units in the 20th century, there has been a growth in the discretion that administrators exercise in the performance of their duties. "Discretion" occurs when an official is "free to make a choice among possible courses of action or inaction."[41] With the increasing range of administrative activities, the exercise of discretion has grown. Legislative, executive, and judicial branches have left many issues in the hands of operating administrators—and the contractors with whom they deal—rather than spell out all possible conditions that should govern their actions. Additional discretion appears when an administrator ignores explicit policies governing certain activities. A local prosecutor exercises discretion when bargaining with a defendant who pleads guilty to a misdemeanor in order to escape prosecution on a felony charge. Police officers generally exercise discretion when encountering someone who seems intoxicated; the officers can drive the person home and make no record of the occurrence, take the person to a hospital, or make an arrest and put the person in jail. Social workers can choose to be strict or lenient in supervising the personal affairs of welfare recipients: by overlooking or enforcing regulations when a client earns a bit of money on a part-time job, or when an unwed mother begins living with a man.

Administrative discretion can be good or bad depending on its use and the observer's perspectives. It may be good to introduce flexibility into a bureaucracy that would otherwise be unyielding in handling the varied needs of its clients. If everyone were ticketed for driving over the speed limit, there might be more work than the authorities could handle, unhealthy public attitudes toward the law, and no opportunities to combat rush-hour congestion by urging drivers to go "faster." The problem with discretion, however, lies in the opportunities for discrimination. The prosperous drunk is likely to be sent home in a taxi while the skid row character goes to jail. Plea bargaining is thought to favor the white or wealthy rather than the poor and black. Administrative flexibility is more acceptable for welfare recipients who deal with lenient social workers than for those who deal with strict moralists. For one commentator, the special problem of discretion is its exercise, at the lowest levels of administration, by personnel who are least educated and most narrow in their consideration of the moral implications that result from their actions.[42]

The units within the conversion process fit no simple pattern. The basic

---

41. Kenneth C. Davis, *Discretionary Justice: A Preliminary Inquiry* (Urbana: University of Illinois Press, 1971), p. 4.
42. Davis, *Discretionary Justice*, p. 88.

model is the hierarchy, but there are so many qualifications of the hierarchy that it hardly stands as a common trait. Three other intellectual roots for the organization of administrative units raise conflicts with the hierarchical model and with each other. They are the concern for political accountability; the separation of powers, or checks and balances; and the concern for professional competence. These show their influence in the numerous mechanisms that provide legislators and citizens with access to administrative decisions; in structures that thwart the "political" control of personnel-selection; and in the ambiguous borders between the control responsibilities of the executive, legislature, and judiciary. The hierarchy fails for reasons of managerial ineptness as well as for notions of organizational propriety. Hierarchies are not sensitive to the complex values and motivations of organizational members, to the likelihood of conflicts within organizations over matters of policy, or to the chief executive's inability to gather adequate information about the goals and resources relevant to policy decisions.

The principal units of administrative systems and of their executive, legislative, and judicial controllers illustrate the diverse theories and the many particular stimuli that motivate those who design administrative units. The federal government includes numerous kinds of units on the periphery of the conversion process of its administrative system, including government corporations, federally aided corporations, government contractors, and such hybrids as the Office of Economic Opportunity, and presidential commissions. The OEO first appeared in the executive's "staff" (the Executive Office of the President), even though it was a service-providing "line" member of the administration. Presidential commissions show how a chief executive can put together representatives of several governmental and private institutions to handle a particular task that has a profound—but perhaps temporary—meaning for the nation.

The administrative control mechanisms of the federal government also present great diversity. Principal control mechanisms in the executive branch are the White House Office, the Office of Management and Budget, and the Council of Economic Advisors. In the legislative branch are the legislative, appropriations, and special investigating committees, plus the General Accounting Office. In the judicial branch, there is the federal district court system, plus special courts for claims, customs, patents, and the military. Not clearly in any branch of government, but exercising a wide range of controls over the administration, is the Civil Service Commission.

In state and local governments, there are further varieties in the structures and procedures of administrative and administrative-control units. These illustrate, as in the case of the federal units, the numerous influences brought to bear on those who establish—and help to evolve—each unit. There is no central architect of public administration in the United States who operates with consistent standards. The building and changing of administrative organizations is a continuing process. Insofar as it reflects various demands and influences from clients or prospective clients and from those who design organizations, the process of organization-building is as much a part of politics as are other features of policy-making.

At the conclusion of this chapter, we have seen a reminder that the issues of administrative discretion and control are not resolved simply by the creation of structures in executive, legislative, or judicial branches. Left unresolved are questions about how much control is possible, or desirable. We return to these issues in Chapter 6.

5

The Personnel of Administrative Agencies

This chapter focuses on the elemental actors in the administrative system —the administrators themselves. In viewing administrators, we look at those things they bring to the job, including social background, education, values, attitudes, beliefs, and skills. We also examine the techniques that administrative agencies use to select their personnel and to deal with the tasks of training, promotion, and dismissal. A further consideration in this chapter is a personnel issue that has achieved the status of a major controversy, especially in local political arenas. This is the role of collective bargaining in public administration.

Some agencies have devised programs to identify the traits they wish their personnel to possess, and they seek those traits in the employment market. From among their existing personnel, agencies select some persons for further training or promotion to leadership positions and other persons for reassignment or dismissal. Yet, not all agencies use sophisticated personnel procedures. Even the most sophisticated agencies may not find all the skilled personnel they desire, may not hire those who are available, or may not make the most efficient use of these skills. Administrative personnel are chosen only partly according to a well-reasoned design. To some extent, administrative agencies cannot control the skills, values, and attitudes that employees carry through the door.

Insofar as administrators help to convert inputs to outputs, it makes sense to place this chapter in Part One with other elements of the conversion process. The reader may profit, however, from viewing some of its information as inputs or outputs. For example, skills, values, and attitudes are inputs that administrators carry with them to their agencies. Also, when we discuss government employment of the disadvantaged, we deal with some opportunities (outputs) that administrators provide to important segments of the population.

RECRUITING, SELECTING AND TRAINING POLICY-MAKERS FOR ADMINISTRATIVE AGENCIES

Some of the most controversial issues in administrative organizations concern the methods used to select administrators. President Andrew Jackson was the first to raise personnel policies to the status of a major reform issue. His own policies—especially as adopted by subsequent chief executives—became the targets of reformers in later generations. Some reformers have been concerned with personnel policies for their own sake, without reference to their influence on other features of the administrative system. Others have assumed that the nature of personnel—and the methods used to select them—influences the nature of services provided by government departments. Jackson himself sought to change the substance of government programs by changing procedures used to select administrators. He wanted personnel that were responsive to the elected chief·executive and that permitted him to transform the public's mandate into government programs. Despite a reaction against the excesses of "Jacksonian" personnel techniques, many contemporary reformers have "returned" to the belief that elected chief executives should exercise control over their subordinates. However, there are significant differences between the proposals of Andrew Jackson and those of present-day reformers. While Jackson—and even more so some of his adopters—sought political control over the entire administrative corps, modern reformers concede the protections of the merit system for the vast majority of government employees. However, they would enhance the executive's control over those administrators in high-level policy-making positions. The executive would have an integrated policy-making team, with members appointed on the basis of their willingness to accept the chief executive's leadership. Also, contemporary reformers see the personnel task as more complex than it was viewed in Jackson's day. It is not simply a matter of giving the power to hire and fire to the chief executive. There is a need to forecast personnel needs, to compete with private enterprise for the desired skills, to train new employees, to provide sufficient rewards, and to allocate personnel to the positions where they can make the greatest contribution to the administrative system. A study published by the Brookings Institution listed several components to be included in an effective personnel program for high-level positions:

1. Analyze future needs for higher personnel and evaluate prospects of meeting such needs.

2. Compete successfully with other employers for superior personnel.
3. Make systematic, reliable, and valid evaluations of employees' performance and potential—as a basis for development and promotion.
4. Develop and train enough superior employees to fill most higher jobs—employees whose professional skills are excellent and up to date and whose perspectives are broad and mature.
5. Select the best candidates from a reasonably broad area of consideration for promotion or appointment to higher jobs—with reference to the particular needs of each job.
6. Provide advancement in compensation at a rate consistent with the employee's professional development and rates of advancement offered by competing employers.
7. Provide flexibility of assignment to meet needs of the program and also changing circumstances of the employee.
8. Compensa e personnel at fair market value for their services.
9. Retain and use to fullest advantage those employees who make a valuable contribution to organization goals.
10. Motivate personnel to give a full measure of cooperative effort.
11. Shift substandard personnel to jobs they can do effectively or discharge them.[1]

Any evaluation of the personnel procedures that are employed by administrative agencies are complicated by differences between career and political appointees. Both categories include people who are at the highest levels in administrative units and who are involved in policy-making. However, the two groups differ in their overt alignment with political parties and involvement in election campaigns, as well as in the kinds of job protection they enjoy. Control over political appointees is generally given to popularly elected executives, while control over the career service is typically held—or shared—by an institution protected from partisanship. The goals of the Brookings study are suitable for both career and political positions; but their detailed applications would vary. The procedures used for evaluating, advancing, and retaining employees could include or exclude partisan criteria.

---

1. David T. Stanley, *The Higher Civil Service* (Washington, D.C.: Brookings Institution, 1964), pp. 7–8. Copyright © 1964 by The Brookings Institution. The "GS" rating of a position refers to its level in the General Schedule classification. The higher the rating, the more status, "importance," and salary are assigned to a position. The specific meaning of the term "high-level administrator" varies with the studies that supplied the information used in this chapter. W. Lloyd Warner et al., *The American Federal Executive* (New Haven, Conn.: Yale University Press, 1963), examines federal administrators at the levels of GS 14 and above. David T. Stanley, *Higher Civil Service,* considers levels GS 15 through GS 18. Dean E. Mann, *The Assistant Secretaries: Problems and Processes of Appointment* (Washington, D.C.: Brookings Institution, 1965), considers departmental assistant secretaries, under secretaries, and their equivalent positions in the independent offices.

"NONPOLITICAL" PERSONNEL
PROCEDURES IN THE
NATIONAL ADMINISTRATION

The United States Civil Service Commission is the central personnel unit of the national government's administrative organization.[2] (Its activities are summarized in Chapter 4, pp. 139–40.) The Commission is primarily concerned with lower-level positions. In the policy-making categories examined by the Brookings project, selection is largely decentralized. The heads of departments and agencies have virtual control over the choice of their immediate subordinates. When looking for such personnel, they tend to promote individuals from within their own organizations or to solicit applications from other agencies of the federal government, from state or local administrations, or from private industry. The main sources are their own organizations or other units of the federal administration. Of the high-level administrators studied by the Brookings project, only 11 percent first entered the federal service at the level of GS 15 or above;[3] the large majority were appointed to these policy-level positions from subordinate places in the administration.

Two devices are used by federal agencies to support and purchase work done by outside institutions and permit the agencies to avoid many details of recruiting and selecting personnel; these two devices are grants-in-aid and federal contracts. By giving grants to state or local governments, federal agencies make an important contribution to the provision of certain public services without having to worry about recruiting personnel who can do the work.[4] By giving contracts to universities or to private industry, federal agencies can likewise "pass-on" their personnel choices. Contracting is particularly attractive where high-priced skills are involved. The contracting party can pay salaries above the normal federal scales in order to attract skilled individuals who would not otherwise be available.

The lack of central control over personnel procedures for policy-level jobs and the flexibility offered by grants and contracts have wide appeal in administrative agencies. One project of the Brookings institution claimed there were no serious difficulties in *competing for person-*

---

2. For background information on this subject, see Paul Van Riper, *History of the United States Civil Service* (Evanston, Ill.: Row, Peterson, 1958).

3. Stanley, *Higher Civil Service*, p. 95.

4. State and local agencies that receive federal grants must use employment criteria subject to certain standards of the U.S. Civil Sevice Commission. The recruiting and selection of specific persons, however, is left to the recipient agency.

nel with private industry.[5] It also criticized several efforts to centralize personnel procedures for policy-level positions. Such a change would deprive agency heads of control over their subordinates and would weaken the concept of an agency "team" united by common program perspectives. Moreover, a central mechanism might move personnel from one agency to another simply to relieve their present supervisors of difficult employees. If agency administrators themselves keep control over high-level appointments, they can elevate the agency's own needs to a foremost position in the selection criteria.[6]

With respect to the *evaluation* of current employees and their further *training*, the Brookings study found civilian agencies are far below desired performance. Its standard of excellence is the military, which assigns its officers to long periods of formal schooling and which makes periodic evaluations to decide about promotion or retirement. Civilian agencies have been slow in realizing the value of employee training paid for by the government. In 1963, the training expenditures reported by the Civil Service Commission were only $35 million, or $14 per employee. In that year, only 24 employees from grades GS 15 and GS 16 were assigned to long-term (more than 120 days) training. Recently, there have been marked increases in employee training. Programs include Executive Seminar Centers and the Federal Executive Institute. The Institute adjoins the campus of the University of Virginia in Charlottesville and provides graduate-level courses to selected groups of upwardly mobile federal executives. Yet, many civilian executives still have negative attitudes toward extensive training programs. Some agency heads feel that if they grant a leave for training they indicate overstaffing and lose opportunities to get additional personnel. Budget officers have cut agency funds on the grounds that training is a sign of overstaffing.[7] Individual employees feel they will lose their chance for promotion if they take training leave. To a large extent, the statement of President Andrew Jackson ("the duties of all public officers are . . . so plain and simple that men of intelligence may readily qualify themselves for their performance") prevails despite the technological transformations that have occurred in public administration. Some administrators and legislators oppose the use of any government money for training civilian employees.

The potential magnitude of selection and training problems for high-level personnel are made evident by the number of persons who

---

5. Stanley, *Higher Civil Service*, p. 81.
6. Stanley, *Higher Civil Service*, p. 97.
7. Stanley, *Higher Civil Service*, pp. 86–88.

might be involved. A federal "Task Force on Career Development" reported that the federal administration employed (in 1967) about 761,000 persons in professional, administrative, and technical occupations.[8]

In most matters of evaluation and retention, procedures favor the employee. After a person has survived a probationary period, it is difficult to identify unsuitable characteristics and dismiss the employee from the service. The procedures require formal charges and permit an appeal by the person being dismissed. The experience is said to upset other employees in an organization, to distress the leadership, to produce a general malaise, to increase voluntary resignations, and to reduce efficiency. "There are ways to do this, but they are expensive and they make us sick to our stomachs."[9] Some officials employ informal techniques to urge unwanted employees to leave. These include unpleasant assignments and social rejection. These techniques may serve their immediate purpose; however, they also reduce the morale of other employees who wonder if informal, unchallengeable procedures will someday be directed against themselves.

The lack of any systematic procedures for evaluating the work of civilian administrators is one of the factors that discourages any greater centralization of the personnel system. Without a surefire way for making evaluations in the Civil Service Commission, the task is left to the agency heads. Presumably, they have insight into their agency's special requirements and perhaps have some knowledge of personalities that is helpful in identifying those employees to be promoted and those to be kept in menial tasks or even dismissed. However, the size of most federal agencies precludes any real control over personnel evaluation by the agency head. Moreover, the procedures used to select employees for promotion are often indirect or even haphazard. They include reports from agency clients, length of service, or performance on particular occasions that are noted by the press or by the employee's superiors. There are serious problems of sampling that make it unwise to generalize about an employee's performance on the basis of individual observations. Length of service may testify to nothing more than the employee's success in not offending anyone; it says nothing about the person's contributions to the agency. Some indirect measures of performance include academic degrees and professional certification. These do show that an employee has certain academic experiences and has passed the screening procedures

8. Roger W. Jones, "Developments in Government Manpower: A Federal Perspective," *Public Administration Review* 27 (June 1967): 134–41.

9. Stanley, *Higher Civil Service,* p. 112.

of a professional body. They also suggest general competence. However, some schools and professional organizations are more lax than others in granting their *imprimatur*. And even the most prestigious certificate may not indicate that an individual can perform the specific responsibilities that are assigned.[10]

COLLECTIVE BARGAINING IN THE PUBLIC SERVICE: CONFRONTATIONS WITH PERSONNEL ADMINISTRATION

An aspect of personnel policy that is an increasing problem for administrative agencies is their relations with the unions and union-like organizations of employees. The difficulties include challenges of established antiunion or antistrike statutes and political squeezes between the citizens and legislators who are outraged at the suspension of public services and the public employees who are outraged at their own lack of desirable salaries or working conditions. Moral confrontations occur between those who argue that government employees should have the same rights to organize and bargain collectively as do employees in the private sector and those who argue that the state's sovereignty cannot be compromised by granting public employees the right to thwart the policies of constitutional offices.[11]

A basic problem of both the employees who organize and of those administrators who must deal with them reflects the insensitivity of earlier civil service reformers to the collective demands of employees. The "merit system" and related mechanisms come down on the side of the individual rather than the group. Its features include open competitive examinations, criteria rewarding individual excellence, and employee classifications on the basis of objective analysis of performance. Against these principles, union demands are in the tradition of a closed shop, of recruitment on the basis of union membership or occupational license, of promotion on the basis of seniority, and of collective negotiation of employee classifications and working conditions.

Along with the individualistic tradition of civil service reformers, some political theories have lead otherwise prolabor politicians to op-

---

10. David T. Stanley, "Excellence in Public Service—How Do You Really Know?" *Public Administration Review* 24 (September 1964): 170–74.
11. This section relies on Frederick C. Mosher, *Democracy and the Public Service* (New York: Oxford University Press, 1968), chapter 6; and Neal R. Peirce, "Employment Report," *National Journal* 7 (August 30, 1975): 1239–49.

pose collective bargaining with public employees. "To the extent that [employees' organizations] can advance the interests of their members they deprive political representatives, who are responsible to the whole people, of power over public policy."[12] President Franklin Roosevelt wrote:

[Collective bargaining] has its distinct and insurmountable limitations when applied to public personnel management. The very nature and purposes of government make it impossible for administrative officials to represent fully or to bind the employer in mutual discussions with government employee organizations.[13]

The unions of government workers, plus employees' organizations and professional associations that behave like unions, have not been confined by these principles or by the antistrike laws that exist in many jurisdictions. Government unions, especially at state and local levels, are now, the fastest growing sector of the union movement. From 1968 to 1972, the percentage of state and local employees in unions or employee organizations rose from 26 to 33, while organized employees in the private sector declined from 27 to 23 percent. Prominent unions or union-like organizations include the American Federation of State, County, and Municipal Employees with about 700,000 members; the American Federation of Teachers with about 450,000 members; and the National Education Association with 1.7 million members. Numerous private-sector unions have representation in the public sector, with the Teamsters enrolling some 200,000 members from police, fire, sanitation, and other units.

Along with growing size, there is also growing militancy among public-employee unions. Although many of them exist in jurisdictions that formally outlaw the strike for government employees, there were 36 recorded strikes in 1960, 42 in 1965, and over 350 in five of the six years between 1969 and 1974. In 1955, there were 7,000 worker-days lost to strikes in government, and over 1 million worker-days in six of the eight years between 1967 and 1974. In many actions, the leaders take care to avoid the term "strike." However, slowdowns or sick leaves that occur in a cohesive manner during crucial periods of collective bargaining leave no doubt about their purpose. Some "strikes" take the form of strict enforcement of regulations that are otherwise slighted for purposes of convenience. Local police officers have enforced parking

---

12. Mosher, *Democracy and the Public Service*, p. 178.
13. Mosher, *Democracy and the Public Service*, p. 177.

regulations with unusual thoroughness, sometimes against the vehicles of prominent citizens or of the policy-makers themselves. In the summer of 1968, the air traffic controllers of the Federal Aviation Agency expressed their displeasure by refusing any of the customary deviations from strict safety requirements. The resulting delays at the major airports led Congress and the Budget Bureau to release additional funds for recruiting and training new traffic controllers. One observer of the traffic controllers' activities saw in it a strategy for the employees of other federal agencies:

If it is obvious that airways traffic control cannot stand still until such time as war expenditures are reduced (enough to permit increased expenditures for air safety), it is equally obvious that official exhortations to make do with inadequate funding will not suffice for the Post Office, the National Park Service, the National Institutes of Health, or other agencies. The problem for these other agencies is to find ways to dramatize their plight.[14]

One of the features in confrontations between public agencies and their employees is the nature of employees' goals. While most are interested in wages or fringe benefits, some focus on the ways that services are administered. The air traffic controllers defended their demands for additional personnel in the name of improved air safety. Likewise, welfare workers and nurses have gone on strike (or taken equivalent actions) while demanding reduced caseloads in order to provide better service for their clients. And teachers have gone on strike to reduce the number of pupils in a classroom. During the fall of 1968, New York City teachers stayed out for 11 weeks over the decentralization of policy-making and over the school board's use of "nonprofessional" standards for assigning teachers.

Strikes and other work sanctions are not the only weapons of employees' organizations. Where government workers are numerically strong and are unified behind certain proposals, they can mount an awesome force in election campaigns. This force assures a receptive hearing from elected executives and legislators. Strikes, slowdowns, or sick-calls may reflect the demands of certain labor categories who cannot mobilize the support of the whole government workforce. Also, the unresponsive nature of many local legislatures may affect the greater tendency of local (rather than state or federal) employees to strike.[15]

---

14. Karl M. Reppenthal, "No Money for Safe Landings," *The Nation* (August 26, 1968): 142–44.
15. Mosher, *Democracy and the Public Service,* p. 191.

One feature of the merit system, designed some years ago to protect government agencies from control by political parties, is now said by unions and other representatives to deprive administrators of their political rights. When the Hatch Acts were passed in 1939 and 1940, the spectre of boss-ruled parties thriving off the patronage of government jobs was still very much alive. The acts sought to protect government employees from partisan political pressures. The covered employees could not be subject to party fund-raisings, and they could not serve as candidates or workers in partisan election campaigns.

Now the more vocal concern has become the rights—rather than the protection—of civil servants. In an era when advocates urge the maximum participation of administrators in the policy-making of their agencies (see pp. 204–206), it is also felt that individual administrators should have the same rights as other citizens: to campaign for partisan office or to work openly in someone else's campaign. In recent years, the Hatch Acts have been challenged in the federal courts and have been the targets of new legislation in Congress. Prominent among the advocates of change are the unions of government employees, the AFL-CIO, and the American Civil Liberties Union. In 1972, the U.S. District Court in the District of Columbia struck down key provisions of the Hatch Act for being vague or overbroad, when measured against guarantees of the First Amendment to the Constitution. In 1973, however, the Supreme Court reversed that decision. The Federal Campaign Act of 1974 loosened some of the controls on federal employees, but they still may not seek a partisan office. The employees of many state and local governments continue to face strict controls patterned after the original Hatch Acts.

PERSONNEL PROCEDURES FOR POLITICAL APPOINTEES IN THE NATIONAL ADMINISTRATION

The civil service reformers of the 19th century portrayed hordes of office-seekers descending on newly elected presidents. In their cartoons, the chief executive was unable to attend to important business because of the job applicants. Today this is a false image. Some people—including a fair number of professors—do hint clearly at their availability during these times when administrations and parties change in Washington or state capitals. However, the president must search for talent and may have to persuade the people chosen to leave well-established situations in business or in their professions. To the prospects, the president offers the opportunity to serve the administration, at times a substantial reduction in salary, and a substantial increase in personal expenses.

Recent presidential candidates have postponed decisions on political appointments until after the election. Although this delay has disturbed some observers of the presidential transition, the campaign itself has consumed the most important resources of the candidates and their assistants. One of John Kennedy's aides said that "Kennedy wouldn't have won" if his staff had devoted any more attention to post-election matters.[16] Eisenhower, Kennedy, Nixon, and Carter detailed a group of advisors to concentrate on high-level personnel immediately after their elections. The central figures in Eisenhower's group were Herbert Brownell and Lucius Clay. Brownell was experienced in Republican party politics as a former national party chairman and campaign manager for Thomas Dewey. Clay was a military associate of the president-elect, had been active in the 1952 political campaign, and was chairman of the board at Continental Can Company. The key people in Kennedy's personnel team (the "Talent Hunt") were his brother and campaign manager Robert Kennedy and his brother-in-law R. Sargent Shriver. Nixon's team had Californians and New Yorkers drawn from his former close associates. The Carter group had a heavy representation of Georgians. The practice has been to solicit names of prospective appointees from contacts in politics, business, the professions, and universities; screen the qualifications of various prospects; clear them with political leaders and professional or business associates; and make recommendations for each cabinet position.

There is no question about the direct involvement of the president-elect in the selection of cabinet secretaries and the heads of major independent offices. There have been differences, however, in their involvement in making appointments just below those levels. President Eisenhower left the selection of subordinate appointees to the new cabinet secretaries and agency heads. This was consistent with his policy of delegating decisions and permitting administrators to operate their own organizations. This policy disappointed some Republican members of Congress who could not get presidential intervention for the sake of a "deserving constituent." On some occasions, Eisenhower's staff urged a department to take "political considerations" into account; but the president-elect did not involve himself directly. Generally speaking, Kennedy exercised more control over subordinate appointments than did Eisenhower. Indeed, Kennedy's first announcement—made even before

---

16. This section relies on Mann, *Assistant Secretaries*, pp. 72ff.

the announcement of a secretary of state—was G. Mennan Williams as assistant secretary of state for African affairs. This presidential concern may have won some credits among elites in the new African states, but it also signaled to the State Department that Kennedy would make decisions formerly delegated to the secretary. President-elect Kennedy appointed Chester Bowles as undersecretary of state and Adlai Stevenson as ambassador to the United Nations. Also, each of Kennedy's cabinet secretaries was assigned a member of the personnel team to review candidates available for subordinate appointments.

Presidents have used a combination of occupational competence and political acceptability as personnel criteria. The Kennedy team asked about a prospect's "judgment," "toughness," "integrity," "ability to work with others," "industry," and "devotion to the principles of the president-elect." The team also asked whether their appointments would enhance the administration's prestige "nationally," "in their states," "in their communities," or "in their professional groups." With the press of time and many prospects to be reviewed, however, evaluations were simplified to "highly qualified," "qualified," or "some qualifications" with respect to competence; and "good Democrat," "political neutral," "Republican," or "politically disqualified" with respect to partisanship.[17]

As presidents pass the period of inauguration, they change procedures for political appointments. Without the crush of numbers, they no longer require a special task force. Eisenhower, Kennedy and Nixon assigned the review of later political appointees to the White House Office. As the presidents themselves concentrate increasingly on substantive problems, their cabinet secretaries take a prominent role in personnel decisions, most of which involve the selection of replacements for subordinates who resign.

Congress also has a role in political appointments. The Constitution gives Congress the power to determine procedures for filling appointive positions. In some positions, Congress gives the appointment to the president alone. Within some cabinet departments and independent offices, administrative assistant secretaries do not require senatorial confirmation. These are typically named by immediate superiors to serve as personal assistants. All department secretaries, under secretaries, and assistant secretaries, as well as ambassadors, the heads of most independent offices, and federal judges, are subject to senatorial confirmation.[18]

---

17. Mann, *Assistant Secretaries*, p. 73.
18. Mann, *Assistant Secretaries*, p. 35.

Most of the time, the Senate makes only perfunctory examinations of candidates. The individual is introduced to the Senate committee that has charge of legislation for the nominee's department. There is seldom any searching probe of the person's background or intentions and often no formal record of the committee meeting. The nominee's name may go before the Senate with no debate and be approved by unanimous consent.[19] Most of the time, senators grant the president considerable discretion over personnel. They seldom offer any public opposition to appointments.[20]

When opposition to an appointment does come from the Senate, it can take several forms. It can be a serious effort to block an appointment or merely the attempt of one senator to record opposition. Some opposition may be designed to elicit policy commitments from the nominee. Few candidates for administrative posts actually are rejected by the Senate. Yet, this is not the full record. Some nominations are withdrawn by the president because of the fears of embarrassment over a formal rejection. Some nominees withdraw themselves—like Theodore Sorrenson, tabbed by President Carter as head of the Central Intelligence Agency—when intensive opposition appears in the Senate. Some nominees are never formally submitted because key senators expressed intense opposition during a preliminary clearance.

SIGNIFICANCE OF ADMINISTRATORS' PERSONAL TRAITS IN ADMINISTRATIVE ORGANIZATIONS

It is impossible to say just how much the personal traits of administrators influence the activity of administrative agencies. At the present time, there simply is not enough information about the backgrounds, values, or skills of administrators to attempt the evaluation. Most of the information to be reported in this chapter concerns large groups of government employees. There is not enough data about the personnel of individual agencies to do a comparative analysis that would show the correspondence between administrators' traits and the policies of administrative agencies. Even our descriptive effort must be limited to the administrative agencies of the national government. The most valuable data focus on federal employees in high-level professional or technical

19. Mann, *Assistant Secretaries*, pp. 135–52.
20. Mann, *Assistant Secretaries*, p. 149.

positions or on those having policy-making responsibility. These personnel are the most likely to shape the decisions of their agencies.

The information available shows that administrators at policy-making levels differ from the general adult population in their social backgrounds and educational experiences. However, they do not differ markedly from individuals in positions of responsibility in other branches of government or in large business firms. Some studies indicate that, among government administrators, a *higher* proportion have advanced education and a *lesser* proportion come from upper-class families, than do members of the legislative branch or executives of large private firms. Yet, the differences are not great. In these and other traits, the high-level personnel of public agencies are more like their counterparts elsewhere in government or business than any of these groups are like adults in the society as a whole. Generally speaking, responsible positions in many fields attract persons with more-than-average education and from upper-income families. There is no indication that the personal traits of government administrators are so different from those of other policy-makers that their presence is likely to distinguish the decisions of government agencies from other institutions.

The multiple influences on agency policies provide some check against whatever influences may come from the personal traits of administrators. Moreover, control procedures found in many agencies reduce even further the influence that is open to personal traits. The personal attributes of administrators must "compete" for influence over policy with formal and informal communications from the legislative, executive, and judicial branches of government, from officials at other levels of the federal system, and from clients and other members of the public. Moreover, different aspects of the administrators' own characteristics may compete with one another for influence over their decisions. The "interests" identified with their family's social status, for example, may conflict with the professional orientation that they acquired as part of their formal training. Within one administrative unit, the personal interests of administrators may compete with one another and make it unlikely that anyone's personal interest can shape the agency's decision. Most administrative agencies have procedures that guard against the overt influence of personal interests on official decisions. These include multiple decision-makers within individual agencies; the separation of powers, or checks and balances, that surround an agency with several executive and legislative supervisors; and conflict-of-interest procedures used to screen out applicants who would have a substantial financial stake in the agency's policies.

It is still helpful to describe the personal traits of administrators, even though we can find little discernible impact of these traits on the outputs of administrative organizations. The composition of the public service has significance for questions of employment opportunities. *To what extent do the children of different social classes or ethnic groups have equal opportunities to enter public employment and reach policy-making levels?* For some groups that have been the target of severe discrimination in private industry, the government may be the most likely source of jobs commensurate with their skills and training. The opportunity for government employment is one of the major outputs an administrative organization provides to such groups in the population. There are also significant questions about the public-mindedness and dedication of government employees. These require information about the personalities, values, and aspirations of administrators.

WHO ARE PUBLIC ADMINISTRATORS?

Compared to the population as a whole, high-level administrators[21] in the federal government come disproportionately from communities having large population, from families in the middle and upper ranges of occupational status, and from Protestant religious groups. This combination of traits suggests that high-level administrators enjoyed a number of childhood benefits. These benefits increased the likelihood of cosmopolitan rather than parochial perspectives and made available attractive educational opportunities and career prospects in science, the professions, or management. The administrators' own educational experiences complement their middle- and upper-class backgrounds. Almost all of them graduated from college, and a sizable proportion have advanced degrees. A high percentage received their precollegiate education in private high schools and took their college degrees at the most prestigious colleges and graduate schools.[22]

Although the backgrounds of high-level administrators differ markedly from those of the "average citizen," they are not very different from the backgrounds of people in other positions of responsibility in government or private industry. Table 5–1 brings together data from

---

21. See Note 1 of this chapter.
22. Warner et al, *American Federal Executive,* chapters 2–4; Mann, *Assistant Secretaries,* chapters 2–3; and Stanley, *Higher Civil Service,* chapter 3. Also, for a study of the changing composition of the U.S. Foreign Service with respect to the undergraduate backgrounds of recruits, see Martin B. Hickman and Neil Hollander, "Undergraduate Origin as a Factor in Elite Recruitment and Mobility: The Foreign Service—A Case Study," *Western Political Quarterly* 19 (June 1966): 337–53.

TABLE 5–1

The Social Backgrounds of Elites in the 1960s

	Federal Political Executives	Top Federal Civil Servants	Business Executives	Congress		Military Leaders			General Public
				House	Senate	Army	Navy	Air Force	
Religion:									
Roman Catholic	19%	N.A.*	9%	12%	21%	11%	10%	16%	36%
Jewish	4	N.A.	5	1	3	—	—	—	5
Protestant and other	77	N.A.	87	87	77	89	90	84	56
Education:									
No college	2	4%	9	7	4	N.A.	N.A.	N.A.	83
Some college	5	13	16	14	13	N.A.	N.A.	N.A.	9
College degree	93	83	74	79	83	N.A.	N.A.	N.A.	8

SOURCES: Adapted from David T. Stanley et al., *Men Who Govern* (Washington, D.C.: Brookings Institution, 1967), pp. 15–18; and W. Lloyd Warner et al., *The American Federal Executive* (New Haven, Conn.: Yale University Press, 1963), pp. 29–36.
* Because the table is compiled from different sources, it has been necessary to leave some cells with data missing. These are designated as N.A. (not ascertained).

several studies of elites' backgrounds. The information is dated, but it has not been challenged by more recent materials. All of the elites come from social groups that have had more advantages than the average citizen.

There are some differences in the traits of high-level government administrators in civilian posts and those of other elite groups. There is a higher incidence of Catholics among government administrators and a higher incidence of laborers' sons; this suggests the relative "openness" of the federal bureaucracy, as compared to private industry. The higher incidence of advanced education testifies to the skills found in the bureaucracy and suggests that many administrators overcame their family or cultural disadvantages by their own hard work in school.

The traits of people elevated to the highest positions in federal administrative agencies reflect to some extent the influence of the particular president who appointed them. President Eisenhower appointed a proportionately lesser number of Catholics and Jews than Democratic presidents, perhaps because there are fewer Catholics and Jews among Republicans than among Democrats. Among the Democratic presidents, the Kennedy and Johnson administrations appointed proportionately more Catholics and Jews than did the earlier Roosevelt and Truman administrations. This may reflect the increasing acculturation of Catholic and Jewish families and the greater likelihood that their children will have the social and educational advantages that help prepare them for high government positions. The lower incidence of appointments made from within the federal bureaucracy during the Eisenhower administration suggests both the distrust of bureaucrats thought to be loyal Democrats and the great numbers of out-of-power party members who wanted federal appointments after their victory. After 20 years without a presidential victory, there were many Republicans who considered themselves suited for a federal appointment. The higher incidence of persons with doctoral degrees among the appointees of the Kennedy and Johnson administrations may reflect a propensity to recruit from university faculties, as well as the increasing importance of administrative tasks that require technical expertise.

CAREER ROUTES AND SUCCESS IN ADMINISTRATIVE AGENCIES

An individual's career route is one background element that may affect one's administrative decisions. The first job, the length of time spent in earlier occupations, and pre-executive experiences within the administrative organization may shape the way an administrator views work. If large numbers of government administrators follow similar career paths and if these paths differ significantly from those followed by elites in the private sector, then the discrepancies in experiences might lead to perspectives—and perhaps behaviors—different from those found in large private organizations. Family background influences the nature of one's early career. Thus, family backgrounds may affect the behavior of administrative agencies through its prior influences on the early career choices of persons who become high-level administrators.[23]

Of all occupations, the professions most consistently supply individuals for high-level positions in the federal administration. One study showed that 46 percent of the persons who were high-level administrators (GS 14 and higher) started their careers in a profession and that over 40 percent were in professional classifications 15 years after starting their careers. Many of those who began their careers in the categories of laborer and white-collar moved into the professional category before reaching their present administrative positions. A breakdown of the profes-'onal category shows that about one-third are engineers and that another one-third are either lawyers or scientists. Other professionals are physicians, professors, accountants, and public school teachers.

There are some differences in career paths within the federal administration and between the federal administration and large private firms. Within the federal administration, political appointees are the most likely to come from the professions; foreign service officers mostly progress through administrative positions; and other nonpolitical civil service administrators are about evenly divided between administrative and professional backgrounds. Of the political appointees, 59 percent had been in professions 15 years after beginning their careers; 40 percent of the civil service executives and only 20 percent of the foreign service executives were in professions at that point. Nonpolitical civil service and foreign service personnel are more likely to work their way through the minor administrative positions in government organizations or to transfer into government from managerial positions in the private sector. Only 24 percent of business leaders began their careers as professionals. In contrast to the 25 percent of government administrators who began in white-collar occupations (clerical and sales), 44 percent of business leaders began in such occupations. Business leaders enter management positions more rapidly than do their counterparts in government; after 15 years, 82 percent of business leaders were minor or major managers,

---

23. See Warner et al., *American Federal Executive*, chapter 10.

while only 47 percent of government administrators were in such positions.

These findings have serious implications for the common stereotypes of government administrators as bureaucrats who glory in redtape and of business leaders as more flexible individualists. It is business leaders who follow the route of white-collar→minor manager→major manager through the business bureaucracies; while government officials —especially political appointees—more often are educated in a professional or graduate school and then transfer into the government at a level where they enjoy prestige, discretion, and responsibility for policy decisions. If any class of leaders shows the behavioral affects of a bureaucratic career, it is more likely to be the person in business rather than in government.

The wide-ranging occupational experiences of upper-level government administrators also suggests a breadth of conception and an understanding of different circumstances. A survey of the top three ranks in the federal civil service found that 83 percent had worked in two or more organizations and that 97 percent had changed occupations during their careers. A common pattern is a shift into administration from a technical or professional specialization. Almost two-thirds of senior administrators had some experience in the private sector, suggesting substantial familiarity with the problems of business in the higher echelons of government.[24]

Within the federal government, career paths show the influence of the parents' social and economic characteristics. Among persons who have reached high-level positions in the federal bureaucracy, the children of laborers and farmers are more likely to be in the lower echelons of the policy-making corps (GS 14 and GS 15), while the children of professionals and executives are more likely to reach positions of GS 16 and above.[25] Major executives' children who became high-level political appointees reached such positions five years earlier in their careers than did the children of laborers. A father's occupation seems more relevant for one's first career opportunity. The children of laborers and white-collar employees were the least likely to begin their careers in the professions—the route that seems most propitious for subsequent career advancement. Over half of the children born into lower-status families began their careers as laborers or white-collar employees, while over half of those born into professional homes began their careers as pro-

24. Lloyd G. Nigro and Kenneth J. Meier, "Executive Mobility in the Federal Service: A Career Perspective," Public Administration Review 35 (May/June 1975): 291–95.
25. Warner et al., American Federal Executive, pp. 157–63.

fessionals. The children of lower-status homes were less likely to reach as high positions in the government; and they usually took longer to reach their positions.

GOVERNMENT EMPLOYMENT OF THE SOCIALLY DISADVANTAGED

One of the questions that is properly asked about administrative agencies is *To what extent do they include members of groups that are discriminated against in the private sector?* The answer to such a question has several implications. First, it indicates the commitment of administrative agencies to provide some opportunities to individuals who are socially disadvantaged. If this commitment is sizable, it can provide an important "output" of the administrative system: opportunities for employment and even influence over policy for those individuals who are shut out of many nongovernmental opportunities. Second, the employment of the disadvantaged stands as one device that can provide members of these groups with the feeling that they can better develop their opportunities within the established order rather than by seeking drastic change. Thus, the employment policies of administrative organizations may lessen—or aggravate—whatever tendencies toward nihilism and violence may develop among disadvantaged groups. Third, the employment of individuals from all groups suggests the efforts of government recruiters to search all potential labor markets. Where government employment is skewed against disadvantaged groups, large pools of labor probably remain untapped. These pools may require "cultivation" with special educational and employment opportunities. If they remain unexploited, however, administrative agencies deprive themselves of important resources.[26]

The efforts of blacks, women, and other underprivileged groups to increase their shares of social benefits have led them to demand more and better jobs in government. Their claims bear some resemblance to the traditional demands for special privileges that have come from veterans and the supporters of victorious political parties. More than these groups, however, blacks, women, and other underprivileged minorities raise the issue of a *representative* bureaucracy.

---

26. This section relies on Samuel Krislov, *The Negro in Federal Employment: The Quest for Equal Opportunity* (Minneapolis: University of Minnesota Press, 1967), p. 94. See also Samuel Krislov, *Representative Bureaucracy* (Englewood Cliffs, N.J.: Prentice-Hall, 1974).

It is difficult to define precisely the notion of a representative bureaucracy. In one sense, a representative bureaucracy is impossible to achieve; the bureaucracy of a modern government must include a disproportionate number of highly educated and well-paid lawyers, accountants, scientists, engineers, and managers. A more relevant conception of a representative bureaucracy has ample numbers of certain groups, especially in jobs considered important. The groups identified as sensitive, like blacks and women in recent years, earn their designations in the political process. The prominent demands of blacks and women for numerous high-ranking positions—and to a less prominent extent the demands of Spanish-origin people, Oriental-Americans, and native Americans—reflects their heightened political consciousness and organizational clout. Yet to be heard from perhaps, are the descendents of Eastern and Southern European immigrants.

There has been a positive response to demands for special consideration, but not without challenge from those who prize a neutral bureaucracy or one selected purely on merit. Official policies require personnel officers to display "affirmative action" in recruiting women and minorities according to established "goals," but they seek to avoid specifying quotas for various groups. The programs to recruit women and minorities benefit from the large size of American bureaucracies and the certain turnover of personnel for reasons of death, retirement, or changing career aspirations. This allows some flexibility for affirmative action in behalf of some groups without constant collisions with the members of other groups seeking to protect their positions. The element of opportunity means that newer and expanding agencies, or those with low status in the eyes of nonminorities, recruit the highest incidence of minorities. The Office of Economic Opportunity, ACTION, departments of Health, Education and Welfare, and Housing and Urban Development have recruited the highest percentages of minorities in ranking positions.

Blacks in Government

In recent years, the incidence of nonwhites in government employment has resembled their proportion in the total population. By this measure alone, nonwhites have "equal" access to administrative systems. Yet, their skewed distribution among job categories testifies to continued disadvantages. Nonwhites are employed mostly in low-wage, low-status positions. They face overt discrimination in some agencies of the federal government and of numerous state and local governments.

An increasing number of middle- and upper-level positions in the federal administration are being filled by blacks. During 1961–65, blacks filled 28 percent of the new positions. While there was an actual decrease in blacks at levels GS 1 through GS 4, there was an increase of 50 percent at the GS 5 through GS 11 levels, and a tripling at the GS 12 through GS 18 levels. Even after this progress, however, blacks comprised only 1 percent of all those in the GS 12 through GS 18 positions and comprised over 32 percent of those in GS grades below the salary level of $5,000.[27] More recently, the U.S. Civil Service Commission has published information for "minority groups" employment in the federal government, which combines blacks and Spanish-surnamed employees. From 1967 to 1974, these employees increased slightly from 18.9 to 21.0 percent of the total. They continued the trend of showing actual declines in the lowest paid federal grades and greatest relative increases in the top grades: from 3.3 to 4.9 percent of all employees in the GS 12 through GS 18 grades. Now there is a new problem of blacks in middle- or upper-level positions who feel they are hired as symbols rather than as skilled professionals.

Negroes all too often find that their newly created posts have no real duties. Often the accoutrements of office are obviously beyond the level of work demanded. The Negro bureaucrat at the upper reaches is often given extra status, a fancier desk, than he would receive on the merits of his position. The suspicion that he is there to perform the function of Art Buchwald's Negro PhD with an engineering background who speaks ten languages—to sit by the door to convince everyone of the egalitarian principles of the business office in which he is employed—haunts virtually every major Negro bureaucrat.[28]

The geographic distribution of blacks in the federal service raises another question about their "progress." *Is the increase in black employment more a function of residential concentration in Washington than a reflection of deliberate policy?* During 1965, blacks comprised about one-fourth of federal employees in the Washington area, but only one-eighth of *total* federal employment. Actually, a combination of population concentration and deliberate policy may explain the increased employment. Blacks have not moved to Washington by accident. A factor in their migration is the attraction of federal employment. All regions have shown some recent increases in black employment. Even Mississippi experienced a 450 percent increase in the number of black federal employees during 1964–65.

Generally speaking, blacks have found the most employment opportunities in those offices that have black clients and in new government

27. Krislov, *Negro in Federal Employment,* p. 101.
28. Krislov, *Negro in Federal Employment,* p. 100.

agencies or programs. Black representation is relatively high in welfare, housing, and urban affairs agencies[29] and in those units of the State Department dealing with African affairs.[30] A significant exception to the principle of black–clientele–black–employment opportunities has occurred in the Department of Agriculture. The political impotence of the black clients (concentrated in the rural South) limited the opportunities for black employees. As late as 1965, the U.S. Commission on Civil Rights reported:

> In some programs, effective service to Negroes has been made dependent upon the number of Negroes employed, on the untenable theory that Negro farmers should be served only by Negro staff.[31]

Even in recent years, some offices in the Department of Agriculture have not permitted black employees to serve white farmers, have isolated blacks in separate offices and at segregated meetings, and have provided black staff members with less in-service training than that provided to whites. Where equal opportunity is provided in the Agriculture Department, it is likely to be in newer programs dealing with food inspection and consumer services.[32]

It is a mistake to ascribe the low incidence of blacks in high-level jobs entirely to discriminatory policies. To be sure, some discrimination is probably at work. However, the low incidence of blacks in responsible jobs is due partly to their lack of preparation. To reverse this situation, it may be necessary to affect major changes in the colleges and universities that train people for government employment and to affect some changes in the black subculture.

In 1966, the chairman of the U.S. Civil Service Commission described some far-reaching goals of its equal opportunity program: "eradicating all vestiges of prejudices, a complete review of federal employment practices, and heavy emphasis on training and development of employees."[33] Training and development of employees may be the most difficult goal; it may require more than the simple willingness of colleges and universities to admit qualified black applicants. Because of educational disadvantages that limit the skills of many black high school graduates, as well as the graduates of predominantly black colleges, it has been ruled necessary to pursue "affirmative action" policies by so-

---

29. Krislov, *Negro in Federal Employment,* p. 127.
30. Krislov, *Negro in Federal Employment,* p. 134.
31. Quoted in Krislov, *Negro in Federal Employment,* p. 133.
32. Krislov, *Negro in Federal Employment,* pp. 132–33.
33. Warren I. Cikins, "Graduate Education, Public Service, and the Negro," *Public Administration Review* 26 (September 1966): 183–91.

liciting applications from prospective black candidates and by providing special opportunities that will make up the deficiencies of earlier schooling. Not only are large sums of money required, but educational institutions must also move from their concern for "equal opportunity" to willingness to provide "special opportunities." For those who must provide the funds for these programs (i.e., the government itself or private foundations), there is the question of which institutions should be aided. One sentiment is to "minimize . . . duplication and overlap and [seek] the gains due to having available the best minds and physical plant."[34] This means a concentration of resources at prestigious—largely white—institutions. Another feeling is to provide resources to the predominantly black institutions. They already serve the greatest concentration of black students; but many of them lack strong programs relevant to the needs of administrative agencies. Other barriers to equal employment opportunities may lie in the black community itself. Generations of discrimination have not prepared black families to place a high value on academic accomplishment.

Despite the problems, government agencies generally offer more attractive employment opportunities to blacks than does the private sector of the economy. The U.S. Civil Rights Commission has surveyed government and private employment in metropolitan areas around the country. In Detroit, Philadelphia, and Memphis during 1967, for example, 24 to 31 percent of the state government employees in upper-level categories—"managers," "officials," "professionals," and "technicians"—were black; in the private sector, only 3 to 6 percent of the employees in these categories were black.[35]

Women in Government

The status and problems of women in administrative agencies are similar to those of blacks. The exclusion of women from certain positions raises similar questions about discrimination and about the failure of administrative agencies to exploit potential resources. The number of women in white-collar federal positions is about the same as the proportion (49 percent) of women in the population.[36] As in the case of blacks, the problem is not so much their number as their distribution. As of 1974, women were only 4.5 percent of the federal employees above the

---

34. Cikins, "Graduate Education, Public Service, and the Negro."

35. *For All the People By All the People: A Report on Equal Opportunity in State and Local Government Employment* (Washington, D.C.: U. S. Commission on Civil Rights, 1969), p. 23.

36. This section relies on Warner et al., *American Federal Executive*, chapter 11.

level of GS 12, a figure that increased by only 0.5 percent in the 1959–74 period. Also like blacks, women have been employed disproportionately in certain kinds of jobs where the clientele would anticipate—and perhaps appreciate—them. They are concentrated in child welfare, public assistance, and vocational rehabilitation.

Women who do reach policy-level positions in the bureaucracy have no obvious traits of family background that distinguish them from male colleagues. More than the average adult in our society, they come from middle- and upper-status families in medium or large cities; their fathers were professionals, executives, or white-collar employees; and they have college, plus some graduate education. In these traits, they resemble male administrators. Two other characteristics of women executives are more distinctive. First, women are slightly older than men at comparable positions. This may reflect discrimination in selection or promotion, the time that women must spend on other aspects of their social roles (e.g., raising a family), or several "false starts" before selecting the route of education and employment that is suitable. In any case, the greater age of women at comparable administrative levels indicates special difficulties that are not encountered by their male colleagues. Second, women executives are more typically single. The choice of career instead of family is one of several difficult choices that many women face.

These 145 women who have become federal executives (as of 1959) bucked a system which began working against them when they were born, around 1910. They selected not to play the highly patterned woman's role in our society. They went to college, they elected to enter the professions; many of them made, what was for some of them, the hard choice of a career rather than marriage; some had the energy and intelligence to combine marriage and career. They had the determination to stay within their chosen way of life until they achieved positions of equal responsibility with men in government.[37]

VALUES, ASPIRATIONS, AND PERSONALITIES IN ADMINISTRATIVE AGENCIES

The backgrounds and educational experiences of high-level administrators suggest what kinds of family, educational, and career experiences provide the most likely routes to responsible positions in administrative agencies. From their backgrounds alone, we cannot infer that govern-

---

37. Warner et al., *American Federal Executive*, p. 187.

ment administrators have any peculiar values, aspirations, or personality traits that set them apart from individuals having responsible positions in other large and complex institutions.

It is very difficult to obtain information about the values, aspirations, and personalities of government administrators. Detailed psychological research is time consuming and expensive. However, a group of scholars headed by Professor W. Lloyd Warner conducted intensive interviews with a random sample of 257 civilian administrators in the federal government at the levels of GS 14 and above.[38] The interviews included Thematic Apperception Tests and lasted three to four hours. The sample is large enough to tell us something about the general tendencies in the federal bureaucracy. However, it does not have enough respondents in each occupational subgroup to permit analysis of categories within the federal service. Moreover, it includes no business executives who can serve as a standard of comparison with the government administrators.

The personal values, aspirations, and personalities of federal administrators—as reported by Professor Warner and his colleagues—suggest that they are persons of large perspective. They see themselves as functioning within a complex and demanding set of institutions and as being responsible for programs with great social value. They view their authority as coming from outside of themselves. Authority is a source of support as well as instruction; they generally accept authority as legitimate, although sometimes resent intrusions on their own activity. By and large, they accept the restrictions of large organizations, and they accept the need for coordination and cooperation. They show the traits of group workers rather than individualists.

High-level administrators also tend to be individuals of lofty ideals. They aspire to community improvement more than to self-aggrandizement. Along with this idealism, government administrators also have strong needs for achievement. This combination of traits may add up to public-minded realism. Their need for achievement, as well as their appreciation for organizational constraints, may temper their idealism so that goals come within the range of feasibility. Perhaps because of this, their goals are usually expressed in concrete terms that are relevant to their field of specialization. Instead of abstract principles that do not lend themselves to clear definition or attainment, they desire improved services in education, health, welfare, transportation, or resource development.

---

38. This section relies on Warner et al., *American Federal Executive*, chapters 12–14.

Their values also reveal a great respect for the institutions of government and a strong motivation to serve the interests of the public. They appear more oriented to public service than to private gain.

Plato's conception of the ideal ruling group was that of a class of men dedicated to the pursuit of wisdom and knowledge, with a taste for every type of knowledge. Such men, endowed with unquenchable curiosity, possessing courage and self-respect, sought after justice and truth. Not being concerned with the pursuit of wealth, nor allied with property, they could achieve objectivity. For them, to govern was a matter of duty and obligation—a sacred calling. They possessed the capacity for temperance, self-control, and a respect for authority. But above all they were dedicated to the pursuit of wisdom and ultimate truth.

The ideology of federal executives comes very close to this ideal. The emphasis upon intelligence, intellectual values, and culture, the notion of restraint, the drive for self-respect and the respect of others, the concept of duty and obligation—all are strikingly reminiscent of the Platonic concept of the State. Even more significant is the emphasis in the federal executive ideology upon the search for justice and fair resolution of problems. Fairness to others, concern for the public welfare, honesty, and "goodness" are characteristics held to be decisive.[39]

The data on high-level government administrators are not without contradictions. They show values and attitudes which appear strange in combination with one another. Yet, this is to be expected. Administrators in policy-making roles must live within the constraints of large organizations, of active clientele groups, and of legislators who may at anytime insert their own desires into agency considerations. Yet, administrators also have powerful motivations and strong ideals of public service. It seems inevitable that many administrators will experience internal conflicts. Intensive interviews reveal not only an expressed ease about their dependence on a large system, but also a drive for independence and anxiety about the dependence that is necessary. Administrators both need and reject authority. Occasionally they show their rejection with expressions of resentment and ineffectual behavior.

In situations in which he is working closely with others, he tends to be more at ease, to initiate more freely, to activate rather than be acted upon. This disposition to avoid "going it alone" is especially noted in areas calling for achievement that must be solely self-directed; here considerable anxiety arises.

In general, the career civil service executive possesses psychological characteristics that may be described thus: he possesses lofty aspirations, the majority of which stem from external influences, from heroic figures or models,

---

39. Warner et al., *American Federal Executive,* pp. 235–36.

and from demands made upon him by the system and by his role as a career man. . . .

Yet the career civil service executive frequently experiences feelings of inadequacy and lack of insight into the means to be used to realize his lofty aspirations. . . . [In some cases] he responds with feelings of hostility which in most instances take a hidden form such as resentment, or failing in tasks of "going it alone," or movement into fantasy and the realm of "magical" solutions.[40]

A survey of 405 senior executives of 52 agencies found that the large majority express liberal democratic opinions with respect to such issues as upholding fair-play rules of the game; allowing freedom of speech; protecting due process; and the equality of various political, social, and economic groups. They also feel that politics offers meaningful opportunities for citizens to influence government. In these traits, senior administrators resemble other elite groups of high income and high educational and occupational status in the private sector. Yet, the senior administrators are not homogeneous. Those with more formal education are the most likely to express liberal democratic views, and those in social agencies are more likely to express such views than those in defense-related agencies. Of most concern, perhaps, is the finding that senior administrators with the longest service are less likely than their young colleagues to express respect for democratic values or to state that the political process offers a meaningful opportunity to change public policy.[41]

SUMMARY

This chapter examines selected aspects of the procedures that administrative organizations use to select and assign their personnel and looks at the nature of the personnel themselves. The primary focus is career and political appointees at upper levels in the federal bureaucracy. People at these levels are most likely to influence the nature of administrative decisions and, thereby, to affect interactions between their agencies and other actors in the administrative system.

There is a prevailing decentralization and a resulting lack of uniformity in the personnel procedures for high-level career positions. Most

---

40. Warner et al., *American Federal Executive*, pp. 194–96. Note that Warner's use of the term "executive" is equivalent to our term "high-level administrator."

41. Bob L. Wynia, "Federal Bureaucrats' Attitudes Toward A Democratic Ideology," *Public Administration Review* 34 (March/April 1974): 156–62.

agency heads have the responsibility for filling positions immediately beneath them. They frequently promote people from within their own units. When they consider outsiders, they generally look to people they know in other federal agencies, in state or local governments, or in private firms.

Procedures for upper-level political appointments are organized by each president to suit his view of a proper job. Recent presidents have sought help from a screening team of individuals who are sensitive both to occupational competence and political acceptability. These procedures last only until the bulk of top appointments are filled. This is usually at the time of—or shortly after—the inauguration. After this, the president becomes preoccupied with the problems of program development and implementation. Aides in the White House Office and the top administrators in each department handle the continuing problems of replacing those political appointees who leave office.

Studies of administrators' social backgrounds and educational and career experiences show marked differences between high-level government administrators and the "average citizen." Administrators are more likely to come from a middle- or large-size city, to have a father employed in middle- or upper-status occupations, and to affiliate with a Protestant religious group. The administrators are also more likely to complete four years of college and some postgraduate education and to begin their careers in one of the professions—most likely engineering, law, or science. Although high-level administrators differ greatly from the general public, they differ much less from other occupational groups which occupy positions of responsibility. In their social backgrounds and educational attainments, for example, government administrators show greater resemblance with groups of "business leaders" than do either of these groups show with the general public.

The occupational disadvantages of two social groups—blacks and women—are evident in their distribution within administrative units. Both groups are represented disproportionately at the lower levels. Where they are in high-level positions, they are most likely in agencies that serve the specific interests of blacks or women, respectively. In recent years, however, there have been sizable increases in the number of black and female employees in administrative positions, agencies, and geographic regions that had seen few such employees earlier.

There is little information about the values, attitudes, and personalities of administrators. The information that is available ascribes to them a high regard for serving the public, an acceptance of the restraints that come along with large organizations and a pluralist political system, and an appreciation for the need to coordinate and cooperate with other administrators. There is a correspondence between this information about the federal employee and the public's image of the federal servant as described in Chapter 7. Federal administrators also have strong motivations to improve services within their fields of specialization. However, there are signs of conflict within administrators between the needs for achievement and the restraints felt from large organizations and the political process.

Several personnel issues generate political controversies. The control of appointments to government offices is a topic that has set Jacksonians—and now some neo-Jacksonians—against civil service reformers. There are sharp disagreements about the rights and prerogatives of government employees' unions and about the policies pursued by agencies to recruit members of minority ethnic groups.

6

The Management of Government Agencies

The conversion process of the administrative system is not a simple mechanism that ingests resources and demands and subsequently produces the outputs of public policy. We have already seen that rational decision-making is a complicated process, employing an elusive set of procedures. In addition, actors in the environment of the system can impose their own preferences on administrators who themselves have a variety of backgrounds and numerous preferences of their own. It is often difficult for agency personnel to agree upon a precisely worded policy that includes a clear statement of goals. Many government programs operate either without any long-range goals or with goals that are too vague to serve as precise targets of policy.

In addition to the problems of policy-formation that we have previously discussed, administrative units must also cope with internal problems of policy-implementation. Our concern in this chapter is the capacity of agency directors to obtain the cooperation of their subordinates. *What techniques can directors employ to develop the full potential of their subordinates for the support of a common effort? Can members of other governmental branches count on administrative implementation of legislative and executive decisions? What factors interfere with the smooth operation of administrative procedures?* The basic discussion in this chapter should lead to other questions: Do the techniques of agency management threaten the individual rights and privileges of government employees? To what extent can superiors deny administrators the opportunities to express their professional opinions about agency policy? Should administrators abandon their own professionally determined manner of providing services when their "political" superiors establish contrary policies? Can administrators be stripped of political rights enjoyed by other citizens, e.g., to campaign actively for candidates seeking public office or for passage of certain bills in the legislature?

It is difficult to distinguish between the preferred control mechanisms because they maintain the department head's control over his or her subordinates (and perhaps lessen control over the bureaucracy by other branches of government) and the mechanisms that impinge unduly on the freedoms of administrative subordinates. Two issues are of concern here: *administrative control* and the *personal rights of subordinate officers*. As we shall see in a later section, sociologists and psychologists have disagreed about which management techniques succeed in boosting work output and simultaneously respect or threaten the worker's individuality. One school of thought—often called the *human-relations* approach—believes that productivity and respect for the worker's individuality can go hand-in-hand. The research findings of this school discredited an earlier *scientific-management* approach that urged detailed, authoritarian control over an organization's members. More recent findings, however, advise against any uncritical acceptance of human-relations techniques that rely too much on the self-direction of subordinate administrators.

Issues of administrative management become especially sensitive when they are affected by larger public controversies. Some of the sharpest disputes in public administration reflect competing pressures to loosen and tighten the policy-control of superiors over subordinates. Controversies in many cities demonstrate conflict between proponents of professional management and of neighborhood control. When the lawyers of the Civil Rights Division of the U.S. Department of Justice accused Attorney General Mitchell of failing to pursue an aggressive policy against racial discrimination, their public presentation reflected a breakdown in internal management that had important consequences for the policy-making process. When the U.S. Post Offices closed in 1970, the whole country saw that existing mechanisms to deal with employee demands were not able to cope with the new era of militance among government workers. Since 1970, citizens in various states and communities have become more accustomed to civil service conflicts. Public school teachers, police, sanitation workers, and other public servants are striking with increased frequency. The number of government worker-days lost to strikes increased from 901,000 in 1971 to 2,299,000 in 1973.

Sophisticated social critics concern themselves not only with the character of public policy that is desirable, but with the problems of implementing policy through administrative agencies. Ralph Nader, for one, has made the public aware that it is the work of agencies, and not law, per se, which defines the nature of policy. The work that he and others have done in behalf of consumers has aroused more awareness of the role played by administrators in keeping policy responsive to the political process. But administrators do not always live up to these expectations. The *ombudsman* is a foreign invention—seeming to operate effectively in Scandinavia and New Zealand—that has been adapted by certain American states and localities as an aid to citizens who feel that administrators are not delivering the benefits due to them. The quality of administrative implementation is important in judging the quality of democracy. As we state this maxim, however, we leave unresolved the conflicts likely to arise between the rights of citizens and of civil servants.

ADMINISTRATIVE UNITS AS COMPLEX SYSTEMS

Throughout most of this book, we view administrative agencies as parts of a larger entity that we call the administrative system. Now it is helpful to remind ourselves that agencies themselves are complex organizations, having numerous elements that relate to one another in various ways. Superiors do not control actions of subordinates by merely issuing orders and monitoring performance. Subordinates and superiors respond to numerous stimuli. Administrators are motivated by economic, social, psychological, philosophical, and/or political stimuli. They see themselves in specific "roles" and, thus, may perceive the demands of numerous constituencies with differing viewpoints. Because of these varied orientations, two administrators may interpret and respond to a given set of instructions in contrary ways. At times, and in all honesty, personnel may not even "see" information that passes before their eyes, especially if such communication runs counter to their own preferred course of action. We have already seen that conflict occurs within administrative units between individuals and between groups who have different commitments and pursue different goals (see Chapter 3, pp. 59–62).

Relationships between administrative superiors and subordinates are affected by several factors. To sort out the problems that agency heads encounter in controlling their organizations, we will discuss *authority, communications, incentives,* and *leadership.*

Authority

Authority delineates the sources of influence within administrative organizations. It answers the question, "Why does X control the behavior of Y?" Many scholars have attempted to define the nature of authority and have produced long lists of factors that give some people a measure of control over others. The items most relevant to relationships in administrative units are formal power, wealth, expertise, respect, and affection.

Formal Power

Formal power reflects the provisions of constitution, statutes, or regulations that permit one person to exercise certain controls over others. In each administrative unit, certain officers have the formal power to appoint new members to the organization, promote or increase the salary of those who are already in the organization, authorize the expenditure of funds for various purposes, and approve the provision of services to clients. The chief officer of an administrative organization is likely to possess some of these powers. However, others may exercise control over budgetary or personnel matters or the agency's services to clients. In hospitals and universities, for example, it is the physicians and professors—not the head administrators—who control the distribution of medical treatment and academic grades. Many agencies have a budget or personnel officer who must certify, independent of the agency head's judgment, that fiscal or personnel actions are proper.

An officer's possession of formal power may provide *direct influence* over the behavior of other people in the organization. Budgetary officers may allow or prevent the spending of funds in certain ways by other officers. An official with the power to approve the hiring, promotion, or assignment of personnel can influence certain programs by the staff allocated to them. At times, formal power permits an officer to exercise *indirect influence* over matters that are, technically, outside the officer's own domain. Logrolling occurs in agencies as well as in the legislature. Individuals with different powers cooperate in administrative agencies, with each obtaining some measure of authority over the other because of decisions they may render at another time or for a different purpose. These relationships may persist over such a long time and may become so embedded with personal feelings that an officer's authority can depend on respect and affection, as much as it does on formal powers.

Wealth

In administrative agencies, as elsewhere, the person who controls the funds is important. The person's authority may come partly from the base of formal power and partly from the bases of respect, affection, or expertise. At the heart of this influence over others, however, is the commodity the officer can withhold or make available. Like others who possess authority, the budget officer may use resources in ways that maximize or minimize control over others. The officer may be "hard-nosed" and measure expenditures carefully; even when spending money, the budget officer may pare down the amounts or examine in detail the plans of program officers. Or the budget officer may ignore program content and focus only on the bare legal requirements of financial accountability: Is the money being spent according to the most obvious of the statutory requirements?

Expertise

Expertise is the source of the specialist's authority. Sometimes this authority is bolstered with formal powers; for example, only physicians can prescribe for a hospital's patients. Often, the title of "expert" is bestowed as a result of formal training. Sometimes, however, the designation comes gradually to a person who demonstrates an understanding of a particular problem more thoroughly than others.

Respect and Affection

Respect and affection can be intertwined with the bases of formal power, wealth, and expertise in providing the foundation of a person's authority. Especially in small or closely knit organizations, personal attachments may grow around other kinds of relationships.[1] Individuals may win respect simply because of their age or their seniority in an agency. Others benefit from their demonstrated skill in handling a certain kind of problem. For some, their most polished skills are those of gracious manners or conviviality; such people may gain authority in an agency's policy-making process simply because they have great personalities and have affective standing in the eyes of colleagues who have gained their own authority as a result of formal power, wealth, or demonstrated expertise.

To be sure, personal feelings can be negative as well as positive and can generate organizational discord rather than harmony. Likewise, other sources of authority can assert negative influences: a person with formal powers may lose subordinates' respect because the person demonstrates a *lack* of expertise or because, in a declining economy, the person has lost control over sufficient wealth to meet demands. The formal powers retained by such officeholders may continue to give them a role in policy-making, even when they can do little more than thwart the creative urges of their colleagues.

---

1. George Homans, *The Human Group* (New York: Harcourt, Brace, 1950).

Communications

Communications link the members of an administrative organization. As is known by any listener or purveyor of rumors, however, communications can do their job poorly or well. In order to control what gets said to whom, government agencies devise formal rules of communication. If everyone in the organization communicated with everyone else:

> the organization would be Babel . . . each communicator communicates with a defined and usually limited number of others. . . . A low-level employee may do little more than communicate with fellow employees and his immediate superior, and any communications he has with more senior persons in the organization is likely to be indirect and carried out by his superior. A superior has contact with his subordinates, with his peers, and with his superior. He may also have contact with a personnel officer, a budget officer, and other representatives of higher echelons in the organization. . . . In general, the more senior a person is in his organization, the more widespread are his formal communications. The more complex his responsibilities, the more people from whom he must get information and the more to whom he must give information.[2]

This passage describes proper communications in a pure hierarchy. As noted earlier, however, the hierarchy does not always perform as designed (see pp. 101–104). Even when an agency's communications are limited by rules that define appropriate "channels," several pitfalls can block effective transmission. The targets of the communication may not perceive the message as its sender intended, or they may not comply with the instructions received. People can avoid seeing messages that are sent to them, especially if the messages threaten a preferred course of action. At times, the failure to see may be intentional; but, at other times, it reflects the defense mechanism of *selective perception* that keeps an unpleasant message below the threshold of awareness. An employee may see but not recognize a hostile message, or the employee may forget it. Related to this is the administrator's capacity to read a preferred message in an ambiguous communication. Some messages are intentionally vague because the policy-makers who originated them cannot agree about the details of a precise formulation. When superiors allow the "technical details" to be ironed out by subordinates, they invite their subordinates to define important phases of the operation. If it is a controversial issue, subordinates may disagree among themselves and

---

2. James W. Davis, Jr., *The National Executive Branch* (New York: Free Press, 1970), pp. 99–100.

continue the chain of ambiguous communications. They will pass discretion further down the line to operating officers. This procedure may produce inconsistent provision of agency services to different clients.

Many organizations suffer from an *information overload*, i.e., more communications than its members can actually handle. The agency library may contain information relevant to a current problem, but the staff may be unaware of the information and not have time to make a detailed search. Also, if personnel are not cognizant of the available information, an agency may even initiate new research on a subject already investigated in an earlier project. (For a discussion of costs of information in an administrative agency, see pp. 62–63, 75–76.)

Pitfalls in the communications network of an agency put a burden on the superior officers. In order to maintain control over their organization, they must recognize which subordinates are tempted to exploit an ambiguous policy statement. Agency heads may attempt to guard themselves against insubordination by making sure a document has no loopholes that are likely to be exploited. Yet, a study of presidential leadership emphasizes that communications alone will not guarantee a superior's control when dealing with administrators who wish to act in a contrary manner. In anticipation of conflict, the president must be certain that a communication is unambiguous *and* must couple the communication with auxiliary bases of political power. The president must be certain that the formal presidential powers provide means to insist upon compliance, and the president must be sure that the instructions are "legitimate." Legitimacy—the widespread acknowledgment of proper action—will allow the president to discipline an errant subordinate without loss of the president's own political following.[3]

Incentives

Incentives are rewards offered by an organization in order to elicit the cooperation of its members. The most obvious incentive is an attractive salary with periodic increments. Other incentives include the direct provision of material benefits the employee would otherwise acquire with personal funds: use of an agency car, a housing allowance, insurance, and other fringe benefits. Some incentives have appeal mainly because of the status they confer on the person who receives them;

---

3. Richard Neustadt, *Presidential Power: The Politics of Leadership* (New York: Wiley, 1976). See also Karl W. Deutsch, *The Nerves of Government* (New York: Free Press, 1963).

these include a chauffeur for the agency car, a desirable title, and various accoutrements that go with an elevated position in the agency.

In most private firms, a superior can use incentives in a flexible manner to reward or stimulate certain individuals: a well-timed raise in pay, a subsidized vacation, or rapid promotion. In the public sector, incentives are not so readily available. Most are standardized by the regulations, statutes, or in the case of some state governments, the constitution. Such documents clearly define the salaries for certain positions, criteria for awarding promotions, kinds of transportation used by government employees, and amounts allowable for hotel rooms and meals. Likewise, there are precise regulations that govern status symbols for persons in each rank: the size and nature of one's desk (wood is more desirable than metal or plastic); the size of one's office; whether the carpeting merely surrounds one's own desk, or is wall-to-wall and extends to the secretary's antechamber; the presence of flags behind one's desk; a conference table in the office; and the size of the conference table.

Due to the position of public administration in the political system, the most visible incentives (salary and fringe benefits) are often made the subject of public controversy. Employees with the most clout in the legislature seem to be offered administration's most lucrative incentives. There are more election votes among lower-level employees than among middle- and upper-level employees. Also, employees at the bottom of the hierarchy are more often organized into unions or employee associations that are aggressive on bread-and-butter issues. The salaries and fringe benefits of lower-level employees are generally better —relative to comparable levels in the private sector—than those of middle- and upper-level employees.

The codification of incentives does not mean that an agency head is *entirely* without discretion in the distribution and amounts of rewards. The agency head can offer a choice assignment in a short-term effort to reward an employee for a job well done or in a long-term strategy to groom a promising subordinate for an eventual promotion. A patron can help proteges build an impressive set of credentials by giving them opportunities to prove themselves in challenging (but not impossible) assignments or by rotating them among various units so that they can become familiar with the full range of agency operations. Conversely, the head can block the career of errant subordinates who might otherwise be scheduled for assignments that would advance their standing. The agency head can also approve or reject an employee's request for a subsidized trip to a professional convention at an attractive resort; this is not unlike the corporation's trip to a "watering hole" for a job well done.

A leader's incentives are limited by their compatibility with the desires of other subordinates. To be of use to the leader, an incentive must offer a desired commodity. For some employees, the willingness of the boss to consult with them on important decisions is sufficient incentive to maintain their agency loyalty. Some personnel are stimulated by the prospects of salary, promotion, choice assignments, status symbols, or friendly encouragement by the boss. Certain of these incentives may influence some people at one point in their career, but these same incentives may have no effect at a later time. As a person's salary increases, for example, there may be diminishing incentives attached to each additional dollar. Once a person occupies an executive suite and feels the first ulcer pain, the prospect of further promotion may lose its appeal. As with communications, the successful use of incentives depends on the skill of the agency head. The better the agency head understands the desires of subordinates, the better the agency head will be able to tailor the incentives to fulfill those desires.

Incentives can also emanate from an administrator's colleagues or from subordinates. Respect, conviviality, or social rejection may result if an administrator meets or fails to meet the informal norms of a work group. These norms may compete with those of superiors in regulating the amount of work to be done, the treatment extended to clients, and the acceptance of other agency policies.[4]

Leadership

Leadership is a summary label for all the material discussed in this chapter. The effective leader of an administrative unit uses authority, communications, and incentives to guide and control subordinates. The leader puts it all together. It is already evident, however, that good leadership is not a simple process. There are various bases of authority, plus different kinds of incentives and communications. Authority may be questioned; communications can go astray; and the available incentives may not satisfy the desires of subordinates. There is no assurance that the holder of a formal position will be an effective leader. Just before Harry S Truman left the presidency, he said:

He'll sit here, and he'll say, "Do this! Do that!" And nothing will happen. Poor Ike—It won't be a bit like the Army. He'll find it very frustrating.[5]

---

4. See, for example, F. J. Roethlisberger, *Man-in-Organization* (Cambridge, Mass.: Harvard University Press, 1968).

5. Thomas Bailey, *Presidential Greatness* (New York: Appleton-Century-Crofts, 1966), p. 78.

Truman was speaking from governmental experience, but without intimate knowledge of field command in the military. From his own vantage point, General Eisenhower could have responded that, in the army, directives are not always administered with utmost efficiency.

The leader's role is ambiguous. A leader cannot expect that orders will be obeyed on the basis of words alone. At the very least, the leader must be sensitive to the complex nature of organization and of the larger environment in which it operates. An agency head in the national government, for example, must recognize that subordinates respond to their own sense of proper action, to professional standards acquired in their training or previous experience, to the demands of clients, and to the propensities of actors in the U.S. Congress, state and local governments, and numerous interest groups. As stated in a classic study of leadership:

> All leaders are also led; in innumerable cases, the master is the slave of his slaves. Said one of the greatest German party leaders referring to his followers: "I am their leader, therefore I must follow them."[6]

A recent study of a man with a reputation for strong leadership described his tactics with the terms "compromise," "bargain," "cajole," "swap," "bend," "plead," "amend," "coax," and "unite."[7]

The leader of an administrative agency must contend not only with the sensitivities of "subordinates" and other actors in the environment but also with established procedures and previous commitments that minimize discretion. In Chapter 3, we examined the elements that inhibit the use of "rational comprehensive" decision-making and encourage and use of mutual adjustment and routine decision-procedures. Although such compromises and routines limit the leader's options, they do not reduce the leader to an automaton who has no options. However, they do put a premium on the leader's capacity to identify those opportunities when previous commitments and routine procedures permit the formulation of a major new policy.

There are considerable differences in the operating styles of administrative leaders. The elements that caution against a simple-minded notion of arbitrary command do not prevent some leaders from being more forceful than others. Numerous studies describe variations in leadership style. One study contrasts "authoritarian" and "participative";

---

6. Georg Simmel, "On Superordination and Subordination" quoted in John Manley, "Wilbur D. Mills: A Study in Congressional Influence," *American Political Science Review* 63 (June 1969): pp. 442–64.

7. Manley "Wilbur D. Mills," pp. 442–64.

another compares "get-the-work-out" and "human-relations" styles of leadership.[8] It is frequently observed that no particular style is uniformly more effective than others.[9] Situational traits vary markedly from one administrative setting to another. It is a prime task of a leader to determine the important constraints in any situation, what is worth fighting for, and what tactics will be most effective.

THREE MODES OF ORGANIZATIONAL CONTROL

Agency heads have many choices in attempting to influence the behavior of subordinates. Choices depend partly on the resources available and partly on their opinions of what will effectively shape workers' performance. Some assessments about useful control procedures are both personal and haphazard. Most governments, however, do not allow their administrators to operate with complete freedom. Proper techniques of agency management are the subject matter of executive manuals and training sessions and are often reduced to statements of do's and don'ts. Over the course of the 20th century, the prescriptions offered to agency managers, and the assumptions about employee motivation and behavior upon which those prescriptions are based, have changed. The changes did not occur in government alone, but they have reflected widespread attitudes about the control of people in public and private organizations. Indeed, much of the impetus for public-management theory has come from prior developments in large business firms. Research into employee performance on the industrial assembly line and in the management sectors of large merchandising operations, investment banking units, and insurance companies has found its secondary influence in the management manuals of national, state, and local governments.

Scientific Management

The first major approach in 20th-century management theory carries three distinct labels: *classical theory,* due to its seniority; *scientific management,* based on its pretentions at precise measurement and prescription; and *Taylorism,* in honor of its creator and most prominent

---

8. See Davis, *National Executive Branch,* pp. 110–13.
9. James D. Barber, *Political Leadership in American Government* (Boston: Little, Brown, 1964), Introduction.

advocate.[10] Advocates of this approach assume that employees are motivated primarily by economic incentives, that the performance desired by an organization can be defined in precise terms and taught to employees, and that physical fatigue is the most important limit on employee compliance. Scientific management had its most direct applications to the highly repetitive work of an industrial assembly line. The clipboard and the stopwatch were its most famous symbols. "Time-and-motion studies" were designed to measure how quickly employees could perform each of the tasks that comprised their particular job, how heavy a load they might carry, and how physical fatigue diminished their productivity. By watching employees and testing various procedures for each of their tasks, Taylor's "human engineers" produced such findings as:

1. The two hands should begin and complete their motion simultaneously.
2. Smooth, continuous motions of the hands are preferable to zigzag or straight-line motions involving sudden and sharp changes in direction.
3. Proper illumination increases productivity.
4. There should be a definite and fixed place for all the tools and materials.[11]

After the "one best way" of doing a job was defined, engineers would scale incentives to the procedure and schedule of work they had established. Piecework was the preferred incentive: an employee would be compensated in a direct relation to the work actually produced. If piecework was not possible either because of the nature of an employee's job or due to an objection by the labor union, then payment by the hour was preferred to payment by the week or month. Work was clearly prescribed and payment offered in response to closely monitored activities. Money was considered as the primary motivation:

> The principal objectives of the employee are to secure maximum earnings commensurate with the effort expended, while working, insofar as conditions will permit, in a healthful and agreeable environment.[12]

What importance did scientific management have for public administration? Some agencies applied its principles to mail-sorting and

---

10. The dominant early work in this field was Frederick W. Taylor, *Scientific Management* (New York: Harper, 1911).
11. See Amitai Etzioni; *Modern Organizations* (Englewood Cliffs, N.J.: Prentice-Hall, 1964), p. 22.
12. Quoted in James March and Herbert Simon, Organizations (New York: Wiley, 1958), pp. 18–19.

other such repetitious tasks. Thus, the time-and-motion study entered the portfolio of the public manager. In more subtle ways, the widespread adoption of "human engineering" in private industry spread to the public sector and influenced the ways in which organizations were designed and managers trained. The principle of hierarchical management and the consequent design of government departments into neat pyramids with precise chains-of-command drew on the precepts of scientific management (see pp. 110–12). Even in dealing with middle- and upper-level government administrators, there was acceptance of Taylor's view of an organization's member as a pliable instrument who would, given appropriate material inducement, perform the assigned tasks. The employee was not seen as a variable personality having needs, preferences, attitudes, and commitments, all of which must be considered by the organization's leaders. Those who designed government departments and trained their managers were concerned with "span of control" (i.e., how many subordinates a manager could supervise) and with other principles of the "one best way" for management: each subordinate should have a single superior; there should be no division of responsibility; there should be no responsibility without commensurate authority.[13] These principles were far too simple to be actually supportive of precise recommendations. To the credit of their creators, however, it must be said that the special studies undertaken to investigate departments did recognize that subtle forces (many of them "political") operate in and around public bureaucracies. A reader who examines some of the theoretical writing and actual recommendations identified as "scientific management" wonders how helpful the theory really was to those who used it—and to some of those who wrote it.

"Economy" and "efficiency" were the prime goals of public-management experts who utilized some of the precepts of Taylor's scientific management. Their emphasis on fiscal matters reflected both the industrial origins of their organizational theory and the fiscal conservatism that prevailed among government reformers from the early part of the century onward.[14] President Taft appointed a commission on economy and efficiency to advise him on management reform in the national government. As did the subsequent series of similar reform groups, culminating in the second Hoover Commission established in the early 1950s, the Taft Commission concentrated on budgetary and per-

---

13. March and Simon, *Organizations*, p. 22. Also, L. H. Gulick et al., *Papers on the Science of Administration* (New York: Institute of Public Administration, 1937).
14. See Richard Hofstatder, *The Age of Reform* (New York: Knopf, 1955).

sonnel instruments that would both increase the president's control over the sprawling administration and save money.

A recurrent theme in the literature of scientific management is that a manager can learn everything for the job. There was, presumably, "one best way" of doing a job. Academic texts and courses in public administration offered POSDCORB as an acronym that represented each major component of management science: planning, organizing, staffing, directing, coordinating, reporting, and budgeting. These are procedures that superiors use to control subordinates. In discussing these procedures, textbooks and manuals minimized any concern with the leader's sensitivity toward the goals, motivations, or norms of employees. Problems involved in maintaining efficient communications, designing effective incentives, or providing leadership to a diverse and demanding organization were also minimized.

Human Relations

The excessive simplicity in the assumptions of scientific management spawned an opposing body of management literature. Its most common name—human relations—highlights its crucial distinction from scientific management. The new school of thought viewed employees as complex human beings whose personal motives, goals, and cultures would have to be considered by leaders who wanted effective control over their organizations. According to proponents of the human relations theory, there can be no "one best way" of management because an organization's members are not pliable enough to fit precast molds. Likewise, money alone is not a sufficient inducement to ensure the cooperative effort of employees. They also want status, security, respect, freedom to define their own working situation, and an opportunity for the work group to help set the organization's norms.

The human relations challenge to scientific management originated in the late 1920s. As a result of a research project that examined the performance of industrial workers under a variety of conditions, it was found that several of Taylor's principles did not work as expected. Economic incentives did not assure rates of production that utilized employees' full physical capacity. Moreover, it was discovered that formal leaders were competing with informal leaders who were recognized as such by the workers themselves. The employees who were influential in defining work norms were not necessarily the supervisors or managers. Informal sanctions were imposed when output went too high or fell too far below the work group's norms. The informal sanctions included the threat of withdrawn affection or respect by one's peers and—under extreme provocation—damage to one's tools or personal property.

The human relations approach emphasized that work output depended upon the quality of relationships among employees and their leaders. The prior concern with "chain of command" and "span of control" was replaced by accentuation on effective communications, attentiveness to employees' motives and morale, consultations between formal leaders and organization members, and employee participation in the definition of their working conditions, e.g., production norms, coffee breaks, parking privileges, vacation schedules, and the promotion of workers to supervisory positions.

For many of the prescriptions of human relations literature, there was a ready market in public, as well as private, organizations. The advice to consult with employees, to recognize the existence of employee groups that set informal norms, and to provide a variety of noneconomic incentives fit the needs of governmental service departments that employ large numbers of highly trained professionals. While much of the writing stressed the contribution of human relations to increased output and efficiency, a substantial portion of the literature went beyond the needs of the organization, per se, to relate them to issues of ethics, morality, and theology. The writing is not without its saccharine qualities:

> The way to make the organization fully rational was to increase by deliberate efforts the happiness of the workers. There are many almost lyric pages in Human Relations writing which depict the worker as anxious not to miss a day at the factory or to come too late lest he miss spending some time with his friends, and even as anxious not to disappoint his foreman who is like a warm and understanding father to him. The work team itself is often referred to as a family. The Human Relations approach maintained that "employees should have a feeling that the company's goal is worth their effort; they should feel themselves part of the company and take pride in their contribution to its goal. This means that the company's objectives must be such as to inspire confidence in the intentions of management and belief that each will get rewards and satisfactions by working for these objectives."[15]

New Synthesis in Management Techniques

At the present time, there is a growing dissatisfaction with both the scientific management and the human relations approaches to administrative control. The problems with scientific management are, essentially, those cited by the human relations school of thought. Even

---

15. Etzioni, *Modern Organizations,* p. 40.

critics of the human relations literature credit it with producing an important awareness of the social and psychological needs of organizational members. However, the principles of human relations are now considered to overlook several problems and to be overly simple. Three criticisms directed at the human relations approach are (1) it substitutes *employee happiness for economic production* as the dominant task of leadership; (2) it deemphasizes the use of material incentives to obtain compliance with organizational goals; and (3) it fails to perceive and cope with persistent conflicts between goals of the organization and goals of the employees.

While these criticisms may be somewhat exaggerated, there is a considerable amount of oversimplification in the human relations literature. In much of human relations writing, there are *implicit* recommendations that the "one best way" to run an organization is to maximize the members' happiness. Moreover, in the fascination with social and psychological incentives, there is minimum attention to economic incentives. This is doubly unfortunate: not only does it overlook the substantial incidence of employees who *are* motivated by considerations of salary and other tangible rewards, but it also places too much emphasis on a kind of incentive that organizations can provide only with great difficulty. Decisions about salary and fringe benefits can be made with clarity, and the rewards can be precisely allocated to deserving employees. If an organization seeks to control its members via intangible rewards, however, it enters a domain where its managers and supervisors may not be able to supply the necessary incentives. Top management can oversee the distribution of material rewards far more easily than it can monitor the distribution of psychological and social gratifications.

A "manipulative critique" attacks both scientific management and human relations, saying that both seek to exploit the employee for the benefit of an organization. Just as time-and-motion studies exploited the fatigue of industrial workers, the human relations expert is said to use the personal needs of employees to profit the employer. Human relations says "happiness," but it means increased productivity. Its concern is not with the employees' emotional and social well-being, except as these will produce more output.[16]

Akin to the manipulative critique is a denunciation of the human relations' equation of employee and organizational interests—that each is bound to the other as one happy family. Some assert that the one-happy-family effort is inaccurate; that is, the organization has its own

---

16. Etzioni, *Modern Organizations*, p. 44.

needs, and these change at different times and for different reasons than do employees' needs. Others contend that the one-happy-family effort may harm the organization by inhibiting changes that would be in its own best interest or, if changes are made, by frustrating employees who view this as a fracture in their organizational family. Other critics maintain that the notion of an organizational family is insulting and unfair to employees. An overdose of human relations resembles the paternalism of an older-style company town. It can discourage employees from nurturing their separate interests and make them excessively vulnerable (both economically and emotionally) to the fortunes of their organization.

At this time, it does not appear as if any one approach is becoming dominant in the field of administrative management. There are several distinct orientations. As might be expected in any literature that has seen two full generations, present-day writers are borrowing in an eclectic fashion from all of their major predecessors, as well as from intellectual currents that have passed through other branches of social science.

One writer describes a "structuralist" approach that seeks to "take everything into consideration."[17] Its proponents view the organization as a system, having an environment and internal components that are dependent upon one another. By this reasoning, every organization may be unique; each may require separate efforts to identify features of environment, employees' traits, and leaders' characteristics, all of which influence one another. Under some conditions a leader might pursue a human relations concern with maximizing worker satisfaction, while elsewhere the leader might profit from a more classical interest in tying wages to output.

Another school of thought views employee conflict as a constant element; persons thrive on competition and will compete for a target defined by their informal groups if the agency does not provide its own target. This is a neo-Hobbesian view of organizational life.[18] In an open culture with strong unions, anything so overt as a Stakanovite Award for extraordinary production may backfire on the management.[19] However, annual salary increments that depend on some reasonable standard of performance may add life to an organization made bland by too much of a human-relations emphasis.

---

17. Etzioni, *Modern Organizations,* especially chapter 4.
18. Michael Crozier, *The Bureaucratic Phenomenon* (Chicago: University of Chicago Press, 1964).
19. After Aleksei A. Stakhanov, a Soviet miner identified with a system of awarding workers who exceed their production quotas.

There is almost an infinite menu from which to choose in the literature of organizational control. If some writers fault leaders for soothing the workers only in an effort to benefit managers, others write that there actually is a common interest between the organization and its members. A widely read author argues that organizations can pursue their own needs while preserving the dignity of their employees. He recommends management techniques that draw heavily from the human relations literature, but that are said to pay off for the employer while they respect the employee's personal drives, and that are wrapped in a citation of the Judaeo-Christian Ethic:

> Most people ideally prefer to be and actually can be self-controlling in the attainment of organizational objectives, given the proper organization of work.... Such assumptions—and they seem generally realistic—underlie the structural arrangements and managerial techniques consistent with the Judaeo-Christian Ethic.[20]

EMPLOYEE-CENTERED ORGANIZATION: THE MINNOWBROOK PERSPECTIVE

Not all modes of organizational control are designed to integrate employees into smooth-functioning units that carry out the missions chosen by superiors. Another approach to organizational control would rely on the choices made by the working administrators themselves. This approach received its most distinctive statement at the Minnowbrook Conference Center of Syracuse University and in a book titled *Toward a New Public Administration: The Minnowbrook Perspective.*

The historical setting of the Minnowbrook conference made itself felt. The initial papers were written in 1968 amidst considerable upheaval in American politics and administration. The influences ranged from the assassination of John Kennedy, riots in Watts and other urban ghettos, the first years of the Johnson administration and the development of community action and its concern for "maximum feasible participation," Vietnam, and the assassinations of Martin Luther King and Robert Kennedy, plus the confrontations at the Democratic convention in Chicago.

It is appropriate to note the incidence of sharp disagreements among the authors and other participants at the conference. Yet, most seemed to share certain points of view.[21]

---

20. Robert T. Golembiewski, *Men, Management, and Morality: Toward a New Organizational Ethic* (New York: McGraw-Hill, 1965).

21. See the review by Victor A. Thompson in *American Political Science Review* 66 (June 1972): 620ff.

1. A perception of revolutionary ferment and change;
2. A perception of government being repressive and unresponsive to demands from racial and low-income minorities;
3. Claims for the maturity of young people;
4. Demanding that social science, including public administration, adopt explicit value orientations, identify with the interests of powerless minorities, and promote equity in income and power;
5. Urging overt political roles for public administrators;
6. Advocating a political process of confrontation rather than negotiation and compromise.

The participants signaled their commitment to confrontation by challenging the leadership of the conference itself:

Why did we have to have formal papers? If we were really the young and the new, why were we so bound by the traditional in our conference arrangements? Who chose the topics? Weren't there more important topics?[22]

In its concern to promote policy-making by administrators, the Minnowbrook perspective criticizes hierarchical controls and offers "confrontation" and "consociated"[23] models of administration. An important concern is the freedom of administrators to express and pursue their political goals:

In searching for the foundations of a new approach to normative theory in Public Administration, this essay has thus far suggested two general guidelines: (1) that such a theory must accommodate the values and motives of individual public administrators to theories of administrative responsibility; and (2) that the essential congruence of administrative freedom and political freedom must be recognized.[24]

Writers saw administrators as policy-makers likely to speak for disadvantaged minorities while "elected officials speak basically for the

---

22. Frank Marini, "Introduction: A New Public Administration?" in Frank Marini, ed., *Toward a New Public Administration: The Minnowbrook Perspective* (Scranton, Pa.: Chandler, 1971), p. 4.

23. "Consociated" models are offered as an alternative to the bureaucratic model, and are said to include a "multivalent authority structure" summarized as "a. no permanent hierarchy; b. situational leadership; and c. diverse authority patterns among various project teams." See Larry Kirkhart, "Toward a Theory of Public Administration," in Marini, *Toward a New Public Administration,* pp. 158–61.

24. Michael M. Harmon, "Normative Theory and Public Administration: Some Suggestions for a Redefinition of Administrative Responsibility," in Marini, *Toward a New Public Administration,* p. 179.

majority and for the privileged minorities. . . ."[25] In instances of conflict with elected officials, administrators should not remain passive:

> Public Administration . . . must find means by which it can enhance the reelection probabilities of supporting incumbents . . . building and maintaining of roads or other capital facilities in the legislators' district, establishing high-employment facilities, such as federal office buildings, county courthouses, police precincts, and the like, and distributing public relations materials favorable to the incumbent legislator. . . . As a consequence it is entirely possible to imagine legislators becoming strong spokesmen for less hierarchic and less authoritative bureaucracies.[26]

This kind of patronage is standard operating procedure in relations between the elected chief executive and members of the legislature. Yet, the Minnowbrook perspective would have administrators disperse patronage and reduce the chief executive's control over the bureaucracy. Just who within the administrative units would have the opportunity to engage in this kind of politics? The conferees did not make that clear.

What is surprising in the papers that advocate more power for undefined personnel in the administration is the virtual lack of concern that the devolution of authority to working administrators may turn against the values expressed by the writers. What would control the brutality of an unrestrained police officer, the racism of a school teacher, the undisciplined infantry lieutenant in Vietnam, or the Air Force general who sought to ignore specific orders of his superiors against bombing? Each of these events was a feature of the era that prompted the Minnowbrook conferees to urge more political and policy-making activity by administrators. Yet, the conferees seemed blind to the possibility that the freedom they urged upon administrators would loosen vital control procedures and unleash more of the forces they abhorred. One writer recognized that the "politics of love" might become a "politics of suppression." But his final sentence could offer only "hope" that things would go the right way.[27]

CONSUMERISM AND ACCOUNTABILITY

The demands of consumers and other citizen groups for administrative delivery of services compete for attention with the rights and privileges

---

25. H. George Frederickson, "Toward a New Public Administration," in Marini, *Toward a New Public Administration,* p. 329.

26. Frederickson, "Toward a New Public Administration," p. 326.

27. Orion F. White, Jr., "Social Change and Administrative Adaptation," in Marini, *Toward a New Public Administration,* p. 83.

of government employees. Herbert Kaufman takes the position that "subordinate compliance . . . is a pillar of democratic government."[28] He reports on a study of devices that agency heads use to monitor the compliance of their subordinates. While Kaufman is sensitive to issues of employees' rights, he is not one to ignore the needs of control.

There is an overlap between the problem of subordinates' noncompliance with instructions and the problem of leadership described earlier in this chapter. Prominent among the causes of noncompliance are the failures of agency heads to communicate their instructions clearly or to make their instructions compatible with their subordinates' time, equipment, and training. It is mostly in another kind of noncompliance—subordinates who refuse to follow instructions that they are able to understand and carry out—where we encounter the sticky problems of conflict between democratic theory and employee rights. Yet, not all cases of willful noncompliance raise serious issues of subordinates' rights. When police officers sleep when they are supposed to be patrolling, they do not raise the same kind of problem as do staff physicians who refuse to perform abortions as a matter of conscience.

There are several means at the disposal of superiors to check on their subordinates' compliance with instructions: routine reports that subordinates file about their activities; inspections by headquarters personnel of operations in the field; and the inquiries made by central budget and audit agencies. There are also the extraordinary investigations that are triggered by a disaster in an agency's domain, like a plane crash, flood, or outbreak of contagious disease. Such inquiries usually deal with the preparation of an agency to deal with emergencies and the compliance of its staff with safety measures and other procedures.

Agency heads do not depend entirely on formal procedures to keep tabs on their subordinates. There is also an administrative grapevine, plus the mass media and interest groups, to convey information about what is really happening at the operating levels of an extensive organization. Kaufman's study of control mechanisms found an agency head's web of personal contacts to be an important source of information, although one that may also carry a fair amount of myth, falsification, innuendo, and partial truth. The media and interest groups did not prove to be major sources of information. Despite the inroads made on the public's awareness by Ralph Nader and other critics of administrative performance, the media and interest groups still concern themselves

---

28. Herbert Kaufman, *Administrative Feedback: Monitoring Subordinates' Behavior* (Washington: Brookings Institution, 1973). Note the difference between Kaufman's use of the term "feedback" and my own.

more with the prominent details of formal policy than with subtle problems of policy delivery by administrative agencies.

All the means of checking on subordinates' activities do not assure agency compliance with official policy. Problems may lie in the office of the agency head where procedures may not be adequate to sift through all the reports and to identify patterns of noncompliance among subordinates that warrant attention. The agency head may be more concerned with acquiring new programs and seeking personal coverage by the media than with seeing to the effective implementation of existing programs. Or the agency head may feel uneasy with formal policy and either permit or encourage personnel at operating levels to do something else. Citizens concerned with administrative compliance will rely on administrators only at their peril. We return to this issue in Chapter 8 and deal with a number of devices—including elections and the ombudsman—that may allow citizens to influence or control the activities of their public servants.

SUMMARY

The conversion process of the administrative system is affected by the personal needs and political demands of the administrators themselves, as well as those of other actors in the environment. Because of this complexity, the control of agencies is no simple task. Authority, communications, incentives, and leadership reflect various aspects of administrative management. These elements also represent extensive fields of inquiry in their own right; in this chapter some of the problems are shown that are pertinent to administrative control. Major disputes appear among three approaches to management that have become prominent in this century: scientific management, human relations, and now an amalgam of several views that are united only in their feeling that earlier approaches were inadequate.

The initial impetus for changes in management technique often comes from the private sector. When each new approach achieves distinction in public administration, however, it is combined with other controversies to make the management of public agencies a subject of political dispute. How much should we pay employees? Should we recognize their rights to bargain collectively or to participate in policy-making for their agencies? Issues like these clothe themselves in the provocative labels of "freedom to bargain collectively," "professional self-determination," "faculty rights," and "patient-physician relationships." With claims of this sort, public administrators manifest their independence from their organization. If agency heads do not succeed in maintaining communications and providing appropriate incentives, latent organizational conflicts spill over into confrontations that involve not only public employees and their administrative superiors, but also the agency's clients, other members of the public, and other branches of government.

The Minnowbrook perspective reflects considerable anger among some scholars and administrators who feel that traditional approaches to organizational control thwart the freedoms of administrators. Yet, there are also those, like Herbert Kaufman, who view subordinates' compliance with instructions as an integral feature of democracy.

Part Two

THE INPUTS
OF THE
ADMINISTRATIVE
SYSTEM

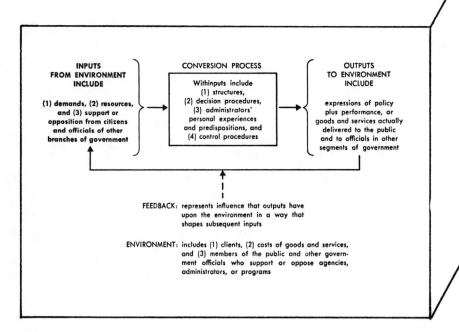

**INPUTS
FROM ENVIRONMENT
INCLUDE**

(1) demands, (2) resources, and (3) support or opposition from citizens and officials of other branches of government

CONVERSION PROCESS

Withinputs include
(1) structures,
(2) decision procedures,
(3) administrators' personal experiences and predispositions, and
(4) control procedures

**OUTPUTS
TO ENVIRONMENT
INCLUDE**

expressions of policy plus performance, or goods and services actually delivered to the public and to officials in other segments of government

FEEDBACK: represents influence that outputs have upon the environment in a way that shapes subsequent inputs

ENVIRONMENT: includes (1) clients, (2) costs of goods and services, and (3) members of the public and other government officials who support or oppose agencies, administrators, or programs

The inputs of the administrative system are the transmissions that come to the conversion process (i.e., administrative agencies) from actors in the environment. These actors include clients of the agencies, government officials in the legislative and executive branches, officers of other administrative agencies, political parties, interest groups, the mass media, and interested citizens. The inputs these actors provide to administrators include demands for services; political support or opposition; and the resources of tax funds, legal authority, and citizens' willingness to accept employment in administrative agencies.

Chapters 7, 8, and 9 deal with various kinds of inputs. Chapter 7 examines the attitudes toward administrators that exist in the political cultures of the United States. These attitudes can make themselves felt in the political support that administrators receive from the public and from legislators and executives who are sensitive to the voters' wishes. Chapter 8 focuses directly on relationships between citizens and administrative agencies and on several institutions that contribute to those relationships, i.e., the mass media, public opinion polls, elections, interest groups, and political parties. Chapter 9 describes two branches of government that figure prominently as providers of demands and resources to administrative agencies: the legislature and the executive.

7

The Status of Public Administration

"Political culture" includes the beliefs, attitudes, and values that affect public affairs. In this chapter, we are concerned with those aspects of the political culture that relate to administrative agencies.[1]

Political culture provides several kinds of inputs to administrative agencies. First, it nurtures those individuals who are eligible to join the bureaucracy. Thus, the attitudes about government bureaucracies that prevail in the culture can shape the behaviors of those recruited to the administration. Popular attitudes make public employment a generally desirable or undesirable career. Prevailing attitudes can pose serious problems for government recruiters, especially if the distribution of attitudes means that the skills most needed by government agencies are found among people who are not favorably disposed to join the agencies. Second, a political culture can influence the elites who allocate resources to administrative agencies. In the United States, elites include elected legislators and executives who make formal decisions about government programs, plus interest-group and party leaders, the corporate leaders who control the mass media, and private citizens who have the skills, money, or time to involve themselves heavily in public affairs. The feelings of these groups can affect the legal authority and the funds given to government agencies.[2]

---

1. See Samuel C. Patterson, "The Political Cultures of the American States," *Journal of Politics* 30 (February 1968): 187–209. This article is valuable in itself *and* for the extensive bibliography cited in it.

2. It is not clear whether officials respond to their own judgments or to those of their constituents in making decisions; available research suggests that this varies with the kind of decisions to be made and with the degree of interest shown by constituents. See Warren E. Miller and Donald E. Stokes, "Constituency Influence in Congress," *American Political Science Review* 57 (March 1963): 45–56. Also see Charles Cnudde and Donald McCrone, "The Linkage between Constituency Attitudes and Congressional Voting Behavior," *American Political Science Review* 60 (March 1966): 66–72.

A search through the commentaries about public bureaucracies does not reveal any consistent set of beliefs, attitudes, or values. Administrative agencies are frequent targets for positive and negative comments. There is no homogeneous attitude about public employees or about the administrative departments of government. Although some statements suggest there is a sizable reservoir of negative sentiment toward administrative processes, many people believe public agencies should be given even greater responsibilities and resources than they have received so far.

Among the terms used to describe administrators are unimaginative, hindering, protectionist, security-conscious, dull-witted, unfit for private employment, harsh, aggressive, empire-building, insensitive to popular values, and aloof. These terms have been used by elected officials and by candidates for office, as well as by political commentators and by private citizens asked for their views in opinion surveys. Yet other people in these same categories use such contrasting terms about public employees as the following: honest, able, well-trained, efficient, dependable, interested in serving the public, personable, and sensitive. Public administrators can see opportunities as well as problems in the political culture.

ASSESSMENTS OF ADMINISTRATIVE AGENCIES IN PAST POLITICAL LITERATURE

The early years of the American Republic passed without much commentary about administrative agencies. The concerns of political writers focused on other features of government, e.g., the division of powers between state and national governments and the powers of the executive, legislative, and judicial branches of government. The Constitution has little to say about administrative departments and agencies. Although it has influenced the evolution of administrative organizations in national and state governments, this is largely the result of the powers assigned to the president and to Congress and, thus, of their roles in administrative development.

The administration is mentioned several times in the *Federalist Papers,* but its position is distinctly subordinated to the constitutional offices. Hamilton mentions the administration more often than other authors, and he gives it a secondary rank below the presidency. He argues that the president should control the appointments of administrators and should be responsible for their supervision. He defends a long term for the president, partly because this would permit long terms for subordinates. "There is an intimate connection between the duration of the executive magistrate (i.e., the president) in office and the stability of the system of administration."[3] While Hamilton acknowledges the importance of administration, he sees the presidency as of greater concern than the administration:

> We cannot acquiesce in the political heresy of the poet who says:
>
> > For forms of government let fools contest—
> > That which is best administered is best—
>
> yet we may safely pronounce that the true test of a good government is its aptitude and tendency to produce a good administration.[4]

At the heart of this early fixation on the roles of the presidency and legislature was the relatively small role that administrators played. In the following passage, Hamilton makes his own estimate about the small numbers of people involved in administration and argues that they are not likely to show any major increase:

> It is evident that the principal departments of the administration under the present government are the same which will be required under the new. There are now a Secretary of War, a Secretary of Foreign Affairs, a Secretary for Domestic Affairs, a Board of Treasury, consisting of three persons, a treasurer, assistants, clerks, etc. These officers are indispensable under any system and will suffice under the new as well as the old. As to ambassadors and other ministers and agents in foreign countries, the proposed Constitution can make no other difference than to render their characters, where they reside, more respectable, and their services more useful. As to persons to be employed in the collection of the revenues, it is unquestionably true that these will form a very considerable addition to the number of federal officers; but it will not follow that this will occasion an increase of public expense. It will be in most cases nothing more than an exchange of State for national officers.[5]

Although Hamilton may have underestimated the size of the administration for the purposes of his argument in defense of a Constitution that was criticized because it would enlarge the national government, he was

---

3. *The Federalist Papers* (New York: Mentor Books, 1961), Number 72.
4. *The Federalist Papers,* Number 68.
5. *The Federalist Papers,* Number 84.

not far from the truth. By 1792, the federal service counted only 780 employees, plus some additional deputy postmasters; by 1801, there were only 2,120 civilians plus another 880 deputy postmasters. Few of these employees were engaged in anything more complicated than tax collecting, record keeping, and copying. The professionals consisted of some physicians and engineers employed by the military, plus surveyors and lawyers. The civil service was hardly the body of expertise that it has become; there seemed little threat that it would challenge the constitutional branches as a maker of important decisions.[6]

Perhaps the earliest—and most profound—concern with the administrative system occurred during the presidency of Andrew Jackson. By 1830, the federal bureaucracy had grown to over 11,000 civilian employees and was populated largely by members of upper-class families appointed during the administrations of John Quincy Adams and James Monroe. To Jackson, the incumbents were aliens both in social class and in partisan loyalties. In his inaugural address and messages to Congress, President Jackson described the character of the administration as a hindrance to reform. Unless he removed large numbers of incumbents and replaced them with his own supporters, he could not count on the departments to carry out his programs. President Jackson felt that the responsibilities of public officials were "so plain and simple that men of intelligence may readily qualify themselves for their performance."[7] He had a dual justification for removing the appointees of his predecessor and replacing them with his own men: (1) the administration's policies should conform with those of elected officials; and (2) government jobs are simple enough to permit frequent turnover without significant loss in expertise.

Perhaps in response to Jackson's personnel policies, some observers noted a decline in the competence of public administrators. In the early 1820s, Alexis de Tocqueville found, "so much distinguished talent among the citizens and so little among the heads of government." Also:

It is a constant fact that at the present day the ablest men in the United States are rarely placed at the head of affairs; and it must be acknowledged that such has been the result in proportion as democracy has exceeded all its former limits.[8]

---

6. See Leonard D. White, *The Federalist* (New York: Macmillan, 1948).
7. From Jackson's *First Annual Message to Congress*, December 8, 1829.
8. Quoted in Franklin P. Kilpatrick et al., *The Image of the Federal Service* (Washington, D.C.: Brookings Institution, 1964), p. 32.

"Jacksonian" personnel administration represents some procedures for appointing and dismissing employees on the basis of "political," rather than "technical" qualifications. It was—and is—practiced to varying degrees by many executives. It is identified with Jackson, not because he was the first to sweep out existing employees when he came to office but . . . because he provided the rationale for political removals and appointments and practiced the art in an overt manner. Actually, he removed no larger a percentage of federal employees than did President Jefferson 20 years earlier.[9] The public service may have reached its most political level at the time of the Civil War. President Lincoln used his powers of appointment and removal to select pro-Union administrators and to assure that government officers would use their powers in support of the Union. The civil service was not freed from political control after the Civil War. It experienced the clash of noble and ignoble values that typified Reconstruction.[10]

Throughout the period from President Jackson to President Arthur, there were several efforts to isolate government employment from the worst excesses of venality and partisanship. Reform at the national level took a major step forward with the Pendleton Act of 1883. Its major features were a Civil Service Commission that would—with some political independence of the president—administer personnel policies; use "merit" as a primary criteria for government employment; employ competitive examinations for the selection of employees; protect "covered" employees from being coerced to support the campaigns of political parties; provide immediate coverage of about 10 percent of federal employees; and give authority to the president to expand the service covered by the act by means of executive orders.

This is not the place to describe in detail the mechanisms of personnel administration as they evolved through frequent amendments of the Pendleton Act, or as they were adopted by many state and local governments (see pp. 109–110 and 160–63). Despite 140 years of talk and activity since Jackson's inaugural message, there are still disputes about administrative organization. By now, however, the administrators of many governments are sufficiently "professional" for most disputes to avoid extreme charges about patronage and venality. Some commentators describe public agencies in the most negative of terms; but other com-

---

9. Kilpatrick et al., *Image of the Federal Service*, p. 32. For a general history of the period, see White, *The Federalist*; plus, Paul Van Riper, *History of the United States Civil Service* (Evanston, Ill.: Row, Peterson, 1958), chapters 2–3.
10. Van Riper, *History of the United States Civil Service*, chapter 4.

mentators would expand the roles that administrators play in policy-making. Some would expand professionalism where a partisan service still exists; but some argue that merit protection has advanced too far. They find chief executives—especially the governors of certain "merit" states—unable to fill important positions with individuals who share their policy perspectives. Like President Jackson, these executives feel they cannot control their administration without having more control over appointments.

CONTEMPORARY VIEWS OF PUBLIC ADMINISTRATION

It is not easy to report a fair representation of the views toward public administration expressed by contemporary observers. Politicians range from outright condemnations of "bureaucrats" and "redtape" to praise for the administrative units that operate their favorite programs. Among political scientists, there is a mixture of respect and reservation about the activities of administrators. Two political scientists who reflect this mixture in their own writings are Norton Long and Emmette Redford.

Norton Long has written numerous articles about administrators. At an earlier point in his career, he described them in positive terms as widely representative of the population in their personal backgrounds, and as infusing professional and creative forces into government. He felt that bureaucracies add to constitutionalism by representing interests that are not otherwise heard in the legislative and executive branches.[11]

According to Long, the bureaucracy's involvement in the policy-making process is inescapable. The bureaucracy contains the highest concentration of information about existing programs; this includes information about the operation of current projects and about the unmet needs not being served. Most proposals considered each year by the legislative and executive branches come from the administrative departments. The administration's expertise makes it representative of interests that do not have adequate representation in the legislature. The departments contain the talents of science, professions, and institutions of learning; more than in the legislature, the values that are identified with these institutions are likely to be voiced in the administration. The departments contain people who are trained to think in terms of general

---

11. Norton E. Long, "Bureaucracy and Constitutionalism," *American Political Science Review* 46 (September 1952): 808–18.

principles and of the implications of policy for those principles, as well as containing people who would pursue the immediate benefits sought by clientele groups. Moreover, the bureaucracy is likely to contain persons coming from a wider range of social and economic backgrounds than is the case in congressional committees. To the extent that these backgrounds are indicative of values, they ensure that the bureaucracy will make its proposals only after extensive deliberation. Because of both wider expertise and more diverse values, the nature of decision-making in the bureaucracy is likely to be more thorough and more responsive to social needs than the legislative process.

In a more recent work, Long paints a depressing picture of urban pathologies and traces many of the problems to local bureaucrats.

The tragedy of the growth of the local public sector is that while it provides income to those it employs, it has no necessary connection with increasing the viability of the local economy and, all too often, is so much dead weight dragging it down.[12]

Long's assessment of the local bureaucracy reflects, in part, the fractured nature of local government in metropolitan areas (see pp. 322–24). Long sees a loss in the urban sense of community. To paraphrase the theme of *The Unwalled City,* the city no longer has walls its citizens feel compelled to defend. The urban area is a hodgepodge of separate entities, with each one of them useful to persons only as it meets certain of their economic needs. The city resembles a market more than a community and cannot call upon the emotional commitments of people who take *citizenship* seriously. City employees have little incentive to show any greater attachment to the community. To them, according to Long, the city is an employer that will pay a salary, but who will not demand high-quality performance. Long writes about "stagnant, costly, unenterprising, consumer-be-damned behavior of centralized, irresponsible, and unresponsive bureaucracies."[13]

Emmette Redford is concerned with the responsiveness of the "administrative state" to the norms of democratic procedures. He sees American society inexorably enmeshed in administrative processes, whether they be with the public agencies of government or the private organizations of big business, labor unions, schools, or charitable foundations. Yet, the administrative state can operate in a way to respect

---

12. Norton E. Long, *The Unwalled City: Reinstituting the Urban Community* (New York: Basic Books, 1972), p. viii.

13. Long, *Unwalled City,* p. 93.

democratic morality. Redford summarizes this morality as concern for individual people in the criteria used in making decisions; as an effort to assign each person's needs equal weight in policy deliberations; and as an effort to make as broad as feasible the opportunities for people to participate in the decisions that affect them.[14] Redford identifies several features that administrative units should have in order to respect the democratic morality. Then he gives the administrative organization of the national government high marks with respect to them. The crucial features include:

1. Sufficient fragmentation of administrative decision-making so that a limited group of individuals does not have the sole authority to make the important decisions for any sector of policy;
2. Wide access to policy-making machinery by citizens who can act through the election of legislators and a chief executive, who can make individual requests of administrators, or who can exert concerted action through group protests or civil disobedience;
3. Adequate control of administrative units by "overhead" institutions that represent the electorate;
4. The interaction of individuals with different perspectives (of social class or professional training) within the arenas in which important decisions are made; and
5. Efforts to keep the personal interests of employees out of policy-making, perhaps by enforcing conflict-of-interest regulations or by a program of professional training that socializes decision-makers into universalist (as opposed to particularist) norms.[15]

Redford has high respect for individual administrators, but he is not content to permit administrators to operate their own agencies without some assurance of external and/or internal controls. A major weakness Redford finds in his study of national administration occurs outside the administration itself—in the structure of Congress. He feels that congressional leadership is not responsive enough to the demands of the broad national constituency. This problem results from the congressional seniority system that puts into positions of importance legislators who are not subject to a wide range of policy demands from their own constituents. Because of this inadequacy in Congress, Redford finds a great burden of administrative control is left with the president. Yet, this individual—even with the assistance provided by the Executive Office—

---

14. Emmette S. Redford, *Democracy in the Administrative State* (New York: Oxford University Press, 1969), p. 6.
15. Redford, *Democracy in the Administrative State,* chapter II.

is overloaded and unable to carry the burden of transmuting citizen demands into administrative policies.

THE PUBLIC'S VIEW OF
PUBLIC ADMINISTRATION

The sophisticated views of political commentators testify only to the availability of certain ideas in the intellectual marketplace. Some valuable information about the public's opinions of administrators comes from a survey, sponsored by the Brookings Institution, that dealt with views toward administrators of the national government. The product of its survey—*The Image of the Federal Service* by Franklin P. Kilpatrick, Milton C. Cummings, Jr., and M. Kent Jennings—reports the attitudes of more than 5,000 people chosen to represent a cross-section of the employed population outside of the federal government, federal civilian employees themselves, students and teachers in high school and college, plus several groups of business and government executives, natural scientists, social scientists, and engineers.[16]

The Brookings study shows no clear set of attitudes held by any large majorities in the population. There is a large reservoir of favorable sentiment toward administrators, but this support is not so widespread or unqualified that the administration can expect unlimited grants of resources. There is a higher regard for some attributes of administrative units than for others. Unfortunately, individuals in upper-status occupations (who are most important as potential recruits or political allies) show the least favorable sentiments toward the administration.

People reveal their sentiments most clearly when asked to compare the public service with some counterpart in their surroundings. In this way, they are least likely to confuse their description by using a wide variety of "unanchored" standards. If people report that some feature of administration is "better" or "worse" than a comparable institution in the private sector, we can see where administration stands in their evaluations. The most useful data in the Brookings survey shows evaluations of top-level people in the federal service in comparison with top-level people in private business.

---

16. This study focuses primarily on the public's view of federal administrative jobs and jobholders. In this section we extrapolate at times from its findings to other features of the public's view about administrative agencies. See Franklin P. Kilpatrick et al., *Image of the Federal Service*.

The general employed public and almost all of the occupational and educational groups within it rank top-level public employees higher than their counterparts in business on the traits of *honesty* and *interest in serving the public*. Most relationships are actually in the middle ranges of a 10-point scale, suggesting the lack of clarity in the public's attitudes. However, federal employees score less favorably than the business people on having the *respect* of respondents, a *drive to get ahead,* and *ability*. These figures are consistent with other information from the same survey. When the respondents were asked in open-ended questions to describe the federal service, the largest number of them listed attributes that could be labeled "good personal character." These traits included honesty, high integrity, ethical standards, and moral fiber. However, the trait of security-consciousness was also assigned to public employees.[17]

Although private employees are viewed more favorably than government employees on the traits of respect, ability, and drive, this finding should not be taken as a sharply negative evaluation of the public bureaucracy. On each trait, the general public ranked the federal service in the upper one-third of the range. In only two cases did subgroups of the general population score the federal service below 5.0 on a 10-point scale: business scientists and engineers gave low marks to federal employees in their "drive to get ahead."

The lack of ambition—and the related trait of security-consciousness—is a component of the public's feeling toward administrators. However, this trait may not reflect a strong condemnation of administrators. When this finding is viewed along with the assessments of honesty, interest in serving the public, and ability, the assessment of low personal ambition suggests that many people respect the administrators without suspecting them of power-mania. The public might approve increased resources for the administrative agencies without fearing that administrators will use the resources in an unrestrained manner.

One of the most important resources that citizens can grant to government is their own talent. To the extent that people will consider a government job for themselves, they show a support for administrative units that may include a willingness to grant other resources, e.g., tax

---

17. These findings are consistent with those observed in other studies of public opinions about government employees or government employment. See Leonard D. White, *The Prestige Value of Public Employment in Chicago* (Chicago: University of Chicago Press, 1929); and Leonard D. White, *Further Contributions on the Prestige Value of Public Employment* (Chicago: University of Chicago Press, 1932); and Morris Janowitz, Deil Wright, and William Delaney, *Public Administration and the Public* (Ann Arbor: University of Michigan Institute of Public Administration, 1958).

money and legal authority. Several questions on the Brookings survey assess the willingness of people to consider employment with the federal government as compared to comparable positions in the private sector.

There is considerable sentiment that favors the government as an employer; but this sentiment is not found among many of the skilled and educated persons that government agencies most want to attract. However, there is some evidence that the *most* talented individuals are the most inclined to accept federal employment. An encouraging sign —from the government's point of view—is the greater appeal of government service for high school, college, and graduate students with the highest academic grades.

What features of government employment are the major attractions and drawbacks? Again, the opinions are consistent with other tendencies already reported. People are most likely to cite security and fringe benefits as the attractions of government employment, while the lack of self-determination, "bureaucracy," and "redtape" are the greatest deterrents.[18] People who prize ambition and drive are more attracted to private than to public employment. Those who are already successful (as shown by incomes) are most likely to be disturbed by problems of self-determination in government, while those with low incomes are most attracted by the security, fringe benefits, and working conditions in government.[19] Even among those with the highest incomes, however, it is only a substantial minority (35 and 27 percent) who cited lack of self-determination and bureaucracy or redtape as undesirable features of federal employment. Federal recruiters may have to work harder in convincing well-trained individuals to consider government jobs; but the level of antigovernment sentiment is not pervasive among them.

The Brookings Institution survey points to more or less positive attitudes toward public administration as stable among large sectors of the American population. Certain sectors of the public are less supportive, however, especially in their attitudes toward particular administrative agencies. Numerous surveys have found central city blacks with predominantly hostile views toward the police.[20] Moreover, a number of polls have found the public generally to be moving in the direction of alienation from the government.[21] Such results are more recent than the

18. Kilpatrick et al., *Image of the Federal Service*, p. 120.
19. Kilpatrick et al., *Image of the Federal Service*, p. 122.
20. See Joel D. Aberbach and Jack L. Walker, *Race in the City: Political Trust and Public Policy in the New Urban System* (Boston: Little, Brown, 1973).
21. See Robert S. Gilmour and Robert B. Lamb, *Political Alienation in Contemporary America* (New York: St. Martin's, 1975).

Brookings' poll and may reflect a lessening in support for administration revealed there. We return to these issues both in Chapter 8 in connection with public opinion polls and in Chapter 11 in connection with the evaluation of administrative outputs.

POLITICAL CULTURES AND ADMINISTRATIVE ORGANIZATIONS IN STATES AND REGIONS

Professor Daniel J. Elazar has sought to identify underlying cultural patterns in almost 360 separate areas of the 48 states. His work is speculative, but it provides some insight into the support offered to the administrative units of different state and local governments.[22] Elazar identifies three principal types of political culture: moralism, individualism, and traditionalism. As he describes them, they form a linear scale on several traits. Two of these traits are relevant for the kinds of support that an administrative organization requires from its environment. In its orientation toward *bureaucracy,* the moralist culture values extensive, well-paid and professional administrative corps at all levels of government. The individualist views government bureaucracy as a fetter on private affairs, but also as a resource that public officials can use to further their own goals; some individualists support political machines that carve up public resources and distribute them as payments to individuals.[23] The traditionalist is most opposed to the growth of bureaucracy as a restraint on the traditional political elite. Thus, a moralistic culture should coexist with a large and well-paid administration, while individualistic and traditionalistic cultures should have smaller and less-well-paid administrative staffs.

On another dimension that is relevant to administrative units, the moralist welcomes public services for the good of the commonwealth; the individualist would minimize public services to permit a balance of satisfactions from activities in the private and public sectors; and the traditionalist would oppose all government activities except those necessary to maintain the existing power structure. Thus, the moralistic culture should coincide with high levels of taxation and government ex-

---

22. Daniel J. Elazar, *American Federalism: A View from the States* (New York: Crowell, 1972).

23. See Edward Banfield and James Q. Wilson, *City Politics* (Cambridge, Mass.: Harvard University Press, 1963), chapters 9 and 13, for a discussion of "private regardingness."

penditure and with generous levels of public service. Individualistic and traditionalistic cultures should score low on taxes, expenditures, and services. Based on several years of observation and on research in state histories and newspapers, Elazar has mapped the cultures that prevail throughout the continental United States. Figure 7–1 shows his designations.

While Elazar's designations of political culture cannot—by the nature of his research techniques—be considered the final word on the subject, they do highlight some prominent regional differences that have long been observed, plus some intraregional variations that suggest the ambiguous nature of political cultures in many areas. The South is the most traditionalistic section of the country, but it has a moralistic component in the Appalachian region and has individualistic regions in the Southwest and border states. Moralism is prominent in New England and in a number of Middle Western states that experienced populist or progressive movements. Individualism is not prominent throughout any large section of the country; it is present as a secondary culture in many areas and appears dominant only in parts of the West.

These dimensions of political culture seem to have some importance for administration.[24] State scores on several measures pertaining to administrative units and their outputs correspond closely with the traits expected on the basis of Elazar's cultural designations. The states that place high on the moralistic end of the scale (and therefore low on traditionalism) tend to show large numbers of state and local government employees relative to population, high-average salaries for government employees, and a high incidence of government employees who are covered by subsidized health and hospital insurance. These states are innovative with respect to the introduction of new programs, and they show high-tax payments relative to personal income, high-government expenditures per capita, and high scores on several measures of educational services public assistance programs, and highway services.

In focusing on the various political cultures of the United States that affect administration, we should not leave the impression that this covers the range of cultural-administrative relationships. Outside the United States the varieties of culture are greater and the influence on

---

24. Ira Sharkansky, "The Utility of Elazar's Political Culture: A Research Note," *Polity* 2 (Fall 1969): Leonard G. Ritt, "Political Cultures and Political Reform: A Research Note," *Publius: The Journal of Federalism* (Winter, 1974), pp. 127–33; and Charles A. Johnson, "Political Cultures In American States; Elazar's Formulation Examined," *American Journal of Political Science* 20 (August 1976).

FIGURE 7-1.

The Regional Distribution of Political Cultures Within the States

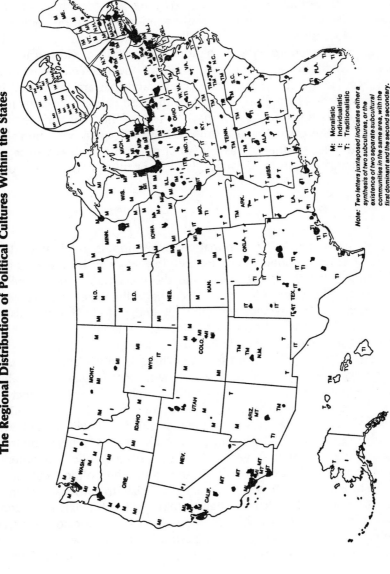

M: Moralistic
I: Individualistic
T: Traditionalistic

Note: Two letters juxtaposed indicates either a synthesis of two subcultures, or the existence of two separate subcultural communities in the same area, with the first dominant and the second secondary.

SOURCE: Daniel J. Elazar, *American Federalism: A View from the States*, 2nd edition (New York: Crowell, 1972), pp. 106–7. Copyright © 1972, by Thomas Y. Crowell Company, Inc., with permission of the publisher.

administration profound. Just considering the countries with highly developed economies, it is possible to find widely differing kinds of relationships between citizens and officials or between the officials of national and local authorities. It was not so long ago that the visit of a Japanese prefectural governor to a local community could be compared to a royal procession.[25] French, as well as Japanese, local officials see themselves as the subordinates of national officials in a wide variety of matters. Their cultures lack the predispositions toward regional or local prerogatives that appear in American culture and that are reinforced by the American federal structure. Specialists in these national cultures may find internal variations, just as we have described internal variations in the cultures of the United States. Culture is an influence on administration, but it is not a straitjacket, and it is not so simple as to be packaged in homogeneous American, Japanese, French, or other national versions.

SUMMARY

This chapter is the first in a group that deals with inputs to administrative units. The focus is on political culture and, in particular, on the attitudes held by sophisticated commentators and the mass public about public bureaucracies. These attitudes may affect the willingness of citizens to seek government employment and the willingness of elected officials to provide funds or legal authority to administrative agencies.

Political cultures in the United States do not contain a single set of attitudes about public administration. There is much ambiguity and no widespread sentiment toward administrators that is clearly favorable or unfavorable. While some sharp sentiments may exist with respect to individual programs or agencies, the attitudes toward administration as a whole are generally mixed, moderate, and permissive. This is evident both from sophisticated commentaries about government administrators and from opinion surveys that measure the public's sentiments toward administration. Because of this ambiguity, the political culture is not likely to restrict the actions of elected officials toward the administration. The data in this chapter suggest that elected officials have considerable "freedom" from public opinion when they allocate resources to administrators. Moreover, prevailing attitudes are not the only factors that influence the resources allocated to administrative units. Elected

---

25. Kurt Steiner, *Local Government in Japan* (Stanford, Calif.: Stanford University Press, 1965), p. 54.

legislators and chief executives respond to numerous other stimuli; they can overlook, modify, or help to shape public demands.

Many people rank federal employees higher than business employees on the traits of honesty and interest in serving the public; but they rank business employees higher on the traits of personal drive, ability, and respect by the public. Perhaps it is most significant that people generally rank *both* federal employees and business employees in the middle ranges on a 10-point scale. There is some tendency for occupational groups that are most needed by the government to rank government service below business, but even here the data are not uniform. A large number of people in the desired occupations rank government employees higher than business employees, and there has been a slight tendency for the most talented high school, college, and graduate students to give government employees higher scores than business employees. Yet, there are threatening signs of hostility or alienation, especially among certain groups in the population. The public's attitudes neither simplify the task of government recruiters nor discourage them. Many people having the skills needed by government are favorably inclined to the prospect of government services; and the attitudes unfavorable to government are not so intense—or so widely held—as to make it impossible for legislators or chief executives to allocate generous resources to administration. On occasion, administrators may use unfavorable poll results in their arguments for more resources, in order to improve services. Yet, sentiments toward administrators are not so clearly favorable that individual politicians cannot benefit from an occasional foray against the "bureaucrats."

8

Citizen Demands
and Administrative Agencies

This chapter focuses on relationships between citizens and administrative agencies and on several institutions said to be transmission belts between them—the mass media, public opinion polls, elections, political parties, and interest groups.

INDIVIDUAL CITIZENS AS PROVIDERS OF INPUTS TO ADMINISTRATIVE AGENCIES

In discussing the roles that individual citizens play as input-providers vis-à-vis administrative systems, it is necessary to distinguish between general tendencies and special cases. Some private citizens are prominent in providing the stimuli that cause administrative agencies to formulate policies and make certain decisions. Moreover, the citizenry as a collective body is valued highly by many administrators. We saw in Chapter 5 that administrators express their sensitivity to public needs. Individuals may receive courteous hearings on matters that affect them personally and may affect an administrator's decision about their cases. Chapter 7 shows that many citizens—when responding to public opinion surveys—give high marks to administrators for the traits of honesty and public-mindedness. When it comes to citizen influence over the major policies that are formulated or implemented by administrative agencies, the evidence is mixed. Moreover, the evidence does not always apply directly to matters of administration. Much of the data come from studies that focus on other aspects of the political process, e.g., studies of popular attitudes and behaviors during election campaigns or in reference to policies being considered by the legislative branch.

There are some data that suggest citizens are largely ignorant of policy matters. They are not familiar with the concepts central to policy debates, and they hold views about policies that appear "inconsistent" or "unreasonable." Although these findings do not by themselves signify a lack of knowledge about *administrative* activities, they do suggest that most citizens are unaware of the most prominent controversies about policy. A group of surveys taken during the 1943–50 period showed that 84 percent of a sample did not understand the concept of "feather-bedding";[1] 51 percent did not know the meaning of "balancing the budget"; 46 percent did not understand *any* of the terms "monopoly," "antitrust suit," "interlocking directorate," or "Sherman Act"; and about 75 percent did not know the meaning of "free enterprise."[2] To answer any of these questions correctly, it was not necessary to provide the pollsters with a learned treatise. Any indication of familiarity was satisfactory.

The findings of inconsistency in policy opinions have shown up in several polls. A survey made in 1956, for example, discovered that *supporters* of welfare programs were more likely to *oppose a tax* that would pay for these programs than were the people who opposed welfare programs. Also, those who were *most in favor of a tax cut* were also more likely to *support* programs that would guarantee employment, low-cost medical care, and federal aid to education.[3] The apparent irony is that many people oppose the taxes that seem necessary to pay for their desires. In contrast to these findings that demonstrate a lack of familiarity with matters of policy, there are some additional data that suggest citizens are selective in their attention to policy. On matters of personal concern, they show awareness of issues and state preferences that are consistent with their economic self-interest. Even in the case of the "inconsistent" views about welfare programs and tax cuts that we just reported, the economic characteristics of people with these views suggest that they may be answering in a reasonable, well-informed fashion. People who express support of lower taxes and improved services tend to have low incomes. They favor services that would help

---

1. Although this term may be unfamiliar to the present generation of undergraduates, it was very salient in an era when government policy toward labor-management conflict was a prominent controversy. "Featherbedding" refers to the practice of requiring more workers on a job than is actually necessary. This data comes from V. O. Key, Jr., *Public Opinion and American Democracy* (New York: Knopf, 1961), p. 183.

2. Robert E. Lane and David O. Sears, *Public Opinion* (Englewood Cliffs, N.J.: Prentice-Hall, 1964), p. 61.

3. Key, *Public Opinion and American Democracy*, p. 167.

them (education, job security, and welfare), while they oppose any increase in their taxes. Perhaps they expect other income groups to pay for the programs. This is not an unreasonable desire, insofar as the tax systems of most state and local governments are regressive and presently take a larger percentage-bite out of low incomes than out of high incomes.[4]

Other opinion surveys support the conclusion that people understand the implications of policies that have important *personal consequences*. One such poll was made in Wisconsin during a political campaign when gubernatorial candidates were debating tax policy. Low-income people were clearly more hostile to a general sales tax "on everything you buy" than were upper-income people, as such a tax would take its heaviest bite out of lower incomes. As expected, increased education added to the tendency of persons to answer in a fashion consistent with their economic self-interest. The well-educated poor were the most hostile to this proposal, which threatened to tax the commodities (especially food) that account for most of their spending. These same low-income people were most likely to switch their support to alternative proposals that were less threatening to their pocketbooks—namely, a sales tax, with food and clothing exempted, plus an increase in the (progressive) state income tax and a reduction in the (regressive) local property tax.[5] This tax package would increase the tax burdens of upper-income persons, but it would reduce those of lower-income citizens. Other research complements these findings by showing that people who feel most involved in an issue are likely to demonstrate the most accurate information about it.[6]

There may be a special meaning in this combination of widespread ignorance about public policies, but "reasonable" responses to questions that are personally significant. Under ordinary conditions, most citizens ignore policy activity. When an issue arises with importance for their own lives, however, they may acquire accurate information and

---

4. Ira Sharkansky, *The Politics of Taxing and Spending* (Indianapolis: Bobbs-Merrill, 1969), chapter II.

5. Sharkansky, *Politics of Taxing and Spending*, chapter II. A "progressive" tax is one that imposes increasingly higher percentage demands on higher incomes; a "regressive" tax, in contrast, imposes its highest percentage demands on lower-income people.

6. Key, *Public Opinion and American Democracy*, p. 190. Also see V. O. Key, Jr., *The Responsible Electorate* (Cambridge, Mass.: Belknap Press of Harvard University Press, 1966); and James L. Sundquist, *Politics and Policy: The Eisenhower, Kennedy and Johnson Years* (Washington, D.C.: Brookings Institution, 1968), especially chapter 2.

perhaps involve themselves in policy-making. They may vote according to candidates' positions on the key issues, join an interest group that pressures elected officials and administrative agencies, or take part in overt demonstrations against administrative units. The Vietnam conflict motivated many otherwise-passive citizens to demonstrate their opposition to conscription and other military policies and to disrupt the proceedings of government agencies. Likewise, policies in the field of public assistance have motivated welfare recipients who are normally apolitical to support the policies that affect them directly or even to engage in violent actions against the property or personnel of welfare agencies. Recent surveys have shown a marked increase both in the public's concern for policy issues and in public dissatisfaction with government services. As we show in later pages of this chapter, some of this dissatisfaction is intense and appears as cynicism and alienation that indicate an unsettling malaise in the administrative system.

Citizen Involvement in Policy-Making and Administration: The Case of Neighborhood Democracy

"Power to the people" is a cry heard with some frequency in the United States. Like other slogans its meaning is not always clear, but it is seldom a sign of support for established bureaucracies. The inner neighborhoods of large cities offer numerous experiments in citizen involvement in policy-making and administration. These offer us the opportunity to see some of the problems involved in self-government, as well as the intensity of certain opponents of established agencies.

Various kinds of neighborhood government have appeared.[7] Some —like block associations—are self-help bodies established by neighborhood residents that have little or no contact with municipal authorities. They focus on clean-up, fix-up, paint-up campaigns and block parties. Others—like "little city halls"—may be the establishment's effort to decentralize some decision-making authority to the bureaucrats working in the neighborhoods, with little or no consultation between officials and neighborhood residents. Often there is a combination of citizen initiative and official responses. Some cities have neighborhood school boards with certain controls over budgetary and personnel matters, but these

---

7. This section relies on Richard L. Cole, *Citizen Participation and the Urban Policy Process* (Lexington, Mass.: Heath, 1974); and Douglas Yates, *Neighborhood Democracy* (Lexington, Mass.: Heath, 1973).

school boards still have to work with city-hall bureaucrats. The goals of neighborhood governments also vary, sometime from one neighborhood to another in the same city. In some, the prominent feature is intense protest, inflamed rhetoric, grudging cooperation with the authorities, and policy demands that would require the economic muscle and regulatory powers of state or national governments. Elsewhere, there is a prosaic concern with clean streets, improved upkeep of private property, or pragmatic efforts to channel citizen complaints to the proper officer in the city's bureaucracy.

The varied map of neighborhood government is matched by varied evaluations. In judging their success, it is necessary first to adopt one of several perspectives: as a citizen, as an established bureaucrat, as the mayor or members of the city council, or as an abstract standard of political theory. We can judge experiments according to their contributions to citizen involvement in public affairs, the substantive improvement of certain local services, or the citizens' sense of satisfaction with their services.

The record of accomplishing these goals shows some consistent patterns from one locale to another. Citizen trust in local government has shown some increase in places having neighborhood institutions. On the other hand, the record of actual citizen involvement in these institutions is not impressive: turnout rates for neighborhood elections has ranged between 1 and 5 percent; residents and officials have not scored well in surveys designed to tap their knowledge of what neighborhood programs actually exist; and studies of citizen boards show their members preoccupied with long lists of petty issues and having poor records of decision follow-up. Some shortcomings may reflect the inherent weakness of neighborhood bodies to make or implement major policies. Successful projects in education, welfare, policy, housing, and jobs may depend on the resources or statutory powers that neighborhood bodies do not control. The fragmented nature of government in the metropolis defies coordination by neighborhood bodies having limited authority and political leverage; by powers divided between agencies jealous of their independence; and by local bodies responsible, in part, to state and national agencies. The political support for neighborhood autonomy is not dependable. In some communities, the enthusiasm of black elites for home rule at the neighborhood level has evaporated as they gain control of the mayor's office and acquire an appreciation of authority centralized in their own city hall. In the discussion of outputs in Chapter 11, we return to the subject of neighborhood government and report some findings of program changes associated with community action programs.

THE MASS MEDIA AS INTERMEDIARIES
BETWEEN CITIZENS AND ADMINISTRATORS

The mass media can add to the information citizens have about public affairs and can enhance their influence on administrative agencies. The mass media—including newspapers, popular journals, radio, and television—carry inputs between people and administrative units. The media also have their own influence on administrators. First, they provide information about public affairs. Second, they help shape the agenda of public debate by emphasizing some issues and making them more important than others. Third, they originate some issues by "campaigns" against social problems, the failures of government programs, or the malfeasance of certain officials. The operators of newspapers and broadcasting networks liken themselves to other "muckrakers" who have been responsible for major innovations in public policies.[8] However, it is not clear how often the media influence policy. The events surrounding one television documentary illustrate the analytic problems involved in attributing policy influence to the mass media.

In May of 1968, CBS broadcast "Hunger in America." It illustrated in powerful detail the horrors of starving children and the inadequacies of existing government programs. The television program had an immediate effect on some administrators, if only to force some defensive public statements. The secretary of agriculture identified some factual errors in the telecast and condemned it as "a biased, one-sided, dishonest presentation of a serious national problem.[9] However, over the succeeding months, the federal government took several steps to increase the flow of food to the poor.

It is not possible to identify the specific impact of "Hunger in America." Coming as it did in the midst of numerous other expressions about the same social problem, it probably added some pressure to Congress, to the president, and to the Department of Agriculture. Yet the media joined a gang-attack that was already underway. In the preceding year, a private foundation sponsored a survey by several promi-

---

8. Classic examples of "muckraking" literature include the following books: Upton Sinclair's *The Jungle*, which aided the campaign to begin the regulation of food processing by the federal government; Michael Harrington's *The Other America*, which informed and aroused readers about the condition below the "poverty line" in the United States and helped in the development of the programs of the Office of Economic Opportunity; and Ralph Nader's *Unsafe at Any Speed*, which provided much of the evidence—and passion—for the federal auto safety regulations.

9. Elizabeth B. Drew, "Going Hungry in America," *Atlantic* (December 1968): 53-61.

nent physicians and local practitioners in the "Delta" counties of northwestern Mississippi. Their report to the Senate Subcommittee on Employment, Manpower, and Poverty then provoked other prominent groups and individuals. The subcommittee attracted a great deal of press coverage, partly because Robert F. Kennedy was a member of the subcommittee and (at the time) a potential candidate for the presidency. The food problem was made a target of the "Poor People's Campaign," which itself was stimulated by public reaction to the assassination of Dr. Martin Luther King. Labor unions also joined the issue. The Citizens' Crusade against Poverty (with support from the United Auto Workers) published a critical assessment of the federal government's food programs entitled "Hunger, U.S.A." Undoubtedly, the media did increase popular interest in the food problem by popularizing an issue that had been raised by others. The media also illuminated some administrative and legislative arrangements that limited the effectiveness of the Agriculture Department's policies. Food programs were developed to relieve the surplus problems of farmers as well as the hunger of poor people; administrators and legislators who were directly involved seemed more oriented to agricultural than to social considerations. Part of the hassle that CBS entered was between House and Senate Agriculture Committees, which included Mississippians Jamie Whitten and James Eastland (frequently accused of being short on social conscience) and the Senate Labor and Public Welfare Subcommittee on Employment, Manpower, and Poverty, chaired by Joseph S. Clark and including Robert F. Kennedy.

Several factors keep the media from exercising continuing control over either the public or administrative agencies.[10] These include people's lack of reliance on the media as their source of political information, the lack of attention to public affairs that is evident in much of the mass media, and the media's lack of ability to force their political interpretations on citizens who are inclined in other directions.

The media do not have a captive audience of vulnerable personalities. Instead, citizens are involved in a network of relationships with one another that provide their own kinds of information. For many people, political discussions with compatible friends, family members, or co-workers are viewed as more reliable sources of political information than can be found in the media. Many individuals distrust the political messages included in the media they otherwise enjoy, and they erect "defense mechanisms" against undesirable information. The phenom-

---

10. This section relies heavily on Key, *Public Opinion and American Democracy*, chapters 14–15.

enon of "selective perception" leads individuals to overlook items of "fact" or "opinion" that challenge their own views.

From many newspapers or broadcasting stations, there is little *useful* information about administrative agencies or other aspects of politics. Most of the media are organized for commercial rather than political purposes. Local newspapers or television stations carry wire-service copy on national or international news, usually in small proportion to the space (or time) devoted to sports, advertising, or recreational material. Local political news is likely to be thin, perhaps, because the manager wishes to avoid sensitive issues or lacks a news-gathering staff. Under these conditions, news about administrative agencies may be especially limited. Without the excitement guaranteed by election campaigns or the involvement of prominent personalities, the media are not likely to view administrative events as "newsworthy." Even news that is concerned with personnel appointments to major offices or changes in regulatory policies is likely to receive little coverage in local newspapers or television stations. If citizens wish to make intelligent assessments of administrative affairs, they may have to get their information from other sources.

Administrators and other policy-makers often credit the mass media with a powerful role in public affairs. At times, they are obsessed with the media's influence on their reputations or the fate of their policies. Presidents Johnson and Nixon, Vice President Agnew, and Secretary of State Kissinger sought to manage the media with selective handouts of vital information and occasionally villified those reporters and commentators who described their activities in uncomplimentary terms. Numerous figures throughout the bureaucracies of national, state, and local governments repeat these patterns on their own smaller stages by seeking to put the best face on their activities for the benefit of the media and occasionally becoming preoccupied with the adversary relations that develop between themselves and the media.

PUBLIC OPINION POLLS AS INTERMEDIARIES BETWEEN CITIZENS AND ADMINISTRATORS

The public opinion poll is another institution that transmits citizens' opinions to administrative units. Polls are taken on a variety of subjects, e.g., support for political candidates and incumbent officeholders, plus various approaches to public policy. There seems to be no lack of information about the public's approval or disapproval of personalities and programs. However, the quality of poll results does not assure public influence over administrative units or over other branches of government. Much of the time, opinion polls do not tell officials what the public is thinking about the problems that the officials currently face. It is rare that an issue presents clear and simple alternatives that lend themselves to polling. The questions on many polls are too general to help the policymaker. Opposition to an increase in taxes, for example, does not signify that the public will not oppose an increase of a certain percentage—as applied to people with certain kinds of income—if the increase in revenues will be used to support certain kinds of public services. The public's support for a certain politician does not identify which programs are receiving support. Moreover, most surveys do not indicate how seriously people stand by their opinions. Many respondents may have thought for the first—and last—time about an issue on being questioned about it. Administrators must keep these limitations in mind when they ponder the implications of public opinion surveys for their agency's program. Most of the time administrators seek new programs—or try to maintain or enlarge existing programs—without any certain measure of the public's opinions. The information that administrators do have about public opinions comes only partly from polls. Other sources are informal solicitations of agency clients or a casual reading of editorials.

A technical problem with public opinion polls is the need to match a population surveyed with a jurisdiction having control over public policy. Nationwide surveys do not usually include enough people from individual states or communities to reveal how such discrete populations feel about issues. Surveys of individual states or cities are available on an occasional basis, but their expense keeps officials from having a running account about how their constituents feel about issues currently on the policy agenda.

In 1970, the Urban Observatory—an institution jointly supported by the Departments of Health, Education, and Welfare and Housing and Urban Development, plus the National League of Cities—surveyed the populations of ten cities. The purpose was to gauge citizen attitudes with respect to city governments and services.[11] The surveys showed how citizens ranked local services as to their importance and their feelings toward the critical issue of more services vs. lower taxes. By and large, citizens of all the cities gave similar weights to various service needs.

---

11. Floyd J. Fowler, Jr., *Citizen Attitudes Toward Local Government, Services, and Taxes* (Cambridge, Mass.: Ballinger, 1974).

There was almost universal concern about the drug problem; somewhat less concern about maintaining the quality of housing; little concern about crimes which do not threaten people (like gambling or prostitution); and little concern about reforming the nature of the school system in fundamental ways. There was widespread dissatisfaction with the property tax as a source of local revenue. Residents of different cities disagreed about the issue of services vs. taxes. In six cities (Albuquerque, Atlanta, Denver, Kansas City [Mo.], Nashville, and San Diego), more people wanted services improved than taxes cut; in four other cities (Baltimore, Boston, Milwaukee, and Kansas City [Kans.], majorities felt that local taxes were too high.

While some surveys are useful in pinpointing citizen attitudes toward concrete issues that lie within the authority of elected officials or administrators, other surveys tap underlying currents. Nationwide surveys, taken since the 1950s, find a marked increase in citizens' sense of alienation from politics. Expressions of distrust for the government appeared in 25 percent of those people surveyed in 1972; individual feelings of powerlessness in 28 percent; and feelings of the meaningless nature of political activity in 52 percent. Each of these measures approximately doubled since the middle or late 1950s.[12] Pollster Louis Harris found an increase in "powerlessness, cynicism, and alienation" over the 1966–73 period going from 29 to 55 percent of the population.[13] Such attitudes are heavily represented in all social groups and all regions of the country, but they appear most frequently among the poor and the least educated. At the same time, there is increasing disatisfaction with the major political parties. As yet, there is no evidence that large numbers of voters prefer a nondemocratic alternative to the American political process,[14] although some concern is appropriate.

What has produced this alienation? What can be done about it? Explanations cite the war in Southeast Asia and the unsettling domestic changes of the 1960s. Such explanations point to problems in charting a simple course—via changes in public policy—toward a repair of the body politick. Consider the improvements in civil rights and social welfare policies. Many whites feel that such programs went too far, were too costly or wasteful, and caused a breakdown in respect for hard work and

---

12. Robert S. Gilmour and Robert B. Lamb, *Political Alienation in Contemporary America* (New York: St. Martin's, 1975), p. 17.
13. Gilmour and Lamb, *Political Alienation in Contemporary America*, p. 141.
14. Norman H. Nie, Sidney Verba, and John R. Petrocik, *The Changing American Voter* (Cambridge, Mass.: Harvard University Press, 1976), p. 2.

law and order. On the other side, many blacks find that the programs were not ambitious enough, were not administered in a way to deliver the benefits promised by the political rhetoric, and then were weakened or curtailed under the pressure of the white establishment. In his controversial study of American cities, Professor Edward C. Banfield describes living conditions of the urban poor that improved according to objective measures, even while the level of satisfaction deteriorated in poor neighborhoods.[15]

ELECTIONS AS INTERMEDIARIES BETWEEN CITIZENS AND ADMINISTRATORS

Elections are frequently cited as the principal device for citizens to enforce their will upon public officials. The chief executives and members of the legislatures at all levels of government in the United States are subject to periodic election. Even those localities that employ city managers as chief executive officers make them the subordinates of an elected council. In state governments, election often extends to the heads of major administrative units. Presumably, elected officials control administrative agencies and employ their control to produce the kinds of policies desired by the electorate. Yet, the character of elections—as well as the imperfect mechanisms that elected officials use to control administrators—limits the usefulness of elections as a means of control over administrative agencies. In most cases, a voter cannot signal support for or opposition to a government program by a vote. The citizen is limited to voting for a person, but without indicating to that person which policies to support.

Part of the voter's problem lies in the political parties. As we see in a later section, they are not so tightly organized that they can discipline individual candidates to support a party program. Thus, a voter cannot be sure by a party label alone which kinds of policies the candidate will support once in office. A second limitation on the election's utility lies in the complexity of the campaigns run by individual candidates. Each candidate typically supports more than one program. We can see the difficulty if we imagine even a simple campaign where two candidates opposed one another on only three issues. The presidential campaign of 1964 provided a convenient example. It was an unusually clear campaign

---

15. Edward C. Banfield, *The Unheavenly City Revisited* (Boston: Little, Brown, 1974).

in terms of the policy choices given to the voters. Among the issues expressed in the campaign, the voters could choose, for example, between Johnson and Goldwater on the issues of civil rights, of the war in Vietnam, and of welfare policies. Most observers agree that Johnson took more "liberal" positions than his opponent on civil rights and welfare issues and that he took a more "restrained" position with respect to extending the war in Vietnam. The problem in interpreting an election comes when the pundits must determine which policies were supported by the majority that voted for the winning candidate. Despite the clarity of Johnson's victory in 1964, the election results alone did not indicate which positions the electorate supported. It is possible that only a *minority* of Johnson's supporters agreed with his civil rights platform. Most citizens could have agreed with Goldwater on this—or any other—issue, but they voted for Johnson because they felt he took the better position on the one issue (e.g., the war) they felt to be most important. When dealing with a presidential election, we usually have a large volume of poll results that we can compare with the election outcome in order to gain some insight into the voters' policy preferences. However, these are not available for most state or local elections; the victorious candidate can read into a victory any combination of policy preferences, and the loser cannot present substantial evidence to the contrary.

Even where election results can be compared with opinion surveys, they may result in little citizen control over the policies of the winning candidate. The statements of the campaign may not stay relevant beyond the first crisis that the new government enters. Again, the Johnson-Goldwater campaign provides an example. Although Johnson indicated his own opposition to expanded American participation in Vietnam, conditions after the election allowed him to claim a release from his campaign statements. Although some voters felt Johnson had gone beyond his "mandate," others felt the conditions justified the subsequent war policies. Moreover, there were no control mechanisms to keep Johnson and his administrative subordinates from pursuing policies that ran counter to their campaign "promises."[16]

---

16. See Robert A. Dahl, *A Preface to Democratic Theory* (Chicago: University of Chicago Press, 1956), p. 127. There is some evidence that a candidate's policy position can attract the support of marginal voters for him (i.e., those who shift from one party to another) in sufficient numbers to give him victory. (See Sundquist, *Politics and Policy,* especially chapter X.) However, this does not counter the argument presented in this section that election results alone (i.e., without carefully analyzed public opinion or preference polls) cannot indicate the policy preferences of the electorate.

The 1972 presidential election also showed the weaknesses of citizen control over policies via the electoral route. The magnitude of the Nixon-Agnew victory was outstanding at 60.7 percent of the vote. Moreover, the policy differences between the Republican and Democratic tickets were clear, with President Nixon committed to a different kind of withdrawal from Vietnam and to different approaches to welfare and school integration than was George McGovern. Yet, it is not clear that the Republican candidate's votes provided him with a mandate for his policies. Much of the Nixon vote was an anti-McGovern vote, reflecting generalized feelings of confidence in the candidates, rather than a selection or rejection of their policy positions. In addition, as the Nixon-Agnew administration became mired in the scandals of bribery, tax evasion, ITT, milk fund, Watergate, the Ellsberg break-in, and others, the 1972 landslide dwindled in importance, as President Nixon's popularity in the polls dropped to the point where only 25 percent of the population approved of his actions. With the resignations of both Agnew and Nixon recorded less than halfway through the four-year term, only the most contorted argument could claim that President Gerald R. Ford could read any policy directives from the "mandate" of 1972.

INTEREST GROUPS AS INTERMEDIARIES BETWEEN CITIZENS AND ADMINISTRATORS

Much of the literature about interest groups (sometimes called lobbies or pressure groups) concerns their relations with legislatures. However, interest groups also deal with administrative agencies. Even if a group is successful in the legislature, this does not guarantee that agencies will provide the services it desires.

Several factors make the administrative system an arena for interest-group activity separate from the legislature. These include discretion that is provided by the legislature to administrators; contingencies that were not foreseen by the legislature, but provide administrators with some additional discretion; and the difference between legislative and administrative procedures that might alter the relative influence among interest groups that had prevailed in the legislature.

Most agencies operate with substantial grants of discretion included within their basic legislation or assumed by the administrators because conditions arise that were not foreseen by the legislature. Legislatures do not expect to provide for all possible situations by their statutes, and they permit administrators to operate within broad standards. The basic statutes establishing the National Aeronautics and Space Administration (NASA), for example, authorize the agency to:

1. Research for the solution of problems of flight within and outside the earth's atmosphere, and develop, construct, test, and operate aeronautical and space vehicles;
2. Conduct activities required for the exploration of space with manned and unmanned vehicles;
3. Arrange for the most effective utilization of the scientific and engineering resources of the United States and for cooperation by the United States with other nations engaged in aeronautical and space activities for peaceful purposes;
4. Provide for the widest practicable and appropriate dissemination of information concerning NASA's activities and their results.[17]

The administrators of NASA read this in a way to permit significant programs that are, at most, tangential to the exploration of space. They subsidized research to measure changes in the quality of lifestyles in the United States[18] and supported university curricula to train public administrators, as well as natural scientists and engineers.

The values and attitudes of administrators can shape the ways in which agency powers are employed, and these values may differ from those that prevailed in the legislature. Because of this, the constellation of groups that influences the legislature may not control an administrative unit. Studies of regulatory commissions suggest that consumer groups may win strong statutory controls over business firms. Yet, business firms gain enough influence in the administration to weaken the regulation that actually occurs.[19]

Many—perhaps most—agencies welcome the appearance of groups that represent their clientele or other interested segments of the population. Sometimes out of respect for the democratic norms of popular access, and sometimes because legislation requires it, administrators establish formal procedures for interests to express their preferences. These procedures include opportunities to petition the agency; opportunities to explain one's desires at an informal conference or a formal

17. *U.S. Government Organization Manual, 1965–66* (Washington, D.C.: U.S. Government Printing Office, 1965), p. 462.

18. See, for example, Raymond Bauer, ed., *Social Indicators* (Cambridge, Mass.: MIT Press, 1966).

19. Murray Edelman, *The Symbolic Uses of Politics* (Urbana: University of Illinois Press, 1964), especially chapter 2; also see Marvin Bernstein, *Regulating Business by Independent Commissions* (Princeton, N.J.: Princeton University Press, 1955).

hearing; and the advanced notice of impending changes in policy with provision for interested parties to express their grievances. Some agencies establish advisory bodies selected to represent various segments of their clientele and invite them to assess agency policies on a continuing basis. Some procedures are more elaborate than others and provide more certain opportunities for affected interests to impress their desires upon administrators. One author has written that interest groups are offered the most generous opportunities to express themselves where the following conditions prevail:

1. Where a large number of people or a great magnitude of resources will be affected by the administrators' policy;
2. Where the administrators can delay the implementation of their policy without causing substantial harm;
3. Where interests are given the status of legal recognition, i.e., where provisions in a statute require the consultation of certain groups; and
4. Where the impending policy decision will have the effect of finally disposing of an issue, without affected parties having the opportunity to prevent the loss or recoup their losses at a later hearing.[20]

Administrators' Pursuit of Interest-Group Allies

Administrators do not always wait passively for interest-group allies:

A first and fundamental source of power for administrative agencies in American society is their ability to attract outside support. Strength in a constituency is no less an asset for an American administrator than it is for a politician, and some agencies have succeeded in building outside support as formidable as that of any political organization.[21]

Administrative agencies use several techniques to develop a constituency. They keep the mass media informed about their activities that have widespread public interest, and they maintain frequent contacts with the interest groups directly affected by their programs.

An allied interest group can help an agency in several ways. First, the group can take a position on an issue that coincides with a position held by administrators, but that the administrators cannot take publicly because it would offend their chief executive or important members of

---

20. William W. Boyer, *Bureaucracy on Trial: Policy-Making by Government Agencies* (Indianapolis: Bobbs-Merrill, 1964), pp. 79–80.

21. Francis E. Rourke, *Bureaucracy, Politics and Public Policy* (Boston: Little, Brown, 1969), p. 11; this section relies on Rourke, chapter II.

the legislature. Second, interest groups can support an agency's requests for funds or statutory authority with the executive and the legislature or can help the agency resist undesirable directives from the executive or the legislature. An interest group can make an argument and build public support for a position that cannot be articulated by an administrator who is currently the target of executive or legislative hostility.

Some agencies are so well endowed with the support of interest groups and private citizens that they seem virtually impervious to direction from the executive and legislative branches. The Federal Bureau of Investigation built up a great reservoir of goodwill among associations of local police departments (whose members are trained at FBI academies and whose analyses are done in FBI laboratories) and among many private citizens (long-accustomed to watching the FBI capture society's offenders on television shows put together with agency cooperation). One sign of the power of the FBI was the tenure of its former director, J. Edgar Hoover, who held the post of director from the Coolidge administration until his death in 1972. Presidents kept him in the office beyond the "mandatory" retirement age for federal personnel. Agency reputations are not immortal. This was apparent in the fall in the FBI's status during the interim directorship of L. Patrick Gray and later during extended revelations of extralegal activities that occurred under J. Edgar Hoover.

Agencies also run a risk when they acquire close relations with interest groups. In exchange for political support, a group might win control of an agency program. The agricultural education programs of some state universities seem tailored to the demands of certain groups that are important in state politics. These may be thought of as "loss leaders," i.e., programs that an agency is willing to lose to the effective control of a farm group in order to receive the legislative support of that farm group for the university's total program.[22] One study of the early years of the Tennessee Valley Authority found close alliances between the TVA and certain groups in its region and found what appears to have been an effective veto by the interest groups over the agency programs.[23]

Some alliances between administrative agencies, interest groups, and other organs of government are so strong that they are labeled "subgovernments." This term is applied to the military-industrial complex: a network of military and civilian personnel in the Department of Defense, defense contractors and the interest groups that represent them,

---

22. Rourke, *Bureaucracy, Politics and Public Policy*, p. 22.
23. See Philip Selznick, *TVA and the Grass Roots* (Berkeley: University of California Press, 1949).

and members of Congress. They are allied partly by the economic incentives of defense contracts that appeal to industry and to the members of Congress whose districts will benefit from employment and capital expenditures, and partly by the incentives of improving the military posture of the United States. Some commentators accuse this conglomerate of applying irresistible pressure on the president and Congress for increased expenditures on military hardware. These pressures have implications not only for the size of the military budget and the economic transactions it can trigger, but also the flexibility of United States foreign policy. It is said that the State Department is hard-pressed to negotiate for arms control with the Soviet Union when the incentives are so great for a continued arms buildup. It is difficult to assess the accuracy of these allegations. However, the mutual economic-political incentives in arms escalation has bothered officials at the highest levels of government. One of the surprising features of President Eisenhower's farewell address was his warning of the "acquisition of unwarranted influence ... by the military-industrial complex."[24]

Government Interest Groups

One kind of interest group that may have special advantages in the administrative system is the professional association that represents administrators themselves. It seems most likely to understand the policy-making process and most likely to have information about concrete policies that matches that of the policy-makers. However, the administrators' professional association may fall short of its potential because of its members' own inhibitions. If they feel "political action" is outside the bounds of professional norms, then their organization may exercise no substantial influence over policy.

A study of the Oregon Education Association describes several features that limit the potential of an interest group composed of government employees. One problem lies in the nonpolitical nature of most members' goals. Most join for the purpose of improving their own teaching and advancing their profession. Others join because they are "expected" to join and feel pressure from local school officials. It is only a small minority who join for political reasons, i.e., to support a group that will lobby for salary increases and improved working conditions.[25]

---

24. Douglass Cater, *Power in Washington* (New York: Vintage Books, 1964), chapter II.

25. Harmon Zeigler, *The Political Life of American Teachers* (Englewood Cliffs, N.J.: Prentice-Hall, 1967), pp. 57–59.

With these different motivations among the members, it is difficult for the organization to maximize its resources for political activity. Another limitation comes from the mixture of teachers, principals, and superintendents in the same organization. Insofar as much of the teachers' political efforts might be directed against the principals and superintendents (or against an alliance of these and school boards), the mixed composition of the association severely limits its political usefulness. Finally, a large number of teachers do not feel they should engage in political activity. The notion that "teaching is above politics" or that lobbying is "unprofessional" limits the pressure that can be mobilized. The apolitical norms of the teaching profession are most inhibiting with respect to the teachers' use of the classroom as a political platform. By supporting "professional norms" (which include—for some people—political neutrality), the association may actually *depress* the political involvement of members who would otherwise be more active. Teachers who are active in the Oregon Education Association *are less expressive* about politics than teachers who are not active members.

It appears that the ideology of the organization as it is perceived by the active members is one of caution.... The more experienced teachers are less [politically] expressive [than the less experienced teachers, and] those who are active in the organization are considerably less expressive than those who are not active in the organization. The educational association does not generate the same political interest among its members that other kinds of organizations do. The organization doesn't instruct its members to keep their mouths shut, but it is apparent that the official ideology of the organization, as it is perceived by those who are in a position to understand it best, is acceptance of things more or less as they are.[26]

Many government personnel feel it is quite proper to lobby their interests in the arenas where important decisions are made. The unions of government employees are certainly in this category (see pp. 163–66). Policy-making officials also have their interest groups. The National League of Cities and the U.S. Conference of Mayors represent urban governments before state and federal legislatures and administrative agencies. They frequently support new legislation that would establish—or enlarge—federal aids, and they testify before appropriations subcommittees to support funding for existing programs. An offshoot of the U.S. Conference of Mayors provides special help to municipal legal officers. The National Institute of Municipal Law Officers (NIMLO) provides "the

---

26. Zeigler, *Political Life of American Teachers*, p. 110.

strength flowing from joint support of many municipalities where the protest of a single municipality would be ineffective." Among its services, NIMLO helps draft local ordinances and then helps defend the ordinances against court challenges.[27] There are also separate organizations for social workers, public health physicians, highway administrators, state departments of agriculture, and public safety officials. Although local and state boards of education may protest their own employees' involvement in "lobbying," school boards themselves (along with educational associations and teachers' unions) send their lobbyists to state capitals and to Washington.

With the large annual increases in federal aid for state and local governments that marked the 1960s and early 1970s, the interest groups of state and local officials increased their staffs and the scope of their activities. The increasing size of these interest groups may have been partly a cause and partly an effect of the increasing federal aid. The staffs and budgets of the United States Conference of Mayors and the National League of Cities went from 15 employees and $200,000 in 1954 to 200 employees and $7 million in 1973; the Washington Office of the National Governors' Conference went from 5 professionals and $260,000 in 1967 to 12 professionals and $400,000 in 1972; the National Association of Counties increased its budget from $18,000 to over $1 million between 1957 and 1972.[28] These representatives of states and localities are labeled public interest groups, with their acronym PIGS taken as an accurate measure of their appetites and success in pursuing federal money. The totals made available to states and localities have gone from $10.9 billion in 1965 to $60.5 billion in 1977.

The competition between government interest groups—not only the PIGS but also the various representatives of state and local bureaucrats, legislators, and council members—is as much a feature of the Washington scene as is their coordinated pursuit of resources. The multilevel nature of American government assures some competition between states, cities, and counties. The differences between large and small municipalities, central cities, and suburbs assures some competition between the U.S. Conference of Mayors (representing the largest cities) and the more broad-based National League of Cities. Also, tensions between elected officials and bureaucrats causes competition between the groups

---

27. Clement E. Vose, "Interest Groups, Judicial Review, and Local Government," *Western Political Quarterly* 19 (March 1966): 85–100.

28. This discussion relies on Donald H. Haider, *When Governments Come to Washington: Governors, Mayors, and Intergovernmental Lobbying* (New York: Free Press, 1974).

representing general governments or elected officials and various professional associations of administrators. Partisan differences add their own spice to the pot. In some years, Republicans have taken a leading role in the National Governors' Conference, while Democrats have dominated the U.S. Conference of Mayors. Each of these groups has felt itself more or less influential in the White House depending on its partisan character. Big-city programs had center stage during the Johnson administration, with the states coming back stronger in the Nixon years.

The federal agencies should not be slighted in any description of government lobbying. Their principal targets are the committees that handle their legislation and appropriations. Although the U.S. Congress has objected and even outlawed the expenditure of public money for lobbying activities, an aide of President Johnson noted that there were about 40 "congressional relations people" in "key roles" in the departments and agencies. They carry their unit's message directly to important legislators and enlist additional support from nongovernmental interest groups. A study of the legislation dealing with the Model Cities program in 1967 found that the following advocates had been recruited to support the administration's position: U.S. Conference of Mayors, National League of Cities, AFL-CIO, National Governors' Conference, American Institute of Architects, Mortgage Bankers Association; representatives for local civic groups, banks, and construction firms; and the heads of some prestigious corporations (General Electric, Westinghouse Electric, Detroit Edison, Allied Chemical, Chicago and Northwestern Railroad, Goodyear Tire and Rubber, Kaiser Industries, Continental Illinois National Bank and Trust Company, Chase Manhattan Bank, Neiman-Marcus Company).[29]

Limitations on the Influence of Interest Groups

Groups take advantage of numerous opportunities to express their demands to administrators. However, any effort to assess the role that interest groups play in administrative systems must reckon with several factors that limit their influence. Administrators themselves seem to dominate the relationships. The status of interest groups is ambiguous. Intermingled in their reputation is the image of selfish lobbyists who would gratify their own group's interest at the expense of the public. There have been episodes of deceit on the part of interest groups, heavily

---

29. Legislators and the Lobbyists (Washington, D.C. Congressional Quarterly Service, 1968), pp. 65–72.

financed campaigns designed to defeat politicians who had opposed group demands, and overt attempts to bribe government officials. Policy-makers are sensitive to these aspects of interest-group traditions. If "undesirable pressures" are perceived the official may terminate the access a group has enjoyed and frustrate its campaign to influence policy.

Lobbyists themselves admit their secondary status in relations with government officials. In response to a question about the influence of various participants in policy-making, more than one-half of 114 lobbyists surveyed named the president or administrators as the most important actors, about 20 percent named the voters as most important, 10 percent named Congress, and only one of the respondents gave the lobbyists first rank.[30]

POLITICAL PARTIES AS INTERMEDIARIES BETWEEN CITIZENS AND ADMINISTRATORS

Political parties also transmit information between citizens and policy-makers. However, a major factor that inhibits party participation in the policy decisions of administrative agencies is the lack of mechanisms to discipline their members on policy issues or to guarantee party unity in the legislature.

American parties lack several devices that parties in other countries use to enforce concerted action. There is no central control of financing or nominations, and there are no other incentives strong enough to assure that state and local organizations will support the positions of national party leaders.[31]

The decentralized structure of American parties is largely responsible for their lack of policy-discipline. Party candidates or incumbents owe their obligations to a variety of state and local parties, each of which has its own constituency of voters' attitudes, beliefs, and policy preferences. Nominations for state, local, and congressional campaigns come from these state or local organizations, which may be nothing more than personal organizations focused on the career of one politician. The nomination of presidential candidates also depends on decisions made in these state and local parties. There is no cadre of national officers who

---

30. Lester W. Milbrath, *The Washington Lobbyists* (Chicago: Rand McNally, 1963), pp. 351–52.

31. See James MacGregor Burns, *The Deadlock of Democracy: Four-Party Politics in America* (Englewood Cliffs, N.J.: Spectrum Books, 1963).

control political resources necessary to state organizations and who might issue policy directives to prospective party nominees. National party leaders lack any formal control over state or local nominations. Some members of Congress and governors campaign openly in opposition to the presidential nominee of their own party. At one time, this was solely a Democratic problem, with liberal presidential nominees expecting to write off the support of conservative southerners. But the 1964 presidential campaign saw Republicans, Governor Nelson Rockefeller, Governor George Romney, Senator Jacob Javits, and Mayor John Lindsay refusing to endorse the candidacy of Barry Goldwater.

Party leaders view their ideological diversity as an asset and perpetuate it by trying to cast a broad appeal with ambiguous platforms. Partly because of their ideological diversity, American parties are most likely to be governed by pragmatic officeseekers who put a premium on flexibility and on the capacity to make such adjustments in their policy positions as are necessary for electoral success. The parties are unlikely to develop strong, permanent staffs that would desire—or be able—to maintain a coherent set of principles on matters of public policy.

In recent years, the parties have become even less prominent in the electoral process. The percentage of voters identifying themselves as independents has gone from 23 in 1952 to 38 in 1974. In the same period, the percentage identifying themselves as strongly partisan has declined from 37 to 26.[32] In the same period, voters have shown more familiarity and concern with issues and more consistency—on a liberal-conservative spectrum—in their feelings about issues in such fields as welfare, taxation, defense, and foreign policy. Yet, the parties themselves have not become more consistent on policy issues. Each has distinctive liberals and conservatives among its leading advocates, who blunt the parties' capacity to offer clearly different alternatives to the voters, and then—in the case of the victorious party—to implement the voters' mandate into policy.

Despite the barriers to strong political parties, elected chief executives assume the roles of party leaders and use existing party loyalties to improve their control over the agencies. When such executives make appointments to high-level positions within their administration, they typically appoint members of their own party. At the national level, 89 percent of Franklin Roosevelt's appointments to ranking administrative positions were made from among Democrats; 84 percent of President

---

32. Nie, Verba, and Petrocik, *Changing American Voter*, p. 49.

Truman's appointments were Democrats; 76 percent of President Eisenhower's appointments were Republicans; 81 percent of President Kennedy's appointees were Democrats; and 84 percent of President Johnson's early appointments were Democrats.[33] In some state and local governments, the elected chief executive has an opportunity to fill not only some high-level positions, but also a large number of middle- and low-range positions with people who demonstrate at least a minimum of party loyalty.

The practice of appointing fellow partisans to administrative jobs has a long history in the United States and is justified with claims that it improves the government, as well as the party. Presumably, a chief executive is more able to count on cooperation from subordinates if they are linked with party ties. Fellow partisans are more likely to share the executive's policy orientation and to help compile a record of administrative accomplishments that will appeal to the voters at the next election.

The appointive power that remains in the hands of chief executives is only a vestige of what they formerly had. Several changes in government programs and the public's regard for partisanship have limited the executive's freedom. Nonpartisan criteria are now required for over 90 percent of the civilian positions in the federal government and for many positions in state and local governments. For a number of positions, it is necessary for the chief executive to balance several positions in boards or commissions with appointees of different parties. Government services are increasingly technical and require professional expertise in many administrative positions. A chief executive must often weigh professional competence above partisanship in selecting department heads, even when the law permits the use of partisan criteria. In many instances, the only feasible partisan standard holds that the "right person" not be uncompromising in support for the opposition. A politically neutral or even bland member of the opposition party may be selected over a fellow partisan if the position calls for special competence. Sometimes a chief executive feels constrained to "balance" the administration even when there is no legal requirement for this. President-elect Eisenhower seemed intent on appointing a Democrat as secretary of labor in 1952; and President Nixon announced ahead of time in 1968 that his ambassador to the United Nations would be a Democrat.

---

33. David T. Stanley et al., *Men Who Govern: A Biographical Profile of Federal Political Executives* (Washington, D.C.: Brookings Institution, 1967), p. 24.

The Machine as the Archetype of Party Government

The machine is one kind of political party with strong discipline and a tradition of using its control of elective offices to staff and control administrative agencies. However, "machines have always been something of a genetic 'sport' among American political parties."[34] They were never "typical" of party organizations, and now they seem to be declining in number.

Several resources seem necessary for a party to operate as a well-disciplined machine. These include a large number of voters who desire tangible rewards, such as jobs, food, help in finding a place to live, assistance in time of trouble with the police, welfare payments, or assistance in completing the forms necessary for welfare assistance. The voters who support a machine have only a secondary interest in the values of middle-class reformers—proper forms of government; efficiency in conducting public business; professional administration; and fair election procedures.[35] A machine also needs resources to "pay off" its voters and its ward and precinct organizers. These rewards include money, government jobs, and nominations for elected positions. Machines offer protection to bootlegging, gambling, narcotics, or prostitution. They also receive "kickbacks" from contractors and public utilities that do business with the government or need a franchise in order to serve the public.

The machines earned their reputation for graft and corruption partly because of charges that they "fix" elections, partly because of the protection they provide to criminal elements, and partly because of the favoritism in the provision of benefits to certain groups and individuals. Some machine politicians claim there is a difference between "honest graft" and "dirty graft." While both are illegal activities, some are less undesirable than others. Honest graft involves the use of information and power to profit the machine in ways that do not offend the morals of most voters. It consists of knowing where roads, bridges, or public buildings are to be constructed, buying the land before that information is made public, and then selling it for a large profit. It also includes selecting a site for public construction near land already owned by friends of the machine and thereby enhancing their property value. Kickbacks from firms chosen to undertake public construction are also

---

34. See Frank J. Sorauf, *Party Politics in America* (Boston: Little, Brown, 1968), p. 58.

35. Edward C. Banfield and James Q. Wilson, *City Politics* (Cambridge, Mass.: Harvard University Press, 1963), chapter 9.

included in honest graft. If a profit were to be made anyway, then why shouldn't part of it go to the machine? Admittedly, the border between "honest" and "dirty" graft is hard to define. Contractors make the entire community pay for the kickbacks to the machine. Instead of taking the kickback out of their own profit, they increase the total cost of the project or lower expenses by using inferior materials or workmanship. Also, the whole community must pay for the increased land prices caused by the advanced purchase of land to be bought by the government. And if sites for public facilities are chosen for the profit of the machine rather than on service-related criteria, then the clients of the prospective facility suffer inconvenience.

Graft that is outright "dirty" involves the protection of criminal activities that offend large segments of the public. Here, too, there may be problems defining the borders of dirty graft. A numbers or book-making syndicate that satisfied the public's needs for gambling without rigging the odds too much or without investing its profits in local narcotics or prostitution might be considered "honest graft" in some communities. Substantiated charges of involvement in prostitution, however, have aroused otherwise quiescent voters and shaken some of the strongest machines. "Machines and their leaders could afford to ignore charges of being crooks, but not charges of being pimps."[36]

From the perspective of one who appreciates a well-run organization, the political machine is a marvel to behold. The party organization is virtually the government. Its candidates are elected to be chief executive and a majority of the city council, and it appoints the chiefs and subordinates in administrative organizations. Its diverse segments are united by a common loyalty to the success of the machine's candidates at the next election, and all can be counted on to mobilize the voters' support. Between elections, the ward and precinct units serve the voters with personal favors. If the mayor or the machine boss (who may not be the same individual) wishes to change certain policies, this person gets the cooperation of the majority on the council and lieutenants in the administration with a speed and harmony that is unknown where political conditions show the plurality and confusion that is more typical of democracy.[37]

The demise of big-city machines is a product of several factors. Some are local in nature, and some reflect basic changes in American

---

36. D. W. Brogan, *Politics in America* (New York: Harper, 1954), chapter IV, especially p. 147.

37. Robert K. Merton, *Social Theory and Social Structure* (Glencoe, Ill.: Free Press, 1957).

politics and economics. The Depression was a major blow to most machines. Immediately, it created a magnitude of poverty and personal distress much too large for the machine's resources of food baskets, jobs, and rent money. In the long run, the Depression led to federally organized, financed, and supervised old-age insurance, unemployment compensation, and public assistance. These provided a level and consistency of benefits that no machine could match and took over a principal device machines had used to attract large blocs of voters. While the machines were losing their welfare role, local governments also began to provide a range of services requiring the employment of skilled technicians and professionals. City hospitals, universities, and welfare organizations, plus an increased concern for excellence in the public schools, raised demands for highly trained employees who could not be recruited from ward and precinct workers.[38] Civil service reforms also took hold at the local level and increasingly required that middle- and low-level jobs be filled without regard to partisanship. Today there remain few big-city or state parties that merit the designation "machine." The machine of Chicago's late Mayor Richard J. Daley was a prominent exception. To be sure, some other local and state parties unite many individuals in their support for certain candidates or policies. But the interlocking machine, with its "boss," mass electorate, control of the administrative apparatus, and tangible benefits for voters and precinct workers, is more a feature of American history than a contemporary reality.

ADMINISTRATIVE AGENCIES AS COLLECTORS OF INFORMATION

Government agencies are not merely the recipients of information about their environment. Beside their role as the receivers of demands from citizens, from lobbyists, and from the representatives of political parties, agencies also seek their own information. A prominent example is the *Report* of the National Advisory Commission on Civil Disorders. The Commission is one of those groups described in Chapter 4 as an "administrative hybrid." It was appointed by the president and included members of the legislative branch, state and local chief executives and administrators, and representatives of private industry. It was not an agency in the usual sense of that term. It carried out in a prominent way

---

38. However, the custodial positions at municipal hospitals and universities may still provide some job resources for local machines.

the tasks of information-collection and formulation of proposals that frequently occur in administrative agencies. The prominence of the problems in this case seemed to require the special attention of the president and a commission of prestigious individuals. In response to the riots in Newark and Detroit during 1967, this body tried to answer the questions: What happened? Why did it happen? What can be done to prevent it from happening again? The Commission's *Report* has several implications for the relationship between the public and policymakers in administrative agencies and in other branches of government. First, it represented a major effort to understand conditions in black ghettos. The Commission found:

- Pervasive discrimination and segregation.
- Frustrated hopes raised by the legislative and judicial victories of the civil rights movement, but not realized for most individual blacks.
- A climate that tends toward approval and encouragement of violence —created by white terrorism directed against nonviolent protest, and by the defiance of law and federal authority by state and local officials resisting desegregation.
- Frustrations of powerlessness that lead some Negroes to the conviction that there is no effective alternative to violence as a means of redressing grievances.
- A new mood of racial pride.
- Hostility and cynicism directed toward the police.[39]

Second, the *Report* was an effort to affect the opinions of both white and black Americans. Its style was calculated to shock many whites into a feeling of guilt and responsibility for the plight of blacks and to generate conditions that would permit passage of ameliorating social legislation:

Race prejudice has shaped our history decisively; it now threatens to affect our future. . . . White racism is essentially responsible for the explosive mixture which has been accumulating in our cities since the end of World War II.[40]

The "public opinion environment" that surrounds each administrative unit is actually quite diffuse and presents several alternatives to the administrators. Some administrators "tune" to a conception of the "general public," while others concern themselves with particular groups. Often it is not possible to serve them all. When the Interstate Commerce Commission permits a larger-size trailer truck to operate on the highways, for example, it may help the truckers; but it may hurt the railroads

---

39. *Report* of the National Advisory Commission on Civil Disorders (New York: Bantam Books, 1968), pp. 10–11. (Hereafter cited as *Report.*)
40. *Report,* p. 10.

by adding to the truckers' competitive advantage in the transportation industry and may also inconvenience—or endanger—the drivers of automobiles.

Only a minority of administrative units make major investments in gathering information about the public. One study found that 60 percent of upper-level administrators in a sample rely on newspaper comment, letters of complaint, and clients' grievances.[41] In the haphazard way that many units gather their information, their image of the world may be shaped by which administrator receives a particular bit of information and by the nature of that official's responsibility for policymaking.

The nature of an administrator's job may have something to do with the way information is gathered about the public. One study categorizes the personnel in administrative agencies as "politicos," "professionals," and "administrators." "Politicos" make policy, defend the agency against the outside world, and are responsible to its external pressures; in this position, they are most likely to see a variety of interests relevant to the agency and to consider the broadest needs of the constituencies in making their decisions. A "professional" is a person with technical or scientific training who is typically in contact with only a portion of an agency's work and is likely to view the needs of clients as the same as those of the particular groups encountered. "Administrators" have the most confined training and work assignments. They supervise subunits within an organization and manage specific projects. With less of a cosmopolitan training than "professionals" and with more restricted responsibilities than "politicos," the "administrators" are inclined to take the most narrow view of the interests served by an agency's programs.[42]

THE OMBUDSMAN

Until now we have concentrated on citizen inputs to the administrative system that concern large numbers of people or broad issues of public policy. Another mechanism—the ombudsman—has appeared in several foreign countries, plus some American states and localities, to facilitate the complaints of individual citizens about their personal problems with the bureaucracy.

---

41. Robert S. Friedman et al., "Administrative Agencies and the Publics They Serve," *Public Administration Review* 26 (September 1966): 192–204.

42. Friedman et al., "Administrative Agencies."

The creation of the ombudsman reflects the broad extent of government services available to citizens, as well as the extensive network of government regulations. There are many opportunities for a citizen to feel deprived of a benefit or unfairly trapped by regulations. Departments generally have their own procedures for reviewing subordinates' decisions upon the appeal of a citizen. In certain cases, however, these procedures themselves may fail to satisfy a claimant, or their complexity may discourage a citizen from using them. The ombudsman is available to simple appeals from the public and is responsible for sorting out the merits of a complaint and trying to set things right. Typically the ombudsman is a person of public prominence and status and has a staff to help with the details. Usually the legislature appoints the ombudsman for an extended term. Thus, the appointee should be able to acquire the respect of administrators while being independent of the agencies subject to review.

The powers available to the ombudsman vary from place to place. Generally unable to order a change in administrative decisions, the ombudsman must rely on persuasion and the threat of adverse publicity. In order to avoid being swamped by crank or repetitive complaints, the ombudsman usually has discretion over the cases to be pursued. At times, the proposed creation of an ombudsman has rankled administrators who fear the annoyance of additional reviews or a threat to their independence. Some research on ombudsmen, however, indicates that agency heads welcome the ombudsman's inquiries as an additional device to monitor the work of their subordinates. The ombudsman's inquiries typically do go to agency heads and most often are satisfied by means of agency compliance. Sometimes an inquiry about an individual case leads an agency to reconsider the merits of a more general matter. Professor Larry B. Hill's research in New Zealand over the course of ten years has found 80 cases of reform in administrative procedures and 87 cases of policy changes that were initiated by an ombudsman's inquiry.[43]

SUMMARY

This chapter focuses on relationships between citizens and administrative units and on the roles of the mass media, public opinion polls, elections,

---

43. Larry B. Hill, "Institutionalization, the Ombudsman, and Bureaucracy," *American Political Science Review* 68 (September 1974): 1075–85; see also the correspondence between Frederick C. Thayer and Larry B. Hill in *American Political Science Review* 69 (June 1975): 580–83.

interest groups, and political parties as intermediaries between them. Because of shortcomings in their interest and information, most individuals require some organized intermediary between themselves and the conversion process of the administrative system. On occasion, the mass media have added significantly to the public's information about a social problem or a public policy and have generated strong pressure on policy-makers. However, the media suffer from some of the same problems as individuals. They have other functions that distract them from the role of political intermediary. Commercial and recreational functions consume many resources which might otherwise be employed in politics. Also, citizens "protect" themselves from mass media just as they protect themselves from other involvements in politics. Many people do not consume the political news and editorials which the media provide. Because of selective perception, some fail to see items that would challenge their own views.

Public opinion polls also serve as intermediaries between citizens and administrators. However, the polls typically do not indicate that the public has taken a clear position on one side or another of an issue. Moreover, the questions asked on most polls are not precise enough to inform the policy-maker about the feeling of the public on the specific issue being faced. Responses may not indicate support or opposition to an entire program, but rather support or opposition for certain aspects. The polls also fail to indicate how seriously individuals take the positions they announce. In many cases, respondents may think of an issue for the first—and last—time when they are approached by the interviewer. Polls that show support or opposition to a candidate—or an incumbent —do not provide the specific information needed by a policy-maker. Individuals can be reacting to any of several positions the politician has taken; generalized support or opposition does not signify support or opposition for any policies. The same difficulty limits the electoral process as an intermediary between citizens and government policy-making. Elections do let the people decide about certain personnel. However, they do not show which of several campaign statements about policy actually won popular support.

Interest groups seldom appear dominant in the administrative system. The status of lobbying is ambiguous, and many officials take a guarded position in their dealings with interest groups. Officials in all branches of government receive a variety of demands, and they have some preferences of their own. Thus, interest groups cannot write their wishes on a clean slate; they must compete with directives that come to administrators from the legislature and the chief executive, from other administrative units, from officials at other governmental levels, and from the personal and professional values of the administrators themselves.

Political parties concentrate on winning elective offices and filling appointed positions, rather than on realizing policy desires. Their self-limitation reflects, in part, their inability to control party voters, candidates, or officeholders. There is little to assure a party leadership that its members—even within the leadership cadre—are united on important policy issues. A political machine is a party organization that combines a disciplined control of executive, legislative, and administrative units, typically in city governments. However, the machine has become a rare and declining feature of American politics. Its demise reflects several social and political changes that have withdrawn the types of resources the classic machine needed. The development of merit systems and the spread of public services requiring technical and professional personnel removed the machine's control over government jobs that could reward large numbers of precinct workers and voters. And as the federal government provided massive cash doles for the needy, for job placement and training, for unemployment compensation, for retirement programs, and for low-cost public housing, the machines lost control over welfare benefits.

Administrative agencies are not passive in their relations with citizens. They actively seek the support of interest groups, lobby in behalf of their own programs with the legislative and executive branches, and collect reams of information about social and economic conditions and about the problems that might be alleviated by public services. Thus, some of the "inputs" that seem to come from the environment of the administrative system are actually solicited and nurtured by the administrators who are, ostensibly, their targets.

Yet, other citizen inputs come to administrators in those countries, states, and cities that have created an ombudsman. This office acts on individual complaints of citizens about improper treatment at the hands of administrators. Although the ombudsman does not have the power to alter administrative action, the weight of the office can be an impressive tool to even the balance between citizens and administrators.

9

Executives, Legislators, and Administrators

The executive and legislative branches are major sources of inputs to administrative agencies. They transmit demands and resources that take the form of statutes, executive orders, committee reports, and informal communications. These transmissions authorize or instruct administrative units to engage in certain activities, to hire personnel, and to pay their bills. These demands and resources from executive and legislative branches are not simply inputs to administrative agencies. Many get their start in the administration and are sent from there (as outputs) to the legislature and the executive for consideration. Among these outputs that go from administrative agencies to the executive and the legislative branches are proposals for new legislation, for personnel standards, and for budgets. Here our concern is with inputs to administrative units; in Chapter 11 we shall return to administrative relations with the legislative and executive branches and consider as administrative outputs the transmissions that stimulate subsequent inputs from the other branches.

It is no simple task to describe relationships among executives, legislators, and administrators. Their activities reflect the formal directives of the Constitution and of statutes, plus a variety of informal arrangements that have evolved over the years. There are some general tendencies, but numerous variations. Some variations reflect institutional peculiarities of the federal government or individual state or local governments. Other variations reflect the nature of the issue, the actors' view of the issue, and the intensity of their feelings.

There is general consensus about one feature of relationships between administrative agencies and the legislative and executive branches: they have changed markedly since the nation's founding. The administrator should no longer be considered the insignificant subordinate of legislators and executives. The changes that have occurred since 1789 are a profound example of relationships within the administrative system changing in response to environmental changes.

When the framers of the Constitution wrote their document, they concentrated on the legislative and executive branches and paid little attention to what was then a small cadre of administrators. The government they described resembles contemporary institutions only in their gross outlines. The magnitude and nature of government has changed dramatically. The federal administration has increased from a staff of 780 civilian employees in 1789 to a staff of 2.5 million in 1977. At the end of the 18th century, the principal activities were postal service, revenue collection, diplomacy, and a rudimentary armed service. Now there is space exploration, the administration of numerous health and welfare services, vast conservation and recreational programs, research and development in the natural and social sciences, the development of air, sea, and land facilities for transportation and communication, and global military responsibilities. State and local governments have accepted major responsibilities in education, transportation, recreation, health, and welfare that were inconceivable in the 18th century. One significance of this growth lies in the problems they raise for the chief executive and the legislature. The scope of activities has far outreached the capacity of these elected officials to initiate policy; it may even outreach their capacity to be thorough in their supervision and control of policy-makers in the administration! However, the legislative and executive branches still have some impressive powers of their own. And they still have the choice as to where and when to employ their powers.

Changes in the relationships between the executive, legislative, and administrative branches are not just features of the past. The Nixon presidency was an occasion for sharp controversy about the powers of the executive branch: first its authority to control administrative spending through the mechanism of impoundment and then the whole series of issues given the label of "Watergate." Much of Watergate concerned the illegal tactics of White House staffers to ensure the president's re-election and then to cover up earlier transgressions. Several related incidents had direct implications for executive-administrative relations: one particular event was the involvement of L. Patrick Gray, acting head of the Federal Bureau of Investigation, in the cover-up and the damage done to the Bureau's morale; another was the president's loss of status and his failure to achieve certain measures he had pursued actively, like executive reorganization or special revenue-sharing; related to this was the executive's preoccupation with its own defense, and a lack of attention given to domestic policy innovation or to filling high-level administrative positions in the face of turnover.

LEGISLATIVE WEAKNESS IN RELATIONS
WITH ADMINISTRATIVE AGENCIES

The major problems the legislature faces are the fragmentation of its energies and a lack of information about policy issues. Fragmentation is a general term that covers a number of difficulties: the diffusion of legislative resources into two houses that—in a formal sense—duplicate each other's responsibilities; the diffusion of the members' interests between policy-making and a number of other responsibilities; and their failure to accept the discipline of any integrating mechanisms (e.g., a political party) that might coordinate them. The information the legislature gathers is impressive in its own right, but it is lacking in comparison to what is assembled by the administrative agencies and to what seems necessary for the control of administration.

Aside from formulating policy or supervising ongoing programs, legislators must also accommodate constituents who wish assistance in dealing with administrative agencies. This typically requires individual legislators and their staff assistants to tend to a much broader field than any of them can master. Constituents seek government jobs and contracts, assistance in qualifying for routine services, or help in appealing their cases after being denied their first application. State legislators, for example, deal with constituents who are denied admission to the state university or mental hospital, or who are denied release from the same state mental hospital or a parole from the penitentiary. Legislators also service local governments. Members of Congress arrange appointments for local officials with federal granting agencies and often lend their physical presence to the meetings. At the state level, legislators introduce "local bills" to the legislature, testify in behalf of their community's needs, and steer the bills through committee. Where the state government controls many functions in the local community, state legislators are kept as busy as the delegates from city hall and the county courthouse. Legislators must also attend to their own political careers. Many of their service activities have political payoffs. Whenever a legislator assists a constituent or a local government, the legislator can expect some goodwill in return. Other duties are more directly linked with reelection. They include speaking engagements and tours of the constituency. Legislators feel a continuing need for exposure—to express their views or to solicit funds for the next campaign.

While legislators dissipate their resources to a number of distinct activities, administrators concentrate theirs by specializing in the affairs of a single agency—or more likely a single program. For many administrators, specialization begins in college or in graduate school and continues throughout their career. Few legislators have the knowledge to match the full range of their responsibilities. Most are content to serve a "generalist" function in supervising "specialists" in the administrative organization. It is related to the "representative" nature of legislators that, like the rest of us, they are somewhat lacking in the specialized knowledge that can be found in administrative agencies. Yet, legislators are also limited in what they can do for us by having a complete understanding of their decisions.

The informational dependence of legislatures reveals itself in the procedures used to elicit the views of administrators on proposed bills. Many bills originate in the department that will be given responsibility for administering the program. A legislator typically refers ideas to the administration for evaluation and modification. One study of legislative-administrative relationships in the city of Los Angeles found that 25 percent of the bills considered by the council originated in the city departments, and almost all others were referred by legislators to the relevant departments for their comments. Lobbyists recognize the importance of the administrator's review: "If the administrators oppose us, we're sunk." "We find the Council checks with the departments on our requests and lets itself be governed by what they say." Almost all of the bills opposed by administrative agencies were defeated in the city council.[1]

SOURCES OF LEGISLATIVE STRENGTH IN RELATIONS WITH ADMINISTRATIVE AGENCIES

The legislature is not without resources to supervise or control administrative agencies. In Congress, committees, seniority, and staff assistants provide some opportunities for legislators to acquire information about administrative activities. Committees provide opportunities for specialization paralleled to the specialization of administrative units. A committee's jurisdiction usually includes a number of administrative units that pursue a related set of programs. Privileges of seniority protect a member's committee seat allowing the member to accumulate information over the years. Congressional committees also have professional staff assistants who gather information for the members, conduct formal hear-

---

1. Harry W. Reynolds, Jr., "The Career Public Service and Statue Law-making in Los Angeles," *Western Political Quarterly* 28 (September 1965): 621–39.

ings, draft legislation, and write committee reports. State legislatures are not as well equipped. Many legislatures lack seniority guarantees, and as a result, members are shifted from one committee to another, losing the benefits of information gained in past sessions. In some states, even committee chairmen do not have continuing rights to their committee assignments. The lack of seniority-guarantees in many state legislatures reflects the unattractive nature of the seats and the high turnover. The staff assistance and future political opportunities for legislators in many states are also markedly inferior to those of members of Congress. In some states, the legislators have no offices or secretaries of their own. Without seniority or other features that allow the members to increase their expertise, state legislatures are likely to depend heavily on policy recommendations that come from administrative agencies.

Even when they are dependent on administrators' information, legislators can assert a strong negative role in policy-making. And although they may not develop fully mature proposals with their own resources, they do prompt administrators to innovate. When the legislature refuses to accept an administrator's proposal for new authority or for a certain level of expenditure, the administrator may be powerless. The administrator *can* appeal the decision of the legislature. A successful appeal, however, may require sufficient time for a change in the political environment that occasioned the first decision of the legislature. Some administrators evade the legislature. They cite an existing statute to justify new activities, or they transfer funds from one activity to support an activity that had not received an adequate budget on its own merits. Such evasions are often contrary to law or at least to prevailing norms that define "proper" relations between the administration and the legislature, and most administrators seem unwilling to use these methods. If discovered, an administrator might be subject to public rebuke and face the loss of legislative support in the future. Administrators who lose rapport with the chairmen and members of key legislative committees may also lose standing with superiors in the administration and in the executive branch.[2]

Legislative importance in policy-making is shown by the resources administrators use to persuade the legislators to agree with their policies. If the legislature were a rubber stamp for the recommendations of the administration, then government agencies would not lobby so heavily.

---

2. Ira Sharkansky, "Four Agencies and An Appropriations Subcommittee: A Comparative Study of Budget Strategies," *Midwest Journal of Political Science* 9 (August 1965): 254–81.

The study of the Los Angeles City Council—which found heavy legislative reliance on the recommendations of the administration—also described a number of tactics administrators use to strengthen their own recommendations. These include:

1. Personal visits with individual council members;
2. A continuing release of written material on the bills of interest to the administration;
3. The use of newspapers, the Mayor's office, interest groups, and prestigious private citizens to communicate circumspectly to the council; and
4. The careful timing of certain major proposals according to crises in the community that might emphasize their worth.[3]

A legislature can exercise some control because administrators fear the legislature's ultimate negative decision and because administrators try to anticipate and accommodate the wishes of the legislators. No administrator knows when a legislative committee will begin a prolonged inquiry into agency affairs and decide to concentrate its energies on controlling the agency. Some administrative units receive exhaustive reviews. Their experience warns other units of what might happen. A study of relations between NASA and Congress found 5,371 pages of published testimony concerning the agency's budget for fiscal 1964, resulting in a budget cut of $600 million. "A thorough reading of the hearings, reports, and floor debates . . . indicates that the agency was not being given just an across-the-board cut. Rather, it was being explicitly told to absorb the cut by dropping, postponing, diminishing, or not expanding various activities or construction projects." During the 1959–63 period, NASA was called before 12 different committees and many more subcommittees. Beside the appropriations committees in the House and Senate, they included the space, government operations, and armed services committees in both houses, plus the Senate Small Business Committee, Senate Judiciary Committee, the Senate Committee on Foreign Relations, and the Joint Committee on Atomic Energy.[4]

EXECUTIVE WEAKNESS IN RELATIONS WITH ADMINISTRATIVE AGENCIES

The president has nominal control over most administrative units of the federal government. However, a number of formal exceptions, plus some

3. Reynolds, "Career Public Service," pp. 621–39.
4. Thomas P. Jahnige, "The Congressional Committee System and the Oversight Process: Congress and NASA," *Western Political Quarterly* 21 (June 1968): 227–39.

political deficiencies, combine to weaken the president's influence over policy-making. Some formal exceptions limit the president's powers of appointment. Members of independent regulatory commissions, for example, have fixed terms, and the president's removal powers are limited by the need to cite certain causes for each dismissal. The president also must share most appointments with the Senate. Generally, this is a nominal requirement, but Senate opposition has led the president to withdraw some major nominations. The greatest formal inhibition on the president lies in the need to share the roles of policy-initiation and supervision with the legislature. An uncooperative committee in either house can keep a president's bill from being considered on the floor.[5] A committee can also support an administrator who would challenge the chief executive.

The president's need to share policy-making with the legislature is only one part of a more general problem: the need to take account of several constituencies when making decisions. It is part of the president's power to affect many different interests by his decisions. One study has identified five constituencies that the president leads—the legislature, administration, political party, citizens of the United States and the organizations that represent them, and foreign governments.[6] Another study of the presidency identifies ten roles: chief of state, chief executive, chief diplomat, commander-in-chief, chief legislator, party chief, chief moral leader, chief keeper of domestic peace and tranquillity, chief guardian of the economy, and leader of an international coalition.[7] Each of these constituencies and roles represents a portion of the president's status. But each, too, represents the diverse sets of interests that must be taken into consideration when important decisions are made. A decision made as chief legislator, for example, must not clash so much with the desires of constituents in the administration that the president will lose the support of the administrators on another occasion. The president is hemmed in by the office's vast power. Because so many decisions affect different constituencies, the president is typically constrained from several sides at once. The president is not without power to manipulate within these confines; but this power is tenuous and dependent on the

---

5. Procedures exist for "calling" a bill from a committee, but they are difficult and are seldom employed. See Malcolm E. Jewell and Samuel C. Patterson, *The Legislative Process in the United States* (New York: Random House, 1966), p. 260.

6. Richard Neustadt, *Presidential Power: The Politics of Leadership* (New York: Wiley, 1964, 1976), p. 7. In the latest editions revised from 1960, Neustadt suggests the addition of yet another constituency: state and local governments whose demands on the White House increased greatly with the spurt in intergovernmental programs beginning in 1964. See his chapter 1.

7. Clinton Rossiter, *The American Presidency* (New York: Signet, 1966), chapter 1.

president's ability to *persuade* the members of different constituencies that these decisions have some benefits and only minimal costs for their own interests.

Constituent relations are relations of dependence. Everyone with any share in governing this country will belong to one (or two, or three) of his "constituencies." Since everyone depends on him, why is he not assured of everyone's support? The answer is that no one else sits where he sits, or sees quite as he sees; no one else feels the full weight of his obligations. Those obligations are a tribute to his unique place in our political system. But just because it is unique, they fall on him alone. *The same conditions that promote his leadership in form preclude a guarantee of leadership in fact.* No man or group at either end of Pennsylvania Avenue shares his peculiar status in our government and politics. That is why his services are in demand. By the same token, though, the obligations of all other men are different from his own. His Cabinet officers have departmental duties and constituents. His legislative leaders head *congressional* parties, one in either House. His national party organization stands apart from his official family. His political allies in the States need not face Washington, or one another. The private groups that seek him out are not compelled to govern. And friends abroad are not compelled to run in our elections. Lacking his position and prerogatives, these men cannot regard his obligations as their own. They have their jobs to do; none is the same as his. As they perceive their duty, they may find it right to follow him, in fact, or they may not.[8]

State governors seem to have even more problems than the president in controlling their administrations. Almost all the governors face severe formal limitations on their powers of appointment. The heads of many departments are named by direct election. Most states have separate elections for the attorney general, treasurer, secretary of state, auditor, and superintendent of public instruction.[9] Appointments of other department heads are made by boards or commissions over whom the governor has only limited control.

If the proposals of the executive threaten the established activities of administrative agencies, the executive may be drawn into a squabble that drains away public standing. Administrators can openly dispute the executive's position or can supply information to interest groups or legislators who oppose the executive. At times like this, the executive's best weapon may be informal power to persuade the policy-makers within the administrative organization. Aiding this power of persuasion is the

---

8. Neustadt, *Presidential Power,* pp. 7–8.
9. Joseph A. Schlesinger, "The Politics of the Executive," in Herbert Jacob and Kenneth N. Vines, eds., *Politics in the American States* (Boston: Little, Brown, 1965), pp. 207–38.

executive's prominent public position, the claim to represent "all of the people," and the technical arguments that are provided by aides. Yet, the weaknesses of persuasive power are the time that it consumes and the publicity it may give to the executive's problems. Executives have won confrontations with administrators, but the time and political costs involved may lead them to concede all but their most-vital concerns to the administration.[10]

The lofty position of the chief executive can mean isolation from many administrative arenas where important decisions are made. The chief executive may have direct access to department heads, but the operating bureaus are submerged within the departments. Unless the chief executive is willing to break through the hierarchical lines on the organization chart, the executive is separated from most policy-makers in the administration. One study of presidential relations with bureau chiefs estimated that 125 separate bureaus make essential decisions in the administrative organization of the national government. "The bureaus are, in fact, the bureaucracy. . . . In non-foreign affairs and non-military programs, they are the units of government closest to the citizen and also to Congress." A study of 20 bureaus done in the mid-1960s found that their chief administrative officers had served a total of 170 years as bureau heads, but that they had met a total of only 79 times with the president. This averages to one meeting every two years for each bureau head. If meetings with the Internal Revenue Commissioner were excluded (25 visits in about four years), the average falls to one meeting every three years. These meetings include ceremonial and social functions as well as policy sessions. Except for social or ceremonial occasions 7 of the 20 bureau heads had no contacts with the president; and 2 had no contacts with the president at all.[11]

SOURCES OF EXECUTIVE STRENGTH IN RELATIONS WITH ADMINISTRATIVE AGENCIES

Despite the handicaps, chief executives (state governors, as well as the president) have certain policy-resources that the legislature lacks. The

---

10. See Neustadt, *Presidential Power,* for the best-known general discussion of this point.

11. David S. Brown, "The President and the Bureaus: Time for a Renewal of Relationship?" *Public Administration Review* 26 (September 1966): 174–82.

executive branch is organized in a fashion that is at least nominally hierarchical (see pp. 101–104). The single executive can probably make decisions with greater speed and with greater certainty that colleagues will cooperate than can any single legislator. The staff agencies of the executive possess a level of information superior to that directly available to the legislators. The president's status as the chief executive helps recruit additional civilian advisors on matters of special concern. The chief executive can also attract the mass media—and through them, the public—in ways not possible for individual legislators.

The chief executive may dominate policy-making by concentrating the resources of unity, information, and prestige. The outside borders of control are defined by the "program" on which the executive chooses to concentrate resources. Outside this scope, an executive may be heavily dependent on the proposals of administrative units. The notion of "program" is flexible. Administrative proposals may work their way into the executive's program or may be considered by the legislature with the passive consent of the executive. Even within the scope of his own program, however, the executive may leave the details of planning, bill-drafting, and implementation to the administration.

The record of the Nixon administration demonstrates the capacity of the chief executive to develop the strengths of the Executive Office. Between 1970 and 1974, the White House Office grew from a staff of 311 to 583, and the total staff of the White House Office grew from 1,945 to 4,626.[12] While the Executive Office grew by 137 percent, the total civilian staff of the national government was declining by 1 percent. As we have seen elsewhere, President Nixon added to the powers of the Office of Management and Budget, created the Domestic Council, and sought to broaden his control over policy by unprecedented impoundments of funds appropriated by Congress. Among teachers of political science and public administration, there were many who approved these additions to the president's powers in principle, even though—being mostly Democrats and not enamoured of Nixon personally—they were reserved in their public praise.[13] To these observers, the presidency was the one opportunity for focused authority and leadership in an otherwise divided government. Those who wanted government to do something saw their best chances for success in a strong presidency. Yet, President Nixon may

---

12. Except for the staff of the Office of Economic Opportunity that was formally attached to the Executive Office.

13. James L. Sunquist, "Reflections on Watergate: Lessons for Public Administration," *Public Administration Review* 34 (September/October 1974): 453–61.

have produced too much of a good thing in centralizing power in the White House. Even cabinet members found it impossible to penetrate Nixon's staff and get time on his calendar. Along with all the other particulars grouped under the general label of Watergate, there was a presidential office that ballooned to uncontrolled size and contributed to the separation of the president from the administration.

Professor Richard Neustadt authored the most influential book of the 1960s that called for a strong presidency. In a new edition in 1976, he continued to see a strong presidency as the best chance for integrated policy-making in a government with too many centers of power. Yet, he also saw great danger in his own prescriptions. In his view, President Johnson and President Nixon were preoccupied to the point of obsession with their own power, and:

set themselves on disastrous courses, leading one to premature retirement, the other to forced resignation, and in the process either damaged or demolished (history will tell) their dearest policy objectives: Johnson's Great Society at home, Nixon's balance-of-power in the world.[14]

Even before the actual resignation of Richard Nixon, reactions to Watergate made themselves felt in other chief executives. Several governors found themselves thwarted in efforts to bring more department heads under their direct control. At the national level, President Ford read with sensitivity the mood toward an outsized presidential institution and reduced the size of the Executive Office staff by two-thirds during his first year in office.[15]

VARIATIONS IN RELATIONS AMONG THE EXECUTIVE AND LEGISLATIVE BRANCHES AND ADMINISTRATIVE AGENCIES

In the previous sections of this chapter, we have identified some features that may weaken or strengthen the legislative or executive branches in their relations with administrative agencies. It is more difficult to generalize about the success of individual legislators and executives in their dealings with administrators. Some factors that seem important are the intensity with which each actor adopts a position; the support received

---

14. Neustadt, *Presidential Power*, preface to the 1976 edition.
15. Again excepting the Office of Economic Opportunity.

from other officials, interest groups, or prominent citizens; and the alliances formed against the position.

Not all interactions between the administrative units and the legislative or executive branches are occasions for conflict. Many are informal occasions for helping one another in the common pursuit of improving public service. One study of relations between the House and Senate committees on small business and the Small Business Administration (SBA) found:

the relations since 1961 have been characterized as a "love feast." In that year, President Kennedy named John Horne as head of the agency. According to a number of observers, Horne was one of the most popular administrators on Capitol Hill. They also suggested that relationships between the agency and the committees since then have been not so much the committees' overseeing the agency but rather one of "mutual backscratching."[16]

The small-business committees have "run interference" for the SBA with other committees in Congress and have helped to increase the statutory authority, as well as the funds, of the agency. The committees have also urged the executive superiors of the SBA to pay more attention to the agency's requests. Here is a case where a legislative "overseer" has dealt with the executive in order to help out an administrative agency.

Party Influence on Administrative–Legislative–Executive Relations

From one period of time to another, the positions of administrators, legislators, or executives can change because of the party composition in the executive and legislative branches. One study of budgeting in Congress found that normal procedures were *least* viable following major party changes in the presidency or Congress. During the 80th Congress (1949–50), the newly elected Republican majority made especially large cuts in the budgets submitted by President Truman. In the early Eisenhower years of 1953–55 and in the Kennedy years of 1962–63, there was also a large number of abnormal decisions. Perhaps members of Congress saw the White House developing numerous innovative proposals and felt it necessary to involve themselves heavily in control procedures.[17]

---

16. Dale Vinyard, "The Congressional Committees on Small Business: Pattern of Legislative Committee–Executive Agency Relations," *Western Political Quarterly* 21 (September 1968): 391–99.

17. Otto A. Davis, M.A.H. Dempster, and Aaron Wildavsky, "A Theory of the Budgetary Process," *American Political Science Review* 60 (September 1966): 529–47.

An increase in the status of military policies after 1945 provoked marked change in the relation of certain administrators (i.e., the professional military officers) with policy-makers in the legislative and executive branches. Professional military officers asserted more independence. In previous postwar situations, the services demobilized to small cadres of officers and enlisted personnel and were typically starved for appropriations. In the years following World War I, spending for military *plus* international activities dipped below the sums spent on the U.S. Post Office! After earlier wars, congressional involvement in military affairs was limited to matters of supply and logistics: How much was to be spent to support the armed services and which military bases would remain in operation? Throughout the late 1940s and after the Korean conflict, however, the military and international budgets alone consumed upwards of 47 percent of federal expenditures. As the post-World War II military remained a significant consumer of federal revenue and became a central figure in the country's new prominence in international politics, Congress maintained an interest in military policy. There also developed serious conflicts between military officers and civilians in the Defense Department and White House. Perhaps due to the influence of newly acquired responsibilities, a sense of professionalism became more viable within the military and generated disputes with civilian administrators who had formal responsibilities for making policy. The result was a legislature interested in policy questions and a cadre of military administrators willing—if not anxious—to provide the legislators with alternatives to the proposals offered by the civilian executive. Members of Congress said they could discharge their constitutional responsibilities only if they could compare the "military" recommendations of the joint chiefs of staff with the recommendations of the president that were "compounded of a number of extramilitary considerations."[18] To facilitate its access to the military's recommendations, Congress wrote a clause in the National Security Act of 1949 that permitted a member of the joint chiefs of staff to present to Congress "on his own initiative, after first informing the Secretary of Defense, any recommendation relating to the Department of Defense that he may deem proper."[19]

The postwar opportunities for military officers to influence major

---

18. Samuel P. Huntington, *The Soldier and the States: The Theory and Politics of Civil-Military Relations* (New York: Vintage Books, 1964), p. 415.
19. Huntington, *Soldier and the States*, p. 416.

policy decisions have also presented some difficult choices to these personnel:

The annual psychic crisis of the Chiefs of Staff before the congressional appropriations committees is a new but apparently enduring phenomenon in American government. If the military chief accepts and defends the President's policies, he is subordinating his own professional judgment, denying to Congress the advice to which it is constitutionally entitled, and becoming the political defender of an administration policy. If the military chief expresses his professional opinions to Congress, he is publicly criticizing his Commander in Chief and furnishing useful ammunition to his political enemies. There is no easy way out of this dilemma. Military leaders in the postwar period varied in their behavior from more or less active campaigning against presidential policies ... to the defense of presidential policies which ran counter to their professional judgment.[20]

Changes in the Leadership of Administrative Agencies

It is not only military officers who have to make difficult personal judgments about their relations with legislative and executive "superiors." As noted earlier, both the legislature and the chief executive have grave limitations on their policy roles. Administrators are often left to define their own codes of behavior. The period of transition between one chief executive and another seems most likely to provide such choices to administrators. The loyalties formed under one executive may clash with the postures taken by a new superior. The moral questions raised by such occurrences are made difficult partly because there are so many options and partly because there is only a vague threat of punishment. It is hard to identify, and perhaps harder to punish, an administrator who deviates from the accepted options.

What is a bureau chief to do under such circumstances? Where does his first loyalty lie? To his program principles? To the Secretary? To his clientele and "his" congressional committees? How far can he adapt himself to political redirection without seeming to knuckle under to a serious perversion of the program? Should he adapt himself, resign, or fight a rearguard action? Such moral dilemmas are political variations on the theme of The Caine Mutiny—less dramatic and less publicized but with somewhat similar ingredients. But mutiny on a ship in war-time is a heinous crime, while the penalty for limited mutiny in a government agency is vague and rarely severe. The chances of unpunished success are all too great.[21]

---

20. Huntington, Soldier and the States, p. 417.
21. Rufus E. Miles, Jr., "Administrative Adaptability to Political Change," Public Administration Review 25 (September 1965): 221–25.

A Cost-Benefit Analysis of Legislative "Oversight"

In many areas of policy, the legislative, executive, or administrative personnel have an opportunity to involve themselves in basic decisions, but choose to abstain on account of the "costs" involved. Some costs occur because participants must focus their resources on a limited set of issues and must deprive themselves of opportunities presented by other topics. Other costs occur because an actor does not wish to "poison" other relations with a protagonist. Legislators may avoid giving offense to a chief executive or to administrators, for example, in order to win their support on some other project that is more highly valued. One study of legislative "oversight" (i.e., supervision) of agency programs concluded that the following types of conditions were likely to have a favorable ratio of benefits to costs and to affect legislative involvement in policy-making. A legislative committee is likely to make a formal investigation of agency activities:[22]

1. When the leadership of the majority party believes it can cause sufficient embarrassment, with accompanying profit for itself, to a past or current opposition chief executive who is held responsible for the performance of his agency appointees.
2. When the committee leadership or powerful committee members believe that constituent or group interests important to them cannot be satisfied by informal personal intercessions between legislators and agencies.
3. When legislators perceive that the chief executive will try to diminish their normal opportunities for influencing agency policy.
4. When, periodically, interest builds in the legislature for revising the basic policies under which the agency operates, committee oversight tends to occur as a byproduct.
5. When committee leaders become convinced that interests to which they are opposed will substantially advance their own purposes by exposing dramatic evidence of agency failure, the committee may move first to neutralize or minimize these gains by initiating its own inquiry.

Formal Powers of the Legislative and Executive Branches

The nature of one's formal powers can also affect legislative or executive involvement in an administrative system. The legislature and

---

22. Seymour Scher, "Conditions for Legislative Control," *Journal of Politics* 25 (August 1963): 526–51; these propositions are extrapolated here beyond the context of Scher's study of congressional-committee–regulatory-commission relations.

chief executive have more formal authority in some governments than in others. Among the state governments, for example, there is considerable variation in the power of the governors to appoint the heads of major departments, to veto legislation, to succeed themselves in office, and to formulate the administration's budget.[23] Where the chief executive is relatively weak on these dimensions, the legislature is more successful in having its policies implemented by administrative organizations. A survey of agency heads in 50 states showed that the governor was perceived to exercise the greatest control over agency affairs (as compared with the legislature) where the governor's formal powers were strongest. The power of appointment seems particularly important. Among those agency heads who were popularly elected, only 9 percent felt the governor exercised greater policy control than the legislature. Among those who were appointed by the governor alone—without the consent of a commission or the legislature—57 percent felt the governor exercised more control over policy than the legislature.[24] However, formal authority does not always provide what it seems. The "item veto" has been heralded as a device to permit the chief executive greater control over the expenditures of administrative agencies. It is used, presumably, to veto discrete items of an appropriations act; the executive can deny the funds for certain programs, without having to threaten many other programs by vetoing a whole appropriations bill. The governors of 43 states now have the item veto; it is mentioned in the remaining states as a device to increase the governor's control over the administration. Yet, state legislatures have learned to protect favored programs against the threat of an item veto. A study of the item veto in Arizona found that it was used only 11 times since 1912, and not at all in the 16 years prior to 1965. When the legislature senses that a certain item may draw a veto from the governor, it typically lumps it with items the governor is likely to approve. It thereby structures the "item" so the governor will not veto it, despite opposition to parts of it.[25]

There is no simple answer to these questions: *What are the "typical" relations among administrators and legislative and executive branches? What conditions will provoke the legislative or executive branch to play an assertive role in policy-making?* When conflict arises within the administrative system, there is no clear indication as to who

23. See Schlesinger, "Politics of the Executive."
24. Deil Wright, "Executive Leadership in State Administration," *Midwest Journal of Political Science* 11 (February 1967): 1–26.
25. Roy D. Morey, "The Executive Veto in Arizona: Its Use and Limitations," *Western Political Quarterly* 19 (September 1966): 504–15.

will prevail. The literature is replete with statements of general tendency. Some scholars have also probed the relative involvement of the legislature or the executive under each of certain conditions. However, their conditions do not exhaust the range of contingencies that face policymakers, and their research methods have not been adequate to quiet skeptical social scientists. It is necessary to admit that not much is known about the scope of administrators' autonomy or about the influence of legislators or executives in policy-making.

BUDGET RELATIONS AMONG LEGISLATORS, EXECUTIVES, AND ADMINISTRATORS

Budgeting involves legislators, executives, and administrators in their most regular and continuous relations. Budgeting is a cyclical process that repeats itself once annually (or once every two years in the case of state governments that use a biennial budget period). Members of the legislative appropriations committees, the chief executive and the central budget office, and representatives for administrative agencies deal with one another both formally in budget proceedings and informally as they seek clearance when conditions require deviations from the existing budget. In many cases, budget interactions involve the same personalities for many years at a time. This occurs when the legislature respects seniority and guarantees a member's seat on the appropriations committee and when a central budget office is staffed with professionals who survive turnover in the office of the chief executive. Budgeting differs from the sporadic kinds of legislative-executive-administrative interactions that occur when a controversial issue generates momentary interest in the legislative or executive branches. Moreover, the medium of exchange involved in budgeting facilitates the description and analysis of general patterns and deviant behaviors. By focusing on the decisions made in the executive and legislative branches about the budget requests of administrative agencies, it is possible to discern which actors seem to prevail in the outcomes.

Chronology of Budgeting

The budget calendar of the federal government provides a convenient device to identify the principal administrative, executive, and legislative actors in budgeting and to note some important features of their interactions. Although calendar details vary in state and local governments, some general features tend to be constant. These are the initiation of requests by administrators, subsequent reviews by upper levels of the administration and of the executive budget staff, and final review in the legislature.

The major elements of the federal budgeting process consume 28 months. Program planning for fiscal year 1979, for example, was underway early in 1977.[26] The length of time is significant in itself. It underscores both the number of actors who involve themselves in the budgeting process and the importance of giving each one a chance to ask questions and to make evaluations. The time involved in budgeting also has its costs. The months of leadtime between planning and expenditures requires considerable replanning during each budget cycle. When a new president is elected to office, much of the budgetary process for the *coming* fiscal year is already complete. By the time of the inauguration in January, the outgoing president has already submitted a budget to Congress that will provide funds extending 21 months into the new administration. The budgeting-spending process is divided into three segments: the *formulation of the executive budget; congressional action;* and *execution of the enacted budget.*

Formulation in the Executive

The decisions in the *formulation* period begin with agency programming, which then provides the basis for making its financial estimates. The agency defends its own estimates in the departmental budget office. (In this budgeting section, the term "agency" refers to an operating subunit of a major federal administrative department.) The departmental budget office plays an intermediate role between the operating agencies and the Office of Management and Budget (OMB). The hearings of the department budget office provide the agency with its only opportunity to defend its *own* requests. After the department budget office makes a recommendation to the OMB, the agency budget office is then obligated to defend the department's recommendation. Typically, this recommendation is lower than the agency's request. The agency gets an opportunity to defend the budget that the department has recommended for it before the examiners of the OMB. At the next opportunity the agency has to defend its budget, it is obligated to support the recommendation (usually reduced further) made for it by the Office of Management and Budget.

---

26. Fiscal year 1979 runs from October 1, 1978 to September 30, 1979.

The formal rules obligate the agencies to accept the successive recommendations of the department budget office and the OMB. However, there are certain opportunities to evade these rules. Agencies vary in their assertiveness, with some being more prepared than others to exploit their opportunities for self-expression. For those who are willing, it is possible to mobilize support at the presidential level while the agency's budget is still within the formulation period; later it is possible to mobilize the support of interest groups or legislators in the appropriations subcommittees.

Although the president does not play a continuing role in the formulation of agency budgets, the president does have an opportunity to review the decisions made by the OMB and to hear appeals from the agencies. With more than 100 agencies and a budget totaling over $400 billion, it is obvious the president cannot give equal (or in many cases any) attention to all who would desire additional funds. One of the devices agencies may employ to attract the president's attention is the influential individual or organization. Most agencies have a *coterie* of clientele groups, and some have developed efficient media of communications that inform the groups when the agency is threatened with an insufficient budget. In certain agencies, however, there is a feeling of impropriety about interest groups. According to this view, each of the agencies is part of the "president's team" governed by the Office of Management and Budget. To seek a redress of the Office's recommendations would be to work against the team.

A problem for all participants in the budget process is the proportion of government funds that is "uncontrollable." These represent commitments to established programs that benefit individuals, state and local governments, the payment of interest on government debt, and the fulfillment of contractual obligations. The Office of Management and Budget reported that almost 75 percent of the 1976 federal budget was uncontrollable, a proportion up from the 59 percent in 1967. Because of these continuing commitments of available revenues, budget-makers have proportionately less opportunity to create new programs or to add new features to existing programs that have proved attractive. As we see in a later section, much of the activity of administrative, executive, and legislative participants in the budget process consists of formal actions to continue programs considered to be commitments.

Congressional Action

Members of Congress have long felt themselves dependent on the executive branch's formulation and justification of the budget. While specialized appropriations subcommittees have allowed certain House members and senators, plus their professional staff aides to become familiar with the details of agency requests, many legislators have felt unable to deal with the aggregate budget or with the setting of priorities from one field to another. The work of each subcommittee was considered and passed by the entire Appropriations Committee and then by each house in sequence, with no formal consideration of the entire budget. Moreover, the executive's increase in analytic capabilities, including PPB, left the legislature with a feeling of being increasingly dependent on the recommendations of the Office of Management and Budget, without a comprehension of the elaborate procedures and arguments used to justify those recommendations.

A major result of Congress's budget malaise was the Congressional Budget and Impoundments Control Act of 1974. Besides dealing with the issue of impoundments, to be considered later, the Act established new Budget Committees in the House and Senate, a Congressional Budget Office with impressive expertise in economic and policy analysis, elaborate procedures for congressional review of the overall budget, plus a restructuring of the fiscal year to allow the meshing of these new procedures with the traditional review of each budget category by appropriations subcommittees.

This is not the first effort to improve congressional scrutiny over the budget. Reforms in 1947 and again in 1950 required the consideration of the entire budget, but they fell into disuse because of the task's magnitude. Now the task has grown further with the size and breadth of the federal government's activities. However, the reforms of 1974 were designed with the weaknesses of the earlier efforts in mind. Table 9–1 portrays the calendar of these procedures, which first occurred during 1975.

The important new procedures are the first and second resolutions, due in April and September. Their purpose is to consider overall program needs and revenue projections, and to make a congressional decision on the total budget—including the size of the deficit to be permitted. The first resolution establishes targets for the appropriations subcommittees, and the second—passed after the subcommittees have finished their work on the details of agency requests—establishes the final totals and the permitted deficit. After this resolution, any spending proposal that would go beyond its limits can be ruled out of order in either house.

One attraction of the new procedures is that they are not so rigid as to break down in the face of changing realities. Exempt from the limits of the second budget resolution are "uncontrollable" items like social security and unemployment, which would be allowed to rise as

Table 9–1
Congressional Budget Calendar

October-December: Congressional Budget Office submits five-year projection of current spending as soon as possible after Oct. 1.

Nov. 10: President submits current services budget, showing projected spending for existing programs.

Dec. 31: Joint Economic Committee reports analysis of current services budget to budget committees.

Late January: President submits budget (15 days after Congress convenes), including current services, new and enlarged activities.

Late January-March: Budget committees hold hearings and begin work on first budget resolution.

March 15: All legislative committees submit estimates and views to budget committees.

April 15: Budget committees report first resolution.

May 15: Committees must report authorization bills by this date.

May 15: Congress completes action on first resolution. Before adoption of the first resolution, neither house may consider new budget authority or spending authority bills, revenue changes, or debt limit changes.

May 15 through the 7th day after Labor Day: Appropriation subcommittees and Congress complete action on all budget and spending authority bills.

• Before reporting first regular appropriations bill, the House Appropriations Committee, "to extent practicable," marks up all regular appropriations bills and submits a summary report to House, comparing proposed outlays and budget authority levels with first resolution targets.

• CBO issues periodic scorekeeping reports comparing congressional action with first resolution.

• Reports on new budget authority and tax expenditure bills must contain comparisons with first resolution, and five-year projections.

• "As possible," a CBO cost analysis and five-year projection will accompany all reported public bills, except appropriation bills.

August: Budget committees prepare second budget resolution and report.

Sept. 15: Congress completes action on second resolution. Thereafter, neither house may consider any bill or amendment, or conference report, that results in an increase over outlay or budget authority figures, or a reduction in revenues, beyond the amounts in the second resolution.

Sept. 25: Congress completes action on reconciliation bill or another resolution. Congress may not adjourn until it completes action on the second resolution and reconciliation measure, if any.

Oct. 1: Fiscal year begins.

SOURCE: Adapted from *Congressional Quarterly Almanac 1975* (Washington, D.C.: Congressional Quarterly Service, 1976), p. 918.

high as demand required. Also the resolution is entirely a matter of congressional action. It does not require the president's signature, and it can be revised whenever Congress feels the situation warrants it. Another attraction is the staff assistance that Congress has provided itself to operate the new procedures. By late 1975, the Congressional Budget Office employed almost 200 people on its own budget of $6 million. Its various staff divisions concentrate on economic forecasting and policy analysis in the areas of taxes, energy and physical resources, human resources and community development, national security and international affairs, and general government.

Some potential weaknesses in the reform appeared when it was given its first test. It is not clear how it will weather the tough realities of congressional politics. During the first use of the procedures in 1975, the passage of the second resolution came only on a close vote in the House in the middle of December, some two months after its due date. Moreover, it faced strong opposition from both left and right, with liberals feeling that it did not allow enough spending for social programs and conservatives feeling it was too generous. This close test in 1975 signaled trouble for the future. Previous congressional budget reforms failed when members would not lessen their support of individual programs for the sake of a united congressional control over budget totals.

Even with the new procedures, the most detailed examination of agency budgets by Congress takes place between the first and second resolutions, in the specialized subcommittees of the House of Representatives Appropriations Committee. The House examines budgets before the Senate does, owing to custom and to an interpretation of a constitutional provision that gives the House precedence in money bills. When the agency budgets are in the congressional stage, there are opportunities for assertive agencies to indicate their true desires. Although it is against the regulations for agencies to ask Congress for funds that have not been recommended by the OMB, it is proper for agencies to respond accurately when a legislator asks them about their "real needs." An agency that wants a larger budget than recommended may plant a question with a cooperative legislator—perhaps through the intermediary of a friendly interest group.

When the appropriations subcommittees examine agency budgets, they seem to be most thorough in their investigation of the assertive agencies. In dealing with these agencies, the subcommittee members ask more questions during the hearing; they are more likely to demand that the agencies justify certain portions of their request; they are more likely to ask the department secretary and budget officer about the agency's budget; and they are most likely to reduce the agency's request and add special restrictions to the agency's use of its funds in the committee report or in the appropriations act. Thus, the assertive agencies get some rough treatment from Congress. But over the long run, the assertive agencies can increase their budgets more than timid agencies do. The treatment of assertive agencies can fail to cancel the impact of their more aggressive requests and tactics. While the agencies that ask for the largest increases and pursue their goals most aggressively may suffer the largest cuts, they may also have the largest increases remaining after the fray.[27]

Budget Execution

It is actually the Office of Management and Budget that has the last say about an agency's expenditure. The office makes apportionments of the funds voted by Congress. The OMB cannot increase an agency's appropriation above the congressional figure; but it can reduce the agency's appropriation either to reserve funds for contingencies, to save money as part of a general economy drive, or to hold the agency at a certain level of program development. Thus, the OMB can enforce its original budget recommendations for an agency or even reduce an agency's actual spending below the OMB's own earlier recommendation (see pp. 133–34).

Nature of Budget Decisions in the Executive and Legislative Branches

Incrementalism is the prime feature of budget decisions in both federal and state governments. Its principal rule is that previous decisions are generally legitimate; concentrate investigations on the increments of growth that are requested.[28]

The use of incremental budgeting in the federal government is evident in the participants' fixation on the "base" of expenditures established by earlier decisions. Agency personnel are concerned with the percentage of increase over their existing budget that they should request for the coming year; reviewers in the departmental budget offices and in the

---

27. Ira Sharkansky, "An Appropriations Subcommittee and Its Client Agencies: A Comparative Study of Supervision and Control," *American Political Science Review* 59 (September 1965): 622–28.

28. This section draws on Ira Sharkansky, *The Routines of Politics* (New York: Van Nostrand-Reinhold, 1970), chapter 4.

OMB calculate their actions in terms of percentage cuts to be imposed on the agencies' requests. Members of the House of Representatives discuss their own percentage changes in the president's budget. Senators talk about the percentage changes they will make in the House decision.[29]

A continuing controversy in incremental budgeting concerns the size of the increment. It is routine that calculations begin from the base of a previous budgetary decision; but it is less regular that the size of the increment is stable from one period of time to another or from one actor to another within a year's budget cycle. As might be expected, the spenders typically request larger increments than budget-reviewers will grant. A study of federal agencies provides some information about the increments voted.[30] Annual requests were made by 24 agencies that averaged at least 10 percent above previous appropriations; 11 made annual requests that averaged at least 20 percent above their previous appropriations; and the annual requests of 2 agencies averaged at least 75 percent above earlier funds. The Appropriations Committee in the House of Representatives permitted annual growth rates in excess of 10 percent for only 12 of the agencies and an annual growth rate in excess of 20 percent for only 1 of them.[31] The Appropriations Committee in the Senate typically serves as a court of appeals to the House decisions. The Senate concentrates on the grievances that agencies hold after their House experience, and it typically adds to the House grant. The House appropriation is the "base" from which the Senate works, and the increment between the House and Senate figure is usually small. For only 10 of the 36 agencies in the study did the Senate provide an average of 5 percent more of its request than did the House, and for only 2 of the agencies was the Senate's generosity as much as 10 percent above the House grant.[32]

State governments provide a useful laboratory for the observation and analysis of incremental budgeting. Their many agencies and diverse economic, social, and political environments provide opportunities for several variants of incremental budgeting to show themselves; the multiplicity of conditions provides the opportunity to see what types of situations give rise to which varieties of incrementalism.

As in federal budgeting, the common ingredient of incremental-

29. Aaron Wildavsky, *The Politics of the Budgetary Process* (Boston: Little, Brown, 1974).

30. Richard F. Fenno, Jr., *The Power of the Purse: Appropriations Politics in Congress* (Boston: Little, Brown, 1966).

31. Fenno, *Power of the Purse,* chapter 8.

32. Fenno, *Power of the Purse,* chapter 11.

ism in state governments is a fixation upon the increment between previously made decisions and the current request. When administrators in state agencies plan their requests, their paperwork requires them to list current and previous expenditures and to compare these figures with their estimates for the coming year. Budget examiners in the executive and legislative branches are most likely to question the funds that would increase appropriations and to cut from these requests in order to minimize budget growth.

If anything can be said about the differences in incremental budgeting at state and federal levels, it is that state personnel seem to be even more fascinated with the dollar-increment of change in an agency's budget proposal. Studies of federal budgeting indicate that budget-reviewers often question the substance of programs that are to be purchased with the budget increment. One study of state decision-makers, however, indicates a narrow fixation on the dollar-amount of the increment, with virtually no attention paid to the substance of the program at issue.[33] There are several possible explanations for the narrower inquiry of budget-makers. The central budget offices of state governments have fewer investigatory resources than does the U.S. Office of Management and Budget, so their inquiry must be more cursory. State legislators have less staff assistance than do members of Congress, and members of appropriations committees are themselves less well prepared to make a detailed investigation of agency programs. Many state legislatures have high rates of turnover and are without a well-developed seniority system. Thus, the members of state appropriations committees are likely to be inexperienced at their work.

By looking at relationships among the nature of agency requests, the governor's recommendations to the legislature, and the subsequent actions of the legislature, we can see how the governor and the legislature actually make their budget decisions in an incremental fashion.[34] Administrative agencies and the governor play the most consistent roles in the state budgeting process. In each of 19 states reported in Table 9–2, the agencies requested a sizable increase (14–53 percent) over their current appropriations, and the governors pared the increase in their recommendations (by 4–31 percent). Agencies requested an average 24 percent increase over their current budgets, and the governors' recom-

---

33. Thomas J. Anton, *The Politics of State Expenditures in Illinois* (Urbana: University of Illinois Press, 1966), pp. 253–55.

34. Ira Sharkansky, "Agency Requests, Gubernatorial Support, and Budget Success in State Legislatures," *American Political Science Review* 62 (December 1968): pp. 1220–32.

TABLE 9–2

Annual Percentage Changes by Stages in the Budget Process of Major Agencies, by State

State, Showing Years of Budget Analyzed and Number of Agencies	Agency Request as Percentage of Current Expenditure	Governor's Recommendation as Percentage of Agency Request	Legislature's Appropriation as Percentage of Governor's Request	Legislature's Appropriation as Percentage of Agency's Current Expenditure	Legislature's Appropriation as Percentage of Agency Request
Florida 1965–67, n = 39	120%	90%	93%	109%	84%
Georgia 1965–67, n = 26	153	86	100	139	87
Idaho 1967–69, n = 23	119	93	92	109	86
Illinois 1963–65,* n = 37	118	83	102	108	85
Indiana 1965–67, n = 47	123	83	103	112	86
Kentucky 1966–68, n = 28	120	90	93	109	84
Louisiana 1966–67, n = 32	121	90	101	110	91
Maine 1965–67, n = 17	114	85	108	109	92
Nebraska 1965–67, n = 10	122	87	119	124	104
North Carolina 1965–67, n = 61	120	84	105	112	87
North Dakota 1965–67, n = 21	124	74	111	111	82
South Carolina 1966–67, n = 29	117	96	104	116	99
South Dakota 1967–68, n = 25	136	82	98	109	80
Texas 1965–67, n = 41	128	82	104	117	86
Vermont 1965–67, n = 17	121	87	106	115	91
Virginia 1966–68, n = 57	120	92	100	114	91
West Virginia 1966–67, n = 43	125	88	92	101	81
Wisconsin 1965–67, n = 26	115	96	98	111	94
Wyoming 1967–69, n = 13	133	69	109	112	75

SOURCE: Ira Sharkansky, "Agency Requests, Gubernatorial Support, and Budget Success in State Legislatures," *American Political Science Review* 62 (December 1968): p. 1223.

*The Illinois data come from the appendix of Thomas J. Anton's *The Politics of State Expenditure in Illinois* (Urbana: University of Illinois Press, 1966). All other data come from the official budgets and financial reports of the states.

mendations trimmed an average 14 percent from their requests. The legislatures' final appropriations typically remained close to the governors' recommendations, but appropriations varied from a cut of 8 percent below the recommendation to an increase of 19 percent above the recommendation. Six of the legislatures cut agencies' budgets below the governors' figures, and 11 appropriated more than the governors asked. In only one case, however, did a legislature (in Nebraska) give more money to the agencies than they had requested themselves. The overall average legislative grant for the coming period was 13 percent below the agencies' requests, but that was 13 percent above the agencies' current budgets.

When we examine the response of governors and legislatures to the budgets of individual agencies, we find that the *acquisitiveness* of the agency requests plays a crucial role in the decision of other budget-makers. In most of the states examined, the governor and legislature direct the greatest percentage cuts at the agencies that request the greatest percentage increases. However, it is these acquisitive agencies that come out of the legislature with the greatest increases over their previous budgets. Both the governor and the legislature are using similar incremental decision rules: *cut the agencies that ask for a large increase, but do not recommend a budget expansion for those agencies that ask for no increase.* The absolute size of agency budget requests does not appear to influence the decisions made by the governor or by the legislature. Budget-reviewers in the governor's office and in the legislature are more likely to respond to the *percentage increment of change requested* (i.e., agency acquisitiveness) than to the sheer size of the request. The failure of either the governor or the legislature to impose additional funds on those agencies that do not ask for them illustrates how much the executive and legislative branches let program-initiation pass over to administrative organizations.

The Sources of Incrementalism

There are several reasons for the popularity of incremental decision-making among budgeteers. One reason lies in the appeal of routines in comparison with the rational assessment of the whole budget document. Rather than attempting the impossible task of considering all the issues that are relevant to a budget, officials in administrative units, as well as in the executive and legislative branches, have grown used to conceding the propriety of expenditures destined for existing programs; they focus attention on the increment that represents a growth in expenditure (and presumably a change in the agency's program). To do otherwise would continually reopen past accommodations between the parties interested in each item of an agency's program. This would make each item always controversial, would preclude administrators or clients from "counting on" the continuation of current programs, and would require an extraordinary magnitude of investigatory resources just to supervise each part of every agency's program and to prepare the information necessary for an annual decision.[35]

A second reason for incremental decision-making lies in the commitments built into each budget. In some cases, relatively little in an agency's expenditure can be changed from one budget period to the next. As noted above, the Office of Management and Budget considered some 75 percent of the national government budget for 1976 to be "uncontrollable." Some parts of an agency's budget may represent "earmarked funds." These moneys cannot legally be spent for any other than certain purposes and, thus, are not likely to be challenged by either the executive or legislative branches. There are also commitments to government employees and to the clients of public services that limit a serious inquiry into an agency's established level of expenditure. Large numbers of employees cannot be threatened with dismissal or transfer during each year's budget review, and large numbers of citizens cannot be threatened that major components of their public services will be curtailed or shifted in their character. These inflexibilities, reflecting common agreements as to what is "practical," impose real limits on the thorough review of an agency's budget.

A factor that weakens the position of many newly proposed activities—and thereby strengthens the role that incrementalism can play in budgeting—is the lack of acceptable measures of performance. The officials in charge of existing programs have acquired some indicators of their workload, and they can emphasize those that maximize their program's appeal to the reviewers in the legislature and the executive. Those who propose new activities, however, may not be able to offer more than hopes and expectations to the budget reviewers. New programs lack a prior history of experience and have not yet generated a record of success in dealing with clients.[36]

Another reason for incremental budgeting lies in the lack of innovative drive that characterizes many governmental arenas. Budget growth tends to be slow because few major proposals can survive all

---

35. Allen Schick, "Control Patterns in State Budget Execution," *Public Administration Review* 24 (June 1964): 97–106.

36. Herman Mertins, "Comments," Conference on Public Administration, Meadowbrook Conference Center of Syracuse University, September 1968.

the veto points in the administrative agencies and in the legislative and executive branches. The constitutional framers set out to design a conservative government, and they seem to have been successful. State governments tend to make only occasional spurts in spending. A period of dramatic growth tends to be short and to be followed by stability. After a surge of innovation in several programs, both the legislature and the executive may tire of the political costs involved in getting lots of people to agree to major changes in programs. Administrators themselves might tire of the expansion necessary to accommodate new programs. Often this means severe competition for new personnel and the need to integrate the new personnel—or perhaps new units—into the existing fabric of supervision, coordination, and control. Programs that grow rapidly may get out of touch with their top administrators; duplications in activities and lack of central control may bring charges of "inefficiency" or "waste." It is often difficult to define these charges with precision. In any case, "inefficiency" and "waste" are powerful accusations in American politics. They may be sufficient to lead some legislators, executives, and administrators to slow or stop the growth in new programs.

Variations in Incremental Budgeting

The rules of incrementalism in government budgeting set outside limits to the percentage of change that is feasible; they do not define precisely the direction and magnitude of the change that will occur. Incremental routines lead budget reviewers to reduce the estimates of growth-oriented agencies and to withhold increases from the agencies that have not sought more funds. Nevertheless, these decision-rules are not uniform. Some governors and legislatures are more or less likely than their counterparts in other states (or in their own states during other years) to grant or withhold increments. In some years, dramatic events, such as war or economic crisis, stimulate officials to be unusually generous—or stingy—in dealing with agency budgets. Sometimes even the "base" of appropriations for existing programs is subject to scrutiny and reduction. By examining the nature of budget relationships among agencies, the governor, and the legislature, in conjunction with several other characteristics of each state in a normal year, we can gain some insight into the elements that influence budget decisions. Actually, the findings are not crystal clear. Although some relationships prevail between the nature of budget decisions and several traits of the state's politics and economy, there are many instances of budget decisions that do not correspond to the general patterns. Deviations from incremental budget routines are not governed by objective forces of economics or politics. Instead, they appear to develop individually in the context of each state.

The governor's possession of strong formal veto powers and state government expenditures that are high in comparison with other states are often associated with strong gubernatorial restraint against agency budget-development.[37] The already high expenditures may incline the governor against further large increases in state spending; and the power of a veto may strengthen the governor's resolve to impose a severe review on the agencies when they submit requests. In contrast, the governor is unusually generous toward agency requests for budget expansion where there is relatively intense party competition. A competitive party situation may lead the governor to decide for the sake of career—and party—by supporting innovative agencies.

Where the legislature is particularly restrictive against agency budget-development, there tends to be both relatively high state government expenditure and debt and a low incidence of state administrators who are separately elected. Like the governor, the legislature appears to resist an acquisitive agency in the face of already committed state resources (i.e., high expenditures and debt). With a scarcity of separately elected agency heads, administrators may lack politically independent advocates who can promote their budget through the legislature.

Innovative administrators have not rested in the face of incremental budget routines. They have devised several techniques to permit examination of the whole of an agency's budget—including the "base" of its current appropriation—and to compare the usefulness of each component of the budget against the other components of the budget. These changes in budgeting represent the efforts of reformers to replace "satisfactory" procedures with those that are "optimal" or "rational." Program-Planning-Budgeting represents a major effort in this direction. It is described in Chapter 3 along with other techniques of decision-making.

General Accounting Office: Administrative Nemesis with Little Public Renown

It is not only the budget-maker who sits astride the financial separations of power, or checks and balances. In the national government, the auditing unit—General Accounting Office—is situated in the legisla-

---

37. Sharkansky, "Agency Requests, Gubernatorial Support and Budget Success."

tive branch and provides administrators with daily reminders that another branch is monitoring their activities. The GAO is a little-known
actor with great importance.[38] To journalists and political scientists—
and thus to much of the population—the auditor arouses far less interest
than members of the legislature, heads of administrative agencies, the
chief executive and presidential staff, candidates for public office, and
functionaries of the major political parties.

The range of the auditor's work and the impact on other parts of
the political process depend on how broadly the auditor's task is defined. There is much dispute about the breadth of this task among GAO
personnel and other actors in the legislative, executive, and administrative branches. At one extreme, auditing is limited to reviewing and certifying the reliability of the financial accounts compiled by administrative
departments. At another extreme, the auditor performs important tasks
in the expenditure process, program planning, evaluation, and implementation.

The most elementary feature of the auditor's work in the national
government is the verification that expenditures are made within the
scope of existing legislation. Typically, this occurs a long time after the
legislative and executive branches have approved a program and after
administrators have begun to operate. Despite the lateness of its entry
into the expenditure process, the audit unit can throw a large monkey-
wrench into a program's machinery. Without the auditor's approval,
the Treasury will *not* pay for goods ordered or services rendered. With
no payments forthcoming, any subsequent operations are unlikely. The
importance of this function is that it allows the auditor to determine
just what kinds of activities are authorized—or not authorized—by
existing statutes. This is not always an easy task. Administrators often develop programs that differ in detail from those described in the statutes.
Also, different statutes may apply to the same program, and some in-
consistencies may appear in their language. For clues to legislative "intent," an auditor may go beneath formal enactments to debates on the
floor of Congress or to statements in committee hearings or committee
reports. This kind of a search increases the alternative standards open to
the audit unit and broadens its discretion with respect to the activities
it will allow.

---

38. See Richard E. Brown, *The GAO: Untapped Source of Congressional Power*
(Knoxville: University of Tennessee Press, 1970); and Ira Sharkansky, "The Politics of
Auditing," in Bruce L. R. Smith, *The New Political Economy: The Public Use of the
Private Sector* (London: Macmillan & Co., 1976), pp. 278–318.

When auditors move out from a narrow consideration of the "legality" of expenditures to a consideration of their "efficiency," an extensive set of opportunities opens up. The GAO does not have the authority to stop expenditures it finds inefficient. It does inform administrators, Congress, and the press about inefficiencies, however, and it becomes a persuasive force that program administrators must recognize. Moreover, along the way to judging the efficiency of expenditures the auditor acquires the skills and information of a systems analyst; these provide the auditor with other powers. The auditor may quarrel with administrators' decisions about the activities that will accomplish certain goals for certain costs and under certain conditions. When auditors take this kind of a posture, they are a long way from the accountant's green eyeshade and into the thick of program debate.

Relations between the GAO and administrative departments are generally cooperative. Reports of illegal or inefficient operations are welcomed by the president, the Office of Management and Budget, and administrative superiors who are interested in credible information about their subordinates' activities. Yet, there are times when the GAO runs into the barrier of strict formality on the part of administrators. Some information about agency programs is denied to the GAO by officials who cite "executive privileges" and the need to keep certain business within the administration. To the administrators who cite these protections, the GAO is an arm of Congress that—with certain information at its disposal—would help legislators gain undesirable advantages in the persistent clash of constitutional branches across the separation of powers.

TENSIONS AMONG EXECUTIVES, LEGISLATORS, AND ADMINISTRATORS

The separation of powers or checks and balances, have exhibited a shifting equilibrium since the adoption of the Constitution. One crisis or near-crisis after another has surfaced over the years to demonstrate the persistence of tension within the government and to define, by the nature of its resolution, the powers of one branch in relation to others. Several episodes from the 1960s and early 1970s demonstrated the continuation of tension and the evolving definition of powers. They include two conflicts between the GAO and certain legislators on one side and executive plus administrative personnel on the other; and a head-on conflict between President Richard Nixon and the Congress that had striking implications for administrative agencies.

GAO Inquiries and Administrative Claims of Privilege

Disputes between the GAO and administrators have occurred prominently in connection with the Defense Department's research, development, and procurement. The Defense Department is especially concerned that GAO inquiries do not open alternative courses of action in addition to those already chosen by the Department. It wants GAO reviews limited to the adequacy of management procedures as applied to existing programs or to programs that have been included in the president's budget. Under certain conditions, the Department would accept GAO reviews of the planning *procedures* used when the Department "establishes objectives, identifies alternatives, and reaches conclusions and recommendations." The Department does not release detailed information about alternatives to current policy. In the Department's official view, it is most desirable for Congress to review the Department's recommendations directly, without independent analyses of policy alternatives by GAO. By making separate program assessments and recommendations, the GAO would burden Congress with too much information and might also threaten the Defense Department with the administration of a program it did not want.[39]

The Defense Department reinforces its preferences about the analyses of the GAO by control over the kinds of information needed to make program assessments. The Department normally withholds all information except that pertaining to the programs finally adopted by the administration. Moreover, the Department releases to the GAO only certain types of internal reports pertaining to those programs. The GAO does not have "ready access to uncensored files of the Department"; its activity is limited by the kinds of documents the Department is willing to release. However, the Department's attitude is flexible and subject to change in response to political pressure. When numerous legislators expressed an intense interest in the MBT-70 (Main Battle Tank), the deputy secretary granted the GAO complete access to all documentation in the Department's files. At the time, the Department insisted this was

---

39. See, for example, *Capability of GAO to Analyze and Audit Defense Expenditures,* Hearings before the Subcommittee on Executive Reorganization of the Committee on Government Operations, U.S. Senate, 91st Congress, 1st Session, September 16–25, 1969 (Washington, D.C.: U.S. Government Printing Office, 1969), pp. 235–37. (Hereafter cited as *Capability of GAO.*)

a "special one-time action and was an exception to the general guidelines."[40] It appears that the breadth of congressional interest and its insistence on administrative candor was a principal feature in this breach of executive privilege.

The Philadelphia Plan

In another prominent instance of legislative-executive-administrative conflict, the GAO tried to outlaw an important item of the president's domestic program. It was a case of the legislature's "guardian of the Treasury" saying that "money cannot be spent" for certain purposes, and the administration responding with a "Dammit, yes!" Most of the time the adverse rulings of the GAO are accepted with little more than grumbling in the affected agency and among the clients and contractors who are affected by the decision. In the case of the Philadelphia Plan, however, the agency involved fought the decision through the highest levels of the Nixon administration and won a ruling from the attorney general that set the executive branch squarely against the GAO.

The details of the Philadelphia Plan are numerous and complex, and they shifted between an original plan and a revised version that was developed—still unsuccessfully—to satisfy the comptroller general about its legality.[41] Only the basic dimensions of the plan are relevant to our purpose: it consists of certain language written into government contracts (first attempted for a federal building project in Philadelphia) to require genuine efforts on the part of the contractor to employ members of minority groups. The issue gained its political importance from (1) the virtual lack of blacks among certain categories of skilled workers in construction projects; (2) the focus of militant and moderate black organizations against the alleged discriminatory practices of craft unions and contractors; and (3) the widely perceived conservative record of the Nixon administration on racial policies. Because of the "southern strategy," the administration was said to be ignoring the needs of black Americans. The Philadelphia Plan was an important—some said the *most* important—move of the administration in the direction of equal economic opportunity.

The clash with the GAO rested upon the comptroller general's claim that the plan was contrary to the precepts of the Civil Rights Act of 1964; in particular, Section 703 (j) states that the act does not require

---

40. *Capability of GAO*, p. 243.
41. See James E. Jones, Jr., "The Bugaboo of Employment Quotas," *Wisconsin Law Review* 1970, No. 2: 341–403.

an employer to grant preferential treatment to any individual or group because of race, color, religion, sex, or national origin. The GAO alleged that the Labor Department would "obligate bidders, contractors or sub-contractors to consider the race or national origin of their employees or prospective employees."[42] The Labor Department responded that the plan only required contractors to take "affirmative action" that would achieve reasonable goals of "minority manpower utilization." The debate set labor *and* management of the construction industry and some conservative Republican and Democratic members of Congress in support of GAO against an alliance of President Nixon, Attorney General Mitchell, numerous black organizations, and liberal Republican and Democratic members of Congress. The protagonists drew fine distinctions between "quotas" and "goals"; and they tried to distinguish the responsibility of contractors from the discriminatory actions of the labor unions with which they must deal. In a memorandum to the Labor Department, the comptroller general recognized that the attorney general had supported Labor's finding of legality for the plan, but held to the earlier position of the GAO "until the authority (for the plan) ... is clearly and firmly established by the weight of judicial precedents or by a judicial statute."[43] The comptroller general invited clarification of the legality of the plan either by congressional action or by a suit in federal court. Over the period of October to December in 1969, Senator Ervin's Subcommittee on the Separation of Powers conducted hearings on the subject of the Philadelphia Plan; the Senate then passed and later withdrew an amendment to an appropriations bill that would have approved the comptroller general's position. In a memorandum addressed to the Congress, the comptroller general then indicated he would henceforth allow federal expenditures under the plan.

The GAO is a major tool of Congress in dealing with administrative agencies. It is symptomatic of the pluralist nature of American politics, however, that the GAO is not the well-controlled representative of a united legislature. In its dealings with the Defense Department and with the Philadelphia Plan, the GAO found both supporters and antagonists in the Congress. Some members of Congress wanted the GAO to be more aggressive in controlling administrative departments, and some

---

42. *The Philadelphia Plan: Congressional Oversight of Administrative Agencies* (The Department of Labor), Hearings before the Subcommittee on Separation of Powers of the Committee on the Judiciary, U.S. Senate, 91st Congress, 1st Session, October 27, 28, 1969 (Washington, D.C.: U.S. Government Printing Office, 1969), p. 133. (Hereafter cited as *Philadelphia Plan*.)

43. *Philadelphia Plan*, p. 133.

felt the GAO had already gone too far in limiting the administrators. The GAO has demonstrated enough independence in its dealings with members of Congress and the executive branch to be considered an important and distinct source of inputs in the administrative system.

President Nixon vs. Congress and Administrators: The Case of Impoundment

In the spring of 1971, the Nixon administration announced it was withholding from the agencies some $12 billion, most of which had been appropriated by Congress to support highway and urban programs. Members of the administration defended this action by arguing that the programs in question were "scheduled for termination" and that it was pointless to pour more money into programs with little or no future. Congressional critics charged that the executive branch alone could not determine program termination; that impoundments of this kind threatened the constitutional separation of powers.[44]

Executive impoundment of funds did not begin with the Nixon administration. In 1803, President Jefferson informed Congress of his refusal to spend $50,000 that had been appropriated for gunboats to patrol the Mississippi River. Impoundment became a major tool of the president in the early years of World War II. Franklin D. Roosevelt withheld funds from several programs not related to the war effort in order to control inflation.

After the war, major presidential impoundments went beyond the control of inflation. In 1948, Harry S Truman withheld $735 million that would have increased the Air Force from 48 to 58 groups, on the ground that the additional groups were unnecessary. President Eisenhower impounded $137 million that had been appropriated for the development of the Nike-Zeus antimissile system, with the argument that additional tests should precede further action. A major executive vs. legislative squabble occurred in 1961, when President Kennedy refused to spend $180 million that Congress had added to his request for the B-70 bomber. The executive argued that added funding was not justified because the United States already had an advantage over the Soviets in bombers and missiles. In an attempt to curb the inflationary pressures generated by the escalation in Vietnam, Lyndon Johnson withheld $5.3 billion from domestic programs during 1966 alone. The programs suf-

---

44. See Louis Fisher, "Presidential Spending Discretion and Congressional Controls," *Law and Contemporary Problems* (Winter 1972).

fering the most were highways, housing and urban development, education, agriculture, plus health and public welfare.

The Nixon administration introduced two new elements to the impoundment issue. First, President Nixon impounded more funds than his predecessors: at least $12 billion in 1971 and 1972. Second, President Nixon used impoundment to promote his domestic priorities over those of Congress. This occurred first when the president reduced grants for health research, Model Cities, and urban renewal. During that same period, he allowed spending to proceed for preferences of his own, such as the supersonic transport, a new manned bomber, a larger merchant marine fleet, and the Safeguard Anti-Ballistic Missile (ABM) system.

The impoundment controversy between the Nixon administration and Congress did not occur in a political vacuum. It paralleled a growing sense of outrage over the revelations of executive involvements in wiretaps and bugging, the break-in to the office of Daniel Ellsberg's psychiatrist, and the cover-up of a White House role in the Watergate break-in. At the same time, there was a long standing congressional malaise among members of Congress over their declined status in budget-making. In July 1974—just one month before Nixon's resignation—the large Democratic majorities in the House and Senate passed the Congressional Budget and Impoundments Control Act of 1974. This both fashioned the reforms in the evaluation of budget proposals described earlier and established stronger constraints against presidential impoundments of funds appropriated by the Congress.

SUMMARY

This chapter focuses on input relations between the legislative and executive branches and the conversion process of the administrative system. The inputs include formal directives and expressions of desire, plus the authority to spend money, hire personnel, and conduct programs. We shall see in Chapter 11 that many of the proposals coming as outputs from administrative agencies provide the substance of the formal decisions that are made by legislators and executives, and sent by their administrators. The circularity of this process testifies to the dependence of elected officials on the administrators' recommendations.

Among the factors that help to make legislators and executives dependent upon proposals coming from the administrators are the dramatic growth in the scope and complexity of government programs; the fragmentation of institutions and interests apparent in the legislative and executive branches; and the related gap in knowledge that separates those legislative and executive officials who allegedly control the policy-making process from the administrators. The legislatures and chief executives of federal, state, and local governments spend much of their time reviewing, modifying, or rejecting proposals that come from the administration.

This is not to say that elected legislators and chief executives are helpless in the presence of demands from the administration. The specialized committees in the legislature and the staff aides of the chief executive provide important resources. These facilities—which seem stronger in the federal government than among states or localities—can subject the administrators' proposals to an intensive inquiry. And they may prompt administrators to focus their own attention on social or economic problems that are selected by legislators or by the chief executive. The GAO serves the Congress as a formidable collector of information and as an important control agent vis-à-vis the administration. The GAO shows a willingness to enter disputes that involve administrative agencies, the executive branch, and powerful interest groups. On these occasions, it stands as a semiautonomous source of inputs for the administrative system.

In part of this chapter, we examined budget activities among federal, state, and local governments. Budgeting represents the most regular of interactions between legislature, executive, and administrators. Moreover, it is conducted with a medium of exchange (dollars and cents) that permits a clear description of general patterns of interaction and an identification of unusual activities. The findings reported for budgeting include the following:

1. The legislative and executive branches at the federal level are better organized and better staffed for budgeting than are their counterparts in most state governments.
2. Legislative and executive branches generally grant renewal of existing budget levels. They pay most attention to the increments of new money that are sought, rather than to the base of funds that had been appropriated to support existing programs.
3. Some agencies are more likely to have cuts made in their budget than are others. Acquisitive agencies suffer the most severe cuts in the short term, but an acquisitive strategy seems to be the only route to long-term budget expansion. This is further testimony to the dependence of the legislature and

executive on the initiative of administrators. If no initiative is taken by the agencies, elected officials will seldom impose new funds on them.

There are no fixed descriptions for the powers of legislative, executive, or administrative branches in policy-making. Conflicts continue, and the resolution of each conflict adds one more bit to the evolving definition of *who has which powers?* We find indications of the ongoing process of changing the administrative system in the redesign of budgetary reviews to favor Congress, plus recent disputes over the powers of the General Accounting Office to obtain information from the agencies, and over the president's power to impound funds appropriated by Congress.

Part Three

THE OUTPUTS
OF THE
ADMINISTRATIVE
SYSTEM

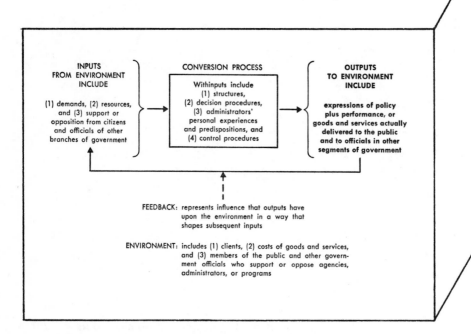

INPUTS FROM ENVIRONMENT INCLUDE	CONVERSION PROCESS	OUTPUTS TO ENVIRONMENT INCLUDE
(1) demands, (2) resources, and (3) support or opposition from citizens and officials of other branches of government	Withinputs include (1) structures, (2) decision procedures, (3) administrators' personal experiences and predispositions, and (4) control procedures	expressions of policy plus performance, or goods and services actually delivered to the public and to officials in other segments of government

FEEDBACK: represents influence that outputs have upon the environment in a way that shapes subsequent inputs

ENVIRONMENT: includes (1) clients, (2) costs of goods and services, and (3) members of the public and other government officials who support or oppose agencies, administrators, or programs

This section completes our coverage of the administrative system. Our concern is with the outputs of the system: the transactions that emanate from the conversion process (which we define as the "line" agencies of government) to citizens, politicians, and other government officials. Some of these transactions carry tangible public services such as the schools, highways, welfare payments, hospitals, parks, regulation of business practices, and fire and police protection that citizens receive from government. Other transactions carry economic resources from one administrative organization to another—the federal grants to the states and localities and the state aids to local governments represent both the outputs of one administrative system and the inputs to another. Still other outputs are the technical assistance and the program requirements that accompany intergovernmental payments. Another class of outputs includes the information and advice that goes from an administrative agency to the public and to members of the legislative and executive branches. This includes published studies, campaigns to influence the thinking of citizens and politicians, proposals for new legislation, budget requests, and the testimony administrators give at legislative hearings. These outputs constitute much of the "stuff" that forms the decisions of legislators and the chief executive.

Many outputs of agencies influence persons in the environment of the administrative system and then "feedback" to the conversion process through their effect on subsequent inputs. Citizens respond to the nature of public services or to the public statements of administrators by shaping their own later demands for additional service. Members of legislative and executive branches consider administrators' testimony and use the information to formulate the laws, instructions, and requests that flow from them into the agencies. Feedback is integral to the concept of systems theory: it provides the principal justification for many decisions taken within an agency about the outputs that should be produced. Yet, we pay little attention to feedback, aside from noting its importance. The inputs that come to an administrative agency as a result of its earlier outputs look very much like inputs that come in response to other stimuli felt by individuals in the environment. When legislators, executives, and members of the public supply inputs to administrators, they do so in response to many other influences besides those coming from the administration. To date, there has been little success in identifying those stimuli going to agencies that reflect the prior influence of the administrators themselves, as opposed to those that reflect other influences.

Chapter 10 focuses on intergovernmental relations. These include "vertical" relations among administrators at different levels of the federal structure and "horizontal" relations among the administrators of different states and localities. Through these relations, outputs are carried *from* some administrative units, and inputs are carried *to* others. The placement of Chapter 10 in the output section is arbitrary. The reader should recognize that one unit's intergovernmental output is another's input.

Chapter 11 discusses other varieties of outputs. One issue in that chapter is the variety and diversity of outputs and the intellectual problems inherent in efforts to classify and analyze them.

10

Intergovernmental Relations

The federal nature of American government means that administrators in most agencies at each level of government must reckon with demands from officials in other levels of government. Moreover, these officials are not simply other actors who must be given recognition in the rituals of public administration. Due to certain guarantees that are integral to the meaning of federalism and due to political customs that bolster these guarantees, the representatives of other governments have special status.

Every major government in the world has a central unit and local units of government. However, a "federal" arrangement is peculiar in providing certain assurances to both levels of government. It is common to speak of the American national and state governments as "superior" and "subordinate" to one another; but this terminology is inaccurate. On some dimensions, the national government (often called the "federal" government) has prerogatives reserved to it alone. The states, however, are not the creatures of the national government. They have a prominent independent role in any amendments to the basic structure of American government (i.e., the Constitution); and they have important guarantees of equal representation in the Senate, of proportional representation in the House, and of a role in selecting the president.[1]

The constitutional structure of federalism helps to protect the

---

1. Provisions dealing with elections to the Senate and the House do not guarantee any powers to state governments, per se, but they provide that representatives from a large number of states must accept whatever proposed legislation is enacted into law. The persons who speak for interests that occur in only a few of the states cannot grant the national government major new powers or cannot circumscribe those that are currently held by the states. Likewise is the case of the electoral college. The requirement that a victorious presidential candidate receive a majority of electoral votes (which are allocated on the basis of separate victories in each of the states) gives little real power to state governments, per se, but it encourages presidential candidates to solicit the support of political leaders in numerous states. This—together with the complementary custom that has grown up in preconvention politics—may close the presidency to any candidate who appears likely to reduce substantially the powers of state governments once in office.

interests of the state governments, but it does not protect institutions of local government from either the national or the state governments. The cities are creatures of their state governments and are subject to whatever constraints or liberties are found in state constitutions or statutes. However, local governments, as well as states, benefit from the political customs that respect "localism." The respect for localism exists among officials at all levels of government and has been observed in the United States since the early 19th century.[2] These values overlay the structure of federalism and make local governments, as well as the state and national governments, distinct actors in policy-making.

A feature that heightens the importance of federalism for the administrative systems is the mixture of governmental responsibilities. There is no important domestic activity that is staffed or financed solely by the federal, state, or local governments.[3] The fields that consume most domestic expenditures—education, highways, welfare, health, natural resources, and public safety—are funded with a combination of federal grants or loans and state and local taxes or service charges. Even when some programs involve *local* implementation with some *federal* funds (e.g., public housing and urban renewal), the *state* legislature and executive also retain a role, i.e., the legal prerogative to permit local participation in the federal program and to define conditions under which participation may occur.[4]

THE MEANING OF FEDERALISM FOR ADMINISTRATORS

The combination of a viable federal structure, localistic political values, and the sharing of responsibilities for major domestic services means that administrators at any level of government produce outputs for—and must be alert to inputs coming from—actors at other levels of government. Often the inputs to an administrative unit are the outputs of an administrative unit at another level of government. Both inputs and outputs go "up" and "down" the relationships among federal, state, and local governments. Federal grants and program requirements are outputs from

---

2. See Alexis de Tocqueville, *Democracy in America* (New York: Vintage Books, 1959), p. 282.
3. Morton Grodzins, "American Political Parties and the American System," *Western Political Quarterly* 13 (December 1960): 974–98.
4. Edward C. Banfield and Morton Grodzins, *Government and Housing in Metropolitan Areas* (New York: McGraw-Hill, 1958).

federal agencies, but they are inputs to state and local administrative agencies. The demands and/or intransigent policies of state and local administrators are outputs of their agencies, but they are inputs to federal agencies. It is not simply the prominent officials, such as chief executives or legislators of other governments, who might impinge on an administrative unit. The list of important actors includes administrators within one's own field of service at different levels of government, plus the staff agencies of the chief executives and the legislatures at other levels, and the courts of other governments. Federal administrators, for example, must contend with decisions—or anticipated decisions—of administrators, executives, legislators, and judges of each state and local government that draws financial assistance from the federal agency, that receives information or advice from the federal agency, or that must adhere to program standards developed by the federal agency. The federal administrator may hear from state and local officials directly or through federal legislators or interest groups who serve as intermediaries. For state and local administrators, intergovernmental relations may take the form of requests, demands, or appeals sent to the federal agency, legislature, executive, or judiciary. In many respects, state administrators stand in similar relations to local agencies as federal administrators stand in their relations with state or local agencies—as providers of funds, information, advice, and program standards. Figure 10–1 depicts in outline form the principal actors and flows of communication that may affect administrative units at any level of the federal structure.

The exchanges of demands, instructions, money, and technical assistance between governments do not pass without sharp political disputes. Much of the interaction occurs between administrators of national, state, and local governments. State educators, for example, deal mostly with the U.S. Office of Education, on one side, and local superintendents, on the other. When the administrators seek altered statutes or funds from Congress, they deal with members of committees or their staffs that specialize in education. This near monopoly of intergovernmental relations by program specialists in administrative and legislative branches does not please chief executives. Governors and mayors often feel themselves confined to a ceremonial role where they have too little control over what happens. Not only do they object to their lack of controls over intergovernmental programs, but they feel that budgetary commitments represented by intergovernmental programs limit their overall control of state or local resources. Governors and mayors welcomed the innovation of revenue-sharing as a device to give them control over intergovernmental finances not committed to certain adminis-

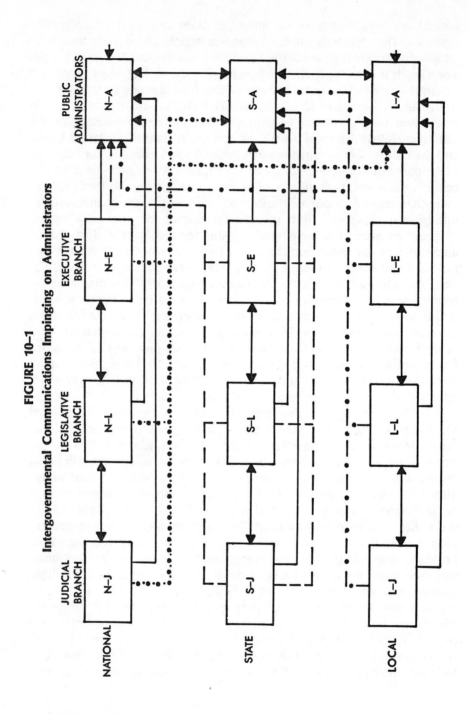

FIGURE 10–1

Intergovernmental Communications Impinging on Administrators

trative units. However, revenue-sharing did not soothe other conflicts of intergovernmental relations: (1) those between governors and mayors themselves over state vs. local government control of national-local aids or (2) those between representatives of large and small cities over the kinds of national and state aids available to each.[5]

Some intergovernmental relations do not involve units that are "superior" or "subordinate" to one another. These connect administrators of different state governments or of different local governments. These "horizontal" relations transmit information and advice pertaining to one another's experience or establish formal or informal arrangements in which different state or local administrative agencies share resources to attack common problems. The horizontal relations are important in carrying—or blocking—program innovations from one political arena to another. They are vital to an understanding of why some state and local governments provide the types of services they do.

Because of the input *and* output nature of intergovernmental relations with respect to different administrative agencies, this chapter is placed tenuously—and in full recognition of the arbitrary nature of the choice—in this "output" section of the book.

TYPES OF INTERGOVERNMENTAL RELATIONS: FEDERAL TO STATE AND LOCAL

Of all the forms of relations among federal, state, and local administrators, grants-in-aid have attracted more attention than others. This attention is warranted, insofar as grants probably account for the greatest tangible resources in intergovernmental relations. Yet, grants are not the only cause for relations among federal, state, and local administrators. There are other kinds of financial assistance and nonfinancial relations. Among other financial aids are federal loans, guarantees of loans contracted from normal financial sources, shared taxes, tax credits, and the feature that permits deductions of state and local taxes from federally taxable income. Federal agencies also provide training and other technical assistance for state and local personnel.

---

5. See Donald H. Haider, *When Governments Come to Washington: Governors, Mayors, and Intergovernmental Lobbying* (New York: Free Press, 1974); and Kenneth C. Olson, "The States, Governors, and Policy Management: Changing the Equilibrium of the Federal System," *Public Administration Review* 35 (December 1975): 764–70.

Financial Aid

Financial aid is the single most prominent feature of federal relations with state and local administrators. In 1977, aids amounted to $61 billion, and 23 percent of state and local expenditures. Federal grants-in-aid were the typical form of assistance until 1972. They had several distinct features, each of which had implications for administrators.[6] Each federal program supported a specific state or local program; they did not provide "general support" of state or local activities. They typically required that recipient agencies submit detailed applications for the funds, provided some of their own resources to support the aided activities, and administered the program according to prescribed standards. The "purpose" nature of federal grants-in-aid and the requirements that came along with the money were frequent sources of conflict between federal, state, and local administrators. It was alleged that the federal carrot led recipients to undertake activities that were not in their own best interests and that requirements were frequently inconsistent with their social or economic problems. Federal money was not "free." If the aided program was not uniformly popular in a state or locality, the recipient agency encountered some political costs, as well as benefits.

Federal grants-in-aid are older than the Constitution, although they have reached great heights only since the 1930s. Throughout the late 18th and most of the 19th century, land grants were given to state governments. Of the 1 billion acres that passed from the control of the federal government during the 19th century, about 230 million acres went to the states. Many land grants were devoted to education. Each new state received a grant for the support of primary education as it was admitted to the Union. The "land-grant" colleges of many states trace their origin to the Morrill Acts of 1862 and 1890. The states were expected to sell or lease the land, with the proceeds used to support educational programs. As the supply of public land dwindled in the late 19th century, the emphasis shifted to money grants. The first regular and continuing money grant began in 1887 for the support of agricultural experiment stations.

The grants-in-aid programs enacted during each decade of the 20th century represented in microcosm the contemporary policy-orientations of American governments. Until World War I, the grants emphasized agriculture and other rural problems. Typical of that period were the Smith-Lever Act of 1914, which established cooperative agricultural

---

6. See Deil S. Wright, *Federal Grants-In-Aid: Perspectives and Alternatives* (Washington, D.C.: American Enterprise Institute for Public Policy Research, 1968).

extension programs; the Smith-Hughes Act of 1917, which established a program for supporting vocational education (with heavy emphasis in agriculture and home economics); and the Federal Aid Highway Act, which authorized the secretary of agriculture to cooperate with state highway departments in the construction of rural post roads. This act was supposed to "get the farmer out of the mud."

In the decade of the 1920s, the aura of "normalcy" and the reliance on private enterprise helped retard the development of new grant programs. Increased funds were appropriated under existing grants, but there were no authorizations for new programs. The 1930s emphasized programs to alleviate the personal hardships of the Depression. Among the major grant programs enacted during 1933–38 were welfare payments for the aged, for the blind, and for dependent children; health services for mothers and children; employment security; and public housing. Some agricultural programs were also begun during the 1930s to cope with economic problems in that sector. Programs were established for surplus commodity distribution and soil conservation.

The period of World War II did not invite major new domestic activities. The total funds provided to states and localities decreased from $2.4 billion in 1940 to $800 million in 1946. With the continuing mobilization of the late 1940s and 1950s, federal aids took on labels that made them part of the defense effort—for example a program to aid school districts suffering population increases because of federal installations, typically those of the Defense Department and its contractors; the Interstate and *Defense* Highway Act of 1952; and the *Defense* Education Act of 1957. It is debatable as to how important the highway and educational activities were to the defense effort or whether they were merely made more attractive to Congress by being identified as such.

In the 1960s and 1970s the program emphasis of new grant programs was urban affairs and education urban affairs, and environmental protection. The Elementary and Secondary Education Act of 1965 was largely responsible for pushing educational grants from $610 million in 1965 to $2.5 billion in 1968. The education category of federal grants increased relative to other categories from 6 to 15 percent of the total. Also during the 1960s, direct grants to cities increased in volume and were joined by grants to private organizations in urban areas.

The emphasis shown by the total amounts of grants spent on various programs has also changed over this century, but the change has been cyclical, rather than unidirectional. Early in the century, benefits to veterans, education, and agriculture dominated the few programs in existence; together they amounted to about $3 million annually. The major educational programs helped support land-grant colleges. As total grants increased, educational grants diminished in relative importance. After World War II, pressures mounted for an increasing scope and magnitude of educational aids. However, some participants in the policy-making process opposed any large increase in federal expenditures; some opposed federally mandated racial integration that might come along with the grants; some opposed federal grants to schools supported by religious institutions; and some opposed federal grants that would *not* aid schools supported by religious institutions. Although federal aids to education increased somewhat in the 1940s and 1950s, the opposition confined the increases to programs with circumspect objectives: aid to federally impacted areas[7] and the program for "defense" education.[8] It was not until the breakthrough of the Elementary and Secondary Education Act of 1965 (which combined aid to public schools with certain aids to schools supported by religious institutions and which was passed after the courts had resolved the basic problem of racial integration) that education's share of total federal grants moved dramatically upward.

The importance of health, welfare, and labor grants in the Depression was evident in their spurt upward during the 1930s. In 1935, grants in this category consumed almost 99 percent of the total federal allocations to state and local governments. They have remained important in the total dollars involved (moving from $2.2 billion in 1935 to $25 billion in 1977), but they have diminished in relative importance. These programs developed in such a massive way during the 1930s that they obscured other changes taking place at the same time. Grants in agriculture increased to more than ten times their original amount during the 1930s: from about $12 million in 1930 to $143 million in 1940. During the same years, however, their percentage of total grants dropped almost in half: from 11.4 to 6.0 percent. Likewise for grants in the fields of commerce, housing, and transportation. They almost doubled in dollar amounts: from $80 million in 1930 to $154 million in 1940; but they declined from 76.5 to 6.4 percent of total grants!

Every department of the federal government provides some grants-in-aid to state and local governments. Even such "nondomestic" units as the Departments of Defense and State offer grants-in-aid to state governments for the National Guard and international cultural affairs.

---

7. That is the "impact" on school population due to federal installations or federal contractors.

8. "Defense education" covered a variety of programs, including foreign languages and natural and social sciences.

Changes in program emphases testify to the flexibility of federal grants-in-aid. Because they provide aid to specific kinds of activities rather than general support to state and local governments, policy-makers in the national government can regulate with some precision the kinds of state and local activities that receive funds. Depending on the assessment of need and performance, the funds appropriated for each program can be increased in small or large amounts, can be passed over with no increase, or can be forced to endure a decrease. Each program can receive additional features that reflect newly apparent service problems. For each feature, the matching formula can be adjusted to make the component more or less attractive to potential recipients and, thereby, to affect the speed of adoption. When members of Congress are especially anxious to have all states take immediate advantage of a new program, they set the federal-state matching formula at an irresistible level. And in order to elicit cooperation on individual components of a program, new bonus offers of aid can be extended in exchange for compliance with special regulations. When the Interstate Highway program was first enacted in 1953, the federal-state matching formula was set at 90–10; this meant that state highway departments would receive $.90 worth of federal highway money for each $.10 of their own money. By not taking immediate advantage of the program, a state would lose a considerable amount of its citizens' federal tax money that would pay for highways in other states. After the program was underway for several years, Congress added other features (e.g., billboard controls) and auxiliary grants for state compliance. Moreover, the administration has adjusted the flow of highway grants to changes in the economy. Allocations have been speeded up during periods of unemployment and slowed down at other times to curb inflation. Some observers also claim that presidents have slowed the allocation of highway funds in order to elicit cooperation from Congress on the other aspects of their programs.

Some developments in federal grant programs during the late 1960s altered relationships among federal, state, and local administrators. There was an increasing use of "project" grants. These required federal approval of state or local applications on a project-by-project basis. They differed from "formula" grants that provided funds to state or local agencies according to a formula established by Congress or the administration. Under a formula grant, the decisions on individual projects were left to the state or local agencies. A study of grant programs enacted between April 1964 and January 1966 found that individual formula programs increased from 64 to 91, while project programs increased from 126 to 226 programs. The increasing emphasis given to project grants increased the discretion available to federal administrators and reduced that left to state and local administrators.[9]

In a contrary move, there was also some experimentation with "bloc" grants. These financed a broad function of government (e.g., health or crime control) and provided the recipient agency with discretion in their use. These grants had wide appeal among state and local administrators, who desired both an increase in federal support and an opportunity to decide their own priorities. Of greater significance, however, was the introduction of general revenue-sharing in 1972.

Revenue-Sharing

Revenue-sharing began with annual grants of $2.6 billion to the states, with two-thirds earmarked for local governments. By 1977, the annual revenue-sharing allocations to state and local governments were some $7 billion. The allotments to individual states and localities reflect various criteria, with revenue increasing with the size of population, the effort of a recipient government in taxing its own population, and its poverty as reflected by income per capita.

Revenue-sharing differs most dramatically from traditional grants-in-aid by its lack of "strings." The money goes to states and communities as a matter of right, without detailed applications. Recipients can spend money at their discretion, subject only to the following restrictions:

State governments have no program restricting their expenditures, but local governments must spend their allotments within certain "priority" areas: public safety, environmental protection (including sanitation), public transportation, health, recreation, libraries, social services for the poor and aged, financial administration, and "ordinary and necessary" capital expenditures;

Discrimination on the basis of race, color, national origin, or sex is not permitted in any program financed with revenue sharing funds;

Revenue sharing funds may not be used to match federal funds provided under other grant programs;

Construction workers paid with revenue sharing funds must receive at least the wage prevailing on similar construction activity in the locality;

Recipient governments must publish plans and publicly account for the use of revenue sharing funds.[10]

---

9. Wright, *Federal Grants-In-Aid*, p. 61.
10. *The Budget of the United States Government, Fiscal Year 1974* (Washington, D.C.: U.S. Government Printing Office, 1973), p. 163.

While the lack of detailed controls on revenue-sharing appeals to elected officials of state and local governments, this feature disturbs certain administrators and interest groups. Administrators of individual programs and their supporters have no guarantee that the money will be spent on their favored projects. With the traditional grants-in-aid, program supporters concentrated their efforts at the national level and counted on state and local officials to carry out requirements in the federal statutes. The lack of program-specificity also poses a threat to the state and local officials who originally welcomed the greater flexibility. Without support from program-oriented interest groups in Washington, the sums distributed under general revenue-sharing may be especially vulnerable to the periodic efforts of the White House to dampen inflation by holding back on allotments of federal aid.

The explanation of revenue-sharing owes something to the traditional inclinations of Republicans who controlled the national executive branch in 1972, as well, perhaps, as to some political needs of key Democratic legislators and to contemporary problems in the nation's economy. Deterioration in the international economic position of the United States and serious problems with domestic inflation and unemployment led the Nixon administration to become active in national economic planning and control, with some of that planning directed toward reforms in federal aids for state and local governments. The president's efforts to decentralize the administration of federally supported programs via revenue-sharing reflected the calls for decentralization heard from Republicans since the 1930s. Yet, the change in policy represented by general revenue-sharing could not come from the White House alone. It required the support of a Democratic Congress, and a change in heart of then Chairman Wilbur Mills of the House Ways and Means Committee who earlier spoke strongly in opposition to revenue-sharing. Mills' shift came early in the presidential campaign of 1972, when he may have been seeking some credit with local politicians and taxpayers for the Democratic candidate, who—in the preconvention circumstances—might have become himself! Whatever his reasons, Mills was known as a shrewd leader who was often responsible for the success or failure of major legislation in the revenue field. Any explanation of revenue-sharing must take account of his reasoning as well as the president's.

Growth in Financial Aids

There is no disputing the fact that financial aids have grown over the years; but the appearance of growth varies with the techniques used to measure it. During the 1900–77 period, the sheer magnitude of federal contributions increased by about 20,000 times: from $3 million annually to $61 billion. However, these figures do not correct for obvious changes in the value of the dollar, the number of people who are served by federally aided programs, the pool of economic resources from which federal aids are taken, or the level of state and local government activities the recipients support with their own funds. When these corrections are made, the magnitude of recent increase appears more temperate. Table 10–1 shows federal grants in 1932, 1936, 1946, 1967, 1969, 1974, and 1977 computed in two ways. The measurements agree in showing a marked increase during the Depression, a fall in magnitude during the Second World War, and an increase since World War II. The growth appears almost shocking when viewed in raw dollar amounts, but corrections for other economic, social, or governmental happenings place the growth in perspective. The role of federal grants in state and local affairs has expanded, both absolutely and relative to state and local revenues. However, administrative agencies in state and local governments still receive the bulk of their financial resources from their own sources.[11]

Other Federal Aids to States and Localities

Grants-in-aid and revenue-sharing are only two devices that federal agencies use to provide resources for state and local agencies. Federal loans, loan-guarantees, tax credits, and the deductibility of state and local taxes from federally taxable income are additional kinds of aid. Some are mixed with grants-in-aid to provide different options within the same basic program. In the public housing program, for example, a federal guarantee for loans arranged in the private market supports the bulk of most project costs, while an outright grant pays for additional costs. Some programs make available a direct loan from the federal Treasury if a federal guarantee will not help a recipient agency contract for a commercial loan at a desirable interest rate. The unemployment compensation program combines a federal tax credit with a grant-in-aid. Employers are exempt for up to 90 percent of a federal payroll tax for the money they pay as state tax to support unemployment compensa-

---

11. See Ira Sharkansky, *The Maligned States: Policy Accomplishments, Problems, and Opportunities* (New York: McGraw-Hill, 1978), chapters 5, 7.

TABLE 10–1

Changes in the Magnitude of Federal Grants to State and Local Governments, 1932–77

	Total (in millions of current dollars)	As Percentage of State and Local Expenditures
1977	$60,523	23.0%
1974	48,293	23.3
1969	20,255	17.4
1967	15,240	16.3
1946	855	7.8
1936	948	12.4
1932	232	2.8

SOURCES: U.S. Bureau of the Census, *Historical Statistics on Governmental Finances and Employment, Census of Governments, 1962* (Washington, D.C.: U.S. Government Printing Office, 1964), vol. 6, no. 4; and *Budget of the United States Government: Special Analysis, Fiscal Year 1975 and 1977* (Washington, D.C.: U.S. Government Printing Office, 1974 and 1976).

tion; and an amount up to the remaining 10 percent of the federal tax is available to the state employment agency for administrative costs.[12]

Many taxpayers are not aware of the federal aid for state and local governments written into the income tax code. In computing the income subject to federal taxation, a citizen can deduct any amounts paid as state or local income, sales, excise, or property taxes; this provision lightens the burden of state or local taxes and, presumably, allows states and localities to levy higher rates of taxes without encountering severe resistance from their residents. Moreover, any income received from interest on state or local government bonds is not subject to federal taxation; this permits state and local agencies to pay lower than commercial interest rates for the money they borrow.[13]

Several other federal programs provide subtle forms of aid to state or local administrative agencies. The direct provision of federal

---

12. See James A. Maxwell, *Tax Credits and Intergovernmental Fiscal Relations* (Washington, D.C.: Brookings Institution, 1962).

13. Tax deductibility lowers the burden of state and local taxes by excusing the taxpayer of that portion of federal income tax that would be due on the money paid out in state and local taxes. If the taxpayer is in an income bracket where 25 percent of income is paid to federal income taxes, then the federal government pays, in effect, 25 percent of the taxpayers' state and local taxes. The no-tax feature applied to the income on state and local government bonds makes these bonds more attractive to investors than are the bonds of private firms, and they permit state and local agencies to borrow money at lower than commercial rates of interest.

benefits to institutions or private citizens relieves states and localities of service demands that otherwise would come to them. In this category are both student grants and federal grants, loans, or loan-guarantees to institutions of higher education (both public and private). Many federal "research contracts" also provide financial aid to colleges and universities; they allow researchers to hire student assistants (and thereby subsidize the students' education) and support sophisticated research to enrich the intellectual climate and the educational offerings of the institutions. The federal social security program is another direct service that may alleviate demands on state and local authorities for welfare and health programs; "social security" is actually the popular designation for a series of programs that provide insurance coverage for old-age pensions, disability pensions, and hospital and physician charges.

The Advisory Commission on Intergovernmental Relations (ACIR) is a research agency of the federal government whose purpose is to provide information and technical assistance to state and local governments and to facilitate the administration of federal programs in a way that is most helpful to the states and localities.[14] The Commission itself includes 23 officials of national, state, and local governments, plus 3 members representing the public. A professional staff does detailed analyses and prepares recommendations for review by the commissioners. The statute that established the ACIR outlined its duties as follows:

1. Bring together representatives of the Federal, State and Local governments for the consideration of common problems;
2. Provide a forum for discussing the administration and coordination of Federal grant and other programs requiring intergovernmental cooperation;
3. Give critical attention to the conditions and controls involved in the administration of Federal grant programs;
4. Make available technical assistance to the executive and legislative branches of the Federal Government in the review of proposed legislation to determine its overall effect on the Federal system;
5. Encourage discussion and study at an early stage of emerging public problems that are likely to require intergovernmental cooperation;
6. Recommend, within the framework of the Constitution, the most desirable allocation of governmental functions, responsibilities, and revenues among the several levels of government; and
7. Recommend methods of coordinating and simplifying tax laws and administrative practices to achieve a more orderly and less compet-

14. This discussion relies on Deil S. Wright, "The Advisory Commission on Intergovernmental Relations: Unique Features and Policy Orientation," *Public Administration Review* 25 (September 1965): 193–202.

itive fiscal relationship between the levels of government and to reduce the burden of compliance for taxpayers.

The Commission publishes detailed studies that deal with specific topics of use to federal, state, and local policy-makers, but that remain outside of prominent and highly volatile public controversies. The list of its publications includes *Coordination of Federal Inheritance, Estate and Gift Taxes; Investment of Idle Cash Balances by State and Local Governments; Interest Bearing U.S. Government Securities Available for Investment of Short-term Cash Balance by State and Local Governments;* and *Measures of State and Local Fiscal Capacity and Tax Effort.*

There has been some question about the effectiveness of the Commission's work. One survey found only 16 percent of 900 top-level state administrators had heard of the Commission and could identify it correctly. At the national level, neither presidents Eisenhower, Kennedy, nor Johnson sought the Commission's recommendations on major policy issues regarding intergovernmental relations. At one time, a staff member reported that several of the Commission's completed studies remained on the shelf because of inadequate printing funds.

STATE AIDS TO LOCAL GOVERNMENTS

The array of state aids to localities includes many of the mechanisms found in federal aids to state and local governments. State aids emphasize revenue-sharing and "bloc" grants, rather than grants-in-aid for specified programs. A fixed portion of taxes that are "shared" revert back to the local government in whose jurisdiction they are collected. Bloc grants and shared taxes, like federal revenue-sharing, provide more freedom to local governments than do grants-in-aid. They are not awarded for specified projects or in response to detailed applications. They go automatically to local governments on the basis of certain criteria and may be used for any program within a generalized function (e.g., "education," "roads and streets") or for the support of any governmental activity. State aids are generally "free" and do not require matching with a certain proportion of locally raised revenues. Local governments receive much of their state aid with few application procedures and few limitations on its expenditure.

State governments use a variety of criteria to allocate financial aids to each local government. Some redistribute economic resources from "have" to "have-not" communities; some merely return to a community a certain proportion of the state tax collected there; some reward communities that show some effort in using their own resources in the support of a program; some award funds "equally" on an arbitrary criterion (e.g., population); and some use special considerations that recognize emergency situations or agreements arranged between state and local agencies.

The concept of "state aid" is necessarily loose due to the wide variety of programs and techniques in 50 state governments. In many states, the aid rendered to local governments is only a small portion of the services state governments provide to local residents. State governments vary in the kinds of services they provide directly and the kinds they leave to local authorities. In the field of education, for example, some state governments pay the entire cost of supporting public junior colleges, while others provide only some of the costs to county or municipal governments. In public welfare, some state governments pay for all aid payments not covered by federal grants, while other states share these costs with local governments. The most complete record of state involvement in the support of public services shows the percentage of total state and local government revenues raised or spent at the state level. Table 10–2 shows this record for each state during 1975.

There is considerable variation in the role that state governments play in raising revenues for themselves and local governments. The na-

TABLE 10–2
Use of Intergovernmental Aids by State and Local Governments, 1974–75

	Percentage of State and Local Revenues Originating at Federal Level	Percentage of State and Local Revenues Originating at State Level	Percentage of State and Local Expenditures Spent by Local Governments
U.S. average	20.6%	42.4%	63.4%
Alabama	27.0	46.9	48.6
Alaska	32.1	46.6	42.0
Arizona	18.5	48.7	64.1
Arkansas	29.0	47.0	47.9
California	18.6	39.5	70.5
Colorado	21.3	41.7	61.1
Connecticut	18.8	41.0	55.9
Delaware	18.8	61.8	45.1
Florida	18.1	44.0	67.5
Georgia	24.7	39.2	55.9

TABLE 10–2 (Cont.)

	Percentage of State and Local Revenues Originating at Federal Level	Percentage of State and Local Revenues Originating at State Level	Percentage of State and Local Expenditures Spent by Local Governments
Hawaii	23.5	59.0	23.0
Idaho	24.7	47.4	51.5
Illinois	18.2	42.3	62.3
Indiana	15.2	48.1	61.5
Iowa	19.6	44.1	61.6
Kansas	19.4	42.9	57.9
Kentucky	25.6	51.2	43.0
Louisiana	22.6	51.0	51.5
Maine	27.0	45.9	44.6
Maryland	19.1	45.2	68.4
Massachusetts	19.0	38.2	61.3
Michigan	20.5	41.3	62.8
Minnesota	19.7	49.5	63.0
Mississippi	28.7	47.7	51.8
Missouri	20.9	37.9	61.3
Montana	26.4	37.6	53.9
Nebraska	19.3	35.8	62.0
Nevada	17.8	42.5	59.9
New Hampshire	23.1	33.6	55.9
New Jersey	17.7	33.6	69.5
New Mexico	27.1	57.6	45.3
New York	17.9	38.3	82.9
North Carolina	26.4	48.9	58.6
North Dakota	21.4	54.3	42.2
Ohio	18.8	39.9	64.9
Oklahoma	25.5	46.5	49.2
Oregon	26.6	38.6	54.4
Pennsylvania	20.6	46.6	58.5
Rhode Island	24.0	47.0	44.5
South Carolina	24.1	53.1	45.7
South Dakota	37.8	36.1	50.6
Tennessee	24.6	40.6	53.5
Texas	20.7	42.8	56.9
Utah	26.9	45.5	51.4
Vermont	27.6	44.5	41.5
Virginia	21.6	46.3	55.7
Washington	21.4	45.0	56.0
West Virginia	29.9	50.4	39.1
Wisconsin	18.1	49.7	65.4
Wyoming	27.4	39.7	49.6

SOURCE: U.S. Bureau of the Census, *Governmental Finances in 1974–75* (Washington, D.C.: U.S. Government Printing Office, 1976).

tionwide average is 42 percent of total state and local revenues coming from the state government. However, the range extends from 33 percent in New Jersey and New Hampshire to 62 percent in Delaware. There is a tendency for low-income states to rely heavily on state-collected revenues. This is evident in the heavy reliance on state revenues in Kentucky, Louisiana, New Mexico, North Dakota, South Carolina, and West Virginia. In these states, there are numerous local governments (especially rural counties) hard-pressed to support a minimum level of public services with the economic resources that lie within their jurisdictions. Perhaps because many local authorities in these states must rely upon state aid, all local governments in these states are inclined to view the state government as a prime source of funds. It is probably easier for the legislature to pass a state aid bill if there is something in it for the constituents of most legislators. On the other side of the income scale, local governments in the well-to-do states of Connecticut, Ohio, New York, New Jersey, Massachusetts, and California carry a larger than average share of state and local financing. Seemingly out of step with the general pattern is Delaware. This state has one of the highest levels of personal income per capita in the nation, but it is also the heaviest user of state government revenues. In this trait, Delaware reflects the pattern of its southern neighbors. Southern states have been "centralized" historically, owing in part to a colonial experience of diffuse population and a plantation economy that did not nurture the development of strong, autonomous towns. Nebraska is another state that deviates from the normal association between low income and high reliance on state revenue. Nebraska ranks below the national average on several measures of economic resources, but it ranks close to the top in the proportion of revenues raised locally. In this case, a strong localist orientation, together with fiscal conservatism, seems to have retarded the development of state revenue sources. Nebraska was one of the last state governments to abandon its reliance on locally raised property taxes.

URBAN-CENTERED OUTPUTS OF NATIONAL AND STATE AGENCIES

Although cities have no constitutional standings in the American federal system, they have acquired a great deal of political clout. A striking demonstration of their real power appears in the efforts of national and state governments to direct massive aid to the cities, especially to the largest cities that seem to present the greatest needs. Table 10–3 shows

TABLE 10–3

Large Cities Receipt of State and National Aids

	Cities of at Least 500,000 Population	All Other Cities
Combined state and national aid as a percentage of city expenditures		
1974–75	50.8%	37.1%
1964–65	24.0	18.1
Per capita receipt of aid*		
1974–75	$362.25	$93.79
1964–65	58.20	18.90

SOURCES: U.S. Bureau of the Census, *Governmental Finances in 1974–75 (and 1964–65)* (Washington, D.C.: U.S. Government Printing Office, 1976, 1966).
* Of necessity, 1964–65 per capita calculations employ 1960 population figures.

the weight of intergovernmental assistance in city budgets. In the largest population group of cities (at least 500,000), 50.8 percent of the expenditures come initially from Washington and state capitals. For all other cities, the percentage is only 37.1. Since the most dramatic take-off of new federal social programs in the 1964–65 period, the largest cities' per capita receipts of intergovernmental aid have grown by 522 percent, while those of other cities have grown by only 396 percent.

The president's budget tabulates a program-by-program record of federal-aid outlays in metropolitan areas. Although this pertains to more cities than those with at least 500,000 population, it does identify the urban programs that receive the most federal support. The proposal for 1975 listed the biggest sums for public assistance, general revenue-sharing, medical assistance, highways and environmental protection. Of the president's proposals for all federal aid to state and local governments 69 percent were programmed for the metropolitan areas in 1975, whereas only 54.7 percent of federal aid went there in 1961.

State governments also deserve credit for their awareness of urban affairs. Cities over 500,000 population received $2.6 billion from the national government during 1974–75, but $7.9 billion from the states. Admittedly, some unknown portion of the states' $7.9 billion initially came from Washington. The states, like the national government, are giving the greatest aids to the largest cities.

State governments are also changing their constitutions and statutes to permit local authorities more flexibility in raising their own revenues. Historically, localities have been limited to the tax on real property. This tax has suffered from sharp political hostility; from its failure to tap the economic resources of individuals who work and shop in the central city, but who reside in the suburbs; from its regressive rate structure;[15] and often from arbitrary and anachronistic assessments of property value. As of 1975, local governments in 28 states collected a sales tax, and localities in 12 states collected an income tax. Agencies of 40 states pursue active programs to improve the administration of local property taxes. These typically involve systematic comparisons between market values, as determined by actual sales and local property assessments. The sales-assessment ratios serve to equalize the distribution of those state aids that go to local governments on the basis of property values and to identify local areas that need additional attention from tax assessors. This can minimize tax competition between local governments and keep assessments reasonably equivalent across the state for properties of similar value.

State governments are also making greater direct expenditures in metropolitan areas. These take the form of state clinics and hospitals, parks, intraurban expressways, and urban branches of state universities. Most states have a Department of Local Affairs. Of these, 26 began during the 1965–69 period alone. Some departments integrate the distribution of state financial aids to local governments, and some offer sizable state supplements for such urban programs of the national government as public housing, mass transit, urban renewal, and worker training.

Explanations of Urban-Centered Intergovernmental Aid

What accounts for this increase in the urban concern of national and state American governments?

Population and Political Representation
Metropolitan population of the United States increased from 96 million in 1950 to 139 million in 1970. Two decades ago, 63 percent of Americans lived in areas designated by the Bureau of the Census as "Standard Metropolitan Statistical Areas." In 1970, this percentage had increased to 69. Due to the advent of court-mandated legislative reapportionments in 1962, these increases in metropolitan populations produced even greater proportional increases in political representation during the 1960s.

---

15. This prevents the local property tax from operating like the state and national progressive income taxes, i.e., increasing in productivity faster than inflation as the inflation moves individuals into brackets where they pay a higher percentage of their income as taxes.

Peculiarities of local government boundaries and local financial options have limited the *public* resources of communities that exist amidst *private* affluence.[16] The abundance of human and material resources in the metropolis should make its problems amenable to solution. Cities have residents with lots of money and the skills needed to plan and implement social programs. The 1970 census reported the median income of white metropolitan area families to be $11,203, compared to $8,881 for nonmetropolitan white families.[17] However, affluence also presents difficulties for urban authorities. Many people come to the cities for the economic opportunities they promise. Urban prosperity attracts the untrained and unsuccessful who want better opportunities. For some newcomers, the cost to the city for providing them with services is substantially greater than the contribution of their skills to the city's economy. Urban slums represent the attractions of the city for the poor, plus the inability of many immigrants to be successful in the urban environment, and provide a stimulus that sends affluent families and business firms to the suburbs. The irony of urban wealth appears in cities with an abundance of wealth that begets poverty and a magnitude of resources not sufficient for local authorities to satisfy intense demands for public service.

The fractured nature of local government in urban areas is an important element in limiting the revenue available to local governments. Boundaries between neighboring cities, counties, suburban towns, school districts, and special districts divide an urban area into a surplus of jurisdictions. Often they compete with each other to keep taxes low. Some local jurisdictions have a greater tax base than required to support their services, so their levies can be low. Other jurisdictions have needs that surpass their resources. While they may raise taxes to the legal or political limits, untapped resources remain in neighboring jurisdictions. One New Jersey school district had an assessed valuation of $5.5 million per pupil, and a neighboring district had only $33,000 per pupil.

State constitutions and statutes add to the problems of urban

---

16. This section relies on Robert L. Lineberry and Ira Sharkansky, *Urban Politics and Public Policy* (New York: Harper & Row, 1971), chapter 2.

17. These figures are for nonfarm, nonmetro whites; for blacks, even sharper differences prevail: $7,140 metro families and $4,605 nonmetro, nonfarm families. Among both whites and blacks, the lowest median family incomes appear for nonmetro farm families: $6,819 for whites and $3,106 for blacks. The figures come from the *Statistical Abstract of the United States, 1972* (Washington, D.C.: U.S. Government Printing Office, 1973), p. 323.

governments by limiting the kinds of taxes they can raise. Restrictions keep most localities to the regressive and unpopular tax on the real property that lies within their borders. The regressive nature of this tax limits its contribution to local treasuries during periods of inflation. An advantage of a progressive tax is that inflation boosts people into higher tax brackets. As a result, tax proceeds can increase dramatically along with inflation. A regressive tax offers no such bonus in the face of inflation. The unpopularity of the property tax dampens the frequent increases needed to keep revenues up to increases in prices and service demands; restrictions to a tax on locally situated real property keep the cities from tapping much of the economic resources (e.g., the income and retail purchases of suburbanites) centered in the urban area.

A Frustrated Reform Movement

The first major response to the problem of surplus jurisdictions in metropolitan areas and the segregation of resources from needs came during the 1950s and 1960s and attempted to integrate the separate jurisdictions. There were several approaches to this goal.

1. Municipal regulation of real estate developments in the rural fringe outside its borders;
2. Development of metropolitan-wide districts;
3. Annexation and city-city consolidation;
4. Consolidation of the city with the urbanized county surrounding it; and
5. Federation of several municipalities.

Few of these reform efforts were successful. Voters tended to be apathetic, and most established elites were hostile. Officials of local governments, political party chiefs, leaders of unions, and the black community were accustomed to the existing structures in which they had come to power and feared dilution of their political bases in any aggregation of diverse communities.[18]

There is also an opposition to integrated metropolitan governments among certain analysts of local affairs. Professor Vincent Ostrom and many of his colleagues in the "public choice" school see benefits in the numerous governments of metropolitan areas. Varied jurisdictions offer maximum consumer choices in their different packages of social

---

18. See Robert L. Lineberry, "Reforming Metropolitan Government: Requiem or Reality?" *Georgetown Law Journal* 58 (May 1970).

services and taxation to potential residents. Smaller governments also avoid diseconomies of scale that appear in large bureaucracies. Studies comparing central city and suburban units have found the smaller police and school departments of the suburbs more efficient, more sensitive to client needs, and more capable of changing programs to cope with unexpected problems.[19]

For a period during the 1960s, the more prominent movement in metropolitan areas created *more rather than fewer* jurisdictions. Between 1964 and 1974, the number of local governmental units other than school districts increased by 6,079. This was largely a result of continued suburban development, but the growth also affected sentiments in the metropolitan core. The central city movements had several names: "decentralization," "neighborhood control," "community control," "control-sharing." Some arrangements would actually decentralize the power to make program decisions; others would merely provide representation on a centralized policy-making body to program clients.

With the failure of metropolitan integration to rationalize local government boundaries, the taxing and spending powers of state (and national) governments came to the fore. State and national governments collect taxes from throughout a metropolitan area, regardless of municipal borders. Moreover, their levies on personal incomes are progressive and help to keep revenue collections current with prices during inflation. Both state and national governments have increased their shares of local financing, and they are distributing these increases to local governments with the largest population.

Some state governments make an effort to keep the proliferation of governments in metropolitan areas from getting worse by controlling the definition of municipal boundaries. Usually, new municipalities are established when voters in an unincorporated area submit a petition to the legislature and hold an election to determine local sentiment. Several states have taken the lead in giving state agencies a role in this process. This hope is to apply well-reasoned standards to the applications for new incorporations and to define the borders of new municipalities in ways that will maximize their efficiency in providing services. The Minnesota Municipal Commission reviews incorporation and annexation proposals; Wisconsin divides the responsibilities between the circuit court and the state director of regional planning; and California has a local agency formation commission in each county. Some of these

---

19. Vincent Ostrom, "Can Federalism Make a Difference?" *Publius: The Journal of Federalism* 3 (1973): 197–238.

units encourage annexations to existing municipalities rather than the creation of new entities; some oppose "gerrymandering," which creates odd-shaped jurisdictions meant to include tax-rich areas or exclude nuisance islands; some use artificial or natural features as boundary lines (rivers, lakes, highways, railroad tracks); and some oppose boundaries that would divide existing commercial districts or residential areas.[20]

EVALUATION AND ACCOUNTABILITY IN VERTICAL INTERGOVERNMENTAL RELATIONS

With so many resources flowing from national to state to local governments, there are obvious opportunities for analytic procedures to maximize effectiveness. One opportunity comes at the point where a granting agency can choose which of several applications to support. Another opportunity comes at the point of follow-up, where the grantor can monitor the recipient's performance in order to determine the merits of continuing aid or advising on program changes. Yet, other opportunities come to a granting agency that would accumulate information on the experience of numerous recipients in order to advise subsequent applicants on program design.

Despite these opportunities for analysis and follow-through, there are problems in the way of too much scrutiny and control. Some problems reflect the political sensitivities of federalism and keep national administrators from laying too heavy a hand on states and localities. Other problems come from the nature of programs themselves. Those which are innovative, or which seek to realize goals that are defined in general terms, leave administrators wondering about the kinds of controls they can impose on applicants for their funds.

The Omnibus Crime Control and Safe Streets Act presented several difficulties that hinder program evaluation and control: disputes over the nature of crime and the types of crime that should be the prime targets of law enforcement; further disputes over the causes of crime and the most effective ways of dealing with them; as well as the disinclination of the new U.S. Law Enforcement Assistance Administration to raise the spectre of federal takeover of police services controlled historically by the state and local authorities. The range of goals con-

---

20. Clarence J. Hein and Thomas F. Hady, "Administrative Control of Municipal Incorporation: The Search for Criteria," *Western Political Quarterly* 19 (December 1966): 697–704.

sistent with the basic legislation included the more effective apprehension of criminals; improved crime detection; the more rapid prosecution of accused criminals; better protections for the civil rights of the accused; programs for corrections, parole, or rehabilitation; or programs to analyze and deal with underlying social and economic causes of crime. Officials argued about the relative importance of white-collar crimes, crimes of violence, and such "victimless" crimes as prostitution and gambling. Much of the activity in the program's early years sought to improve information about crime and crime control. Sample surveys found that citizens reported several times the incidence of crimes appearing in the FBI's Uniform Crime Reports. Other surveys sought reliable information about the incidence of specific crimes and their cost to victims; the apprehension of suspects and the flow of cases through the courts; or the effectiveness of various approaches to punishment and rehabilitation.[21]

INTERLOCAL AND INTERSTATE "HORIZONTAL" RELATIONS

Vertical associations among federal, state, and local administrators and other officials do not exhaust the catalog of intergovernmental relations. The presence of 50 state governments and approximately 78,000 local governments gives rise to numerous opportunities for horizontal relationships among administrators at the same level. While vertical relationships focus on the provision and receipt of financial aid, no single prominent stimulus for horizontal relations exists. The formats for horizontal relations vary with the incentives that prompt them. They include "federations" and "compacts" that permit the joint administration of public services; agreements to share information or technical assistance; reciprocal legislation that permits the citizens of one jurisdiction to receive certain services within another jurisdiction; and the membership of government officials in organizations that seek to develop solutions for common problems. Officials in administrative agencies or in legislative or executive branches usually take the lead in formulating intergovernmental arrangements. On occasion, however, the action of aroused citi-

---

21. See David T. Stanley, "How Safe the Streets, How Good the Grant?" *Public Administration Review* 34 (July–August 1974): 380–89; and Pamela Horst et al., "Program Management and the Federal Evaluator," *Public Administration Review* 34 (July–August 1974): 300–8.

zens imposes intergovernmental unions upon officials reluctant to surrender their autonomy.

Stimuli of Horizontal Intergovernmental Relations

Metropolitan areas are the most frequent settings for horizontal relations among administrative units. This reflects the high density of people and the demands for policy that they generate, plus the obvious feature of many separate governments, each of which has an administrative organization depending partly on activities within another's jurisdiction. Some public services can be provided with greater efficiency if administered on an areawide basis, than if administered in many separate units. If the service units are sufficiently large, they can employ a variety of specialists needed for complete and competent service. In the case of libraries, zoos, and museums, a large tax base can support a diverse collection in a central location with some smaller collections in branch units. In the case of pollution control, wind and water currents do not respect political boundaries. An enforcement agency must have access to violators throughout the area. Likewise in the case of slum control. If a blighted area can spread across a street to another jurisdiction with an inadequate housing code or enforcement program, then one community's slum program will have limited success in controlling the basic problems of crime and disease. In the case of police and fire activities, there is some need for reciprocal rights of pursuit, assistance in apprehending fugitives, or assistance in dealing with major fires. Without these provisions, criminals might evade the law simply by crossing a street, or a community might suffer major fire loss while its neighbor's equipment stands idle.

Not all instances of horizontal intergovernmental relations reflect the problems of metropolitan areas. Some result because features of the environment bring common difficulties to different administrative agencies widely separated or rural in their character. In one form, this is the river or lake that serves as the boundary between different states, yet joins their governments to the problems of pollution and makes the problem more difficult because of the numerous governments involved. The Mississippi River system, for example (with the Ohio and Missouri as major tributaries), flows through or between 19 states! With numerous governments, it is necessary to appease many actors in negotiations. Interest groups that oppose certain policies have that many veto points where a strategy of intransigence can stall a program. The Great Lakes wash the shores of 8 states and present additional problems by involving international relations with Canada. Because Canada, as well as the United States, has a federal structure, Ontario provincial officials, as well as Canadian federal officials, take part in negotiations. Two problems requiring intergovernmental coordination along lakes and rivers are pollution and water use. Pollution control requires the cooperation of governments on either side of a stream, as well as those upstream and downstream. The problems of water use involve diversions by one state or community of resources that another state or community desires for its own use. The Great Lakes states have charged that Chicago's diversion of water from Lake Michigan into the Chicago River (and eventually to the Mississippi) lowers shorelines around the lakes and causes much damage and inconvenience to recreational and port facilities. On the Colorado River, conflicts over diversions for irrigation have prompted interstate compacts that portion out the water to Colorado, Arizona, Nevada, and California.

Instruments of Horizontal Relations

The devices that different state or local administrators develop to resolve their common problems are often informal and designed merely to keep them in contact with one another. In this way, they can share information and perhaps coordinate efforts. However, some devices are very detailed and involve formal commitments from several state or local governments and perhaps from Washington or a foreign government as well.

Several devices attempt to cope with the problems of governmental coordination within metropolitan areas. Called "federations" or "consolidations," these terms imply that general-purpose governments provide a full range of services throughout the urban area. In some places, however, these terms denote governmental entities that handle only some local government functions. In Dade County, Florida, for example, the metropolitan government leaves numerous functions to pre-existing municipalities and the county. Most large metropolitan areas have "special districts" that provide individual services to an extensive area. Districts offer elementary and secondary education, water and sewage, refuse collection, police and/or fire protection, parks, mass transportation, or libraries. Each district may have its own borders that are not coterminous with those of other districts; one district may include several municipalities and parts of other municipalities or the rural fringe and may overlap only partly with the territory covered by another kind of district. Where districts have proliferated, they can provide individual services on an economical basis, but they do not reduce the confusion or inequities that arise from numerous separate jurisdictions. Many citizens do not know which districts include their own residence, much less how they can influence policies within their districts.

Where a metropolitan area spills over into more than one state, it may be necessary to formalize intergovernmental agreements as "interstate compacts." These must be defined in legislation acceptable to the officials of each state and to the United States Congress. The Port of New York Authority is a product of one such compact. It is an agreement between New York and New Jersey that defines the legal authority and financial procedures for developing and maintaining transportation facilities in the New York City area. The Authority owns bridges, tunnels, airports, highways, and port facilities. It raises money by selling bonds that it pays off with tolls and other revenues earned by its facilities.

Some agreements commit administrators to share information used for enforcement programs. The tax officials of different states and the federal government share information about individuals who move from one state to another or business firms that operate in many states. Returns filed by an individual or business for state and federal taxes can be checked for consistency, and an audit performed by one agency may produce information useful to another.[22]

The national and regional organizations of state and local government officials are important media for horizontal relations among state or local governments. These organizations bring their members together for periodic meetings and sometimes provide staff services that compile information and write position papers on topics of common interest. Some attain national publicity. The United States Conference of Mayors includes the chief executives of most large cities; and the Governors' Conference includes all of the state chief executives. Many other organizations exist for the heads of certain administrative departments. These organizations provide an opportunity for policy-makers to get together. Some contacts made at these meetings mature into personal friendships. They provide channels that smooth relations between neighboring jurisdictions and facilitate administrators' job mobility from one state or locality to another. When administrators face an unfamiliar situation, they contact colleagues in neighboring jurisdictions to see if they have worked out a policy to deal with similar situations. Two organizations publish collections of data widely used by state and local administrators

---

22. Clara Penniman and Walter W. Heller, *State Income Tax Administration* (Chicago: Public Administration Service, 1959), chapter IX.

to see how their own activities compare with those across the country. The International City Managers' Association publishes *The Municipal Year Book,* and the Council of State Governments publishes the *Book of the States.*

As we have noted before, organizations of administrators are important not only as media for intergovernmental communications, but also as interest groups that present the demands of administrators to other government officials. They do not always seek more discretion for state or local administrators. At times, the organizations welcome stringent federal requirements for matching funds and see them as program standards that state or local administrators can use to elicit more funds for their legislative and executive branches.

Regional Similarities in Public Policy

One manifestation of horizontal relations among administrative organizations is policy-copying among geographic neighbors. Several features guide officials to their regional neighbors for policy cues: the officials' belief that neighbors have problems similar to their own; the attitude of officials and interested citizens that it is "proper" or "reasonable" to adapt one's own programs to those of nearby jurisdictions; and the structure of organizational affiliations that put officials into frequent contact with their counterparts in neighboring governments.[23] The professional associations of administrators hold both regional and national meetings; however, officials report they are more likely to attend and acquire their contacts at regional meetings. Federal agencies also encourage regional communications by virtue of their field offices. New York, Atlanta, Chicago, Dallas, Kansas City, and San Francisco have acquired the status of regional capitals because they contain the offices of numerous Washington agencies. The personnel in these field offices conduct most of the correspondence between the federal agency and state and local units, and they help to pass the news of problems and solutions from one state government to another within their regions. One study of horizontal relations among administrators questioned the budget officers of 67 major agencies in the states of Florida, Georgia, Kentucky, and Mississippi. The 67 officials made 198 nominations of states that were among the "best sources of information." Of their nominations 87 percent were in the region that includes the 11 states of

---

23. This section relies on Ira Sharkansky, *Regionalism in American Politics* (Indianapolis: Bobbs-Merrill, 1969), chapters 1 and 6.

the Confederacy and the border states of Delaware, Maryland, Kentucky, West Virginia, and Oklahoma. Of the nominations 35 percent were states that bordered directly on the states of the respondents. A survey conducted among school superintendents in Georgia showed comparable results. The superintendents were most likely to contact their immediate or near neighbors within the state. The choice of a contact was often an uncomplicated one, guided by a notion of friends and neighbors within easy reach. One rural superintendent described his daily route as his guide to contacts: "Well, I live in Macon County, so I have to drive [to work] through Marion and Schley Counties. I talk with those three pretty often." Although it is conceivable that southerners are more parochial in their reliance on neighbors than are officials in other sections of the country, administrators elsewhere also refer primarily to states in the immediate or near neighborhood when questioned about the source of their own policy norms.

The question remains: *Which regional neighbors are the targets of administrators' emulation?* From the comments of several officials, agencies that have acquired a reputation for leadership are sought out disproportionately for their advice. There seems to be a two-step communications process: most administrators seek to copy the leading agencies within their region, but the leading agencies either generate their own innovations or take their cues from other leaders outside their immediate region. Jack L. Walker of the University of Michigan has gathered evidence on the timing of innovations in each of the 48 contiguous states. By aggregating data across several fields of service, he ranked the state governments according to their adoption of programs or policies earlier—or later—than other states. His rankings suggest that agencies in New York and Massachusetts play leadership roles in the Northeast, Michigan and Wisconsin in the middle section of the country, California on the West Coast, Colorado in the Mountain region, and Louisiana and Virginia in the South.[24]

The ambiguous regional location of some states provides their administrators with special opportunities. When a state is situated on the borders between different regions, its officials can choose from among several states as the subjects of comparison. When they face a situation where they must plead for additional funds, they can identify themselves as the poor cousin, in comparison with more well-endowed

---

24. Jack L. Walker, "Innovation in State Politics," in Herbert Jacob and Kenneth N. Vines, eds., *Politics in the American States*, rev. ed. (Boston: Little, Brown, 1971), pp. 354–87.

neighbors. But when they find it necessary to defend themselves against public criticism, they can picture themselves as offering better services than other neighbors. Educators in Missouri, for example, often find it necessary to justify their low level of expenditure for public schools. When they are on the defensive, Missouri officials can compare their efforts to such low-ranking neighbors as Arkansas, Oklahoma, and Nebraska, rather than to high-ranking Illinois. When they are on the offensive, Missouri educators ask for funds to help them attain the standards of Illinois.

THE MIXED REALITIES OF INTERGOVERNMENTAL RELATIONS

It is misleading to describe "vertical" and "horizontal" relations among administrative agencies and to imply that relations are clearly one type or another. Relationships among administrators of different governments evolve from concrete problems that affect several jurisdictions; they often combine "horizontal" with "vertical" relationships. "Triangular" relations may also develop; these involve two local governments with a single federal (or state) agency, or two federal (or state) agencies with a single local government. Neighboring localities may develop a joint project under the prodding of a federal grant. Or an integrated set of local programs may receive support from different federal grants offered by distinct agencies. Beyond this level of complexity, a variety of "poly-angular" relations may evolve among a number of federal, state, or local agencies that have a common interest in a particular problem.

It is also an oversimplification to assume that the involvement of a "superior" level of administration permits that organization to control its "subordinate" associates. A study of intergovernmental relations in a rural Indiana county found several federal programs controlled by local commissions that operated with substantial discretion. They were extensions of the federal administrative organization,[25] but their mixture of local considerations with federal standards confound any simple equation of federal involvement with federal control. These units included the Selective Service Board, the Welfare Board, County Agricultural Stabilization and Conservation Committee, and the Civil Defense Board.

---

25. Douglas St. Angelo, "Formal and Routine Local Control of National Programs," *Southwestern Social Science Quarterly* 47 (March 1966): 416–27; see also the discussion of "administrative hybrids" in Chapter 4, pp. 127–29.

These units were responsible for selecting young men for the armed services; deciding on applications for welfare assistance; distributing crop allotments and payments for conservation activities; establishing emergency procedures, and securing federal grants for fire-fighting and hospital equipment. Outside the formal boundaries of government, but still able to affect the local administration of federal programs, were the banks that exercised their approval on all applications for loans arranged by the Federal Housing Administration and the Veterans Administration.

During the era of massive investment in the Cape Kennedy space facilities, east-central Florida experienced a vast expansion of intergovernmental relations. Between 1950 and 1966, the population of Brevard County increased from 23,600 to 221,000. The economy shifted from one based on citrus, cattle, truck crops, fishing, and forestry to one based almost exclusively on the space program. At the end of 1965, the Air Force, NASA, or their contractors employed about 37 percent of the area's labor force. A brief survey of the most prominent interactions provides a rich illustration of the diverse ways in which the administrative agencies of separate governments can come together to make demands on one another and/or to provide one another with benefits. A study of intergovernmental relations conducted in 1966 found the following goals motivating intergovernmental relations:

1. An agency's desire to make life more convenient and agreeable for its burgeoning work force;
2. An agency's concern that projects begun by other units would affect its own programs;
3. An agency's desire to support its own projects with the resources controlled by other governments;
4. An agency's desire to protect its constituents' interests from being disturbed by the projects of other governments;
5. The desire of agency administrators to build rapport with other units of government; and
6. The recognition by agency personnel that they had surplus resources valuable to other units of government.[26]

NASA officials were most prominent in playing the role of a large employer concerned about the convenience of its employees. The agency wanted community amenities that would help it—and its contractors—recruit personnel to the area; and it wanted convenient travel facilities to ensure its employees' promptness and good spirits. It had a

26. Ira Sharkansky, "Intergovernmental Relations in Brevard County, Florida," a report to the Urban Research Institute of Florida State University, 1966.

special interest in travel problems. The main NASA facilities were separated from the mainland by a wide estuary and occupied a series of islands that had received little use before the space boom. Because the facilities were spread north-south over 50 miles, it was necessary to provide numerous roads, causeways, and bridges between each major work site and the communities that house the workforce. In order to stimulate and guide the state, local, and federal agencies that would provide the necessary roads, NASA's Office of Community Services surveyed the travel habits of its own employees and those of other federal agencies and contractors; it provided the data to state, county, and municipal officials and to the U.S. Bureau of Public Roads.

The choice of specific locations for causeways and bridges involved the U.S. Army Corps of Engineers. That agency showed the second motivation for intergovernmental relations: projects of other units affect the Corps' own responsibilities. In this case, the Corps had to review the designs of causeways and bridges to see that they did not interfere with navigation in the Intracoastal Waterway and in other streams in the Cape Kennedy area.

The question of money often generates activity. In displays of the third motivation for intergovernmental relations, several administrators sought the financial resources of other agencies for road and bridge improvements. The county road department requested extra funds from the state road board to acquire rights-of-way ahead of the normal schedule for receiving state road funds. In their turn, state officials argued that federal agencies should pay more than their usual portion for Brevard County road improvements because of the federally induced traffic. Federal agencies did accept some additional financial responsibility, but they hedged against the full state demands with the argument that economic benefits of the space program compensated for state road expenditures.

Together, state and county administrators approached Washington officials in the pursuit of extra federal aid. During March of 1965, a member of the state road board said that a delegation led by Governor Burns would meet with Florida senators and representatives and would try for an audience with President Johnson. This meeting did not occur, but during April, state officials met with Vice President Humphrey during his visit to Orlando (for the purpose of honoring astronaut John Young). Vice President Humphrey then arranged a Washington meeting between the governor, members of the state road board, the chairman of the Brevard County Commission, both Florida senators, the secretary of the air force (which operates Patrick Air Force Base in the Cape area), and the director and associate director of NASA's Kennedy Space Center. From this meeting came a state-federal agreement about the division of costs for certain roads and bridges, an indication of NASA and Air Force willingness to request a budget allocation for roads based upon military needs, and plans for the submission of a supplementary appropriations bill in Congress.

The Orlando meeting with Humphrey produced an incident that showed some of the tensions that might accompany intergovernmental relations. In displays of the fourth motivation for intergovernmental relations (protecting one's constituents from another government's projects), local officials and allied newspaper editors dramatized a *faux pas*. The incident occurred as the meeting began. A security guard could not find the name of the Brevard County Commission chairman on the list of guests and insisted that he leave. In the confusion that preceded the opening of the talks, the commissioner could not establish his identity. In reporting the incident to the press, the commissioner said that he was commanded by the guard: "Out out . . . you, out." Local officials and editors viewed the exclusion as depriving Brevard County of a representative at the discussion that might have long-range effects upon the county's welfare. Worse yet, the meeting was in Orange County, and its host was the publisher of the *Orlando Sentinel,* an Orange County newspaper. In Brevard County, the Titusville *Star Advocate* quoted a local official as saying: "Brevard County is the ninth most populous county in Florida. We've never asked Orange County for help in the past and we don't plan on asking them for help in the future. . . . I feel Brevard County is due an apology for [the commissioner's] ouster from that important meeting." Another Brevard County newspaper, the *Cocoa Tribune,* referred to the Orlando publisher as "The Little Emperor of Central Florida" and speculated that he had contrived the exclusion of the Brevard County official in order to emphasize road projects that would benefit Orange County at the expense of Brevard County. The commissioner himself came to see an advantage in his exclusion from the meeting. In the vice president's embarrassment and apology that followed, the commissioner found other governments more cooperative than he had originally expected.

Decisions concerning roads and bridges provide other examples of intergovernmental relations motivated by officials' desires to protect their constituents. The Bureau of Sports Fisheries of the U.S. Department of the Interior analyzed the design and location of bridges and causeways with respect to their impact on the health of marine life and on recreational opportunities. Municipal authorities opposed the choice of certain locations for new roads and bridges because of their likely impact on local restaurants, motels, and retail shops. The administrators of toll-bridge authorities opposed the development of competing toll-free facilities because of their own obligations to bondholders.

Another display of intergovernmental relations prompted by officials' concern for their constituents surrounded NASA's decision to create a Visitors' Information Center. The Center promised to become the major tourist attraction in the area. A survey by the U.S. National Parks Service predicted that 3.2 million persons would visit the Center annually. Reacting to this prediction, one county editor wrote:

> Three million people will eat a lot of meals in Brevard County. Many of them will want a place to stay overnight. They will want to buy souvenirs, visit our beaches, perhaps stay over long enough to fish or relax in our fine year-around climate.
>
> Their cars will need fuel and probably some repairs and maintenance. They may even want to look around with an eye to choosing a retirement home or looking for a job....
>
> We'd better be ready to render the services they demand and will be willing to pay for.[27]

Not only would communities close to the Center glean more from tourists than towns at the far end of the county, but the Center's exact location would determine which of several routes the national automobile clubs and oil companies would recommend for tourists. If a town did not have convenient access to the Center, it would lose tourist business. Before NASA made a decision about the Center's location, several chambers of commerce urged it for their areas; at least three communities offered free land for the Center, and one offered a vacant supermarket as a suitable building. To avoid the honky-tonkism that would surround a location on a public highway (few major roads in the County were free of strip development), NASA decided to build the Center inside its reservation, with a federally controlled road between it and a major highway. Although this decision did not escape harsh criticism from community newspapers, NASA tried to minimize the controversy. During the course of public presentations, NASA asserted that it would not compete with the private tourist industry. As an appeal to local eateries, the Center would limit its refreshment stands to snacking, rather than lunching or picnicking, facilities. In order to keep all important communities on the tourist routes, NASA would make the Center

---

27. *Orlando Sentinel* (Brevard County Edition), June 5, 1965.

accessible from various parts of the county; to accomplish this, NASA would allow the state road board to build additional highways through its reservation.

While intergovernmental competition and conflict were prominent in the relationships generated by road and bridge developments and by NASA's Visitors' Information Center, most intergovernmental relations in Brevard County appeared amicable. Indeed, that was the assertion of both federal and local administrators. Both NASA and the Air Force made a conscious effort to promote rapport with other units of government. At the Washington level, NASA worked to establish a subregional office of another federal agency (the Department of Housing and Urban Development) in Brevard County. The subregional office was not a usual component of HUD's organization. Rather, it was the Department's effort to help area communities cope with their rapid growth. NASA's involvement came partly from its sense of obligation for the effects of its own growth, partly from its desire to have good working relations with local governments, and partly from the hope that improved community facilities would help it recruit and hold competent employees. HUD's subregional office provided advice and technical assistance to local authorities who wished to apply for federal grants. Its staff listed and described the programs of HUD and other federal departments and indicated the criteria that federal officials were likely to consider when they reviewed local applications for grants. Somewhat in the manner of traveling sales representatives, HUD personnel called upon local authorities in order to acquaint them with new or changing programs. The Air Force's major effort in intergovernmental relations was the Civilian-Military Council of Patrick Air Force Base. This provided an opportunity for base commanders and public relations officers to meet with prominent civilians: e.g., the local clergy, retail business executives, real estate agents, and local government officials. Local government members reported that monthly business meetings were typically short and uneventful, but that the accompanying social hour provided opportunities to discuss items of mutual concern and to arrange joint activities. Once each year the members spent several days together—partly at federal expense—visiting other Air Force installations throughout the United States. Members claim this extended period in close contact allowed them to understand more clearly the views of fellow members and to comprehend the constraints that influence one another's operations. The members trace several instances of intergovernmental cooperation to the friendships that developed out of the Council's programs. A public relations officer for the Air Force cited the Council's program as an explanation for the immediate response that he once received from the County Road Department in response to his call for assistance. During the Cuban missile crisis, it was necessary to close the main highway that ran alongside of the airstrip. "Within a few minutes" of this official's telephone request, the county had a road grader on the scene to smooth a dirt road detour, and police officers appeared to block the highway and redirect traffic.

Many administrators tell stories about the exchange of favors between agencies. Some of these reflect high-level decisions to build intergovernmental rapport. However, lower-level employees also exchange favors for less-complex motives. They do so when they are predisposed to cooperation, and when they have a surplus commodity that can benefit another agency in the area. These exchanges have not been significant in terms of money or working-hours, but they make relations tolerable for the personnel of different units. Patrick Air Force Base loaned personnel and vehicles without charge to help a school construction project that had fallen behind schedule; county personnel and equipment—using materials donated by local businesses—helped construct a swimming pool for noncommissioned officers; and the county donated materials for a refreshment stand on the Air Force Little League field. NASA and the Air Force donated obsolete missiles to local authorities for display purposes, and they allowed local government personnel to attend in-service training courses provided for federal employees. On one occasion, Patrick Air Force Base rescued a local government from embarrassment at the hands of another federal agency. When the Federal Aviation Agency would not allow a new airport to commence operations on the day of its formal opening because its tower operator lacked the proper credentials, the Air Force offered the services of a tower operator. Federal and county officials cooperate regularly in making it convenient for federal employees to file requests for property tax exemptions and to purchase automobile license tags. Both NASA and the Air Force provide temporary office space for county officials and allow their own employees released time to take care of their personal chores.

These descriptions indicate there is no simple pattern of intergovernmental relations. No formal routines prescribe in clear terms how administrators of one government should deal with officials of another unit. Furthermore, each major "instance" of intergovernmental relations is not one event. It is a series of meetings, telephone conversations, memoranda, and informal or formal accords. At times, a government's decisions may influence another government when there has been no real contact. An administrator of one unit may base a decision on anticipations of the likely actions that will be taken by officials of other units. If the officials of different units have obtained sufficient knowledge of each other's environment and modes of action, their anticipations may lead to actions that differ little from what would occur with formal communications.

SUMMARY

Administrators from all levels of government seek to affect the decisions of administrative agencies at other levels of government. Various kinds of intergovernmental aids join the resources of federal, state, and local governments in the support of all major domestic services. Actors at each level of government feel the impact of decisions that flow from administrative decisions at all levels of government.

There are numerous forms of intergovernmental relations. Many involve financial assistance, and even those that are not overtly financial have economic importance for the participants: grants-in-aid; shared taxes; revenue sharing tax credits; federal income-tax provisions that allow deductions for state and local taxes and the exclusion of income earned on state or local government bonds; the direct provision of services from one government to the citizens of another; technical assistance; and informal ties among personal friends in different agencies or through the media of administrators' professional societies. It is not feasible to estimate the economic value of these relations to the providers or to the recipients. The resources involved in federal grants and state aids to localities are considerable. Federal grants for states and localities amounted to $47 billion in 1974–75, and state aids to localities were about $51 billion.

There has been a continuous growth in the magnitude of intergovernmental financial assistance since World War II, although any report of growth is partly a function of the measurements that are used. The kinds of programs added during each decade of the 20th century indicate that intergovernmental relations grow with prevailing policy concerns. Recent programs in the fields of education and urban affairs, for example, reflect the preoccupation with these areas of policy that began during the middle and late 1960s.

Not all intergovernmental relations are vertical. There are numerous horizontal contacts among different states or localities. These arrangements do not emphasize financial "aid," but they often have great economic significance for each of the participants. There are numerous kinds of metropolitan cooperation, interstate compacts, reciprocal agreements on the provision of services and enforcement programs, and informal links on the basis of personal friendships and contacts made through the organizations of government officials. It is often misleading to identify the "type" of intergovernmental relations that prevails at any time or place. Multiple relationships evolve among different governmental units as their officials or clients perceive common interests. Individual problems may generate both vertical and horizontal relations among several units.

11

Varieties of Administrative Outputs

In Chapter 1, we listed some of the outputs that the conversion processes of administrative systems provide to their environments. Now that we have examined numerous features of the environment, inputs from it to the conversion process, and the conversion process itself, we take a final look at several kinds of outputs. This final picture should appear richer—and more complicated—than at our first look.

In discussing the outputs of administrative agencies, we must frequently beg the question as to the origin of these outputs and the influence of administrators upon them. Some only pass through administrative agencies and show little influence from the actions of those agencies. In other cases, an administrative unit may work on a project, producing it in the formal sense, leaving no feature on it that is its own distinctive creation. When some state or local agencies provide services funded and regulated by federal agencies, for example, producing units may do nothing more or less than is required by the federal manual. Or an agency may simply continue producing a service according to procedures devised in the past generation, without the present corps of officials making any alterations in the product. In some cases, administrators might help to create a new program primarily as a response to the demands of citizens, interest groups, or members of the executive and legislative branches. These questions about origins are important for a full understanding of the administrative system. We want to know which transactions are originated or shaped in the conversion process, as well as which are shaped primarily by its environment. If we wish to use our knowledge of administration in order to make adjustments in public programs and policies, we should know whether to apply these adjustments to agencies or to other factors in their environment. For the most part, however, this kind of detailed knowledge has not been collected. We can only raise the question about the true origin of administrative outputs and then proceed to describe several outputs that appear to reflect the activities of administrators and other actors in their environment.

ADMINISTRATIVE EFFORTS
AND PUBLIC SERVICES

Public services include some of the most tangible outputs of administrative agencies, but even they defy clear and unambiguous measurement. We cannot simply equate the policies pursued by administrative agencies with the services that actually are delivered to citizens. We have noted above the possible gaps between "policy" and "performance" (see pp. 11–13). The services delivered, or performance, can be measured in several ways: by the products received by clients; by the improvement in the clients' conditions that results from the service; by the popularity of a service among the clients; or by some standards of quality set by an organization of professional persons concerned with the service at issue. In the case of intangible "services"—such as patriotic or religious utterances or other symbolic acts of administrative officials—their output might be gauged by the indications of satisfaction (and dissatisfaction) that appear in the population. Outputs are frequently measured by policies directed at services (like expenditures) by administrators. Some policies may fail to deal with the needs of agency clients; while other policies may work at cross purposes with one another. Such policies as agency expenditures, the recruitment and selection of a staff, the design of physical facilities, and the purchase of equipment may not make their expected contribution to the services that an agency renders.

Expenditures are among the most evident manifestations of agency policies. Officials pay a great deal of attention to budget-making, and expenditures are widely viewed as a common denominator among the items that actually produce services. Although spending, by itself, does not meet popular demands for services, spending appears to buy many of the things that produce services. Sufficient funds may be a *sine qua non* for public services. However, several other determinants of service outputs may be provided in generous or stingy proportions by different jurisdictions whose total budgets are nearly equal. By varying the allocation of funds among different factors, policy-makers may make a budget of a certain total more or less productive of actual performance. Some of the policies that have important effects on service outputs may be independent of spending levels.

Several aspects of an agency's staff may have a bearing on the quality or quantity of service outputs. The personnel's training, their sensitivity to clients' needs, and their motivation for professional advancement may each affect an agency's ability to make the greatest use of its funds. Staff size and the distribution of personnel among the principal and auxiliary tasks to be performed can affect an agency's service outputs. Professional educators predict that the consolidation of small districts will add to the teaching skills available for each pupil and will increase the quality of school outputs. If expenditures are used to make salary levels competitive with those in other jurisdictions, they may facilitate the policy-maker's search for the "right combination" of training and motivation for each of the principal jobs within the organization. However, salary alone does not guarantee success in obtaining a good staff. Indeed, leadership sensitivity and skill in using financial resources may be the key determinant that may (or may not) translate a good budget into a good staff, and then into public services that meet the needs and/or desires of clients.

The crucial dimensions of physical plant and equipment that may affect service outputs include compatibility with contemporary methods of providing service, flexibility with respect to the multiple needs and changing demands of clients, and durability in the face of heavy use. It is probably true that good education can be provided in an inadequate physical plant if the professional personnel are highly motivated and adaptable. But the nature of the surroundings and the availability of modern equipment should contribute to the capacity of the staff to perform in a superior fashion. However, attractive plant and facilities cannot guarantee success. If quality facilities are available for only a limited range of the school's task, they may not have their maximum impact on overall performance. If the high school gymnasium sparkles, while the library lacks up-to-date science texts, then the money spent on facilities may have a distorted influence on the school's output. The durability of facilities provides yet another dimension that may influence services. If the plant and equipment cannot withstand the use it is given, the cost of maintenance will deplete the investments that can be made in additional facilities or in staff improvement. Later in this chapter, we shall return to these questions about the effects various kinds of administrative outputs have on the services that clients receive.

INFORMATION AS AN OUTPUT

Administrative agencies produce information and ideas for the public and for other branches of government. These outputs often help set the agenda of public discussions, influence the content of "public opinion," and provide the information legislators and the chief executive use to "supervise and control" administrators. This is no place to exaggerate the influence of administrative agencies over public opinion. The image to be presented is *not* that of a monolithic government that exercises subtle but irresistible influence over the minds of men. Administrative units are typically as complex and beset with diversity as the population they serve. This diversity is one of the prime defenses society has against an overbearing opinion machine; because of this diversity, administrators provide opinion-options to their citizens, rather than public opinion per se.

Administrators use several means to present information and ideas to the public. Some are formal announcements and other communications designed to influence public opinion; others are public communications to other government officials that have a secondary function of influencing the public. In many cases, it is difficult to separate the primary and secondary targets of administrators' communications. They may be addressed to other officials and yet delivered in a fashion that guarantees some arousing of public support. Many deliberations are ritualized for the purpose of informing the public about the government's business; thus, the official who routes an in-house communication through the public is only acting according to a format well established in democratic practice. When agency personnel testify at administrative and legislative hearings, make reports to special investigatory commissions, or participate in election campaigns, they are helping to involve the public in governmental affairs. Many of the topics discussed in these forums have enough innate importance to attract attention and to make the public receptive to the information and ideas offered. The topics of peace and war, economic development, unemployment, environmental protection, inflation and interest rates, testing of new drugs and medical devices, and the provision of education and housing are each vitally important to large numbers of people.

Several kinds of public information come from administrators. Agencies describe ongoing programs in order to advertise their availability and the requirements prospective clients must fulfill. Some agencies also publicize their needs for new legislation or increased appropriations. An agency which does not want to advertise its needs directly may inform interest groups of its needs and let them mount the campaign. Agencies also provide much of the information used by elected officials in their public statements and in deliberations about present and proposed activities. Legislators and executives recognize agencies as primary reservoirs of expertise and often use agency speechwriters to compose their own remarks.

Administrators suffer the accusations of those who feel they take unfair advantage of their opportunities to inform the public. They are charged by citizens—and by other government officials—with "managing the news" or with violating "freedom of information." "Managing the news" refers to the selective release of information that benefits the agency providing the information. It was a charge heard frequently during the Vietnam conflict. It was alleged that the Defense and State departments released partial or distorted reports about military engagements or diplomatic efforts. Violation of "freedom of information" is claimed frequently in state capitols and city halls, as well as in Washington. It refers to the efforts of government officials to classify controversial documents as "secret" or "confidential." The U.S. Congress and several state legislatures have enacted "freedom-of-information" statutes. They require that certain information be given to any citizen who asks for it, while they protect other documents from public scrutiny. The claim for an individual's "right to privacy" frequently clashes with "freedom of information" and in many states results in withholding from the public the information contained in tax returns, records of welfare recipients, and other documents pertaining to individual cases.

With all the possibilities that exist for administrators to supply information and ideas and to regulate some mechanisms of public information, there also are many protections that guard citizens from the opinions of administrators. Perhaps the most important of these protections is the diversity among administrative agencies and personnel. There is no single "administrative line" disseminated via the mass media. Representatves of different administrative agencies argue publicly with each other's interpretation of a social problem. Individual legislators and the chief executive challenge agency views and provide additional alternatives for the public to consider. There have been numerous public conflicts among the military heads of the armed services, the civilian secretary of defense, the president, and members of Congress. After the secretary of defense cuts a budget request, for example, a friendly congressional committee will most likely provide a forum for the service head to accuse the secretary of gambling with the national security.

In addition, the diversity of nongovernmental information protects citizens from administrative views. The mass media are themselves a diffuse set of institutions that offer a variety of information and ideas. Individuals also have numerous noninstitutionalized sources of information: friends, family, co-workers, and co-religionists, each of whom can provide information and reinforcement for positions counter to those presented by government officials.

Administrators send many of their "informational" outputs to other branches of government. Indeed, many of the inputs that come to administrators from the legislative and executive branches of government actually get their start as the outputs of the administration. As the administration's outputs, these take the form of requests for appropriations or a change in statutes or as an administrator's advice to a member of another branch about a proposal developed. These outputs of the administration may be so important in the deliberations of other branches that they permit administrators to dominate other officials. Administrators often bolster their reputation for expertise with the political support offered by interest groups or with the support of the communities in which their services are provided. In some cases, these alliances form tightly knit "subgovernments" that present irresistible demands to the legislature and the chief executive. Perhaps the most well-known "subgovernment" is the alliance of military administrators, defense contractors, and the representatives of communities that have defense plants or military bases. Other alliances are formed among agencies that engage in the construction of public works (Corps of Engineers, Bureau of Reclamation, Bureau of Public Roads) and the construction firms, related industries, local communities, and groups of citizens that benefit from their activities.

The outputs that the administrative agencies provide to executive and legislative branches are not limited to policy proposals and relevant information. The implementation of policies provides outputs that are attractive to elected executives and legislators, as well as to private citizens. These outputs appeal to executives and legislators as the products of their own handiwork in helping to build and supply public services. Voters are thought to identify the services received with the elected executive and legislature. Elected officials look to administrators for outputs that will help the politicians secure reelection.

OPPORTUNITIES FOR CHANGES IN OUTPUT

We have seen that numerous features of staff, budgets, and political demands converge to influence the outputs of administrative agencies.

It also appears that patterns of policy or implementation have a way of maintaining themselves. Policy-makers do not often change the bargains among competing interests that allowed programs to be set up. The routines of budget-making usually admit only incremental changes in the overall size of agency resources. The tenure of staff members generally keep new ideas from taking over established agencies, and yet, changes do occur. The administrative system is not closed. Events in the environment work their influence through the addition of new programs and new agencies and through changes felt in established agencies. The U.S. Army Corps of Engineers is a case in point. For many years, the Corps had been the archetype of an entrenched bureau. It offered the tangible benefits of dams, flood control, improved channels and ports in exchange for political support from groups interested in such physical improvements. The exchange of physical improvements for political support provided the Corps with a breadth of influence in Congress sufficient to withstand executive budget-cutters. Even such a master of bureaucratic in-fighting as President Franklin D. Roosevelt was stymied in his efforts to control the Corps.[1]

As a concern with protecting the physical environment began to assume prominence in the United States, the Corps seemed committed to unlimited physical alterations for the sake of economic development. It was a symbol of evil for groups interested in conservation. Yet, recent years have seen major changes in the posture and the outputs of the Corps. Its internal procedures have changed to take even greater account of environmental protection than that required by the National Environmental Policy Act of 1969. It has accepted the principle of natural flood control as at least a partial alternative to dams and levees. Thus, it has cleared flood plains, left—or returned—them to their natural state and turned them into recreational areas that can accept flooding without major damage. The Corps has also pursued comprehensive urban planning, combining concerns of waste water management with solid waste disposal and the siting of power plants. Top echelons of the Corps have pursued extensive citizen participation in planning, even with the reluctance of some of its district engineers. These new ventures have not avoided all attacks from conservationists. Some view the Corps' new ventures as "empire building," suggesting that the Corps is damned if it does and damned if it doesn't. One chairman of its Environmental Advisory Board resigned and charged the Corps with not doing enough,

1. Arthur Maas, *Muddy Waters: The Army Engineers and the Nation's Rivers* (Cambridge: Harvard University Press, 1951).

but a successor—a vice president of the National Audubon Society—defended the Corps' policies.[2]

EFFECTS OF
ADMINISTRATIVE OUTPUTS

After we have identified the diversity of outputs from administrative agencies, we still have questions about their impact on social and economic conditions. Do the programs work? What about their *unintended* consequences? Do they generate additional problems that come back to visit administrative agencies in another guise? For someone interested in the relation between administrative agencies and their environments, these may be the most important questions.

The policies produced by administrative agencies do not by themselves guarantee results. They must interact with whatever social, economic, or political conditions exist in the environment, some of which generate the problems that administrators' outputs are designed to attack.

Who Pays the Bills? Who Gets the Benefits?

One set of output calculations that is especially clouded by a variety of factors concerns the distribution of tax costs and service benefits. *Who pays the bills?* and *Who gets the benefits?* are questions of sharp controversy. In the case of taxes, the questions focus on "progressivity" and "regressivity." A progressive tax takes a larger percentage of the income earned by upper-income individuals, while a regressive tax takes the larger percentage from the income of poorer citizens. The determination of tax progressivity or regressivity involves far more than a consultation of the statutory tax rates. It is necessary to take account of economic behaviors that define the direct liability of persons and their tendency to shift their own tax burden to someone else. Thus, landlords who are directly liable for property-tax payments typically pass the burden onto their tenants as a certain portion of their rent. Likewise, auto manufacturers pay the federal excise tax on each car sold but they shift the burden of that tax to the purchasers.

The statutory rates of some taxes are neither clearly regressive nor

---

2. Daniel A. Mazmanian and Mordecai Lee, "Tradition Be Damned! The Army Corps of Engineers is Changing," *Public Administration Review* 35 (March/April 1975: 166–72.

progressive, but economic behavior works to make certain income groups more likely to feel the burden. The typical retail sales tax, for example, places a flat rate on everyone's retail purchases (2 to 6 percent, depending on the state). The tax works in a regressive fashion, however, because lower-income people spend a larger percentage of their money for taxable commodities. Middle- and upper-income families do not encounter the sales tax when they save and invest.[3]

Overall, the impact of tax policies is a mixture of progressivity and regressivity. Federal taxes—especially the individual income tax—operate in a progressive fashion. State and local taxes, however, are generally regressive. We can balance our concern with *who pays the tax bills* with an assessment of *who gets the benefits of public services*. The determination of benefit distribution is, if anything, even more difficult than the determination of tax burdens. The benefit calculation involves some figuring (and some untested assumptions) about the distribution of direct and secondary benefits and about the distribution of benefits from services that may affect us all equally or differentially. From one perspective, expenditures on national defense benefit us all equally. From another perspective, however, those who work for—or own stock in—defense industries receive more benefits than do the rest of us. The same situation exists in the area of education benefits. We all benefit from the economic vitality that comes with a highly trained population; but those whose skills are more highly prized in the contemporary marketplace seem to receive more than the average benefits from the education that has been subsidized with public revenues.

The Tax Foundation has calculated the distribution of service benefits, by income class, resulting from the activities of national, state, and local governments.[4] The results indicate a "progressive" distribution of benefits, i.e., lower-income families seem to receive a higher percentage of their incomes in the estimated values of government benefits than do upper-income families. Federally funded benefits are more progressive than state and local benefits, largely because of the greater amount of public welfare benefits provided by national agencies. What may be questioned in this study is the allocation of federal spending for defense and international purposes. The calculations for these expenditures reflect the assumption that we all benefit equally: benefits are distributed to each income group according to the number of families

---

3. *Allocating Tax Burdens and Government Benefits by Income Class* (New York: Tax Foundation, 1967). (Hereafter cited as *Allocating Tax Burdens*.)
4. *Allocating Tax Burdens.*

in the group. A different calculation—one that would produce a less progressive distribution of the benefits—would trace the wages, salaries, and profits resulting from defense contracts.

Two political scientists—Bryan R. Fry and Richard F. Winters—took the calculations of the Tax Foundation and produced state-by-state measurements of tax and expenditure distributions.[5] Table 11–1 shows the ratio of expenditure benefits to tax burdens for low-income groups in each of the 48 contiguous states. In all these states, poor families get more in expenditure benefits than they pay in taxes. In the states at the upper end of the scale, however, the poor do better than in the states at the lower end of the scale. In a later analysis, Fry and Winters sought to explain the interstate variations in "redistribution" by reference to characteristics of state economies and politics. Their findings show that states with high levels of political participation, extensive merit systems in the state bureaucracies, and "professional" legislatures tend to provide the greatest benefits (relative to costs) to the lower-income taxpayers. Apparently, lower-income groups get a better hearing in governmental councils where there is active participation in politics and where professionally oriented personnel in legislative and administrative branches have the skills and motivation to recognize and respond to their demands.

A Test of Community Action Programs

Beginning in 1964, the federal government initiated a massive effort to improve the situation of the poor. Numerous acts of Congress and administrative agencies set targets among the urban and rural poor, the old and the young, whites as well as ethnic and racial minorities. The Office of Economic Opportunity was prominent among the units administering the activities, and its community action programs received the bulk of attention from the friends and the opponents of antipoverty activities.

Among the numerous efforts to gauge the results of community action was a series of interviews conducted among the leaders and residents of some 100 neighborhoods. Interviews conducted in late 1968 and early 1969 sought to measure the experience of these neighborhoods since the programs began in 1964. In judging the results of this program evaluation, it is important to recognize that the data represent the perceptions of individuals, rather than objectively determined measures of

---

5. Bryan R. Fry and Richard F. Winters, "The Politics of Redistribution," *American Political Science Review* 64 (June 1970): 508–22.

TABLE 11–1

Redistributive Ratios for 48 States

	Ratio[a]		Ratio[a]
1. Massachusetts	3.320	25. Washington	2.093
2. Missouri	2.712	26. Maine	2.060
3. New York	2.644	27. Tennessee	2.031
4. Oklahoma	2.567	28. West Virginia	2.011
5. Connecticut	2.486	29. Iowa	2.001
6. Rhode Island	2.482	30. Kansas	1.998
7. Colorado	2.464	31. Montana	1.962
8. Oregon	2.446	32. Utah	1.954
9. Kentucky	2.428	33. Maryland	1.923
10. Illinois	2.376	34. Michigan	1.920
11. Wisconsin	2.340	35. North Carolina	1.900
12. California	2.322	36. Florida	1.850
13. Mississippi	2.274	37. North Dakota	1.845
14. Alabama	2.267	38. New Hampshire	1.830
15. Louisiana	2.252	39. Nevada	1.826
16. Ohio	2.242	40. Nebraska	1.813
17. Arkansas	2.212	41. Texas	1.800
18. Idaho	2.205	42. Indiana	1.793
19. Vermont	2.199	43. South Carolina	1.775
20. Delaware	2.190	44. New Mexico	1.720
21. New Jersey	2.135	45. South Dakota	1.715
22. Georgia	2.127	46. Arizona	1.694
23. Pennsylvania	2.107	47. Wyoming	1.660
24. Minnesota	2.098	48. Virginia	1.620

SOURCE: Bryan R. Fry and Richard F. Winters, "The Politics of Redistribution," *American Political Science Review* 64 (June 1970): 515.

NOTE: Alaska and Hawaii have been excluded from the analysis because data for some of the independent variables were not available for the time period considered.

[a] The ratio of expenditure benefits to tax burdens for the three lowest income classes.

change. However, the perceptions and feelings of citizens who are the targets of social programs are an important component of program success or failure. Furthermore, the surveys included community leaders who should be able to report with some accuracy whether certain events had taken place in their neighborhoods during a certain period of time.[6]

The findings point to the great variety of program results in different communities. While some communities were virtually untouched, others reported numerous changes in neighborhood social services. The interviewers presented citizens and community officeholders with check-

---

6. Curt Lamb, *Political Power in Poor Neighborhoods* (New York: Wiley, 1975).

lists of specific reforms in order to see which, if any, had appeared in each neighborhood. Questions dealt with schools, welfare agencies, and the practices of employers. Other questions dealt with political activities and residents' knowledge of political events. For the field of education, respondents reported more change in opportunities for community involvement in decision-making than in the actual components of educational services. In 84 percent of the communities two out of three PTA presidents reported an increase in parent activity. In judging the substantive changes occuring in education, however, an analyst concluded that "the vast majority of poor communities ... are ... served by unimaginative, slow-moving educational institutions."[7] The field of employment showed more change in the statements of prospective employers than in the actual operation of programs to increase the number or quality of jobs for poor people. Three-fourths of all personnel officers acknowledged a responsibility for taking special steps to recruit the hard core unemployed, but only about one-third had provided special training opportunities or had even contacted government officials about job training programs.

Overall the surveys show uneven results with respect to the effects of community action programs. Yet, on the issue of increased political involvement of the poor and its link to improved services, there are some positive findings. Those neighborhoods scoring highest in changed local services tend to have combined protest activity with involvement in conventional politics and have a high incidence of alliances among community organizations. Among the various institutions surveyed, social service agencies were most responsive to protest activities, schools somewhat less so, and private employers the least responsive.

Were the community action programs successful? It is not possible to offer a simple answer, especially in the case of this multifaceted and controversial program. Much of the public argument has included large doses of emotion to compete with the facts available. The results of one kind of analysis—relying on opinion surveys among target populations and community leaders—are mixed in their evaluations. How many of the successes or the failures are due to the original design of the programs? And how much to the efforts—or lack of efforts—among program administrators and clients? These questions are important to the assessment of administrative outputs, but they challenge the technologies of program evaluation.

---

7. Lamb, *Political Power*, p. 18.

The Success of Regulatory Agencies

Ralph Nader is the most active and visible individual in the evaluation of administrative activities. He first became prominent when his book, *Unsafe At Any Speed,* exposed the mechanical dangers inherent in automobiles. His book was a major stimulus for the enactment of federal auto-safety regulations and for the demise of the Chevrolet *Corvair.* With the income from that book and from his popular lectures and personal appearances, Nader founded the Center for Study of Responsive Law. This organization sponsors investigations into a wide range of regulatory activities. Among its major studies have been those dealing with the Food and Drug Administration, the Interstate Commerce Commission, the Federal Trade Commission, and the National Air Pollution Control Administration.[8] Nader's investigators are recent graduates of colleges and professional schools. Nader operates in the grand tradition of American muckrackers. His books provide one horrible example after another, pointing to the failure of regulation to protect the public from ill-conceived products and services and demonstrating the irresponsible actions by the officials of private corporations and government agencies. Several of the books try to clarify the complex details of regulatory statutes and the technical considerations that must go into policies for transportation, air pollution, food safety, and drug effectiveness. What they lack is a sophisticated concern for "how bad" regulation actually is. They do not assess the incidence of regulatory failure in comparison to the incidence of success. Also, they do not assess the benefits from improved regulation in relation to the costs of improved surveillance.

The findings of "Nader's Raiders"—as his investigators are often called—should not surprise a professional political scientist. Several years ago Professor Marver Bernstein described the "life cycle" of a regulatory body.[9] In the early stage of its life, there is enthusiasm about the new statute and agency and about the impending end of antisocial industrial practices. Gradually, this euphoria is replaced by the recognition that a regulatory agency is a guardian, as well as an antagonist, of the regulated industry. This euphoria helps protect the agency from grieved con-

---

8. See Edward F. Cox, Robert C. Fellmeth, and John E. Schulz, *Nader's Raiders* (New York: Grove Press, 1969); John C. Esposito, *Vanishing Air* (New York: Grossman, 1970); James S. Turner, *The Chemical Feast* (New York: Grossman, 1970); and Robert Fellmeth, *The Interstate Commerce Omission* (New York: Grossman, 1970).

9. Marver H. Bernstein, *Regulating Business by Independent Commission* (Princeton, N.J.: Princeton University Press, 1955), chapter 5. See also Murray Edelman, *The Symbolic Uses of Politics* (Urbana: University of Illinois Press, 1964).

sumers. Yet, the findings of Nader and his colleagues come through with a force missing from the learned books of academic political scientists. Nader's reports are written with the conviction that publicity is the necessary first step to a sweeping reform, and Nader himself is a frequent witness at congressional hearings. Some of the most vivid writing describes obvious failures in regulatory policies: the FDA permitted the unrestricted use of cyclamates and monosodium glutamate long after serious research had questioned their dangers; the plight of homeowners who believed the ICC will assure a smooth move of furniture from one state to another; ICC's cooperation in the decline of railroad passenger service; and ICC's failure to protect motorists from unsafe trucks.

From the perspective of the political scientist, some of the most interesting findings of Nader's group concern the procedures of the regulatory agencies that limit their capacity to implement strong policies. In an effort to show that the FTC followed a tactic of *looking for no evil and finding none,* one of Nader's groups reported on the commission's personnel policies. FTC recruited the graduates of mediocre law schools, and—even within this group—failed to make employment offers to the best of its applicants.[10] Their report on the FDA stated the agency was uncomfortable with scientific information that upset certain policies: the FDA dismissed one noted consultant who persisted in making negative reports about some pesticides that the agency had decided to approve. Each of the regulatory agencies seems to concentrate on trivial violations of the statutes in order to create an impressive record of enforcements, while they ignore significant violations that would require intensive investigations and raise political complications. The National Air Pollution Control Administration, for example, conceded that auto emissions accounted for 60 percent of urban air pollution, while it spent less than 3 percent of its budget on this problem.

Nader's findings are valuable in suggesting how numerous aspects of administrative policy and the environment influence outputs. In writing about ICC's failures to regulate safety in the trucking industry, Nader's associates pointed to a collusion between the shippers, truckers, and drivers that work in the common direction of evading regulation. The shippers and truckers want rapid, low-cost delivery of goods, while the drivers want the extra overtime pay they can get only by a violation of maximum number of driving-hours permitted and by use of dangerous stimulants to keep awake through the extra working hours.

---

10. Cox, Fellmeth, and Schulz, *Nader's Raiders,* pp. 140–61 and 226–28.

Nader's investigators know from the experience of existing agencies that statutory reform is not enough. An insipid administration, or one in collusion with the "regulated" industry, will defeat any prospect of achieving success through new laws alone. Like other muckrakers, there is some faith expressed in the value of an alert citizenry, intense leadership, and public exposure of administrative shortcomings.[11] At times, however, there is a call for more sweeping reform of the economic and political systems.

The main reason why citizens have no impact on the corporations which they support and which affect their lives and health is that the large corporate polluter refuses to be held accountable to the public... because their wealth buys legal and scientific apologists, because they are generally bigger and more powerful than government agencies making half-hearted attempts at confrontation, and because they can direct consumer choices away from environmental issues. ...

So long as the crucial decisions remain with a small group of mammoth coporations, there is little reason to expect anything but further deterioration.[12]

Professor Cynthia H. Enloe has tried to identify traits that make for successful regulation in the field of environmental protection. She writes that the quality of an agency's legal mandate is important. The laws must not be so broad as to discourage achievement of their objectives. The U.S. Environmental Protection Agency, for example, was given the task of achieving an unreasonably high standard of air quality in an unreasonably short period of time. The result was that certain targets were not achieved, and some were formally reduced. Therefore the Agency acquired a reputation as a paper tiger. The budget of an agency must match its legal mandate, and its top administrators must have the personal stature and political skills to fend off attacks from hostile pressure groups, legislators, and other agencies. Good luck also helps. Environmental units in the United States suffered from adverse changes in the economic environment. The fuel crisis, inflation, and unemployment of the 1974–76 period weakened the appeal of programs conceived in the rosier economic period of the late 1960s, when it was felt that factories could be ordered to burn natural gas or low-sulfur oil or to install expensive pollution control devices without substantial threat to the high levels of employment.[13]

---

11. Turner, *Chemical Feast,* pp. 252ff.
12. Fellmeth, *Interstate Commerce Omission,* pp. 299–302.
13. Cynthia H. Enloe, *The Politics of Pollution in a Comparative Perspective· Ecology and Power in Four Nations* (New York: McKay, 1975), especially chapter 3.

We encounter difficulties when we attempt to test the influence of administrators' policies on social and economic conditions. As observers of government agencies, we have no more certain idea than do their officials about the policies that should be implemented (see pp. 57–69). Like them, we lack a standard of excellence against which to compare the results of public service. Not only are there disagreements about what kinds of service levels agencies should strive to attain, but there are related disagreements about the proper units to be used in measuring what the agencies actually produce.

Administrators and other policy-makers may make a dent in a hostile environment only with great difficulty. Public policy is only one of the elements that shapes conditions of the population. In the case of policies that promote racial integration, for example, their accomplishments depend partly on the willingness of the dominant racial group to comply voluntarily. Policies to improve education depend on the inclination of various cultural groups to place a value on academic achievement. Government programs to upgrade the occupational qualifications of minorities rely on the willingness of labor unions and employers to accept the products of new training programs.[14]

Programs may accomplish some of their goals but at the price of unanticipated consequences (sometimes called "secondary effects"). Highway programs, flood control projects, and other large-scale construction projects are powerful stimulants that have multiple effects. Aside from their primary goals, they alter existing land-use patterns with implications for housing and industry; they affect the habitat of wildlife and other features of the natural environment. Welfare programs designed to benefit the children of women without husbands have encouraged illegitimate births and the breakdown of families.

The Payoffs from Spending

Some tests of administrative policies have examined statistical associations between one kind of policy—government expenditures—and outputs that clients expect to receive from administrative agencies. In order to accept the influence of expenditures vis-à-vis the problems they are designed to alleviate, the jurisdictions showing high (or low)

---

14. Thomas Sowell, *Race and Economics* (New York: McKay, 1975).

levels of expenditures should show consistently high (or low) scores on most measures of service.

Three studies in different contexts show that relationships between government expenditures and levels of public service are neither strong nor pervasive. A highly regarded study of education finds that school spending bears little relationship to the learning that occurs. More important are traits of the pupil's family and friends. The pupil who comes from a well-educated family and associates with friends who are academically motivated is likely to do better in school than if the situations of family and friends are not supportive.[15] Another study of 163 Georgia school districts show only weak relationships between measures of educational spending and service outputs.[16] Yet, another study of state and local governments' spending and services across the country found that only 16 of 27 service measures (59 percent) showed sizable relationships with government spending.[17] Some of the spending-service relationships were negative. This means that high scores on spending corresponded with low scores on the measure of service. In the highway field, the mileage per capita of rural roads and a measure of traffic safety were negatively related with state and local government highway spending per capita. Apparently it is the low-spending states that developed the most extensive systems of rural roads. Low-spending states also experience the most enviable record of highway safety. In the field of crime control, the rates for rape, robbery, burglary, larceny, and auto theft were low where spending is low, while high-crime rates coexist with high spending. It is unlikely that high (or low) spending brought about high- (or low-) crime rates. The incidence of crime probably works upon the

15. James S. Coleman, *Equality of Educational Opportunity* (Washington, D.C.: U.S. Government Printing Office, 1966).

16. Ira Sharkansky, "Environment, Policy, Output and Impact: Problems of Theory and Method in the Analysis of Public Policy," a paper presented at the 1968 Annual Meeting of the American Political Science Association, Washington, D.C. The paper uses terminology in a different way than does this chapter. The differences in terminology reflect the different focus of the two writings: this book deals with an abstraction of the "administrative system"; the paper deals with the "policy process."

17. Ira Sharkansky, *The Politics of Taxing and Spending* (Indianapolis: Bobbs-Merrill, 1969), Chapter VI. The services actually delivered in different fields are necessarily defined in terms of these fields. Some measurements define the units of service (e.g., miles of highway) in relation to population. Some measures employ the incidence of beneficiaries among people likely to use a service (e.g., the proportion of poor citizens receiving welfare benefits). Others measure the rate at which a program is performed. Other assess services by the frequency with which the population chooses to use a program (e.g., the proportion of a population who attends schools or visits parks). And some assess services indirectly by measuring the continued existence of phenomena (e.g., disease or crime) that administrative outputs are designed to control.

spending level. States with little crime feel comfortable with relatively low per capita expenditures for public safety.

Several social and economic features of the environment show stronger, and more consistent, relationships with services than does government spending. In the field of secondary education, service levels are highest where there is the greatest incidence of adults with at least a high school education. Perhaps the parents' concern for education makes itself felt on their children and on school personnel; their children may be well prepared for school, and they may stimulate administrators to provide a high-quality program. Highway mileage per capita varies directly with the incidence of motor vehicles, while road safety varies inversely with the incidence of vehicles. Perhaps high levels of traffic produce more accidents and, through intermediate influence on the political process, more road mileage.

THE GENERAL ASSESSMENT OF ADMINISTRATIVE OUTPUT: DO WE LIKE WHAT GOVERNMENT IS DOING?

For some readers, the questions about administrative output will not end with the issues of cost-and-benefit calculations, the success of regulatory programs, or the payoffs of government spending. Other concerns deal with more basic issues of legitimacy in the actions of governments: the pursuit for many years of a war halfway around the world in Southeast Asia; the elaboration of welfare programs that consume billions of dollars, support huge, impersonal bureaucracies, and still leave millions of recipients with little income, hope, or self-respect; a growing fear of crime that has ended casual strolling on many city streets and made suburbanites turn their homes into fortresses. In the discussion of the Minnowbrook perspective (pp. 204–206), we saw that some observers would deal with our social problems by allowing more freedom of action to working administrators. But in the treatment of administrative discretion, we saw the problems of free-wheeling officials who exercise some discretion not permitted by the law, or who make their decisions in a manner that discriminates against people on the basis of social status, race, or wealth (see pp. 153–54).

Many of our problems result from the actions or inactions of administrators. However, in the era when *Watergate* means wrongdoing in high places, it is important to remember that administrators are not solely responsible for the shortcomings of government. Virtually all of the scandal emanating from the 1972 campaign centered on the Executive Office of the President, i.e., the *executive* branch.

Some problems reflect conditions that administrators or other officials cannot control within the framework of current practice. Much poverty and related social problems stem from personal difficulties that seem unamenable to any known social technology that would be politically acceptable. To the extent that popular aspirations for social programs develop more rapidly than program accomplishments, then dissatisfaction can grow even while accomplishments also grow. A widely read and controversial book, *The Unheavenly City Revisited,* argues that residents of big city ghettos have never had it so good with regard to income, education, housing, and police service, even while these same people have never been so frustrated and angered by an existence they find less-than-acceptable.[18]

SUMMARY

The "outputs" of administrative systems include the services rendered to the public; agency expenditures and policies concerning staff and physical facilities; the information and advice given to the public and to officials in the legislative and executive branches; financial and technical assistance given to the administrators of other governments; the distribution of tax costs and service benefits to various groups in the population; and the regulation of private industry. The outputs of one moment affect the environment and help shape subsequent "inputs." The services rendered to the public satisfy some needs and leave others unsatisfied and thereby influence subsequent demands. Intergovernmental payments likewise meet some needs more than they do others. They generate some requests for "more of the same" and other demands for additions to or modifications in current programs. Information and advice given to other governmental officials often return to administrators in the form of statutes, executive orders, budget authorizations, or committee reports.

Our concern with the administrative system should not end with a simple description of outputs. A curious reader will ask: "What difference do they make?" Present knowledge allows only partial answers to this question. We can list the kinds of information that administrators provide to the public and to other government officials, but we have no

---

18. Edward C. Banfield, *The Unheavenly City Revisited* (Boston: Little, Brown, 1974).

systematic information about the impact of this information on the actions of the recipients. We can identify the kinds of governments that make relatively great (and little) use of intergovernmental programs. Our information is not good enough, however, for us to predict with any certainty what individual governments will do in response to new programs. Present generalizations are hedged by many deviant cases. In the case of some outputs, we know enough to be skeptical. Ralph Nader reminds us that regulatory statutes are not self-enforcing. Government expenditures were long thought to be the key ingredients in the production of public services. Yet, we are now aware that numerous other outputs—and some features of the environment—also have effects on the services that actually are made available. We realize that an expenditure —or any other single policy—by itself is not likely to produce the intended kind of service. Finally, the satisfaction of public desires depends on aspirations, as well as achievements. To the extent that outputs are evaluated in terms of their meeting demands, the administrator is never likely to satisfy all the judges among the citizens. This book cannot be read as the final description of public administration or related phenomena; but it should impress the student with the sparse nature of knowledge, and to provoke the discovery of more.

Suggestions for Additional Reading

1. THE STUDY OF PUBLIC ADMINISTRATION AND PUBLIC POLICY

Caiden, Gerald. *The Dynamics of Public Administration: Guidelines to Current Transformations in Theory and Practice.* New York: Holt, 1971.

Gerth, H. H., and Mills, C. Wright, eds. *From Max Weber.* New York: Oxford University Press, 1946.

Marini, Frank, ed. *Toward a New Public Administration.* San Francisco: Chandler, 1971.

Ostrom, Vincent. *The Intellectual Crisis in American Public Administration.* University, Ala.: University of Alabama Press, 1974.

Ranney, Austin, ed. *Political Science and Public Policy.* Chicago: Markham, 1968.

Reagan, Michael, ed. *The Administration of Public Policy.* Glenview, Ill.: Scott, Foresman, 1969.

Sharkansky, Ira, ed. *Policy Analysis in Political Science.* Chicago: Markham, 1970.

Simon, Herbert A.; Smithburg, David W.; and Thompson, Victor A. *Public Administration.* New York: Knopf, 1950.

Smith, Bruce L. R., ed. *The New Political Economy: The Public Use of the Private Sector.* London: Macmillan & Co., 1975.

Wade, L. L., and Curry, R. L. *A Logic of Public Policy: Aspects of Political Economy.* Belmont, Calif.: Wadsworth, 1970.

2. COMPARISON IN THE STUDY OF PUBLIC ADMINISTRATION

Aledman, Irma; and Morris, Cynthia Taft. *Society, Politics, and Economic Development.* Baltimore: Johns Hopkins, 1967.

Armstrong, John A. *The European Administrative Elite*. Princeton, N.J.: Princeton University Press, 1973.

Armstrong, John A. *The Soviet Bureaucratic Elite*. London: Stevens, 1959.

Campbell, Alan K., and Sachs, Seymour. *Metropolitan America: Fiscal Patterns and Governmental Systems*. New York: Free Press, 1967.

Chapman, Brian. *The Profession of Government*. London: Allen and Unwin, 1959.

Cockroft, James D., et al. *Dependence and Underdevelopment: Latin America's Political Economy*. Garden City, N.Y.: Anchor, 1972.

Crozier, Michel. *The Bureaucratic Phenomenon*. Chicago: University of Chicago Press, 1964.

Daland, Robert T., ed. *Comparative Urban Research: The Administration and Politics of Cities*. Beverly Hills, Calif.: Sage, 1969.

Due, John F. *State Sales Tax Administration*. Chicago: Public Administration Service, 1963.

Dye, Thomas R. *Politics, Economics, and the Public: Policy Outcomes in the American States*. Chicago: Rand McNally, 1966.

Eyestone, Robert. *The Threads of Public Policy: A Study in Policy Leadership*. Indianapolis: Bobbs-Merrill, 1971.

Fischer, Glenn W. *Taxes and Politics: A Study of Public Finance*. Urbana: University of Illinois Press, 1969.

Gupta, K. R. *Issues in Public Enterprise*. Delhi: S. Chand, 1969.

Heady, Ferrel. *Public Administration: A Comparative Perspective*. Englewood Cliffs, N.J.: Prentice-Hall, 1966.

Hirschman, A. O. *The Strategy of Economic Development*. New Haven, Conn.: Yale University Press, 1968.

Hirschman, A. O. *Journeys Toward Progress*. New York: Twentieth-Century Fund, 1963.

Huntington, Samuel P. *Political Order in Changing Societies*. New Haven, Conn.: Yale University Press, 1960.

Jacob, Herbert, and Vines, Kenneth N., eds. *Politics in the American States: A Comparative Analysis*. Rev. ed. Boston: Little, Brown, 1971.

LaPalombara, Joseph. *Bureaucracy and Political Development*. Princeton, N.J.: Princeton University Press, 1963.

Montgomery, John D., and Siffin, William J., eds. *Approaches to Development*. New York: McGraw-Hill, 1966.

Myrdal, Gunnar. *Asian Drama: An Inquiry Into the Poverty of Nations* New York: Twentieth Century Fund, 1969.

Peacock, Alan T., and Wiseman, Jack. *The Growth of Public Expenditure in the United Kingdom*. London: Allen and Unwin, 1967.

Penniman, Clara, and Heller, Walter W. *State Income Tax Administration.* Chicago: Public Administration Service, 1959.

Pye, Lucian W. *Aspects of Political Development.* Boston: Little, Brown, 1966.

Riggs, Fred W. *Administration in Developing Countries: The Theory of Prismatic Society.* Boston: Houghton Mifflin, 1964.

Rostow, W. W. *Politics and the Stages of Growth.* London: Cambridge University Press, 1971.

Rothwell, Kenneth J., ed. *Administrative Issues in Developing Economies,* Lexington, Mass.: Heath, 1922.

Sharkansky, Ira. *Regionalism in American Politics.* Indianapolis: Bobbs-Merrill, 1970.

Sharkansky, Ira. *Spending in the American States.* Chicago: Rand McNally, 1968.

Sharkansky, Ira. *The United States: A Study of a Developing Country.* New York: McKay, 1975.

3. DECISION-MAKING IN ADMINISTRATIVE AGENCIES

Braybrooke, David, and Lindblom, Charles E. *A Strategy of Decision.* New York: Free Press, 1963.

Cole, H. S. D., et al. *Models of Doom: A Critique of the Limits to Growth.* New York: Universe, 1973.

Crecine, John P. *Government Problem-Solving: A Computer Simulation of Municipal Budgeting.* Chicago: Rand McNally, 1969.

Cyert, Richard M., and March, James G. *A Behavioral Theory of the Firm.* Englewood Cliffs, N.J.: Prentice-Hall, 1963.

Davis, Morris, and Weinbaum, Marvin G. *Metropolitan Decision Processes: An Analysis of Case Studies.* Chicago: Rand McNally, 1969.

Deutsch, Karl. *The Nerves of Government.* New York: Free Press, 1963.

Dorfman, Robert, ed. *Measuring Benefits of Government Investment.* Washington, D.C.: Brookings Institution, 1965.

Downs, Anthony. *Inside Bureaucracy.* Boston: Little, Brown, 1967.

Dror, Yehezkel. *Public Policymaking Reexamined.* San Francisco: Chandler, 1968.

Gore, William J. *Administrative Decision-Making: A Heuristic Model.* New York: Wiley, 1964.

Gore, William J., and Dyson, James W., eds. *The Making of Decisions: A Reader in Administrative Behavior.* New York: Free Press, 1964.

Lindblom, Charles E. *The Policy-Making Process.* Englewood Cliffs, N.J.: Prentice-Hall, 1968.

Logsdon, John M. *The Decision to Go to the Moon: Project Apollo and the National Interest.* Cambridge, Mass.: MIT Press, 1970.

Lyden, Fremont J., and Miller, Ernest G. *Planning-Programming-Budgeting: A Systems Approach to Management.* Chicago: Markham, 1968.

March, James G., ed. *Handbook of Organizations.* Chicago: Rand Mc-Nally, 1965.

March, James G., and Simon, Herbert A. *Organizations.* New York: Wiley, 1958.

Meadows, Donella H., et al. *The Limits to Growth.* New York: Universe, 1972.

Merewitz, Leonard, and Sosnick, Stephen H. *The Budget's New Clothes: A Critique of Planning-Programming-Budgeting and Benefit-Cost Analysis.* Chicago: Markham, 1971.

Rabinovitz, Francine F. *City Politics and Planning.* New York: Atherton, 1969.

Sharkansky, Ira. *The Routines of Politics.* New York: Van Nostrand Reinhold, 1970.

Thompson, Victor A. *Modern Organization: A General Theory.* New York: Knopf, 1961.

Wise, David. *The Politics of Lying: Government Deception, Secrecy, and Power.* New York: Vintage, 1973.

4. ADMINISTRATIVE ORGANIZATION AND ADMINISTRATIVE CONTROL UNITS

Blau, Peter M. *Bureaucracy in Modern Society.* New York: Random House, 1956.

Blau, Peter M., and Scott, W. Richard. *Formal Organizations.* San Francisco: Chandler, 1962.

Brown, Richard E. *The GAO: Untapped Source of Congressional Power.* Knoxville: University of Tennessee Press, 1970.

Dahl, Robert A. *Pluralist Democracy in the United States.* Chicago: Rand McNally, 1966.

Davis, James W., Jr., *The National Executive Branch.* New York: Free Press, 1970.

Davis, Kenneth C. *Discretionary Justice: A Preliminary Inquiry*. Urbana: University of Illinois Press, 1971.

Huntington, Samuel P. *The Soldier and the States: The Theory and Politics of Civil-Military Relations*. New York: Vintage, 1964.

Karl, Barry. *Executive Reorganization and Reform in the New Deal*. Cambridge, Mass.: Harvard University Press, 1963.

Redford, Emmette S. *Democracy in the Administrative State*. New York: Oxford University Press, 1969.

Seidman, Harold. *Politics, Position and Power: The Dynamics of Federal Organization*. New York: Oxford University Press, 1970.

Shapiro, Marshall. *The Supreme Court and Administrative Agencies*. New York: Free Press. 1968.

Smith, Bruce L. R. *The Rand Corporation*. Cambridge, Mass.: Harvard University Press, 1966.

Wilensky, Harold L. *Organizational Intelligence: Knowledge and Policy in Government and Industry*. New York: Basic Books, 1967.

5. THE PERSONNEL OF ADMINISTRATIVE AGENCIES

David, Paul T., and Pollock, Ross. *Executives for Government*. Washington, D.C.: Brookings Institution, 1957.

Golembiewski, Robert T., and Cohen, Michael, eds. *People in Public Service: A Reader in Public Personnel Administration*. Itasca, Ill.: Peacock, 1970.

Janowitz, Morris. *The Professional Soldier*. New York: Free Press, 1960.

Krislov, Samuel. *The Negro in Federal Employment: The Quest for Equal Opportunity*. Minneapolis: University of Minnesota Press, 1967.

Mann, Dean E. *The Assistant Secretaries: Problems and Processes of Appointment*. Washington, D.C.: Brookings Institution, 1965.

Mosher, Frederick C. *Democracy and the Public Service*. New York: Oxford University Press, 1968.

Stahl, O. Glenn. *Public Personnel Administration*. Rev. ed. New York: Harper & Row, 1970.

Stanley, David T. *The Higher Civil Service*. Washington, D.C.: Brookings Institution, 1964.

Stanley, David T., et al. *Men Who Govern: A Biographical Profile of Federal Political Executives*. Washington, D.C.: Brookings Institution, 1967.

Van Riper, Paul T. *History of the United States Civil Service.* Evanston, Ill.: Row, Peterson, 1958.

U.S. Civil Rights Commission. *For All the People ... By All the People: A Report on Equal Opportunity in State and Local Government Employment.* Washington, D.C.: U.S. Government Printing Office, 1969.

Warner, W. Lloyd, et al. *The American Federal Executive.* New Haven, Conn.: Yale University Press. 1963.

6. THE MANAGEMENT OF GOVERNMENT AGENCIES

Argyris, Chris. *Organization and Innovation.* Homewood, Ill.: Irwin, 1965.

Bennis, Warren. *Beyond Bureaucracy: Essays on the Development and Evolution of Human Organization.* New York: McGraw-Hill, 1973.

Caiden, Gerald. *Administrative Reform.* Chicago: Aldine, 1969.

Dvorken, Eugene P.; and Simmons, Robert H. *From Amoral to Humane Bureaucracy.* San Francisco: Canfield, 1972.

Etzioni, Amitai. *Modern Organizations.* Englewood Cliffs, N. J.: Prentice-Hall, 1964.

Gawthrop, Louis C. *Bureaucratic Behavior in the Executive Branch: An Analysis of Organizational Change.* New York: Free Press, 1969.

Golembiewski, Robert T. *Men, Management, and Morality: Toward a New Organizational Ethic.* New York: McGraw-Hill, 1965.

Gross, Bertram M. *Organizations and Their Managing.* New York: Free Press, 1968.

Homans, George. *The Human Group.* New York: Harcourt, Brace, 1950.

Kaufman, Herbert. *Administrative Feedback: Monitoring Subordinates' Behavior.* Washington, D.C.: Brookings Institution, 1973.

Kaufman, Herbert. *The Forest Ranger: A Study in Administrative Behavior.* Baltimore: Johns Hopkins University Press, 1960.

Mouzelis, Nicos P. *Organization and Bureaucracy: An Analysis of Modern Theories.* Chicago: Aldine, 1969.

Schein, Edgar H. *Organizational Psychology.* Englewood Cliffs, N.J.: Prentice-Hall, 1965.

Whyte, William H. *The Organization Man.* New York: Simon and Schuster, 1956.

Zeigler, Harmon. *The Political Life of American Teachers.* Englewood Cliffs, N.J.: Prentice-Hall, 1967.

7. THE STATUS OF PUBLIC ADMINISTRATION

Aberbach, Joel, and Walker, Jack L. *Race in the City: Political Trust and Public Policy in the New Urban System*. Boston: Little, Brown, 1973.

Appleby, Paul H. *Big Democracy*. New York: Knopf, 1945.

Gilmour, Robert S.; and Lamb, Robert B. *Political Alienation in Contemporary America*. New York: St. Martin's, 1975.

Janowitz, Morris, et al. *Public Administration and the Public*. Ann Arbor: University of Michigan Institute of Public Administration, 1958.

Kilpatrick, Franklin P., et al. *The Image of the Federal Service*. Washington, D.C.: Brookings Institution, 1964.

Long, Norton E. *The Polity*. Chicago: Rand McNally, 1962.

Long, Norton E. *The Unwalled City: Reconstituting the Urban Community*. New York: Basic Books, 1972.

Parkinson, C. Northcote. *Parkinson's Law and Other Studies in Administration*. Boston: Houghton Mifflin, 1957.

Peter, Lawrence J., and Hull, Raymond. *The Peter Principle: Why Things Always Go Wrong*. New York: Bantam, 1969.

Woll, Peter. *American Bureaucracy*. New York: Norton, 1963.

8. CITIZEN DEMANDS AND ADMINISTRATIVE AGENCIES

Alford, Robert R. *Bureaucracy and Participation: Political Cultures in Four Wisconsin Cities*. Chicago: Rand McNally, 1969.

Almond, Gabriel, and Verba, Sidney. *The Civil Culture*. Princeton, N.J.: Princeton University Press, 1963.

Altschuler, Alan A. *Community Control*. New York: Pegasus, 1970.

Burns, James M. *The Deadlock of Democracy: Four-Party Politics in America*. Englewood Cliffs, N.J.: Prentice-Hall, Spectrum Books, 1963.

Cater, Douglass. *Power in Washington*. New York: Vintage, 1964.

Caudill, Harry M. *Night Comes to the Cumberlands: A Biography of a Depressed Area*. Boston: Little, Brown, 1963.

Chittick, Wililam O. *State Department, Press, and Pressure Groups*. New York: Wiley, 1970.

Cole, Richard C. *Citizen Participation and the Urban Political Process*. Lexington, Mass.: Heath, 1974.

Devine, Donald J. *The Attentive Public: Polyarchal Democracy.* Chicago: Rand McNally, 1970.

Elazar, Daniel J. *American Federalism: A View from the States.* New York: Crowell, 1972.

Fowler, Floyd J. Jr., *Citizen Attitudes Toward Local Government Services and Taxes.* Cambridge, Mass.: Ballinger, 1974.

Haider, Donald H. *When Governments Come to Washington: Governors, Mayors, and Intergovernmental Lobbying.* New York: Free Press, 1974.

Lamb, Curt. *Political Power in Four Neighborhoods.* New York: Wiley, 1975.

Lipsky, Michael. *Protest in City Politics: Rent Strikes, Housing, and the Power of the Poor.* Chicago: Rand McNally, 1970.

Lowi, Theodore J. *The End of Liberalism.* New York: Norton, 1969.

Milbrath, Lester W. *The Washington Lobbyists.* Chicago: Rand McNally, 1963.

Olson, Mancur, Jr. *The Logic of Collective Action: Public Goods and the Theory of Groups.* Cambridge, Mass.: Harvard University Press, 1965.

Rourke, Francis E. *Bureaucracy, Politics, and Public Policy.* Boston: Little, Brown, 1969.

Salisbury, Robert H., ed. *Interest Group Politics in America.* New York: Harper & Row, 1970.

Scammon, Richard M., and Wattenberg, Ben J. *The Real Majority.* New York: Coward-McCann, 1970.

Selznick, Philip *T.V.A. and the Grass Roots.* Berkeley: University of California Press, 1949.

Truman, David B. *The Governmental Process.* New York: Knopf, 1951.

Watts, William, and Free, Lloyd A., eds. *State of the Nation.* New York: Universe, 1973.

Yates, Douglas. *Neighborhood Government.* Lexington, Mass.: Heath, 1973.

Zeigler, Harmon, and Baer, Michael. *Lobbying: Interaction and Influence in American State Legislatures.* Belmont, Calif.: Wadsworth, 1969.

9. EXECUTIVES, LEGISLATORS, AND ADMINISTRATORS

Anderson, Patrick. *The Presidents' Men.* Garden City, N.Y: Doubleday, Anchor Books, 1969.

Anton, Thomas J. *The Politics of State Expenditures in Illinois*. Urbana: University of Illinois Press, 1966.

Art, Rovert J. *The TFX Decision*. Boston: Little, Brown, 1968.

Bauer, Raymond; Pool, Ithiel de Sola; and Dexter, Lewis A. *American Business and Public Policy: The Politics of Foreign Trade*. New York: Atherton, 1963.

Cronin, Thomas E., and Greenberg, Sanford D., eds. *The Presidential Advisory System*. New York: Harper & Row, 1969.

Eulau, Heinz, and Quinley, Harold. *State Officials and Higher Education: A Survey of the Opinions and Expectations of Policy Makers in Nine States*. New York: McGraw-Hill, 1970.

Fenno, Richard F., Jr. *The Power of the Purse: Appropriations Politics in Congress*. Boston: Little, Brown, 1966.

Fenno, Richard F., Jr. *The President's Cabinet*. Cambridge, Mass.: Harvard University Press, 1959.

Freeman, J. Leiper. *The Political Process*. Rev. ed. New York: Random House, 1965.

Heller, Walter W. *New Dimensions of Political Economy*. New York: Norton, 1967.

Hitch, Charles J. *Decision-Making for Defense*. Berkeley: University of California Press, 1965.

Holtzman, Abraham. *Legislative Liaison: Executive Leadership in the Congress*. Chicago: Rand McNally, 1970.

Hyneman, Charles S. *Bureaucracy in a Democracy*. New York: Harper, 1950.

Loveridge, Ronald O. *City Managers in Legislative Politics*. Indianapolis: Bobbs-Merrill, 1972.

Manley, John F. *The Politics of Finance: The House Committee on Ways and Means*. Boston: Little, Brown, 1970.

Neustadt, Richard. *Presidential Power: The Politics of Leadership*. New York: Wiley, 1976.

Pierce, Lawrence C. *The Politics of Fiscal Policy Formation*. Pacific Palisades, Calif.: Goodyear, 1971.

Sayre, Wallace, and Kaufman, Herbert. *Governing New York City: Politics in the Metropolis*. New York: Russell Sage, 1960.

Schilling, Warner R., et al. *Strategy, Politics, and Defense Budgets*. New York: Columbia University Press, 1962.

Sharkansky, Ira. *The Politics of Taxing and Spending*. Indianapolis: Bobbs-Merrill, 1969.

Sorensen, Theodore C. *Decision-Making in the White House*. New York: Columbia University Press, 1963.

Sundquist, James L. *Politics and Policy: The Eisenhower, Kennedy, and Johnson Years.* Washington, D.C.: Brookings Institution, 1968.

Talbot, Allan R. *The Mayor's Game: Richard Lee of New Haven and the Politics of Change.* New York: Praeger, 1970.

Wildavsky, Aaron. *Politics of the Budgetary Process.* Boston: Little, Brown, 1964.

Williams, T. Harry. *Huey Long.* Boston: Little, Brown, 1969.

Yessne, Peter, ed. *Quotations from Mayor Daley.* New York: Pocket Books, 1969.

10. INTERGOVERNMENTAL RELATIONS

Anderson, Martin. *The Federal Bulldozer.* New York: McGraw-Hill, 1964.

Beer, Samuel H., and Barringer, Richard E., eds. *The State and the Poor.* Cambridge, Mass.: Winthrop, 1970.

Davis, James W., Jr., and Dolbeare, Kenneth M. *Little Groups of Neighbors: The Selective Service System.* Chicago: Markham, 1968.

Derthick, Martha. *The Influence of Federal Grants.* Cambridge, Mass.: Harvard University Press, 1970.

Freedman, Leonard. *Public Housing: The Politics of Poverty.* New York: Holt, 1969.

Graves, W. Brooke. *American Intergovernmental Relations.* New York: Scribners, 1964.

Hansen, Niles. *Rural Poverty and the Urban Crisis.* Bloomington: University of Indiana Press, 1970.

Heller, Walter W., ed. *Revenue-Sharing and the City.* Baltimore: Johns Hopkins University Press, 1968.

Key, V. O., Jr. *The Administration of Federal Grants to the States.* Chicago: Public Administration Service, 1939.

Martin, Roscoe. *The Cities and the Federal System.* New York: Atherton, 1965.

Musgrave, Richard A. *Essays on Fiscal Federalism.* Washington, D.C.: Brookings Institution, 1965.

Patterson, James T. *The New Deal and the States: Federalism in Transition.* Princeton, N.J.: Princeton University Press, 1969.

Reagan, Michael D. *The New Federalism.* New York: Oxford University Press, 1972.

Reuss, Henry S. *Revenue-Sharing: Crutch or Catalyst for State and Local Governments?* New York: Praeger, 1970.

Sharkansky, Ira. *The Maligned States: Policy Accomplishments, Problems, and Opportunities.* New York: McGraw-Hill, 1972.

Sundquist, James L. *Making Federalism Work.* Washington, D.C.: Brookings Institution, 1969.

Wolman, Harold. *Politics of Federal Housing.* New York: Dodd, Mead, 1971.

Wood, Robert C. *1400 Governments.* Garden City, N.Y.: Doubleday, Anchor Books, 1964.

Wright, Deil S. *Federal Grants-In-Aid: Perspectives and Alternatives.* Washington, D.C.: American Enterprise Institute for Policy Research, 1968.

11. VARIETIES OF ADMINISTRATIVE OUTPUTS

Banfield, Edward C. *The Unheavenly City Revisited.* Boston: Little, Brown, 1974.

Bauer, Raymond. *Social Indicators.* Cambridge, Mass.: MIT Press, 1967.

Bish, Robert L. *The Public Economy of Metropolitan Areas.* Chicago: Markham, 1971.

Campbell, Alan, ed. *The States and the Urban Crisis.* Englewood Cliffs, N.J.: Prentice-Hall, 1970.

Coleman, James S., et al. *Equality of Educational Opportunity.* Washington, D.C.: U.S. Government Printing Office, 1966.

Cox, Edward F., et al. *Nader's Raiders.* New York: Grove Press, 1969.

Davis, Frank G. *The Economics of Black Community Development: An Analysis and Program for Autonomous Growth and Development.* Chicago: Markham, 1972.

Dye, Thomas R. *The Politics of Equality.* Indianapolis: Bobbs-Merrill, 1971.

Edelman, Murray. *The Symbolic Uses of Politics.* Urbana: University of Illinois Press, 1964.

Enloe, Cynthia H. *The Politics of Pollution in a Comparative Perspective: Ecology and Power in Four Nations.* New York: McKay, 1975.

Esposito, John C. *Vanishing Air.* New York: Grossman, 1970.

Fellmeth, Robert. *The Interstate Commerce Omission.* New York: Grossman, 1970.

Gardner, John A. *The Politics of Corruption: Organized Crime in an American City.* New York: Russell Sage, 1970.

Gross, Bertram M., ed. *Social Intelligence for America's Future: Explorations in Societal Problems*. Boston: Allyn and Bacon, 1969.

Hansen, W. Lee, and Weisbrod, Burton A. *Benefits, Costs, and Finance of Public Higher Education*. Chicago: Markham, 1969.

Haveman, Robert H., and Margolis, Julius, eds. *Public Expenditures and Policy Analysis*. Chicago: Markham, 1970.

Holt, Robert T., and Turner, John E. *The Political Basis of Economic Development: An Exploration in Comparative Political Analysis*. New York: Van Nostrand, 1966.

Miller, S. M., and Roby, Pamela. *The Future of Inequality*. New York: Basic Books, 1970.

National Advisory Commission on Civil Disorders. *Report*. New York: Bantam Books, 1968.

Neenan, William B. *Political Economy of Urban Areas*. Chicago: Markham, 1972.

Netzer, Dick. *Economics of the Property Tax*. Washington, D.C.: Brookings Institution, 1966.

Pechman, Joseph A. *Federal Tax Policy*. New York: Norton, 1971.

Phelan, James, and Posen, Robert. *The Company State*. New York: Grossman, 1973.

Russett, Bruce M. *What Price Vigilance? The Burdens of National Defense*. New Haven, Conn.: Yale University Press, 1970.

Smigel, Erwin O., and Ross, H. Laurence. *Crimes Against Bureaucracy*. New York: Van Nostrand Reinhold, 1970.

Sowell, Thomas. *Race and Economics*. New York: McKay, 1975.

Steiner, Gilbert Y. *Social Insecurity: The Politics of Welfare*. Chicago: Rand McNally, 1966.

Turner, James S. *The Chemical Feast*. New York: Grossman, 1970.

Index

Aberbach, Joel D., 34, 222
Acquisitiveness, 285
ACTION (American Council to Improve our Neighborhoods), 136, 177
Adams, John Quincy, 215
Administrative agencies. *See* Administrative units
Administrative branch, 16
Administrative coherence, 33–38
Administrative control, 130–48, 156, 187–209
Administrative courts, 32. *See also* Judicial mechanisms for administrative control
Administrative growth: in use of discretion, 154; intellectual roots of, 104–12; physical growth, 148–53, 260, 268–69
Administrative hybrids, 127–29, 253
Administrative organization, 101–4, 112–29, 155–56
Administrative system, 7–8, 13–15, 17–18, 101–4, 112–29, 155–56. *See also* Borders; Comparative analysis; Conversion process; Environment; Feedback; Inputs; Outputs; Withinputs
Administrative units, 16, 42, 112, 148–53, 155–56
Administrators. *See* Public administrators.
Advisory Commission on Intergovernmental Relations (ACIR), 314–15

Affirmative action, 177, 293
AFL-CIO, 166, 247
Africa, 38, 45, 69
Agency for International Development (AID), 16, 51
Agnew, Spiro, 235, 240
Agriculture, Department of, 119, 179, 233, 234
Air Force, 294, 332, 333, 336–37
Alabama, 22, 23, 85, 143, 316, 350
Alaska, 21, 22, 316, 350
Albuquerque, 237
Alesch, Daniel J., 35
Algeria, 44
Alliance for Progress, 50
Almond, Gabriel, 14, 42
American Civil Liberties Union, 166
American Federation of State, County, and Municipal Employees, 164
American Federation of Teachers, 164
American Institute of Architects, 247
American Printing House for the Blind, 123
Anton, Thomas J., 83, 143, 283, 284
Appalachian Region, 52, 224
Appropriations committees, 137–38, 278, 280–81, 282
Arizona, 22, 52, 274, 316, 327
Arkansas, 23, 52, 316, 331, 350
Armed forces. *See* Defense, Department of; Military
Army Corps of Engineers. *See* Corps of Engineers
Arthur, Chester A., 216

Asia, 38, 45, 69. *See also* Less-developed countries
Aspirations in administrative units, 181–84
Atlanta, 130, 237, 329
Attitudes toward public administrators, 212–13, 217–27
Auditor, 288–90
Australia, 31
Authority, 189–91

"Baby boom," 71
Bailey, Thomas, 195
Baltimore, 237
Banda, Hastings, 47
Banfield, Edward C., 223, 238, 251, 302, 358
Barber, James D., 197
Bartlett, Joseph W., 120
Bauer, Raymond, 241
Bernstein, Marvin, 241, 352
Blacks, 176–80. *See also* Philadelphia Plan
Bloc grants, 310. *See also* Intergovernmental relations
Bolivia, 44
Borders of administrative system, 16–17, 55, 120, 129
Boston, 237
Bowles, Chester, 168
Boyer, William W., 242
Brazer, Harvey E., 26
Brazil, 43
Brevard County, Florida, 333, 334, 335, 336
British Commonwealth, 31
Brogan, D. W., 252
Brookings Institution, 158–59, 160–61, 220–23
Brown, David S., 267
Brown, Edmund G., Gov., 88
Brown, Lester R., 126
Brown, Richard E., 289
Brownell, Herbert, 167
Bruhs, F. C., 35
Buck, A. E., 111

Budget: activities, 91–98, 296–97; Congressional budget calendar, 278, 279; Congressional committees, 278; effect of feedback on, 13; reforms, 278–81. *See also* Incremental budgeting; Planning-programming-budgeting (PPB)
Budgeting and Accounting Act of 1950, 91
Budget relations among legislators, executives, and administrators, 275–90
Burch, Philip C., 88
Bureau of the Budget, 133–34. *See also* Office of Management and Budget (OMB)
Bureau of Employment Security, 130
Bureau of Work Programs, 130
Bureaucracy, 16, 217–18, 222
Bureaucratic elite. *See* Elite
Bureaupathic behavior, 67–68
Burkhead, Jesse, 88
Burns, James MacGregor, 248

Cabinet, 112, 114–20, 167, 168, 266, 269. *See also* Cabinet departments by name
Caiden, G. E., 51
California, 22, 24, 45, 95–97, 316, 318, 323, 327, 330, 350
Calmfors, Hans, 35
Campbell, Alan K., 27
Canada, 31, 45, 327
Cape Kennedy, 332–37
Career routes, 173–76
Carter, Jimmy, 50, 88, 98, 114, 119, 167, 169
Cater, Douglas, 244
Cazzola, F., 35
Central Intelligence Agency (CIA), 127, 169
Centralization, 46–47
Checks and balances/separation of powers, 107–9, 141, 170, 288–91, 294–95
Chicago, 36–37, 204, 253, 327, 329

Chief executive, 61, 249–50, 267–68, 273–74, 303. *See also* Executive-administrative relations; President
Children's Bureau, 119
Chile, 45
Cikins, Warren I., 179, 180
Citizens demands, 228–58. *See also* Resources; Supports
Citizens' Crusade against Poverty, 234
City-commission form of government, 146, 147–48
Civil Aernonautics Board, 121
Civil Rights Act of 1964, 292–93. *See also* Commission on Civil Rights
Civil service, 66, 106, 109, 253
Civil Service Commission, 124, 139–40, 142, 155, 160–62, 178, 179, 216
Civil War, 216
Clark, Calvin W., 141
Clark, Joseph S., 234
Classical theory of management. *See* Scientific management
Clay, Lucius, 167
Cleveland, Frederick, 111
Cleveland, Ohio, 130
Cnudde, Charles F., 27, 212
Coastal Plains Regional Commission, 52
Cole, H. S. D., 72, 73
Cole, Richard L., 231
Coleman, James S., 356
Collective bargaining, 156, 163–66
Colorado, 52, 316, 327, 330, 350
Commerce, Department of, 114
Commission on Civil Rights, 179, 180
Commission on Economy and Efficiency, 111
Commitments, 59–61, 64–65
Committee on Administrative Management, 111, 132
Commodity Credit Corporation, 122
Communications, 102–93
Community action programs, 127, 232, 349–51
Community development, department proposed, 119

Comparative analysis: cross-nationally, 28–53; within U.S., 21–28, 44–53, 144–45
Comptroller general, 138
Concentration, 46–47
Conflict within administrative agencies. *See* Administrative conflict
Conflict-of-interest screening, 170
Congress, 108, 122, 123, 124, 133, 134, 144, 168, 233, 247. *See also* Legislative branch
Congressional Budget Committee, 138
Congressional Budget and Improvement Control Act of 1974, 278, 295
Congressional Budget Office, 92, 138, 278
Congressional committees, 136–38, 262–63, 270, 280–81. *See also* specific names
Congressional oversight, 270, 273
Connecticut, 22, 52, 316, 318, 350
Conservation. *See* Growth vs. conservation
Constituents, 219, 242, 261, 265–66
Constitution, U.S., 107–8, 166, 168, 213, 259–60
Constitutions, state, 321–22
Consumerism and accountability, 206–8
Conversion process, 7, 10–11, 54–209
Cook County Democratic party, 37
Coolidge, Calvin, 243
Corps of Engineers, 123, 333, 45, 346–47
Corruption, 39–40, 251–52
Costa Rica, 44
Cost-benefit analysis, 95–97, 273. *See also* Planning-programming-budgeting (PPB)
Costs of incoherence, 36–38
Council-manager form of government, 146–47
Council of Economic Advisors, 132, 134–36, 155
Council of State Governments, 141, 145, 329

Council on Environmental Quality, 136

Cox, Edward F., 352, 353

Crecine, John P., 84

Cronin, Thomas E., 128

Crozier, Michael, 203

Cuba, 45

Cuban missile crisis, 337

Cumberland, John H., 52

Cummings, Milton C., Jr., 220

Cyert, Richard M., 61, 64, 76, 77

Dade County, Florida, 327–28

Dahl, Robert A., 239

Daley, Richard J., 36–37, 38, 253

Dallas, 329

Davis, James W., Jr., 134, 192, 197

Davis, Kenneth C., 154

Davis, Otto A., 270

Dawson, Richard E., 24

Decision-making, 56–100. *See also* Rational decision-making

Decision rules, 79–91, 99

Defense, Department of, 118, 127, 243, 271, 291–93, 308

Defense Education Act of 1957, 307

Delaney, William, 221

Delaware, 22, 24, 316, 318, 330, 350

Demands, 211, 219–20, 228–58

Dempster, M. A. H., 270

Denver, 237

Depression, 90, 132, 149–53, 253, 307, 308, 312

de Tocqueville, Alexis, 215, 302

Detroit, 180, 254

Deutsch, Karl W., 15, 193

Development, 29–30; development administration, 50. *See also* Less-developed countries; More-developed countries

Dewey, Thomas, 167

Discretion, administrative, 153–54, 156, 240–41, 256, 357

District of Columbia, 139, 166, 178

Domestic Council, 132, 135–36, 268

Dominant-party mobilization, 43, 44

Douglas, H. St. Angelo, 107

Downs, Anthony, 62, 75, 76

Drew, Elizabeth B., 233

Dye, Thomas R., 14, 24–26, 28, 141, 147

Eastland, James, 234

Easton, David, 14

Economic development, 21–28, 47–49, 119; Economic Development Administration, 130. *See also* Development

Economic influences on policy, 21–28, 44–53, 224–25, 347–51. *See also* Depression

Economic Opportunity, Office of (OEO), 105–6, 127–28, 130, 132, 155, 177, 233 n.8, 269 n.15

Economic Report of the President, 135

Edelman, Murray, 241, 352

Education, 95–97

Education, Office of, 16, 20, 303

Educational background of administrators, 171–73

Egerton, John, 123

Egypt, 44

Ehrlich, Paul, 70

Ehrlichman, John D., 135

Eisenhower, Dwight D., 111, 114, 116, 167, 168, 173, 196, 244, 250, 270, 294, 315

Elazar, Daniel J., 223

Elections, 238–40, 257

Elementary and Secondary Education Act of 1965, 307, 308

Elite, 32, 33, 38, 43, 212

Elms, Alan C., 61

Employment Act of 1946, 134–35

Energy, Department of, 114, 118, 119

Energy Resources Council, 132

Enloe, Cynthia H., 60, 354

Environment, 7, 9–10, 56–57, 60, 84

Environmental Protection Agency, 136, 354

Ervin, Sam, 293

Esman, Sam, 293

Esposito, John C., 352

Etzioni, Amitai, 198, 201, 202, 203
Evaluation. *See* Intergovernmental relations: vertical; Personnel administration
Executive-administrative relations, 47, 65–67, 132–36, 260, 264–75. *See also* Chief executive; Decision-making
Executive branch, 112–13, 132, 259–60, 358
Executive-legislative competition, 98. *See also* Nixon, Richard M., vs. Congress
Executive-legislator-administrator relations, 259–97. *See also* Executive-administrative relations; Executive-legislative competition; Legislative-administrative relations
Executive Office of the President, 92, 112, 127–28, 132, 133, 135–36, 148 n, 155, 358
Executive Seminar Centers, 161
Expenditures, 148–53, 341–42, 355–57, 359
Expertise, 191
Export-Import Bank of Washington, 122

Family background of administrators. *See* Social backgrounds
Faubus, Orval, 47
Featherbedding, 229
Federal aid, 312–15. *See also* Financial aid and technical assistance; Grants-in-aid; Intergovernmental relations
Federal Aid Highway Act, 307
Federal Aviation Agency, 165, 337
Federal Bureau of Investigation (FBI), 14, 243, 260; Uniform Crime Reports, 325
Federal Campaign Act of 1974, 166
Federal Communications Commission (FCC), 121
Federal contracts, 160
Federal courts, 138–39

Federal Crop Insurance Corporation, 122
Federal Deposit Insurance Corporation (FDIC), 122
Federal Executive Institute, 161
Federal government. *See* Federalism
Federal National Mortgage Association, 122
Federal Power Commission, 121
Federal Prison Industries, 122
Federal Reserve Board, 11, 121
Federal Savings and Loan Insurance Corporation, 122
Federal Security Agency, 118, 119. *See also* Health, Education, and Welfare, Department of
Federal-state-local relations. *See* Intergovernmental relations
Federal Trade Commission (FTC), 121, 352–53
Federalism, 301–5
Federalist Papers, 213–14
Federally aided corporations, 123–24
Feedback, 7, 13, 207 n.28, 299
Fellmeth, Robert C., 352, 353, 354
Fenno, Richard F., Jr., 14, 137, 282
Financial aid and technical assistance: domestic, to poor states, 49, 52–53; federal, to state and local, 311–12, 313; international, to poor countries, 49–51
Fish and Wildlife Service, 123
Fisher, Louis, 294
Flexibility, 126
Florida, 22, 85, 142, 316, 329–30, 332–37
Food and Drug Administration (FDA), 122, 352–53
Ford, Gerald R., 50, 98, 136, 240, 269
Forest Service, 119
Formal power, 190, 273–74
Formalism, 41, 42
Formula grants, 309. *See also* Intergovernmental relations
Four Corners Regional Commission, 52
Fowler, Edmund P., 147
Fowler, Floyd J., Jr., 236
Fox, Douglas M., 37

France, 31, 32–33
Frederickson, H. George, 206
Friedman, Robert S., 255
Fry, Bryan R., 28, 349, 350

Gallaudet College, 123
Gawthrop, Louis C., 66
General Accounting Office (GAO),
    124, 138, 143, 155, 288–90, 291–
    94, 296, 297
General Schedule (GS), 159 n. *See
    also* Personnel
Georgia, 22, 45, 85, 143, 316, 329–
    30, 350, 356
Germany, 31, 32–33
Gerth, H. H., 111
Ghana, 47
Gilmour, Robert S., 222, 237
Goals, 57–61, 92–93, 94. *See also*
    Outputs; Policy
Goldwater, Barry, 249
Golembiewski, Robert T., 204
Gore, William J., 80
Government contracts, 124–27
Government corporations, 122–23
Government interest groups, 244–47
Governors, 145, 266, 274, 283–84
Governors' Conference, 328
Grants-in-aid, 91, 160, 304, 306–10,
    338. *See also* Federal aid; Inter-
    governmental relations
Gray, L. Patrick, 243, 260
Great Britain, 31, 32–33, 34
Great Lakes, 326–27
Greece, 44
Greenberg, Sanford D., 128
Grodzins, Morton, 302
Gross domestic product per capita
    (GDP/c), 45
Growth of administrative units. *See*
    Administrative growth
Growth of population, 70–73, 300
Growth of public-employee unions.
    See Collective bargaining
Growth vs. conservation, 69–73
Grumm, John G., 141
Guatemala, 43

Guinea, 44
Gulick, L. H., 199

Hady, Thomas F., 324
Haider, Donald H., 246, 304
Hamilton, Alexander, 213–14
Hansen, W. Lee, 95–97
Harmon, Michael M., 205
Harrington, Michael, 233
Harris, Louis, 237
Hatch Acts, 140, 166
Hawaii, 21, 22, 317, 350
Heady, Ferrel, 30, 32, 43
Health, Education, and Welfare, De-
    partment of, 118, 123, 124, 130,
    177, 236
Hein, Clarence J., 324
Heller, Walter W., 135, 328
Hickman, Martin B., 171
Hierarchical management, 101–4,
    110–12, 112–14, 128, 199
Higher education, 95–97
Hill, Larry B., 37, 256
Hofferbert, Richard I., 25, 27
Hofstadter, Richard, 199
Hollander, Neil, 171
Homans, George, 191
Hoover, Herbert, 111
Hoover, J. Edgar, 243
Hopkins, Harry, 103
Horst, Pamela, 325
House of Representatives, 301. *See
    also* Congress
Housing and Home Finance Adminis-
    tration, 114, 118, 332
Housing and Urban Development,
    Department of (HUD), 114, 118,
    130, 177, 236, 336
Howard University, 123
Huitt, Ralph, 95
Human relations approach to man-
    agement, 200–1
Human resources, department pro-
    posed, 119
Humphrey, Hubert H., 333
Hunger, 233–34

Huntington, Samuel P., 271, 272
Huntington, West Virginia, 130

Idaho, 22, 24, 317, 350
Illinois, 22, 24, 85, 142–43, 317, 331, 350
Impoundment of funds, 260, 268, 294–95
Incentives, 193–95
Income tax, 24, 320, 348
Incremental budgeting, 83–84, 89–91, 94, 99, 281–88
Independent offices and establishments and cabinet departments, 114–20
Independent regulatory commissions, 120–22. See also Regulatory agencies
Indian Affairs, Bureau of, 16
Indiana, 21, 23, 85, 142, 317, 331–32
Indonesia, 43, 47
Influences on outputs, 345. See also Policy
Information, 192–93, 233–35, 253–55, 258, 342–45
Information cost, 62
Information limits, 62–63
Innovation, 88–91, 288
Inputs, 7, 9–10, 56, 210–97; definition of, 56, 211. See also Demands; Resources; Supports
Interest groups, 240–48, 257–58. See also Government interest groups
Intergovernmental relations, 299–339; horizontal, 299–300, 304, 325–29, 331, 338–39; vertical, 299–300, 304–15, 324–25, 331, 338–39. See also Bloc grants; Formula grants; Grants-in-aid; Project grants
Interior, Department of, 119, 334
Internal Revenue Service, 51
International City Managers' Association, 329
Interstate and Defense Highway Act of 1952, 307
Interstate and Defense Highway System, 90

Interstate Commerce Commission (ICC), 16, 121, 254–55, 352–53
Iowa, 22, 85, 317
Iran, 43
Iraq, 43
Israel, 21,35
Item veto, 274

Jackson, Andrew, 105–6, 158, 215–17
Jacksonianism, 32–33, 105–6, 158, 216
Jacob, Herbert, 21, 141, 266, 330
Jahnige, Thomas P., 264
Jamaica, 44
Janowitz, Morris, 221
Japan, 31, 126
Javits, Jacob, 249
Jefferson, Thomas, 216, 294
Jennings, M. Kent, 34, 220
Jewell, Malcolm E., 265
Job Corps, 127
Johnson, Charles A., 224
Johnson, Lyndon B., 61, 68, 116, 128, 173, 204, 238–39, 247, 269, 294, 315, 333
Jones, Douglas N., 120
Jones, James E., Jr., 292
Jones, Roger W., 162
Judicial mechanisms for administrative control, 138–39
Justice, Department of, 16

Kansas, 22, 52, 317
Kansas City, 237, 329
Karl, Barry, 111
Kaufman, Herbert, 207, 209
Kennedy, John F., 52, 61, 114, 116, 167, 168, 173, 204, 270, 294, 315
Kennedy, Robert F., 167, 204, 234
Kentucky, 22, 45, 52, 130, 143, 317, 318, 329–30, 350
Kenya, 44, 47
Kenyatta, Jomo, 46, 47
Kerner Commission, 128–29
Key, V. O., Jr., 229, 230, 234

Kilpatrick, Franklin P., 215, 216, 220, 222
King, Martin Luther, Jr., 204, 234
Kirkhart, Larry, 205
Kissinger, Henry, 119, 235
Korean conflict, 91, 94, 149–53, 271
Krislov, Samuel, 4, 176, 178, 179

Labor, Department of, 130, 250, 293
Labor unions. See Collective bargaining
Lamb, Curt, 350, 351
Lamb, Robert B., 222, 237
Land grants, 306. See also Grants-in-aid
Lane, Robert E., 229
Latin America, 38, 45, 69
Law Enforcement Assistance Administration (LEAA), 324
Leadership, 195–97
Lee, Mordecai, 347
Legislative-administrative relations, 65–67, 261–64. See also Decision-making
Legislative branch, 136, 259–60. See also Congress
Legislative mechanisms for administrative control. See Congressional committees
Legislative oversight, 270, 273
Legislators, executives, and administrators, relations among, 269–75. See also Budget relations among . . .
Lepawsky, Albert, 111
Less-developed countries, 29 n.10, 38–53
Less-developed states, 44–53
Lincoln, Abraham, 216
Lindblom, Charles E., 58, 80, 81, 112
Lindsay, John, 249
Line units, 16, 55, 299
Lineberry, Robert L., 147, 321, 322
Loans and loan guarantees, 312, 314. See also Intergovernmental relations

Lobbyists, 245–47, 262. See also Interest groups
Local governments, 145–48
Lockheed Corporation, 126–27
Long, Huey, 47
Long, Norton E., 4, 217–18
Los Angeles, 262
Louisiana, 22, 24, 317, 318, 330, 350
Loyalty, 109, 111, 252, 272

Maas, Arthur, 346
McCrone, Donald J., 27, 212
McGovern, George, 240
Maine, 22, 52, 317
Malawi, 47
Malaysia, 44
Mali, 44
Malthus, Thomas, 72
Management, 187–209
"Management by objective" (MBO), 98
Manley, John, 196
Mann, Dean E., 159, 167, 168, 169, 171
Marbury v. Madison, 108
March, James G., 61, 64, 74, 76, 77, 111, 198, 199
Marini, Frank, 205, 206
Maritime Board, 121
Marxism, 38
Maryland, 22, 143, 144, 317, 330
Mass media, 233–35
Massachusetts, 22, 52, 317, 318, 330, 350
Massachusetts Institute of Technology (MIT), 70–73
Maxwell, James A., 313
Mayor-council form of goovernment, 146
Mazmanian, Daniel A., 347
Meadows, Donella H., 70
Meir, Kenneth J., 175
Merit system, 163, 166, 216–17. See also Civil service
Mertins, Herman, 286
Merton, Robert K., 252
Metropolitan areas, 318–24, 326, 327

Michigan, 22, 24, 52, 85, 317, 330
Middle West, 224
Milbrath, Lester W., 248
Miles, Rufus E., Jr., 272
Military-industrial complex, 20, 244, 345
Military intervention, 40
Miller, Warren E., 212
Mills, C. Wright, 111
Mills, Wilbur D., 196, 311
Milwaukee, 237
Minnesota, 22, 52, 85, 317, 350
Minnesota Municipal Commission, 323
Minnowbrook, 204–6, 209, 357
Mississippi, 22, 23, 24, 45, 52, 142, 153, 317, 329–30, 350
Missouri, 21, 23, 52, 317, 331, 350
Mitau, G. Theodore, 143
Model Cities program, 247, 295
Modernization, 39–40
Monroe, James, 215
Montana, 22, 24, 143, 317
More-developed countries, 29, 31–38
Morey, Roy D., 274
Morgan, E. Philip, 50
Morocco, 43
Morrill Acts of 1862 and 1890, 306
Mortgage Bankers Association, 247
Moses, Robert, 37, 38
Mosher, Frederick C., 163, 164, 165
Muckrakers, 233
Muddling through, 126
Multinational corporations, 126–27
Mutual adjustment, 80–81
Myrdal, Gunnar, 51

Nader, Ralph, 122, 207, 233, 237, 352–54, 359
National Advisory Commission on Civil Disorders, 253–54
National Aeronautics and Space Administration (NASA), 241, 264, 332–37
National Air Pollution Control Administration, 352–53
National Association of Counties, 246

National Association of State Budget Officers, 85
National Association of State Conservation Officers, 85
National Association of Housing and Redevelopment Officials, 85
National Audubon Society, 347
National Defense Education Act, 90
National Education Association, 164
National Environmental Policy Act, 346
National Governors' Conference, 246, 247
National Institute of Municipal Law Officers (NIMLO), 245–46
National Institutes of Health, 165
National Labor Relations Board, 121
National League of Cities, 236, 245, 246, 247
National Park Service, 123, 165, 335
National Security Act of 1949, 271
National Security Council, 119, 132
Native Americans, 177
Natural resources department proposed, 119
Navy, Department of, 91, 118
Nebraska, 23, 144, 285, 317, 318, 331
Neighborhood government, 231–32
Nepotism, 41
Netherlands, 126
Neustadt, Richard, 193, 265, 266, 267, 269
Nevada, 22, 143, 317, 327
New England, 52, 224
New Hampshire, 23, 52, 143, 317, 318
New Jersey, 22, 317, 318, 350
New Mexico, 22, 45, 52, 317, 318
New York City, 45, 329
New York State, 22, 24, 37, 45, 52, 317, 318, 328, 330, 350
New Zealand, 31, 256
Newark, 254
Newman, Monroe, 52
Nicaragua, 43
Nie, Norman H., 237, 249
Nigro, Lloyd G., 175
Nixon, Richard M., 50, 53, 61, 126, 130, 167–68, 247, 250; and mass media, 235; and Philadelphia

Plan, 292–94; reforms by, 118–19, 133, 135, 136, 311; vs. (Nixon) Congress, 260, 268–69, 290–91, 294–95. *See also* Watergate
Nkrumah, Kwame, 47
Nonpolitical personnel, 160–63
North Carolina, 22, 52, 85, 123, 317
North Dakota, 22, 45, 142, 317, 318
Nuclear Regulatory Commission, 121
Nyere, Julius, 47
Nystrom, Paul C., 34

Occupational backgrounds of administrators, 174–75
Office of Management and Budget (OMB), 92, 97, 132–35, 142, 155, 268, 276–79, 281, 282, 286, 290, 349–51. *See also* Bureau of the Budget
Ohio, 21, 23, 24, 85, 317, 350
Oklahoma, 22, 52, 317, 330, 331, 350
Olson, Kenneth C., 304
Ombudsman, 37, 255–56, 258
Omnibus Crime Control and Safe Streets Act, 324–25
Orange County, Florida, 334
Oregon, 22, 317, 350
Oregon Education Association, 244–45
Oriental-Americans, 177
Orlando, Florida, 333
Ostrom, Vincent, 104, 125, 322–23
Outputs, 7, 11–12, 56, 298–359. *See also* Goals; Policy; Public services
Ozarks Regional Commission, 52

Pakistan, 43
Panama Canal Corporation, 122
Paraguay, 43
Patrick Air Force Base, 333, 337
Patterson, Samuel C., 12, 265
Pechman, Joseph A., 95, 97
Peirce, Neal R., 163
Pendleton Act, 109, 216
Penn-Central Railroad, 126

Penniman, Clara, 328
Pennsylvania, 22, 24, 317, 350
Performance, 12–13
Personalities of administrators, 181–84
Personnel, 157–86
Personnel administration: evaluation, 161–62; program for high-level positions, 158–59; selecting, 157, 158–62; training, 161–62
Peru, 43
Petrocik, John R., 237, 249
Philadelphia, 180
Philadelphia Plan, 292–94
Philippines, 44
Planning-programming-budgeting (PPB), 91, 92–98, 278, 288. *See also* Budget; Cost-benefit analysis; Decision-making
Poland, 35, 36
Policy, 12–13, 341–42; definition of, 6–7. *See also* Goals; Influences on outputs; Outputs
Policy implementation. *See* Management
Policy-making, 7, 205, 263–64, 265–68
Political accountability, 105–7
Political appointees, 166–69
Political controversy, 101–4
Political cultures, 212, 223–26
Political elite. *See* Elite
Political machine, 250–53, 258
Political parties, 248–52, 258, 270
Polyarchal-competitive, 43–44
Poor People's Campaign, 234
Population growth, 70–73, 320
Port of New York Authority, 238
Portugal, 38
POSDCORB, 200
Postal service, 122, 124, 165, 271
Powell, G. Bingham, 14, 42
President, 111–13, 114, 122, 123, 167–68, 233. *See also* Chief executive; Executive-administrative relations; and individual presidents by name
Problems, 59–61, 69–73. *See also* Rational decision-making

Professionalism, 24, 109–10, 174–75, 250, 271
Program budgeting. *See* Planning-programming-budgeting
Project grants, 309. *See also* Intergovernmental relations
Property tax, 23, 24, 318, 319–20, 347
Prosthus, Robert, 68
Public administrators, 55, 159; activities of, 1–4; attitudes toward, 212–13, 217–27; control of, 2–4, 5–6, 132–36, 138–39; definition of, 4; demands and constraints on, 57; discretion among, 344; impact on policy, 4–5, 17; personal traits, 169–73. *See also* Bureaucracy; Civil service
Public Health Service, 16, 20
Public interest groups (PIGS), 246. *See also* Interest groups; Government interest groups
Public opinion polls, 229–31, 235–38, 257
Public Roads, Bureau of, 333, 345
Public services, 341–42, 355
Public-employee unions. *See* Collective bargaining

Rabinowitz, Francine F., 35
Radian, Alex, 51
Ranney, Austin, 95
Rational decision-making, 57–58, 59–68, 92, 98–99. *See also* Decision-making
Reagan, Michael D., 34
Reclamation, Bureau of, 345
Reconstruction, 216
Redcliffe-Maud, Lord, 34
Redford, Emmette, 217–19
Reform, 91–99, 288, 322. *See also* Budget
Regional consultation, 84–86, 99
Regions, 52–53, 129–31, 223–26, 329–31. *See also* specific names
Regulatory agencies, 352–54. *See also* Independent regulatory commissions

Religious background of administrators, 171–73
Reppenthal, Karl M., 165
Resources, 9, 211, 220–22
Respect and affection, 191
Responsibility, questions about, 37–38
Revenue-sharing, 303–4, 310–11
Reynolds, Harry W., Jr., 262, 264
Rhode Island, 22, 52, 144, 317, 350
Riggs, Fred W., 142
Ripley, Randall B., 134
Ritt, Leonard G., 224
Robinson, James A., 24–25
Rockefeller, Nelson, 249
Roethlisberger, F. J., 195
Romney, George, 249
Roosevelt, Franklin D., 52, 103, 111, 114, 116, 132, 173, 249, 294, 346
Rossiter, Clinton, 265
Rothwell, Kenneth J., 50
Rourke, Francis E., 242, 243
Routines, 81–88, 99. *See also* Incremental budgeting; Regional consultation; Spending-service cliche
Ryder, Norman B., 71

Sachs, Seymour, 27
Safire, William, 61
St. Angelo, Douglas, 331
Salaries of state employees, 24
Sales tax, 24, 153, 320, 348
San Diego, 237
San Francisco, 329
"Satisficing" techniques, 74–79, 91–92
Saudi Arabia, 43
Scandinavia, 31
Scher, Seymour, 273
Schick, Allen, 97, 286
Schiff, Ashley L., 63
Schlesinger, Joseph A., 141, 266, 274
Schultz, John E., 352, 353
Scientific management, 197–200
Sears, David O., 229
Securities and Exchange Commission, 121

Selection procedures. *See* Personnel administration
Selective perception, 192, 235, 257
Selznick, Philip, 243
Senate, 122, 123, 169, 301. *See also* Congress
Separation of powers. *See* Checks and balances
Service outputs. *See* Public services
Sharkansky, Ira, 21, 25, 26, 27, 34, 45, 69, 83, 84, 88, 90, 91, 95, 96, 124, 145, 147, 149, 224, 230, 263, 281, 283, 284, 288, 312, 321, 329, 332, 356
Sherman Act, 220
Sherwood, Robert E., 103
Shriver, R. Sargent, 167
Simmel, Georg, 196
Simon, Herbert, 58, 62, 74, 111, 198, 199
Sinclair, Upton, 233
Small Business Administration, 130, 270
Smith, Bruce L. R., 34, 125, 289
Smith-Hughes Act of 1917, 307
Smith-Lever Act of 1914, 306–7
Smithies, Arthur, 111
Smithsonian Institution, 122
Social backgrounds of administrators, 172, 175–76, 185
Social Security Administration, 119
Socially disadvantaged, 176–81, 185
Sorauf, Frank J., 251
Sorensen, Theodore, 169
South Carolina, 22, 52, 85, 142, 317, 318
South Dakota, 22, 317
South Korea, 43
Southern states, 224
Southwest, 224
Soviet Union, 29, 31, 45, 244
Sowell, Thomas, 355
Spain, 38
Spanish-origin people, 177, 178
Spending-service cliché, 86–89
Spending-service relationship, 355–57. *See also* Cost-benefit analysis
Staats, Elmer B., 34

Staff units, 16, 112–114, 268–69
Stakhanov, Alexei A., 203
Stanley, David T., 50, 159, 160, 161, 162, 163, 171, 172, 250, 325
Starbuck, William H., 34
State aid to local governments, 315–18, 338. *See also* Intergovernmental relations
State, Department of, 116, 118, 127, 168, 179, 244, 308
State governments, 141–45, 316–18. *See also* Council of State Governments
Status of administrators, changing, 271–72. *See also* Public administrators
Status of public administration, 212–27
Stein, Harold, 119
Steiner, Kurt, 226
Stevenson, Adlai, 168
Stokes, Donald E., 212
Subgovernments, 243–44, 345
Sudan, 43
Sukarno, 47
Sundquist, James L., 130, 230, 239, 268
Supports, 9, 211, 220–23
Supreme Court, 166
Sussex University, 71–73
Sweden, 34–35, 45
Synthesis in management techniques, 201–4
Syria, 43
Systems framework, 7–8, 13–15, 17–18, 93

Taft, William Howard, 111, 199
Taft-Hartley Act, 108
Talmadge, Gene, 47
Tanzania, 44, 47
Tariff Commission, 121
Tarkowski, Jacek, 35
Task Force on Career Development, 162
Taub, Richard P., 51

Tax Foundation, 348–50
Tax-benefit ratio, 348–50
Taxes, 23–24, 47–49, 96, 137 n.27, 312–13, 321, 347–50
Taylor, Frederick W., 198, 199, 200
Taylorism. *See* Scientific management
Tennessee, 23, 85, 123, 143, 317
Tennessee Valley Authority, 16, 52, 122–93, 293
Tensions, 79–80, 290–95
Texas, 23, 317
Thailand, 43
Thayer, Frederick C., 256
Third World, 46. *See also* Less-developed countries; Africa; Asia; Latin America
Thompson, Victor A., 66, 68, 204
Toffler, Alvin, 69
Traditional-autocratic, 43
Traditionalism, 38–40, 224
Training. *See* Personnel administration
Transportation, Department of, 118
Treasury, Department of, 12, 116, 118
Truman, Harry S, 111, 173, 195–96, 249–50, 270, 294
Tugwell, Franklin, 70
Tunisia, 44
Turkey, 44
Turner, James S., 352, 354

Unions of government employees, 164, 245
United Auto Workers, 234
United Nations, 168, 250
United States Conference of Mayors, 245, 246, 247, 328
University relations, 126, 160, 161, 243
Upper Great Lakes Regional Commission, 52
Urban affairs, 307, 318–24, 346. *See also* Housing and Urban Development, Department of; Metropolitan areas
Urban Observatory, 236
Utah, 22, 45, 52, 317

Values of public administrators, 181–84
Van Riper, Paul, 106, 160, 216
Verba, Sidney, 237, 249
Vermont, 22, 45, 52, 143, 317, 350
Veterans Administration, 136, 332
Vietnam conflict, 61, 68, 94, 96, 149–53, 206, 231, 239, 240, 294
Vines, Kenneth N., 21, 141, 266, 330
Vinyard, Dale, 270
Virginia, 22, 317, 330
VISTA, 127
von der Mehden, Fred R., 39
Vose, Clement E., 246

Wahlke, John C., 15
Waldemann, Raymond L., 136
Walker, Jack L., 34, 222, 330
Wallace, George, 47
War, Department of, 116, 118
Warner, W. Lloyd, 159, 171, 174, 175, 180, 181, 182, 183, 184
Warren Commission, 128–29
Washington, D.C., 129, 130. *See also* District of Columbia
Washington state, 22, 317
Watergate scandals, 5, 68, 132, 145, 240, 260, 269, 295, 357–58
Wealth, 190–91
Weaver, Robert, 114, 118
Weistrod, Burton H., 95–97
West (United States), 224
West Germany, 45
West Virginia, 22, 23, 45, 52, 142, 144, 317, 318, 330
Western Europe, 31, 38, 43–44
Westoff, Charles F., 71
White House Office, 124, 132–33, 155, 168, 268–69
White, Leonard D., 215, 216, 221
White, Orion F., Jr., 206
Whitten, Jamie, 234
Wiatr, J., 35
Wildavsky, Aaron, 83, 89–90, 93, 282
Winters, Richard F., 28, 349, 350
Williams, G. Mennan, 168

Wilson, James Q., 223, 251
Winters, Richard F., 28, 349, 350
Wisconsin, 22, 52, 85, 142, 145, 317, 323, 330, 350
Wise, David, 61, 69
Withinputs, 10–11, 56
Women, 176, 177, 180–81
Wood, Bruce, 34
Wood, Robert C., 88
World War I, 271
World War II, 91, 149–53, 271, 294, 307, 308, 312

Wright, Deil, 24, 34, 221, 274, 306, 310, 314
Wynia, Bob L., 184
Wyoming, 22, 24, 317

Yates, Douglas, 231

Zeigler, Harmon, 34, 244, 245